The Accounts:

Anglo-Dutch by **William Seymour**
French by **Jacques Champagne**
Prussian by **Colonel E. Kaulbach**

Prologue & Epilogue by **Lord Chalfont**

Edited by Lord Chalfont

WATERLOO
BATTLE OF THREE ARMIES

Alfred A. Knopf   New York   1980

1 On page one: A grenadier of the Imperial Guard
2 On page two: The battle of Waterloo from the French
side at about 7.30 p.m. Napoleon was about to start his last
desperate attempt to force the left-centre of the allied
position. Painting by Sir William Allan

THIS IS A BORZOI BOOK

PUBLISHED BY ALFRED A. KNOPF, INC.

Copyright © 1979 by Sidgwick and Jackson Limited

Design and colour photographs of the battlefield by Paul Watkins
Colonel Kaulbach's text translated from the German by Mark Heller
Maps by Richard Natkiel
Picture research by Anne-Marie Ehrlich

Library of Congress Cataloging in Publication Data
Main entry under title: Waterloo: battle of three armies.
Includes bibliographies and index.
1. Waterloo, Battle of, 1815.
I. Seymour, William, [date]
II. Champagne, Jacques Pierre, joint author.
III. Kaulbach, E., joint author.
IV. Chalfont, Arthur Gwynne Jones, Baron, [date], joint author.
DC242.W37   1980   940.2′7   79–3499
ISBN 0–394–51119–0

Manufactured in the United States of America

FIRST AMERICAN EDITION

Contents

List of illustrations

and maps

Editor's Note

A distinguished European historian, much concerned with the problems of war and peace, once
told me that international conflict would persist
as long as children at school were taught history
from national text books; and he cited the battle
of Waterloo as an example of how history tends to
perpetuate hostility through the fallacy of the
national stereotype.

This book is an experiment in popular military
history. It is an attempt to tell the story of Waterloo
by bringing together, in one volume, the perceptions of three different nationalities involved in the
battle, drawn mainly from their respective national
historical sources. To set the scene, I have written
a prologue incorporating a brief description of the
forces involved in the campaign, and my own
personal impressions of the campaign distilled
from a wide variety of sources, documents and
authorities.

The main body of the book is the detailed story
of the battle woven together from the accounts of
three writers, a German, a Frenchman and an
Englishman. Although this method does not, of
course, eliminate subjectivity or iron out national
perceptions, it places the three images in close
proximity in an attempt to achieve a measure of
internal balance.

The epilogue seeks to draw together the threads
of the narrative. It is unlikely that the professional
student of military history will find here anything
that is startlingly new. However, those whose
impressions of Waterloo have hitherto depended
exclusively on British (or French or German)
historians might possibly find good reasons to
think again.

PROLOGUE
Lord Chalfont

In the introduction to his absorbing account of Waterloo, *A Near Run Thing*, David Howarth quotes from the preface of Serjeant-Major Edward Cotton's much earlier book on the battle. Although he published his work over a hundred years ago, Cotton was nevertheless moved to ask the question which must have been in the minds of more recent historians: '*After the publication of so many accounts of the battle of the 18th of June, it may be fairly asked on what grounds I expect to awaken fresh interest in a subject so long before the public.*' It is a question that even now 'may be fairly asked'. The answer, so far as this book is concerned, lies in the fact that it is an attempt to present the story of Waterloo simultaneously from three individual points of view, filtered through three sets of national historical records, and to establish to what extent this method can be used to resolve some of the inevitable differences of perception.

If, for example, we are concerned with the question of Napoleon's physical health, the difficulties of arriving at an objective assessment are at once apparent. Many French accounts insist that when Napoleon returned to France from Elba at the age of forty-six, *he was in astonishingly good physical health*. Other historians, however, commenting on the Emperor's generalship at Waterloo, suggest that *illness and physical as well as mental exhaustion may have played their part*. There is, too, some disagreement about Napoleon's general performance during the battle. While some historians suggest that he was well below his best as a commander, Jacques Champagne's view, on p. 180 of this book, is that 'Napoleon himself can hardly be found at fault during the whole campaign, during the battle, or even during the retreat. . . .'

On a lighter note, one of the interesting discrepancies among various accounts of Waterloo concerns the reply of the French general Cambronne to the call by British officers for the surrender of the Imperial Guard. According to some French versions his reply was '*La Garde meurt et ne se rend pas*'. What Cambronne, on horseback in the ranks of the 2nd Battalion 1st Chasseurs, actually said, was something quite different. It is fascinating to contemplate in the mind's eye the spectacle of the French general, faced with the certainty of monstrous defeat and the near certainty of death, riding among his men and searching his mind for some suitable, historically memorable reply to the suggestion of an English officer that they should lay down their arms. Something dignified but unyielding seemed to be called for, and certainly 'The Guards will die before surrendering' has a bold and fairly robust ring about it; but Cambronne was clearly a man with a certain panache and economy of style. His considered reply was brief and left no room for ambiguity. '*Merde!*' is what he said, and it seems sad that this single, contemptuously arrogant word has to be concealed, presumably on grounds of good taste, from students of the history of war.

The historical foundation for the battle of Waterloo was laid at the Congress of Vienna in March 1815, when the allies (Great Britain, Prussia, Austria and Russia) had received news of the escape of Napoleon from Elba, where he had lived since his abdication in 1814. Wellington and the Prussian general Blücher were to invade France through Belgium, the Austrians and Russians from the east. Napoleon returned to France on 1 March 1815. He landed near Cannes with 1000 men, and took over a French regular army of about 150,000 first-line soldiers. He immediately began to raise more troops for an early campaign against the allies, and in eight weeks he had increased the strength of the army by 80,000. By the end of April, Napoleon had decided to attack the British and the Prussians in Belgium, hoping to defeat them before the Austrians and Russians could cross the Rhine and join in a concerted allied march on Paris. Accordingly, at the beginning of June he concentrated the Armée du Nord, of approximately 120,000 men, close to the Belgian frontier south of Charleroi. The concentration was a masterpiece of speed and secrecy involving the movement of units and formations over distances of up to two hundred miles. The army was grouped into three columns on a twenty-mile front. It was a highly professional and experienced army that enthusiastically welcomed Napoleon at Beaumont on 14 June.

Napoleon, according to Field Marshal Montgomery of Alamein, had few equals as a military leader 'and no betters'. It is possible that Montgomery's assessment is coloured to some extent by a comparison of the circumstances surrounding his own arrival in the Western Desert in 1942 with Napoleon's in Italy in 1796. When Napoleon took over command of the French army in Italy, at the age of twenty-six, morale was low, the troops were disillusioned and there was a smell of defeat in the air. Within a week Napoleon's inspired leadership had transformed the situation, and the campaign which followed in 1796 and 1797 was a masterpiece of its kind. '*In those years*' wrote Mongomery, '*a great military genius was loosed upon the world, and the world has never been quite the same since.*' In spite of a number of substantial errors of judgement – the decision to invade Spain in !808 and the dis-

astrous march on Moscow in 1812 being the most obvious – Napoleon proved himself to be a master both of strategy and tactics. His method was direct and uncomplicated, constructed around the basic essentials of mobility, concentration and morale – qualities which characterized most of his campaigns in Europe with the Grande Armée and which were still in evidence during his brilliant concentration at the Belgian frontier in 1815.

By that time, however, Napoleon at the age of forty-six was no longer the confident, masterful and dominant genius of earlier years. Most historians are of the opinion that he was in poor health. Following the best traditions of the subjective historical approach, different accounts, depending upon the individual author's general opinion of Napoleon, have suggested that he was suffering from piles, cystitis, hepatitis and venereal disease, and one of the contributors to the account which follows insists that Napoleon was in 'astonishingly good health' at Waterloo, thus demonstrating once more the precarious uncertainty of historical fact. Whatever the accuracy of these various diagnoses, Napoleon was almost certainly suffering, as he prepared to face Wellington and Blücher at Waterloo, from the appalling pains of the duodenal-pyloric cancer which was eventually to kill him.

Opposing Napoleon's 120,000-strong army was an allied force of almost 250,000. Of these, 100,000 belonged to Wellington's 'infamous army' which, although sometimes described as the British army, was polyglot, heterogeneous and largely unreliable. About a third were British troops, most of whom had never been under fire; another third were Dutch-Belgians who had been serving under Napoleon little more than a year before; the rest were Hanoverians, Brunswickers and about 6000 men of George III's German Legion, the only contingent of Wellington's army upon whom he could safely rely in a crisis. The remaining 120,000 troops in the allied armies – Blücher's four Prussian corps – were mainly inexperienced conscripts.

The allied armies were dispersed over a very wide area, a deployment designed to enable them to guard a large stretch of the frontier. They covered a front of about ninety miles, with the 'English' on the right and the Prussians on the left; the depth of the dispositions was about forty miles, from the Franco-Belgian frontier as far back as Liège in the east and Brussels in the west. This meant that at least three days would be necessary to concentrate all the defences at the centre of the line, and six days at either flank. Napoleon thus secured a clear initial strategic advantage; and this he seized with characteristic skill, having secretly assembled his relatively weaker forces on a front of no more than twenty miles in three columns around Beaumont, at the point which is inevitably the weakest in any defensive line – the junction between two commands. Furthermore he was only one hour's march from the forward areas of the allied defences.

The scene was therefore set for an historic encounter. The allied armies were superior in strength, but the French had the supreme advantage of tactical surprise; furthermore the numerical inferiority of the Frenchmen was compensated for by their greater experience and skill. In the imminent battles much would therefore depend upon the quality of leadership on either side, and especially upon the ability of Wellington, meeting Napoleon on the battlefield for the first time, to impose his will upon the man whose ambition was to be remembered as the greatest general in history.

Wellington was a man of a very different breed. Personal ambition meant less to him than duty. As a strategist he was cautious, steady and reliable rather than brilliant, and it is perhaps especially relevant to any analysis of the battle of Waterloo that his tactical *forte* was defence. It is also important to place in its proper context the quality of the troops which he had to command at Waterloo. If, as some historians have suggested, the principal credit for most of Wellington's victories belonged to the British army, he was undoubtedly facing a crucial test at Waterloo, with an army whose general aspect and demeanour were more likely to strike terror into its own commanders than into those of the enemy. Much of the contradiction in the varying accounts of the Waterloo campaign concerns the mistakes and the successes of the various commanders, and specifically those of Napoleon and Wellington. There are, however, certain aspects of the battle – its geographical pattern, its tactical development and its chronological sequence – about which there is less controversy; and it might help the reader of this story of three armies to begin with a brief chronological account of the battle.

Soon after 3 a.m. on Thursday, 15 June, Napoleon's army crossed the frontier into Belgium and advanced north towards Charleroi in three columns. The bridge across the Sambre south of the town was taken by midday and by 3 p.m. the French had occupied Charleroi. By nightfall on 15 June Napoleon had concentrated his army between the 'English' and Prussian forces and was poised to attack either. Meanwhile Wellington, in Brussels, having received firm intelligence of the French

attack at about 3 p.m., decided to march south to Quatre-Bras, where he arrived at about 10 a.m. on 16 June. The French, under Ney, advanced cautiously on Quatre-Bras, which was held by the allied I Corps under the Prince of Orange. Although the advance seemed at first likely to succeed, the arrival of reinforcements from Brussels and Nivelles radically altered the balance of forces and Ney's attack failed.

Meanwhile, eight miles to the east, Blücher had taken up positions around Ligny. At 2.30 p.m. on 16 June, Napoleon attacked. The Prussians fought stubbornly, but by 7.30 p.m. the French had taken Ligny and Blücher's troops were in retreat towards Wavre, allowing Napoleon to concentrate his attention on Wellington. At 7.30 a.m. on 17 June, Wellington, hearing of Blücher's defeat, ordered a retreat from Quatre-Bras, and decided to take up defensive positions at Mont St Jean on the ridge south of Waterloo. The last of his troops reached Mont St Jean at about 6.30 p.m. and the scene was set for the battle of Waterloo. The battlefield covered a front of no more than four miles, between Paris Wood in the east and the village of Braine l'Alleud in the west. The principal features of the terrain were two low ridges, less than a mile apart. Wellington's defensive positions were on the northern ridge, along a track running east from Braine l'Alleud, south of Mont St Jean towards the village of Ohain. The main body of Wellington's troops were on the reverse slopes of the ridge, but there were outposts, about five hundred yards in front of the main defence line, at the château at Hougoumont and the farm at La Haye Sainte. There was also small observation posts further east at Papelotte and Ter La Haye. The total number of troops manning the defences has been variously estimated at figures between 70,000 and 90,000.

Napoleon's force of 70,000 was drawn up on the southern ridge, 1200 yards away from Wellington's forces, with its centre at La Belle Alliance. At 11.36 a.m. on 18 June the first shots of the battle of Waterloo were fired.

As Elizabeth Longford has noted in the second volume of her excellent biography of Wellington, 'there is something so ponderously classical about the battle of Waterloo that it comes as no surprise to find it unrolling in five acts'. The first was the French attack on the outpost at Hougoumont, led by Prince Jérôme, Napoleon's youngest brother, and bloodily repulsed by Nassauers, Hanoverians and units of the Brigade of Guards. Meanwhile the advance guard of the Prussian army, Bülow's 30,000-strong IV Corps, was threatening the

French right flank and Blücher's main body was on its way from the east. In the second act Napoleon's infantry, under d'Erlon, advanced on Wellington's positions, to be defeated at the terrible cost of 7000 British and Dutch-Belgian dead. The third act saw the destruction of Ney's cavalry in a series of violent and costly attacks on La Haye Sainte, which fell at 6 p.m., opening up Wellington's centre. Wellington, however, not Napoleon, was the dominant character in the fourth act. He mobilized all his reserves to reinforce his threatened centre and set the scene for the fifth and final act.

The Imperial Guard, Napoleon's élite troops, had never yet failed in an attack. By 8 p.m., however, Napoleon's soldiers had heard the cry which they had never heard before '*La Garde Recule!*'; and the main force of Prussians under Blücher had arrived to alter decisively the balance of forces. At about 8.15 p.m., Wellington ordered a general advance and the French were crushed between the converging allied forces around La Haye Sainte; shortly after 9.15 p.m., Wellington and Blücher met on the Brussels road between La Haye Sainte and Rossomme. Napoleon, defeated, fled from the battlefield, leaving behind the shattered remains of his army, as well as his dark blue and gilt carriage, a million francs in diamonds and a cake of Windsor soap. He arrived in Paris on the morning of 21 June and on the following day abdicated for the last time. On 7 July, the allies entered Paris.

Behind this apparently simple sequence of events lay a complicated interaction of move and counter-move, based upon the plans and calculations of three experienced military commanders, two of whom may by any criteria be regarded as among the great captains of history.

The short campaign leading up to the battle illustrates perfectly one of the central problems of warfare – the time-space factor. Napoleon's understanding of this was crucial to his success as a military commander. During the Waterloo campaign, he displayed this understanding to the full, especially in his original planning, but in the battle itself there were curious lapses which were to cost him his victory. The combination of superb insights and a brilliant general plan with strange lapses in execution was uncharacteristic and in the end fatal. This was reflected in the Waterloo campaign by the conduct of Wellington and Blücher, who themselves made near-fatal blunders but eventually found themselves poised for victory.

The combined allied armies of Blücher and Wellington outnumbered any force the French could field, but their dispositions in Belgium were well known to the French, who had many sympathizers there. The details of the allied lines of communication were also known. Napoleon calculated that it would take at least twelve hours to concentrate each corps of the two allied armies; and that even when this assembly had been completed it would probably take two more days for Blücher and Wellington to unite their armies, each with its own separate lines of communication. The Prussian line ran through Liège into Germany, whereas Wellington's went from Brussels to the Channel, at Ostend.

With these factors in mind, Napoleon decided to assemble an army in secret near the Belgian border, to strike suddenly across the Sambre at the point where the allied armies had their main junction point, along the Nivelles/Namur road, and to defeat each in turn as they pulled back along their lines of communication, or tried to concentrate to meet him. He calculated that he could cross the Sambre before the nearest allied corps could organize a defence of the crossings and that he could strike the vital separating blow before the allied armies could unite. Once they were separated, he was sure that he could defeat them in detail, even though each one was individually almost as large as the 120,000-strong Armée du Nord. Wellington had 110,000 men and Blücher 117,000, but a French army, with its experienced cadres and its flexible battle tactics, could be expected to prevail over an allied force of similar size; furthermore, the Prussian army contained a large number of inexperienced conscripts, and the cream of the British army had been sent to America. Napoleon therefore relied on the celebrated mobility of his army to implement a novel organization. The Armée du Nord was to be split into three – two wings and a central reserve. Each wing would have one of the allied armies as its target, while Napoleon controlled the reserve to reinforce each wing in turn. This organization gave the French flexibility, but also posed considerable risks if communications between the wings should break down.

The essence of the campaign was, as in so many Napoleonic operations, the concentration of forces close to an unsuspecting enemy. During late May and early June, excellent planning ensured that this was achieved. Troops were assembled from all over northern France, and the allies were kept in ignorance of these movements by the total secrecy of the operation. From 7 June there was total security on the border: even fishing boats in northern French ports were forbidden to sail. By the 14 June, when Napoleon arrived at Beaumont,

5 French officers of the line. Napoleon's army was young
in spirit, well officered and eager to fight

the Prussians were only just beginning to realize the scale of French concentration. And when the French began moving over the border, at 2 a.m. on the 15th, both Wellington and Blücher were taken almost completely by surprise.

The speed and suddenness with which Napoleon was accustomed to open his campaigns often unnerved his opponents; and the Waterloo campaign was no exception. Both Wellington and Blücher reacted hastily and exposed their armies to what could easily have been total defeat. On 3 May, the two generals had agreed to a contingency plan, should the French attack: Blücher was to concentrate three of his corps around Sombreffe while his fourth Corps covered the operation, and Wellington was to concentrate his army towards the Prussians, maintaining communications. As soon as he heard of Napoleon's onslaught, Blücher immediately tried to put his part of the plan into operation. The plan had not, however, taken full account of so rapid an advance by the French. To assemble the Prussian army at Sombreffe against such a powerful, rapidly-closing enemy was practically suicidal. No sooner would the Prussian army be assembled than it would be swept away – as indeed happened the next day.

Blücher's decision to concentrate at Sombreffe was the more dangerous (although he was not to know this) in that Wellington failed to implement his part of the agreed plan. Not until 3 p.m. on 15 May was he informed that Prussian outposts on the Sambre had been subject to serious attack. He had also received reports of sorties by French troops from Dunkirk and Lille, and this may have persuaded him that Napoleon was trying to cut the allied army off from the Channel coast, slicing through its communications with Ostend. Wellington therefore decided to concentrate his army to meet such a threat, and ordered his army to assemble in positions to meet a French advance through Mons. Communications with the Prussians, and especially with the vital position at Quatre-Bras, were not considered in the orders that he issued that afternoon and evening. The nearest troops to Quatre-Bras would be the Prince of Orange's corps at Nivelles.

So, as Napoleon's men crossed the Sambre on 15 June, both allied commanders had already made mistakes. Blücher was ordering his men to concentrate just where Napoleon could strike with his full weight, and Wellington's army had received orders which gave the French every chance of success in their attempt to split the allied armies. Yet the French advance was not without its problems. The Emperor's choice of subordinates

had not been happy. His scheme of operating with two wings and a separate reserve demanded inspired leadership on the wings and excellent coordinating staff-work. Yet Napoleon had chosen Ney to command the left wing, probably for political reasons (Ney had been appointed commander of the Bourbon armed forces, but had deserted to Napoleon when he came back from Elba). Ney's judgement, although he was undoubtedly the 'bravest of the brave' had never been sound, and he was not a thinking general, able to assess his own situation in a broader strategic context. For the right wing, Napoleon had chosen Grouchy, a good cavalry general, but with no experience of commanding an army corps. Soult, the Chief of Staff, was a fine fighting general, but quite unsuited to the detailed staff-work he was now being called upon to undertake. The most surprising aspect of these individual appointments was that more able subordinates (Davout and Suchet, for example) were available. These appointments contained the seeds of other mistakes which Napoleon was to make during the campaign. Although he was still superior to any other general in Europe, Napoleon's instinct for war was clearly losing its edge.

Partly as a result of these problems of command, the actual advance over the Sambre was not as smooth as Napoleon had hoped. The move had been well-planned, but its execution was confused by the late arrival of orders following an accident to an aide-de-camp, the desertion of General Bourmont, commanding one of the leading divisions, and the unexpectedly fierce resistance of the Prussian troops at the one river crossing which was reached according to plan. Even when these initial obstacles had been cleared, there was a lack of urgency by both Ney on the left and Grouchy on the right. Ney reached Gosselies, but not his target of Quatre-Bras; he decided to abandon any further advance when 2000 cavalry and an infantry battalion met allied resistance there at about 8 p.m., when there was still plenty of daylight left. On the right, Grouchy's men reached the outskirts of Fleurus. Napoleon himself arrived to urge them on, but they failed to take the town before night fell. Even so, the 15th had been a good day for the French: they seemed poised to split the allied armies on the next day, when Blücher's suicidal concentration would also deliver the Prussian army into their hands.

It was not until the early hours of the morning of the 16th that Wellington realized his mistake in ordering his initial concentration west of Brussels. He was at the famous ball given by the Duchess of

Richmond when reports were brought to him that the main French forces were advancing through Charleroi. Leaving the dinner table with every appearance of calm, the Duke remarked in private, 'Napoleon has humbugged me, by God! He has gained twenty-four hours march on me.' Fresh orders were issued at once to concentrate the army at Quatre-Bras, but Wellington knew that he was unlikely to be able to stop Napoleon there. He expected to have to fight further back, probably at a position of which he had already taken note, Mont St Jean. In fact, Wellington was fortunate to be able to order a concentration at Quatre-Bras at all, for his initial orders had made no provision for troops to assemble there. In spite of this, however, the Prince of Orange's division had occupied the vital crossroads. The brigade they deployed there fought off Ney's cavalry on the evening of the 15th, and was to play a critical role in the events of the following day.

As the 16 June dawned, all seemed set for a French victory, with the Armée du Nord poised to strike at its disorganized enemy. Yet a combination of bad leadership and poor communications threw away the chance of a crushing victory, although the French had much the better of the day's fighting.

Napoleon's first orders were issued at 6 a.m., outlining his intention to make his main effort of the day against Wellington, as he was sure that Blücher would pull back to avoid a full-scale engagement. These initial orders may have led Ney to think that he was not to move until the Emperor came up with the reserve. At all events, he made no attempt to take Quatre-Bras during the morning, although this had been one of his main objectives and was obviously of vital importance. Napoleon himself went to Fleurus during the morning to confirm reports that the Prussians were not retreating. When he found that they were not, he immediately ordered the reserve to join Grouchy, although he still believed that Blücher must be preparing a rearguard action rather than an extended battle. Eighty thousand French with 210 guns were deployed against Blücher, who by the mid-afternoon had brought his numbers up to 84,000. He hoped for help from Wellington; at 1.30 p.m. the Duke (who had left Brussels at 7 a.m.) had ridden over to the Prussian positions and had promised to help, providing his own troops were not attacked. He had also criticized Blücher's dispositions, on the grounds that they left the Prussian infantry exposed to French artillery fire.

Napoleon, too, was aware of the vulnerability of the Prussians. He planned to hold their left with a cavalry feint, then to pin the right and centre by attacks using the corps of Vandamme and Gérard, drawing in Prussian reserves. Finally, at about 6 p.m., he expected Ney to come over from Quatre-Bras to fall on the exposed Prussian right; at this moment he would send the Imperial Guard crashing through the centre, destroying the whole Prussian army. The plan, however, was ruined by Ney, who had made no attempt to move his men forward on the morning of the 16th – although as late as 2 p.m., only 8000 men and sixteen guns held the crossroads. In a campaign in which time was vital, the delay was decisive. When, shortly after 2 p.m., French troops eventually began to advance, they did so cautiously. Reille, who led the first assaults, was a veteran of the Peninsular War, and was worried that Wellington might, in typical style, have concealed large bodies of troops in the thick woods and high corn surrounding the position. Even so, Reille's 20,000 men seemed bound to succeed; at 3 p.m., however, Wellington himself arrived with the first reinforcements. When these, in their turn, seemed about to give way, the Duke of Brunswick arrived with more help. At this point, Ney received Napoleon's revised plan for the day, which envisaged Ney swinging over to help at Ligny by the late afternoon. Ney at once ordered Reille to redouble his efforts, and called up d'Erlon's corps of 20,000 men, who had so far not seen any action.

D'Erlon's corps did not, however, reach Quatre-Bras. When Napoleon realized that Ney was engaged with the British army there, he sent a messenger to tell Ney that if he were heavily embroiled, he need only send one corps over to Ligny. The message was either oral or badly written (accounts differ on the point); in any case, the crucial fact was that General La Bédoyère, bearing the message, vastly exceeded his authority. He came upon d'Erlon's corps before he had seen Ney, and told d'Erlon to go directly to Ligny, to the village of St Amand, which was in itself a mistake, as Napoleon wanted the corps to go to Wagnelee. At Quatre-Bras, Ney was furious when he heard that d'Erlon had been sent elsewhere. When one of Napoleon's aides arrived carrying a clearer order (sent at 3.15 p.m.) for one corps to be sent to Ligny as soon as possible, Ney's anger completely unnerved the young man, who forgot to hand over the despatch. At the same time, the allies counter-attacked, and Ney, believing himself to be in mortal danger, sent off a message to d'Erlon, ordering him to return at once to Quatre-Bras. D'Erlon was almost at Ligny when he received this message – but he turned back as ordered, without, however, informing Imperial headquarters of this change of direction. This was just after 6 p.m. and d'Erlon did not get back to Quatre-Bras until after the fighting there was over. His 20,000 men would probably have ensured total French victory on either battlefield; yet, due to a combination of misjudgement and poor communications, his men had spent the afternoon marching and counter-marching with less effect than the ten thousand men of the grand old Duke of York.

Meanwhile, at Ligny, Napoleon's plans had been successful, with the exception of the projected envelopment of the Prussian right. Fighting began after 2 p.m.; the French cavalry contained the Prussian left, as ordered, while in the centre, Vandamme's corps engaged the enemy along the line of Ligny brook. On soft ground and amongst small farmhouses, this phase of the fighting was desperate – some French regiments lost half their strength. By 5 p.m. Napoleon had, however, achieved his objective: Blücher's reserves had been drawn in, and 55,000 French troops were pinning down 84,000 Prussians, who were weakening rapidly under the terrible pounding they were receiving (as Wellington had forecast) from the French artillery.

It was at this time that Ney should have arrived to take the Prussians on their exposed right flank. As there had been no message from him, Napoleon decided to send that Guard through the centre without delay. This would probably have destroyed the Prussian army, but from now on, events conspired to give Napoleon less than the complete victory he had hoped for. First of all, at 6 p.m., General Vandamme appeared at Imperial headquarters to report that a large column of troops, reportedly hostile, had come up on his flank. So, the assault on the Prussian lines was postponed while some of the Young Guard were sent to reinforce Vandamme. The approaching column was, of course, d'Erlon's corps, heading for the wrong village. As soon as this was realized, an aide was sent to re-route d'Erlon to Wagnelee, as originally intended, but the man came back with the news that d'Erlon had now changed direction, and was returning to Quatre-Bras! Napoleon could do little about this, for soon after, Blücher launched a counter-attack on the village of St Amand. The Young Guard quickly re-established the French line, but it was not until 7.30 p.m. that the Guard was able to mount its attack on the centre. In pouring rain, the guardsmen took the village of

Ligny and, after a halt to beat off a last despairing cavalry charge led by Blücher himself, they carved a way through the centre of the Prussian position, and the Prussian army fell back in headlong retreat.

The Prussians lost 25,000 men, including deserters, as a direct result of Ligny, and had been driven from the field in disorder; but the two wings of their army had been able to pull out relatively intact. The 16th had been almost completely successful for Napoleon. That it was not completely so was in large measure attributable to Ney's failure to take Quatre-Bras or to support the Emperor at Ligny. Subordinate commanders had also acted strangely. Nor can Napoleon himself be entirely exonerated. He had allowed a whole corps (that of Lobau, which had been the last formation to cross the Sambre) to remain inactive when its presence at Ligny would have compensated for the absence of Ney.

Napoleon now assumed, mistakenly, that the Prussian army was a defeated rabble in full retreat. Gneisenau, the Prussian Chief of Staff, had indeed wanted to retreat directly at Liège. As the Prussian generals struggled, in darkness and with Blücher still absent, to find a rallying point for the retreating army, they picked on Wavre, because it was plainly visible on all maps. So the line of retreat was north, rather than east. When Blücher at length arrived at his headquarters, he decided that Wavre should be the centre of a new Prussian concentration, rather than a mere step on a retreat. He was determined to help Wellington if he could. It so happened that Wavre was within reach of Mont St Jean, where Wellington was to make his stand. After two days of fighting, therefore, the French, although they had kept the allied armies separate, had not achieved their primary aim of preventing an allied concentration.

Nevertheless, as the day of the 17th dawned, the chances of French success were still great. The advantages of their secret concentration and surprise attack, combined with the early mistakes of the allies, had not yet evaporated. Only at 11 a.m., however, when reports indicated that Ney had not yet taken Quatre-Bras, did Napoleon realize that he had an opportunity to catch Wellington's army; he sent Grouchy after the Prussians with 33,000 men while he himself tried to concentrate 69,000 at Quatre-Bras. When he reached there, however, at 1 p.m., Napoleon was astonished to find Ney's troops preparing lunch, while Wellington's army carried out an unhindered withdrawal! The left wing was galvanized into activity but it was not until 2 p.m. that the French were ready to advance.

They were just too late to catch the guns of Uxbridge's rearguard and before active pursuit could begin, a sudden thunderstorm made rapid movement all but impossible. The French could merely follow the allied army along the Brussels road. Ney's inactivity on the morning of the 17th had again been crucial.

By early evening on the 17th, Napoleon was relieved to find that his opponent was establishing his army at Mont St Jean, to fight the next day. The French Emperor was sure that this was a mistake; he still discounted the possibility of Prussian intervention (ignoring reports that Prussians had been seen near Wavre). In any case, Grouchy's 33,000 men should have been adequate to cover the French right flank until Wellington was defeated. At 4 a.m. on the 18th, Napoleon received a despatch from Grouchy reporting that the bulk of the Prussian army was indeed at Wavre. Not until 10 a.m. did Napoleon even reply, and the orders he then sent were indecisive, telling Grouchy to head for Wavre while maintaining contact with the main army. If Soult's suggestion that Grouchy be recalled had been followed, or even if Grouchy had been told to take up a more protective position, perhaps near Wahain, then the two Prussian corps Blücher had promised to send would have found it almost impossible to reach the battlefield at Waterloo. Napoleon's orders, however, allowed Grouchy to stray too far from the main action. Nor was Grouchy himself entirely without blame; he was slow in moving his men during the morning, refused suggestions to march towards the sound of the guns at Waterloo (which must have saved the French cause) and fought an indecisive action against a single Prussian corps at Wavre.

Dismissing the possibility of a threat from the Prussians, Napoleon decided to delay the first major assault until 1 p.m., because the ground, still sodden from the rain of the previous day, was making manoeuvre difficult, and diminishing the effect of his artillery. Wellington had chosen his position at Mont St Jean with some care. The crucial question was whether his polyglot force could resist the attacks of a seasoned French army led by Napoleon. Wellington would probably have made his task easier if he had recalled a force of 17,000 men he had placed ten miles west, fearing that Napoleon might try a flanking march. Napoleon's plan, on the contrary, was for a frontal assault, led by d'Erlon's corps. He thought that this would shatter his opponent, and in the morning estimated his chances of success as ninety to ten. A diversionary attack on Hougoumont at 11.30 a.m. by Prince Jérôme's division of Reille's

7 From the crossroads, the road ran straight across the valley, past La Haye Sainte to La Belle Alliance on the skyline. There the allied soldiers could see the French as they paraded past the Emperor

corps was intended to draw in Wellington's reserves, to weaken the sector of the line which d'Erlon was to attack. Meanwhile, on the left of the French line, d'Erlon's corps was preparing its assault. A centrally sited battery of eighty-four guns made little impact on the main allied formations, protected as they were by the reverse slope, and as d'Erlon's men were on the point of advancing, bodies of troops were seen at Chapelle St Lambert – the Prussians of Bülow's corps. Lobau's men were moved east to deal with this threat, taking up positions between Plancenoit and the Paris Wood. Orders were sent for Grouchy's recall, but he did not receive them until 5 p.m. The French were beginning to run out of time.

At 1.30 p.m., d'Erlon's men moved forward. Three of the four divisions were in huge unwieldy formations, however, two hundred men wide and twenty-four ranks deep, which inhibited movement and the cavalry support which normally accompanied French infantry was reduced to one brigade of cuirassiers. The four divisions had some success, especially on their right, but they could not clear La Haye Sainte on their left, and Picton's division coolly moved in to halt the two central divisions. Their momentum exhausted, the French infantry were taken in the flank by Uxbridge's cavalry. The Scots Greys created havoc, and many of the 92nd Highland Infantry joined in the fray, clinging to the horses' stirrups. The French were thrown back down the slope, but the British cavalry proved impossible to stop. The Union Brigade, 2500

strong, plunged on towards the French central battery. Although they reached it and sabred many gunners, they were by then tired and cruelly exposed. Napoleon launched his lancers and cuirassiers against them with excellent timing and over 1000 of the British cavalry were killed as they tried to escape.

In spite of the disaster which had overtaken the Union brigade, this first phase had been a success for the allies, who had beaten off the first major assault. Now the battlefield quietened, until at about 3 p.m. the only fighting was at Hougoumont. Napoleon realized that the key to Wellington's position was La Haye Sainte and he ordered Ney to take it at all costs.

Ney's first attack on La Haye Sainte was a failure, but in the course of it he thought that he noticed the beginning of a retreat in the allied rear. Hoping to profit from any confusion this might cause, he ordered a brigade of cuirassiers forward to exploit any weakening of the allied line. To attack well-positioned infantry with cavalry alone was extremely dangerous, as Ney must have known. Without artillery or infantry support, this attack was foredoomed: the defending infantry formed twenty large squares around which the horsemen milled helplessly, steadily being picked off by allied artillery and occasionally counter-attacked by Uxbridge's cavalry. To extricate Ney's cavalry, Napoleon sent Kellermann forward with some of the cavalry reserve. Again, however, the movement got out of hand,

and another massed charge, this time of almost 10,000 horsemen, was under way by 5 p.m., only to recoil in its turn. Although unsuccessful in themselves, these charges had exhausted Wellington's cavalry and had drawn in the allied infantry reserves; if the battle had been taking place on only one front, the charges might well have been the prelude to French success. At 4 p.m., however, Bülow's men had begun to emerge from the Paris wood, and by 5 p.m. had taken Plancenoit. The Young Guard had to be sent over to stabilize the situation there. With Lobau's corps already committed against Bülow, Napoleon's central reserve was dwindling fast, and he dared not risk launching it against Wellington until his right flank was secure.

After the failure of the cavalry charges, Ney was ordered to take La Haye Sainte, and eventually, soon after 6 p.m., it fell to a combined attack of infantry, cavalry and artillery. Ney was able to site a battery only three hundred yards from the allied centre, and men of d'Erlon's corps began to advance. This was the moment at which the reserve should have been sent in to exploit the weakness in the allied centre. But Napoleon rejected Ney's appeals. 'Des troupes? Voulez-vous que j'en fasse?' he is said to have told Ney's messenger. This was the critical moment of the Waterloo campaign. Had Napoleon agreed to send in the Guard, then the battle might well have been won. Napoleon, however, no longer trusted the judgement of a subordinate who had thrown away so many chances of victory over the previous three days, and he wanted to make sure that his right was secure against Bülow. So the Old Guard was sent to Plancenoit instead of being used against Wellington's centre.

By 6.45 p.m. Plancenoit had been recaptured, the French right was again secure, and Napoleon could bring some Guard battalions back to augment his reserve. Wellington's situation was still grave (two brigades had been almost destroyed by Ney's forward artillery), but in the hour which had elapsed since the fall of La Haye Sainte a second Prussian corps, under Zieten, had begun to arrive on the allied left. Wellington was thus able to move troops from his left to reinforce his centre: Brunswick and Belgo-Dutch infantry together with some cavalry.

Some commentators have suggested that at this point (about 7 p.m.) Napoleon should have withdrawn his still-intact army. Yet he now had, in fact, little choice. In spite of his efforts of the previous three days, the allied armies were uniting, and his campaign was in danger of failing with all

that implied for his position in France. So, at 7 p.m., Napoleon played his last card. He sent four to eight battalions (accounts vary) forward along the Brussels road to crack the allied centre. The guardsmen left the road soon after they passed La Belle Alliance, and attacked in two main columns. Wellington was expecting the attack; his troops, again positioned on the reverse slope to avoid artillery fire, met the Guard as it reached the crest. Some of the grenadier companies were repelled by the British Brigade of Guards along the Ohain road, the chasseurs of the Guard were halted in cornfields by Adam's Light brigade, and thrust back down the slope after some hand-to-hand fighting.

As the celebrated Imperial Guard drew back from the allied line, the morale of the French army began to evaporate. Wellington ordered a general advance and, as his army came forward down the slope, Napoleon's army started to retreat, except for the Guard, which carried out a model withdrawal, not leaving Plancenoit until 9 p.m. At about the same time, Wellington met Blücher at La Belle Alliance, secure in the knowledge that they had won a great victory. Wellington had said in the early hours of 16 June that Napoleon had gained twenty-four hours march on him. Much of the story of the Waterloo campaign concerns the way in which this advantage gradually eroded between 15 and 18 June.

Until late afternoon on the 18th, French success seemed probable, but when the final hour, from 6–7 p.m., drained away without a determined assault on the allied centre, the advantage swung decisively in Wellington's favour, and Napoleon had lost.

How do the historians of the countries involved in the battle see these events? Wellington's own comment sums up the difficulties of recording, as von Ramke put it, 'how it actually was'. Writing from Paris two months after Waterloo, he said:

The history of a battle is not unlike the history of a ball. Some individuals may recollect all the little events, of which the great result is the battle won or lost; but no individual can recollect the order in which, or the exact moment at which, they occurred, which makes all the difference as to their value or importance.

What follows is yet another attempt to bring together some of these recollections – not so much to try to throw new light on one of the greatest of land battles, but rather to look at it by the existing light of history, from three different and often irreconcilable points of view.

1 FROM ELBA TO MONT ST JEAN

Jacques Champagne

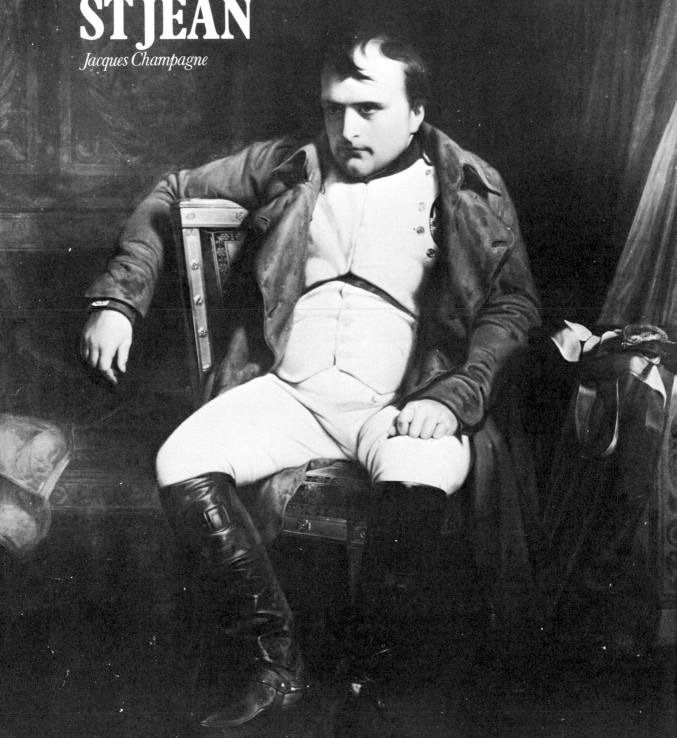

On 18 June 1815 Napoleon's French army faced
Wellington's Anglo-Dutch army at Mont St Jean,
twelve miles south of Brussels and two miles south
of Waterloo. The battle that was to ensue was the
last episode of a momentous chapter in the political
and military history of France. It was also to be
the last major armed confrontation in Europe
between the Great Powers for the next hundred
years.

Known as 'The Hundred Days', this period
began in fact at the end of February 1815 when
Napoleon decided to return to France after a
year's exile on the island of Elba. It was a bold and
calculated step dictated, in his predicament at that
time, both by his personality and temperament.

He was forty-six years old. His first-rate mental
powers were unimpaired. He was in astonishingly
good physical health considering his turbulent
career and meteoric rise to power.[1]

A product of the French Revolution, he had
risen from the rank of artillery lieutenant at the
age of sixteen to that of brigadier-general at
twenty-four and of commander-in-chief three years
later. At thirty, he was First Consul, and Emperor
of France at thirty-five. He, Napoleon Bonaparte,
the little Corsican bourgeois, had become the
equal of monarchs, with a royal and imperial
family, yet remaining a soldier of fortune at heart.

For the next ten years, he had shaped and
mastered the destinies of France and of Europe,
distributing kingdoms and honours at will, whilst
leaving an indelible mark on history as an outstanding military figure, statesman and scholar.[2]

With his fourteen famous marshals,[3] he had
personally fought and won some forty major battles
against the combined forces of Europe before
having to retreat from Moscow. And he had fought
some ten more before being crushed by the forces
of the Holy Alliance of European Powers (always
spurred on and financed by England, mistress of
the seas), compelled to abdicate in Fontainebleau
on 4 April 1814 and exiled to Elba.

By the end of February 1815, his position,
humiliating at first, was deteriorating fast and had
become untenable, even positively dangerous.
King Louis XVIII, barely restored to the Bourbons' throne by foreign powers, had deprived him
of the annual financial support he was entitled to
according to the Treaty of Paris. The King was
also planning to abolish by decree Napoleon's title
to the kingdom of Elba and the hereditary right of
his descendants to it. Both in Vienna and in Paris
plans were afoot to deport Napoleon either to
Malta or to St Helena, or even to make an attempt
on his life on Elba itself.[4]

His private life was in ruins. His first wife, the
Empress Josephine, whom he had divorced because she could bear him no children, had died at
La Malmaison soon after his arrival on Elba. His
second wife, the Empress Marie Louise, and their
child, his only legitimate son and heir, then three
years old, were at the court of her father, the
Austrian Emperor. Napoleon had had no word
from them since he had last seen them on 18
January 1814.[5]

Verbal and written communications from some
of his loyal friends and old advisers were becoming
daily more pressing; they begged Napoleon to
return to Paris before France's Revolution and
independence were irremediably lost, the Empire
was finally liquidated by the Bourbons and their
foreign allies, and he, the Emperor, was forgotten,
if not worse.

The circumstances were propitious. In France,
political and intellectual ferment was ripe at all
levels: in the professions, the clergy and the civil
and military hierarchies, as well as amongst the
millions of ordinary people (workers, peasants and
artisans) whose acquired freedoms, positions and
material benefits were being 'restituted' by the
King to the returning émigrés. Royalist, Bonapartist and Republican conspiracies were overlapping to converge in a dominant liberal theme
against absolutism.[6]

In Europe, the Congress of Vienna was dead-
locked by the discord amongst the major powers
over the re-drawing of the European map. Their
troops were scattered behind the rivers Po, Inn,
Oder and Niemen, and most of their officers were
on long leave. Wellington was in Vienna, Blücher
in Berlin and Czar Alexander in St Petersburg.

Napoleon saw the opportunity and seized it. On
26 February, he left Elba with his escort of only
1,000 officers and men of the Old Guard (his total
military establishment at that time) on board the
brig L'Inconstant, landing three days later at Golfe
Juan, a small beach in the South of France, on
1 March.

Within twenty days (then a record travelling
time in any circumstance) he had reached Paris
without any hindrance from the civil authorities
and with little or no resistance from the Royalist
troops and their commanders.[7] He had rallied
about 40,000 of them to his cause, amidst popular
enthusiasm, chased Louis XVIII, his family and
his partisans out of France, foiled numerous conspiracies and re-established his political and
military authority over the whole of France,
except in the Vendée. He felt entitled to boast: 'I
have regained my throne without one drop of blood

11 and 12 Above: The Congress of Vienna attempted to restore the balance of power in Europe, but while the major powers were in deadlock, and their troops were scattered, Napoleon seized the opportunity to escape from Elba (right)

having been spilt, either on the battlefield or on the scaffold.'[8] But if he had avoided general civil war in France, he had stupefied and shocked the Allied powers. A major military confrontation with the forces of the Holy Alliance was now inevitable despite his hopeful, yet illusory, diplomatic moves for peace.[9]

In Vienna, on 31 March, England, Prussia, Austria and Russia signed a military convention pledging themselves to mobilize immediately against France 150,000 troops each (out of their combined armies of almost 800,000 men) and to place their forces under the supreme command of the Duke of Wellington.[10] All the other European nations, except Spain and Portugal, promised to supply contingents.

Thus, Napoleon needed an army of 800,000 men to be able to fight the combined armed forces of Europe on equal terms. But the French military establishment he found once he was installed in Paris was very far from being adequate for this purpose.

13 Napoleon landing at the Golfe Juan on 1 March 1815.
He arrived with a military escort of only a thousand officers
and men of the Old Guard

In March 1815, the French army numbered
149,200 men of all arms and disposed of 19,000
horses. Of these, 93,900 officers and men (infantry
64,500, cavalry 13,800, artillery 12,000, engineers
3,000, supply 600) and 13,800 horses were immediately available for war. The rest were just
about sufficient to guard the ninety forts and naval
establishments throughout France.

All forts were disarmed, fencing and palisades
having been dismantled and sold, together with the
stocks of provisions. Except for one man o'war and
three frigates based in Toulon, and two frigates in
Rochefort, all ships were disarmed and their
crews had been dismissed. As regards the equipment in stock (apart from that in the hands of the
army), there was sufficient artillery to re-arm the
forts adequately. There were enough sabres for the
cavalry, and there were 150,000 new rifles and
300,000 more to be repaired or in spare parts.

Barely ten days after his arrival in Paris, at the
end of March, Napoleon set in motion a gigantic
reorganization which, in scope as well as in speed,
remains to this day unprecedented in military
history.

He created new cadres for three infantry regimental battalions, for two cavalry squadrons, for
thirty artillery battalions, for twenty regiments of
Young Guard, for ten battalions of transport and
supply, and for twenty marine regiments, thus giving immediate employment to all officers on half
pay of all arms, including shore establishments and
naval crews. He requested and obtained from the
central and local administrative authorities all over
France the recruitment of 200 battalions of National
Guard, each comprising 560 men (two companies
of grenadiers and two of fusiliers). All the veterans
were recalled to arms. No coercion was necessary:
130,000 peasants, artisans and workers from all
over the country left work at the end of the week,
put on their old uniforms and medals and rejoined
their old regiments. The 1813 class (veterans of the
Peninsular War) was recalled: 90,000 men had
joined up by the end of May.

Thirty thousand sailors were also recalled, with
their officers and petty officers as cadres. Out of
100,000 officers, petty officers and soldiers on
pension or invalided out, 30,000 were used for
administrative work in the forts and recruiting
offices all over the country under the direction of
Marshal Davout, Prince of Eckmühl, the War
Minister.

In order to accelerate the production of military
equipment, factory and workshop workers were
exempted from military service. Thousands of
copper plates were melted down, the workshops of

14 and 15 Left: The gates of Grenoble are laid at the Emperor's feet. On his journey through France, Napoleon met with little resistance and by the time he reached Paris on the 20 March (left, below), he had already established his political and military authority over most of France

16 Below: Napoleon's proclamation to the army, written at Golfe Juan. Twenty days later he had rallied 40,000 men to his cause

Au Golfe Juan, premier Mars 1815.

NAPOLÉON,

par la grâce de Dieu, Empereur des Français, etc., etc., etc.,

A L'ARMÉE.

SOLDATS!

Nous n'avons point été vaincus. Deux hommes sortis de nos rangs ont trahi nos lauriers, leur Prince, leur bienfaiteur.

Ceux que nous avons vu pendant vingt-cinq ans parcourir toute l'Europe, pour nous susciter des ennemis, qui ont passé leur vie à combattre contre nous dans les rangs des armées étrangères, en maudissant notre belle France, prétendraient-ils commander et enchaîner nos Aigles, eux qui n'ont jamais pu en soutenir les regards? Souffrirons-nous qu'ils héritent du fruit de nos glorieux travaux? Qu'ils s'emparent de nos honneurs, de nos biens, qu'ils calomnient notre gloire? Si leur règne durait, tout serait perdu; même le souvenir de ces immortelles journées. Avec quel acharnement ils les dénaturent! Ils cherchent à empoisonner ce que le monde admire, et s'ils restent encore des défenseurs de notre gloire, c'est parmi ces mêmes ennemis que nous avons combattu sur le champ de bataille.

SOLDATS! dans mon exil j'ai entendu votre voix, je suis arrivé à travers tous les obstacles et tous les périls.

Votre Général, appelé au Trône par le choix du peuple, et élevé sur vos pavois, vous est rendu: venez le joindre.

Arrachez ces couleurs que la nation a proscrites, et qui, pendant vingt-cinq ans, servirent de ralliement à tous les ennemis de la France. Arborez cette cocarde tricolore, vous la portiez dans ces grandes journées!

Nous devons oublier que nous avons été les maîtres des Nations, mais nous ne devons pas souffrir qu'aucune se mêle de nos affaires. Qui prétendrait être maître chez nous? Qui en aurait le pouvoir? Reprenez ces Aigles que vous aviez à Ulm, à Austerlitz, à Yéna, à Eylau, à Friedland, à Tudella, à Eckmulh, à Essling, à Wagram, à Smolensk, à la Moskowa, à Lutzen, à Wurchen, à Montmirail. Pensez-vous que cette poignée de Français, aujourd'hui si arrogans, puissent en soutenir la vue? Ils retourneront d'où ils viennent, et là, s'ils le veulent, ils règneront comme ils prétendent l'avoir fait pendant dix-neuf ans.

Vos rangs, vos biens, votre gloire, les biens, les rangs et la gloire de vos enfans n'ont pas de plus grands ennemis que ces princes, que les étrangers nous ont imposés, ils sont les ennemis de notre gloire, puisque le récit de tant d'actions héroïques qui ont illustré le peuple Français, combattant contre eux pour se soustraire à leur joug, est leur condamnation.

Les vétérans des armées de Sambre et Meuse, du Rhin, d'Italie, d'Egypte, de l'Ouest, de la Grande-Armée, sont humiliés; leurs honorables cicatrices sont flétries, leurs succès seraient des crimes, ces braves seraient des rebelles, si, comme le prétendent les ennemis du peuple; les Souverains légitimes étaient au milieu de l'ennemi. Les honneurs, les récompenses, leur affection sont pour ceux qui les ont servis contre la patrie et contre nous.

SOLDATS! venez vous ranger sous les drapeaux de votre Chef. Son existence ne se compose que de la vôtre, ses droits ne sont que ceux du peuple et les vôtres; son intérêt, son honneur et sa gloire ne sont autres que votre intérêt, votre honneur et votre gloire. La Victoire marchera au pas de charge, l'Aigle avec les couleurs nationales volera de clochers en clochers jusqu'aux tours Notre-Dame: alors vous pourrez vous vanter de ce que vous aurez fait; vous serez les libérateurs de la Patrie.

Dans votre vieillesse, entourés et considérés de vos concitoyens, ils vous entendront avec respect raconter vos hauts faits; vous pourrez dire avec orgueil: *Et moi aussi je faisais partie de cette Grande Armée* qui est entrée deux fois dans les murs de Vienne, dans ceux de Berlin, de Madrid, de Moscou, et qui a délivré Paris de la souillure que la trahison et la présence que l'ennemi y ont empreinte. Honneur à ces braves Soldats, la gloire de la Patrie, et honte éternelle aux Français criminels, dans quelque rang que la fortune les ait fait naître, qui combattirent vingt-cinq ans avec l'Etranger pour déchirer le sein de la Patrie.

Signé NAPOLÉON.

Par l'Empereur,

Le Grand Maréchal faisant fonction de Major général de la Grande Armée;

Signé Comte BERTRAND.

the Mint were re-established and transformed into engineering plants. By such means, the French factories, which could formerly supply 20,000 new rifles a month, doubled their output. In all the main provincial forts, repair shops were established to refurbish all the old rifles in stock within six months. In Paris itself, the main workshops were ordered to assemble the available spare parts into rifles, to repair the old ones, and to produce new rifles. Parisian coppersmiths, watchmakers, chisellers, carpenters and cabinet makers were all put to work to that end In May, these workshops produced 1,500 rifles a day, and in June, over 3,000.

All clothing workshops had been closed down or abandoned during the Restoration. In April 1815, the Treasury advanced several million francs to the manufacturers to enable them to restart work within a month. The administrative branch of the National Guard was ordered to provide 100,000 uniforms and other equipment for active army service.

On 1 June, 20,000 cavalry horses were delivered to the depots by the civilian population, and 10,000 more by the dismounted gendarmerie. In all, 46,000 cavalry horses were mustered at the depots or allocated to the troops of the line, as well as 18,000 artillery horses.

The Finance Minister, Count Gaudin, Duke of Gaete, and the Minister for the Treasury, Count Mollien, called upon French and Dutch finance houses and on private capital to help finance this fantastic operation. The call was answered to the extent that everything was paid for in cash and even in advance. The Public Debt was funded, pensions were paid and Public Works were restarted. The Treasury sold 4 million of the Government Bonds it possessed at 50 per cent of their value and replaced them by mortgages on the national woodlands. This produced another 40 million francs. The collection of the ordinary tax revenue was accelerated and some regions presented the Treasury with gifts of up to 1 million francs. Lastly, the Treasury still possessed the Crown silverware worth 6 million francs and the 50 million francs in cash which Louis XVIII had left at the Treasury in his precipitous flight from France.

By 1 June 1815, France had 560,600 men under arms, of whom 413,400 had been recruited, conscripted or recalled in the previous two months (that is at a rate of 7,000 a day). The latter were organized into an army of the line (196,000 officers and men) and a special auxiliary army (217,400 officers and men).

The equipment of the French army was of 1815 European standard. The rifles were actually muskets, smooth-bored and muzzle-loading, with flintlock and bayonet. The latest type had grooved (or rifled) barrels, but they were expensive weapons and difficult to combine with muzzle-loading.

The infantrymen carried flints, iron balls three-quarters of an inch in diameter and powder cartridges. They loaded and primed their weapons standing up. Well trained, they could fire one or two rounds a minute, with a range of 200 yards (lethal at fifty). At close quarters, they used bayonets. On the battlefield, in defensive formation, they either held a double line to receive enemy infantry attacks on a wide front, one line firing standing upright, the other one re-loading, crouched on one knee, or, in square formation, the infantry presented a wall of steel bayonets to cavalry charges. In offensive formation, the French infantry advanced in mass columns, marching in mixed, or tight, formations (as opposed to thin-line order), preceded by the skirmishers (*tirailleurs*), who fired as they advanced; then, fanning out, on the double (*au pas de charge*) until the actual hand-to-hand bayonet fighting with the enemy. In counter-attack, when called in in support of cavalry, or when assailed by enemy infantry superior in numbers, the French charged in tight formation with their bayonets crossed.

The artillery guns of the period were generally 12-pounders with a range of 3,500 yards, but really effective at only half that distance. Their recoil action not being absorbed, they had to be wheeled back and aimed again after each shot (solid iron ball, time-fused shell, or 'grape'). Yet trained crews could fire two shots a minute. The French had perfected 3–4-pounder and 8–12-pounder guns which were lighter and more accurate than the 12-pounder since their shells were less affected by the wind in their trajectory. The French artillery was not a separate arm distributed in groups, as required, to infantry and cavalry. Instead, Napoleon had organized his artillery in separate regiments attached to the various army corps, of which they were an integral part. The army corps were therefore strong and autonomous three-arms units, but more cumbersome and slower than infantry–cavalry corps in taking up position on the battlefield or in moving over long distances. On the other hand, their cavalry and infantry were never without artillery support in emergencies when on the move, whether in offensive or in defensive position. The division was the smallest unit to which French artillery was

attached. There were no real artillery duels in battle. The guns concentrated their fire power on the enemy lines prior to an attack and blasted advancing enemy infantry and cavalry to terrible disintegration.

The weapons normally carried by the French cavalryman were the sabre and the lance. Napoleon had reduced the number of heavy cavalry regiments from twenty-five to fourteen. In these, both officers and men wore breast-plates (hence the name cuirassiers) and carried a sabre and a short carbine at the saddle. They formed a homogeneous unit and were never dispersed as divisional cavalry but always kept in reserve for shock attacks, organized in brigades and divisions. On the other hand, Napoleon had increased considerably the number of medium and light cavalry regiments, converting dragoons from mounted infantry to cavalry proper (chasseurs and hussars) serving army corps, each having two to four cavalry regiments attached to it. The rest of the light cavalry was formed into reserve brigades, the dragoons carrying long swords instead of sabres and a pistol at the saddle, and the lancers being used for pursuit, a manoeuvre which could turn an indecisive battle into a rout.

The élite of the French army, the pride of Napoleon and of France, was of course the Imperial Guard. It consisted of men chosen for their height and their strength, their fearlessness, their endurance and their tenacity. Most of them, the Old Guard, carrying the Imperial Eagles, veterans of many campaigns, had remained faithful to the Emperor throughout his exile on Elba. They had been disbanded by Louis XVIII and their pension reduced by half (they were called 'les demi-solde'), and they had welcomed Napoleon as one man when he returned to France. They had put on their uniforms which they had kept at home and joined their regiments spontaneously at the first call. In battle, they were fierce as well as experienced and presented to the enemy an imposing and terrifying spectacle, whether on foot or on horseback, with their eighteen-inch-high black bearskin bonnets adding to their own six-foot stature. Their gunners were the most experienced of the army. Yet their numbers were no longer sufficient to provide a backbone around which to build the military establishment of 800,000 men which Napoleon needed to face the combined armies of Europe.

In that respect, the army which Napoleon had reorganized and re-created could not compare with the famous Grande Armée of the past which had really been destroyed during the retreat from Moscow and the subsequent invasion of France by the Allied armies. About half the troops, up to the rank of lieutenant, were now new conscripts of the 1815 class. The other half (those who had been recalled to the colours) had learned soldiering under enemy fire in 1813 or 1814 and were now taking up arms again after a year's civilian life. Only in the Guard were experienced veterans to be found, and even there 4,000 to 5,000 men, out of a total of 18,500, were new conscripts.

Nevertheless, this was a truly national army,[11] of which Napoleon and France could be proud: young in spirit and physical ardour, well officered by non-commissioned and subaltern officers who were close to the troops, eager to fight with popular support, for Emperor and country, against a new foreign invasion, and to gain rank and glory like their predecessors.

It is significant that on this campaign, which was to be his last and which was to end at Waterloo, Napoleon took only four marshals with him: Soult, a man of action rather than a co-ordinator in the field, as major-general (chief of staff); a reluctant Ney, 'the brave of braves', whom Napoleon recalled at the very last moment (11 June) to take command of the army's left flank; Mortier, suffering badly from sciatica, to command the Grenadier Guards; and, against Davout's advice, Grouchy, whom Napoleon had only just appointed marshal and put in command of the cavalry reserve army corps.

The fact is that Napoleon's choice of high-ranking commanders for his new army, about to go to war in earnest, was hesitant and circumscribed by the circumstances in which he had to make it.

Apart from the generals who had accompanied him to Elba (Bertrand, Cambronne, Drouot), most of the others had joined Napoleon during his lightning march on Paris, more in spontaneous response to the unmistakable and irresistible will of their troops and subalterns than by deliberate choice. All had paid homage to King Louis XVIII only three weeks after Napoleon had abdicated in April 1814, and they had served him for the past year with various degrees of political loyalty according to their position at the court or their distance from it.[12] Ministerial appointments and promotions, royal honours, the pleasures of the court and the leisure of peacetime had been most welcome to many of these famous commanders (who were of Napoleon's age group) as their due for their glorious careers.[13]

Their personal courage and valour on the battlefield were not in doubt. But in the army, the ranks, and their cadres and subaltern officers, who were totally and admiringly loyal to Napoleon and committed to his cause, were distrustful of his high command officers who had so openly served the Bourbon king and paraded at his court of returning *émigrés* while the Emperor was in exile. Houssaye aptly sums it up when he writes: 'Impressionable, argumentative, undisciplined, suspicious of its chiefs, troubled by its fears of treason and thus vulnerable to panic, but seasoned and warlike, feverishly vengeful, capable of heroic efforts and of furious drives, and more impetuous, more ardent to fight than any other Republican or Imperial army – such was the Army in 1815. Never had Napoleon had such a formidable, yet so fragile, instrument of war in his hands.'

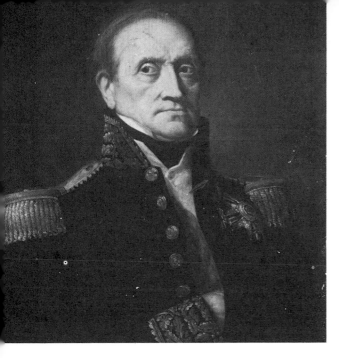

By the end of May, the 196,000 men of the line were fully equipped and ready for war. Napoleon formed them into seven army corps, one infantry reserve corps, four cavalry reserve corps, four observation corps and an Army of the Vendée, as a Royalist rebellion had broken out there in May. These forces were deployed so as to cover all the frontiers, their main strength within a reasonable distance of Paris, Lyon and the Flanders border. The deployment was as follows (for details, see Appendix III, Table 2):

The Flanders Army
(*later called l'Armée du Nord*)
4 Army corps, 1 infantry reserve corps, 1 cavalry reserve corps, and the Imperial Guard. In all, 115,500 officers and men with 350 cannon.

Two covering armies
(*in Alsace and in Chambéry*)
1 Army corps each. In all, 33,120 officers and men with 92 cannon.

Four observation corps
(*based in Jura, Provence, Pyrenees and Gironde*)
In all, 18,540 officers and men with 84 cannon.

The Army of the Vendée
17,000 infantry, cavalry and artillery officers and men with 24 cannon, reinforced by 10,000 men drawn from the Flanders Army (6,900) and the covering armies (3,100); in all 27,000 men with 24 cannon supported by the Gironde observation corps, the National Guard and the Gendarmerie.

The ninety main French frontier strongholds, provincial forts and ports were manned by 150 battalions (85,000 men) of élite National Guard, who were part of the 217,000 men of the auxiliary army garrisoned all over France, also mainly in the proximity of Flanders, Paris and Lyon. These two capital cities had been strongly fortified during April and May under the command of Generals Haxo and Lery of the Royal Engineers.

Napoleon estimated that by the autumn the forces of the European coalition would number about 800,000 men and that he must finish building up the French army to that number by October because, in the end, 'it would be before Lyon and Paris that the destiny of the Empire would be decided. So long as these two strongholds were held in force, the Motherland would never be lost.'[14]

As the enemy forces were already massing on the frontiers of France, Napoleon envisaged two possible plans of campaign. He could, in the first place, stay on the defensive, leaving the onus of aggression clearly, for all to see, on the enemies of France. They would be left to attack the French frontier strongholds, probably around 15 July, and

to attempt to march on Lyon and Paris. The entrenched French army, strongly built up in numbers by then, would engage in an intense and decisive war on French territory.

On the other hand, Napoleon could take the initiative and attack the Anglo-Dutch and the Prussian-Saxon armies before the Russian, Austrian and Bavarian troops had time to arrive on the Rhine. This would mean attacking not later than 15 June the Anglo-Dutch and the Prussian armies who were now garrisoned in Belgium 'commanded by two different generals [see note 10, page 225] and composed of men belonging to different nations divided as much by interests as by feelings'.[15]

Napoleon estimated the Anglo-Dutch army at 103,000 men and the Prussian army at 134,000 men, a total of 237,000 men (see Appendix III). His own army of the line had been depleted by some 20,000 men to form the Army of the Vendée, but, without depleting the forts and strongholds, he still had a Flanders Army of 115,000 men and 350 cannon available to start the campaign. He could attack both enemy armies, separate them and beat them in turn. If this failed, he could re-deploy his Flanders Army with the rest of his forces before Lyon and Paris, the two pillars of the French defence. He opted for this second plan.

On 2 June, according to a most remarkable schedule, minutely detailed and timed by himself, Napoleon ordered all corps of the Flanders Army to begin a vast movement of concentration on the banks of the rivers Meuse and Sambre. On 4 June they were all on the move, replaced as they left their forts and garrisons by the 217,000 men of the special auxiliary army. I Corps started from Valenciennes towards Avesnes; II Corps from Avesnes to Maubeuge; III Corps from Rocroi to Chimay; IV Corps from Thionville to Rocroi; the infantry reserve corps from Soissons to Avesnes; and the Imperial Guard from Paris to Soissons and Avesnes. By 12 June when Napoleon himself arrived overnight from Paris in Laon at 2 p.m., the army was finishing its concentration.

Only Grouchy had not moved his cavalry reserve corps forward from Laon to Avesnes: Soult had failed to give him 'the necessary order'. After meeting the Emperor, Grouchy moved immediately, arriving in Avesnes with his corps during the night of 13–14 June at the same time as Napoleon, who spent the night there. On the 14th Napoleon installed his headquarters at Beaumont, in the centre of his Guard and of his army.

In ten days, Napoleon had moved across France 115,000 infantry, cavalry and artillery officers and

men with 350 cannon who had been garrisoned in French forts between 300 and 1,750 miles away from one another. He had concentrated that formidable force on the Franco–Belgian frontier in an area twenty miles deep and sixteen miles long along the banks of the Meuse and the Sambre. And he had brought this whole army within cannon reach of the enemy forward positions in Belgium, if not entirely without the latter's suspicions or knowledge, certainly without Field-Marshal Blücher, commander-in-chief of the Prussian army, or Wellington, commander-in-chief of the combined Anglo-Dutch-Prussian forces, taking any notice of it or preparing for action.[16]

On the evening of 14 June, the French army was camping in three staging positions: the left flank (more than 40,000 men of I and II Corps) on the right bank of the Sambre; the centre (about 60,000 men of III and VI Corps, the Imperial Guard and the cavalry reserve) with Napoleon's headquarters in Beaumont; the right flank (more than 15,000 men of IV Corps and one cuirassiers division) in Philippeville. In all, 115,000 men (85,820 infantry, 20,460 cavalry, 7,020 artillery, 2,200 engineers and 350 cannon) were concentrated two and a half miles from the frontier in camps established behind hillocks to hide their bivouac fires from the enemy.

On the other side, all was quiet. The enemy forces were in their camps, the Prussian–Saxons to the east, the Anglo-Dutch to the west and north, disseminated on a front some eighty miles long and thirty miles deep. Blücher had forces estimated by Napoleon at more than 120,000 in four army corps under Generals Zieten, Pirch, Thielemann and Bülow, (in all 85,000 infantry, 20,000 cavalry and 15,000 artillery, with 300 guns) along the Sambre and the Meuse, with headquarters in Charleroi, Namur, Dinant and Liège respectively. Each corps needed half a day to assemble and, except for Zieten who was in Fleurus, point of concentration of the whole Prussian army, the three other corps were between twenty and forty miles away from it (Bülow being the farthest).

The Anglo-Dutch army under Wellington had forces estimated by Napoleon at 104,000 men: 37,000 English (22,000 infantry, 10,000 cavalry, 5,000 artillery), 42,000 Germans (32,000 infantry, 6,800 cavalry, 3,200 artillery) and 25,000 Dutch and Belgians (19,000 infantry, 3,000 cavalry, 3,000 artillery) with 250 guns in all. Their ten infantry divisions were organized in two army crops: one in Braine-le-Conte, under the Prince of Orange, the other in Brussels, under Lord Hill. Lord Uxbridge commanded the cavalry, with its assembly point at

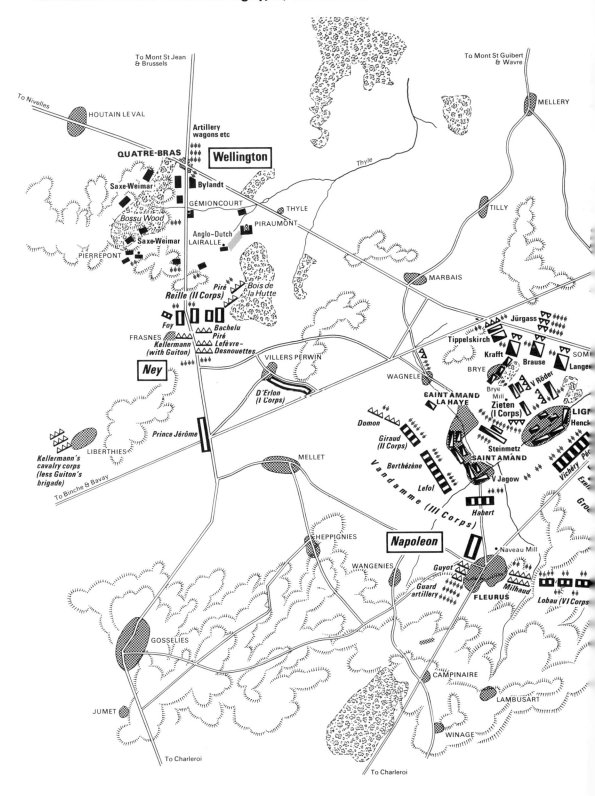

The battles of Quatre-Bras and Ligny, 15/16 June 1815

To Mont St Jean & Brussels

To Mont St Guibert & Wavre

To Nivelles

HOUTAIN LE VAL

MELLERY

Thyle

Artillery wagons etc

QUATRE-BRAS

Wellington

TILLY

Saxe-Weimar

Bylandt

GÉMIONCOURT

Bossu Wood

THYLE

Anglo-Dutch LAIRALLE

PIRAUMONT

Saxe-Weimar

MARBAIS

PIERREPONT

Jürgass

Piré

Bois de la Hutte

Tippelskirch

SOM

Reille (II Corps)

Krafft

BRYE

Brause

Langer

Foy

Bachelu
Piré

Brye Mill

V Röder

FRASNES

Lefèvre-
Desnouettes

VILLERS PERWIN

WAGNELE

Kellermann (with Guiton)

SAINT AMAND LA HAYE

Zieten (I Corps)

LIG

Henck

Ney

D'Erlon (I Corps)

Domon

Steinmetz

Vichéry

Giraud (II Corps)

SAINT AMAND

Exe

Prince Jérôme

Berthézène

V Jagow

Gro

Kellermann's cavalry corps (less Guiton's brigade)

LIBERTHIES

MELLET

V a n d a m m e (III Corps)

Lefol

To Binche & Bavay

Habert

CHEPPIGNIES

Napoleon

• Naveau Mill

WANGENIES

Guyot

Milhaud

Guard artillery

FLEURUS

Lobau (VI Corps

GOSSELIES

CAMPINAIRE

JUMET

LAMBUSART

WINAGE

To Charleroi

To Charleroi

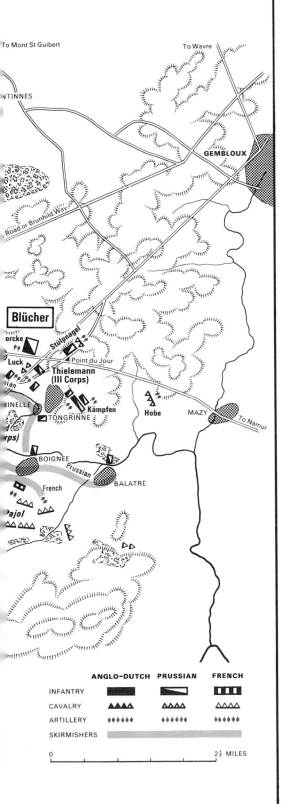

To Mont St Guibert

To Wavre

NTINNES

GEMBLOUX

Road or Brunhild Way

Blücher

orcke
Stülpnagel

Luck
Point du Jour

Thielemann
(III Corps)

INELLE
Kämpfen   Hobe   MAZY   To Namur

TONGRINNE

rps)
BOIGNEE   Prussian

French   BALATRE

ajol

Gramont. Each division needed half a day to assemble, and they were at distances of between six and thirty-two miles from Quatre-Bras, the Anglo-Dutch point of concentration, five miles from the right of the Prussian army.

In these positions, each of the two allied armies needed two whole days to assemble on their line of contact and three more to join up on a single battlefront, where they would have confronted Napoleon with a combined force of 224,000 men and 550 guns – almost twice the French army's strength. Blücher's headquarters were in Namur, forty miles from Wellington's which were in Brussels. The Emperor's mind was made up: since the contact line of the two enemy armies passed through Sombreffe and crossed at Quatre-Bras, he would drive a wedge between them by marching the French left flank on Quatre-Bras and the right on Sombreffe, while he, with his centre forces, would be marching on Fleurus, the apex of this triangle, attacking whoever was encountered first.

At dawn (3 a.m.) on 15 June, the French army began to cross the Sambre in three columns: the left flank (Rcille and d'Erlon), on the bridge at Marchiennes; the centre (Vandamme, Lobau, Grouchy and the Guard), nine miles away on the Charleroi bridge; the right flank (Gérard), four miles further along on the Châtelet bridge. Once again, Napoleon's personally scheduled order of movement was a model of clarity and detail. But there were delays in transmission and execution. D'Erlon started one and a half hours late, at 5 a.m. At that time, Vandamme was still waiting for Soult's orders. And Gérard only arrived at his assembly point at 7 a.m., with the whole of his IV Corps in a flutter.

Two hours earlier, as the corps had begun to move, General de Bourmont (a protégé of Gérard and Grouchy), commanding the spearhead division, had galloped over to the enemy with all his staff: Major de Villoutreys and Captains d'Andigné, de Trélan and Sourda. By 7 a.m., wearing the Royalist cockade, de Bourmont was revealing to the officer commanding the Prussian forward post that the French would attack Charleroi in the afternoon. Later, he told Zieten's aide-de-camp that the French army numbered 120,000 men.[17] Worse perhaps than the value of the information de Bourmont gave the enemy was the effect of his desertion on the morale of the French soldiers and their cadre officers, confirming, as it were, right at the start of the campaign, the suspicions and fears of treason they held in regard to their high-ranking commanders.

When the fighting began in earnest, Zieten's forward positions took the brunt of the French attack and withdrew with 500 casualties. By midday Napoleon had entered Charleroi, acclaimed by the population. Two hours later, he ordered Reille and d'Erlon to march on Gosselies where the Prussians were showing up in force.

At 3 p.m., Ney arrived on the scene. Summoned by Napoleon on 11 June, he had arrived two days later at Avesnes by coach from his manor in Normandy, accompanied by one aide-de-camp and without horses. On the 14th, he had travelled in a peasant's cart to the headquarters in Beaumont, where he had bought two horses from Marshal Mortier who was crippled by an attack of sciatica and was being replaced by General Friant as commander of the Grenadier Guards. Ney had been riding along the army's moving columns since the morning of the 15th when he arrived in Charleroi.

Napoleon said that he was glad to see him. He gave him command of the left flank (I and II Corps, and the Guard's light cavalry, the latter not to be used before the arrival of Kellermann's cuirassiers the next day) and ordered him to attack 'anything you encounter' on the Brussels road and to take up position at Quatre-Bras. A moment later, Napoleon called Grouchy and gave him command of the right flank with orders to push the Prussians towards Sombreffe and to take up position there. These two orders were given verbally and were to be confirmed by Soult the next day.

In the event, neither of these two objectives was reached on 15 June. At 5.30 p.m., after two hours' delay in combining their action at Gilly, Grouchy and Vandamme had to be hurried by Napoleon himself to attack Zieten's and Pirch's corps, who lost 2,000 men in fierce fighting before retreating beyond Fleurus. French General Letort (dragoons) was mortally wounded in this battle during a cavalry charge which wiped out two enemy square formations. But as night was falling, Vandamme refused point blank to give any further support to Grouchy, who wanted to take Fleurus (then occupied only by two Prussian battalions) and to pursue the enemy up to Sombreffe as ordered by Napoleon. Vandamme argued that his troops were tired (which was quite true) and that, in any case, he 'had no orders to take from the commander of the cavalry' (which was a snub, perhaps in ignorance of Napoleon's verbal appointment of Grouchy as commander of the army's right flank).

Deprived of infantry, Grouchy stopped within cannon reach of Fleurus.[18]

Meanwhile, on the left flank, Ney had not advanced as far as Napoleon had wished either. At 1 p.m., French hussars had engaged Prussian cavalry and infantry of the Steinmetz division who were occupying Gosselies. After two hours of attack and counter-attack, Reille arrived in support with infantry and artillery, and Ney with the Guard's light cavalry. Gosselies was taken in an attack which practically wiped out the 29th Prussian Regiment defending it. Steinmetz retreated towards Fleurus. The Brussels road was free and there were still about four hours of daylight left.

But Ney judged that he had already advanced too far in relation to the army's right flank (now almost ten miles away) at the risk of finding the whole of Wellington's Anglo-Dutch army here in front of him. He established his main forces around Gosselies and sent only the Guard's lancers and chasseurs towards Quatre-Bras. At Frasnes, they were received by cannon fire from the 2nd Battalion of Nassauers. Lefèvre-Desnouettes asked for some infantry, and while waiting for this support, which soon arrived, he sent General Colbert with a squadron of Polish cavalry to reconnoitre Quatre-Bras. The position was not occupied by the enemy but Colbert, without support and too far from his division, returned to Frasnes where Prince Bernhard of Saxe-Weimar was rushing two fresh battalions from the Orange corps to reinforce the Nassauer troops. Ney galloped forward to assess the position. The enemy was now established about one mile in front of Quatre-Bras with 4,000 men and eight cannon – quite enough to defend the position against Lefèvre-Desnouettes' 1,700 light cavalry supported by only one infantry battalion. Ney ordered a few probing charges against the Nassauer infantry, and at 8 p.m. he rallied Lefèvre-Desnouettes' division at Frasnes, leaving it there while he went to spend the night at Gosselies.[19]

Although Sombreffe and Quatre-Bras were not in French hands on the 15th as planned, the tactical delays incurred had not impaired the success of Napoleon's strategic plan. Having surprised the enemy, the French army had crossed the Sambre with little difficulty, advanced eighteen miles inside enemy territory, disrupted their opponents' lines of communication and driven a wedge between the Prussian and the Anglo-Dutch armies. Napoleon was now established in the centre of the enemy within a 100-square mile triangle.

At 5 a.m. on 16 June, Napoleon was planning to

advance on Sombreffe and Gembloux with Grouchy and the army's right flank. He would attack and throw back eastwards any Prussian corps he encountered and, rallying his reserves in Fleurus, he would join up with Ney's left flank at Quatre-Bras to march on Brussels by night and arrive there at 7 a.m. on the 17th.

Between 7 and 8 a.m., Napoleon dictated (and Soult dispatched) orders to all commanders to deploy their forces in accordance with this plan. Just before 10 a.m., as Napoleon was preparing to ride to Fleurus and assume overall command, reports reaching him from Grouchy and Ney respectively informed him that the Prussians were arriving in force at St Amand and Ligny, while the Anglo-Dutch were reinforcing Quatre-Bras. The two enemy armies were evidently assembling with the intention of joining up.

Reflecting on the different characters of the enemy commanders, Napoleon judged that Blücher, the impetuous and adventurous hussar, would be more likely to rush to the help of the Anglo-Dutch army if it were attacked first than Wellington, circumspect and slow-moving, would be to succour the Prussians in reverse circumstances. He therefore confirmed his orders to his commanders, particularly to Ney who was 'to assemble the corps of Reille, d'Erlon and Kellermann under his command and to beat and destroy all the enemy whom he encountered coming from Brussels'.[20]

At 11 a.m., Napoleon arrived in Fleurus (evacuated at dawn by the Prussians), where Grouchy was hesitating to march on Sombreffe against enemy forces now entrenched there in considerable force. Surveying the field from the top of a windmill, Napoleon ordered the attack.

It was spearheaded at midday by Gérard, who was thrown from his horse by an enemy charge and was almost taken prisoner. Soon Napoleon realized that he had more on his hands than he had expected: practically the whole Prussian army was here in front of him. Zieten's, Pirch's and Thielemann's corps held Sombreffe on the left, Ligny in the centre ten miles away, and St Amand on the right, with reserves on the heights of Brye; some 85,000 Prussians were therefore facing 60,000 French on a battlefront four miles wide. Napoleon decided to take up Blücher's challenge and to crush him there and then. The Anglo-Dutch would be contained by Ney at Quatre-Bras until, the army's right flank having dealt with the Prussians, Napoleon could join up with Ney and finish

Wellington's army off. Napoleon was not interested in two half victories.

At 2 p.m., therefore, he modified his orders to Ney to that effect. He was instructing him now to continue pressing Wellington vigorously but to execute at the same time an enveloping movement in support of Grouchy, who was attacking the Prussian right flank between Sombreffe and Brye. Napoleon judged that Reille's corps, with 20,000 men, was sufficient for the first purpose (containing Wellington) and that d'Erlon's corps, detached from Ney with 19,000 men, would be sufficient for the second purpose (turning Blücher's right and attacking his rear).

By 3 p.m., the battle was raging along the whole front. Using infantry, cavalry and artillery, Vandamme attacked St Amand and La Haye (where General Girard fell mortally wounded). Gérard engaged the Prussians heavily at Ligny and Grouchy made a diversionary cavalry attack on Blücher's left flank. The Prussian counter-attacks were just as massive and fierce. All positions were taken and re-taken at least four times by charges under devastating fire.

In the midst of it all, at 4.30 p.m., Napoleon angrily sent a third confirming and pressing order to Ney: 'The salvation of France and the fate of the Army depend on your execution of the Emperor's orders.'[21] A copy of this order was dispatched direct to d'Erlon, who was to lead the required enveloping movement on Blücher's flank and rear. Two hours later, as Napoleon was preparing finally to burst through the Prussian centre with the Guard, d'Erlon appeared on the horizon, causing some confusion: Napoleon thought at first that it was an enemy column and d'Erlon, who had got a little lost on the way to Ligny, was himself in a quandary, having been recalled to Frasnes by Ney even as he was marching towards Napoleon according to the Emperor's direct order. In the event, seeing that Napoleon was in any case about to give Blücher the *coup de grace*, d'Erlon decided to make his way back to rejoin Ney.

On the battlefield, the end was in sight. At 7.30 p.m., St Amand and Ligny fell under a terrific French onslaught. Zieten's, Pirch's and Thielemann's corps, decimated and routed, retreated in disorder. Napoleon had lost 8,500 men and Blücher more than twice that number, while at least 10,000 more Prussians and Saxons disbanded and roamed the banks of the Meuse up to Liège. Blücher himself, his horse killed under him, was thrown to the ground and half crippled and badly bruised during a French cavalry charge; he was then run over by a squadron of cuirassiers who did not even notice him as night was falling.

Napoleon returned to Fleurus at 11 p.m., satisfied that he had gained a great victory and that the Prussians were now retreating eastwards, probably towards Namur, their base of operations. But he was both perplexed and angry at having received no news from Ney all day.

In fact, compounding as it were his cautious laxity of the previous evening, Ney had remained inactive during the whole morning of 16 June, quietly awaiting the Emperor's orders at Gosselies, convinced as he was that Quatre-Bras, thinly defended, could be occupied at leisure, if necessary after a brief attack.

At 7 a.m. he received from Soult a dispatch confirming the imminent arrival of Kellermann's corps of cuirassiers promised by Napoleon the day before to reinforce his left flank. He then left for Frasnes without even ordering Reille to get his corps ready to march. He simply told him to execute immediately any orders from the Emperor which might arrive in his absence and to communicate them to d'Erlon. At Frasnes, Ney did not even send a reconnaissance to probe the enemy positions at Quatre-Bras. At 11 a.m., when Flahaut (one of Napoleon's ordnance officers) brought him the Emperor's order to attack and to take up position at Quatre-Bras and beyond, Ney issued his first marching orders of the day: to Reille towards Genappe and Quatre-Bras, to d'Erlon

towards Frasnes and Marbais, to Kellermann and the Guard's light cavalry to escort him (Ney) on the Brussels road, which he evidently thought was open. When Ney received Napoleon's second order confirming the first one to attack Quatre-Bras, he was still waiting for Reille, who only arrived at Frasnes at 1.30 p.m.

At 2 p.m., Ney launched his attack with 19,000 bayonets, 3,500 sabres and sixty-four cannon. His reserves, including 18,000 infantry of d'Erlon's corps, were five miles behind him. The Prince of Orange had only 8,000 infantry and sixteen cannon at that time. The Nassauer troops in the front line were cut to pieces and the Prince of Orange was only saved by the speed of his horse. At 3 p.m.,

Wellington arrived and judged the situation to be critical for his troops, who were only now beginning to receive reinforcements: Dutch, Belgian and Hanoverian cavalry and the Picton infantry division, but little artillery support. Ney charged again, throwing the enemy on to the Brussels road and taking eight cannon.

At 4 p.m., spurred on by Napoleon's second order to take Quatre-Bras, Ney intensified his attacks. The Brunswick corps arriving on the scene was badly mauled (the reigning Prince of Brunswick fell mortally wounded). Picton charged and was repulsed by infantry with heavy losses. His square formations slowed down the French cavalry's subsequent onslaught, but the 42nd and

25 and 26 Two early twentieth-century photographs of
the farm buildings at Quatre-Bras, the centre of fighting
on 16 June

44th Highlanders were breached and the 42nd's colonel was killed.

By that time, Ney felt the need for his infantry reserve. But d'Erlon, on receiving Napoleon's direct order, was now marching on St Amand. At 5 p.m., Ney received the original of that order enjoining him to detach d'Erlon against Blücher's right flank, which was heavily engaged at Ligny. Enraged by this modification of Napoleon's original orders, which was depriving him of his infantry reserve at a time of need (unforeseen by him because of his own laxity and unpreparedness), Ney sent imperative orders to d'Erlon recalling him forthwith to Quatre-Bras in direct contravention of Napoleon's orders.[22]

Under such stress, Ney recovered some of his old impetuous daring for the first time since the beginning of the campaign. He ordered Kellermann and his cuirassiers to execute one of those massive, spectacular and terrifying charges for which they were rightly famous. The rumbling noise that they made increasing with their speed, they rode right over the square formations of the Colin Halkett brigade, crushing the 69th and taking its flag, ruptured the Brunswick squares, and entered Quatre-Bras to find themselves right in the middle of Wellington's army and being shot at from all sides: they faced Dutch, English and Brunswick infantry fire and artillery shells from Major Kulman's batteries. Kellermann's horse was

killed under him. The cuirassiers, protected by their breast-plates from enemy bullets, got their commander back in the saddle in no time, then turned round at speed, taking the advancing French infantry with them in their gallop. Ney, who was in the middle of it all, had had two horses killed under him and was 'brandishing his sword like a madman'.[23] He had just about time to glance at Napoleon's fourth message confirming that the Emperor intended to finish off the Prussian army, that d'Erlon must march on St Amand whatever the situation at Quatre-Bras, and that he, Ney, must at least contain Wellington's army.

By 6 p.m. the enemy had received new reinforcements: Brunswick artillery, Maitland and Byng's brigades and fresh Nassauer troops. Wellington launched a general attack on the French, who withdrew inch by inch. A Maitland battalion was stopped by artillery fire, charged by the lancers and dispersed in disorder while the cuirassiers were overthrowing a Belgian battalion. By 7 p.m., the battle had been neither won nor lost by either side. Two hours later, when d'Erlon, returning from St Amand, emerged at Frasnes, Ney's and Wellington's forces were holding exactly the same positions as they had that morning. The French had lost 4,300 men and the Anglo-Dutch 4,700.

At 7 a.m. on 17 June, in Fleurus, Napoleon reviewed the situation in the light of the reports he had just received. Shadowed since dawn by

Pajol's cavalry corps, the Prussians were retreating on the roads to Liège and Namur. The Anglo-Dutch were in force, forward of Quatre-Bras, with eight infantry regiments, 2,000 horses and artillery. Napoleon decided to join Ney against Wellington whilst keeping Blücher at bay.

At 9 a.m. he rode to Ligny, where he visited the battlefield and gave orders to tend the wounded before reviewing his troops at their bivouacs. He even found time to discuss with Grouchy and several generals the news from Paris about the state of public and parliamentary opinion, and about the activities of Fouché and of the Liberals.

At 11 a.m. he sent a message to Ney ordering him to resume his attack on Wellington pending his own arrival. He then called Grouchy to explain to him verbally both his own plans and the task he was going to entrust him with: while Napoleon, together with Ney, would be dealing with Wellington, Grouchy, with 34,000 infantry and cavalry and 102 cannon placed under his command, was to concentrate all his forces in Gembloux (at an equal distance from Liège and Wavre). He was to reconnoitre the roads to Namur (probable, but not certain, direction of Blücher's retreat), to pursue the Prussians and to discover whether Blücher intended to join up with Wellington, and to stay constantly in close communication with Napoleon's headquarters. These orders were clearly confirmed to Grouchy in a letter dictated by

Napoleon to Count Bertrand (his Grand Marshal) in the absence of Soult, then still in Fleurus (see Appendix II).

'From the first instant,' writes Houssaye, 'Grouchy felt the burden, rather than the honour, of this mission.' Grouchy had been given the most important command of his career at the head of the army's right flank. He was a brilliant cavalry commander with a well deserved reputation as a battlefield tactician. But he was quite conscious of his limitations as a strategist when leading for the first time several army corps (infantry, cavalry and artillery) in isolation from the main body of the army. He also knew by now that Gérard (who had been expecting a marshal's baton after his conduct at Ligny) and the bad-tempered Vandamme (see page 35) would be displeased at being under his command and he was doubtful about the authority he would have over them. On the other hand, Grouchy, extremely deferential to, and terrified of, Napoleon, could not, as a Marshal of France, decline the honour bestowed upon him and refuse the difficult and perilous mission which the Emperor was asking him to accomplish. He therefore set out immediately to obey his orders without a murmur but not without forebodings.

For his part Napoleon considered that, having dealt adequately with Blücher, it was time to deal with Wellington as well. At midday, Napoleon rode towards Quatre-Bras, preceded by Lobau's infantry, the whole Guard, the light cavalry divisions of Domon and Subervie, and Milhaud's cuirassiers. He halted at Marbais at 1 p.m., expecting either news from Ney or the sound of cannon fire. Instead, Napoleon saw a detachment of French hussars rushing back towards him, hotly pursued by English cavalry. He immediately ordered battle positions: Milhaud's cuirassiers on the right, light cavalry left and right, infantry in second line and batteries in the centre.

Ney was still nowhere to be seen. Five hundred hussars were detached towards Frasnes to find him and his corps. An English woman sutler, taken prisoner, brought the news that Wellington (having learned only during the night of the Prussian disaster at Ligny) had ordered a retreat towards Brussels, leaving only Lord Uxbridge's cavalry corps and some artillery as rearguard at Quatre-Bras. From there, two English batteries had already opened fire, apparently on Napoleon himself. The Emperor ordered a battery of the Guard's horse artillery to move forward and to open fire. The light cavalry charged the enemy, followed by Lobau's infantry, and the Anglo-Dutch withdrew in considerable disorder from Quatre-Bras. Dark, heavy clouds were torn by lightning and it started to rain just as first d'Erlon's corps, then Ney, appeared.

Napoleon reproached d'Erlon briefly for his delay in arriving at St Amand the day before. To Ney, he expressed drily his surprise that the Marshal had ignored this very morning's order to attack Quatre-Bras again.[24] Then, wasting no more time in recriminations, Napoleon galloped ahead of the whole army in hot pursuit of Wellington's forces 'at the pace of a fox hunt'.[25] At the village of Genappe, Lord Uxbridge regrouped his main cavalry and installed two batteries on a slope. When the French lancers appeared in pursuit of the Vivian brigade, they were first received by cannon fire and then charged upon by the English hussars (Life Guards), Lord Uxbridge leading the attack. There was a brief and bloody street battle in the village between French lancers and hussars on the one hand and English hussars and Life Guards on the other. The English got the worst of it and retreated. After Genappe the appalling weather, rather than the English haste or the French ardour, slowed down the pace. The infantry was marching calf-deep in water on the flooded roads or sinking knee-deep in the soaking fields. The cavalry could hardly move and the artillery was completely stuck. All this impeded both the French pursuit and the retreat of the English cavalry under intermittent fire from the French.

It was 6 p.m. when Napoleon arrived at the head of his army on the heights of La Belle Alliance, opposite the village of St Jean, two miles south of Waterloo and twelve miles south of Brussels. The Brunswick infantry, in considerable disorder, and the English cavalry rearguard were crossing the valley separating La Belle Alliance from the plateau of Mont St Jean, when they seemed to halt as they approached the neighbouring Forest of Soignes.

The rain had stopped. Through the damp mist hanging over the scene, Napoleon could discern masses of infantry and cavalry. Was it an army corps taking up position to cover Wellington's retreat, or was it more? Napoleon ordered Milhaud's cuirassiers to feint a new charge on the English rearguard, which had been protected until then by about fifteen guns. Wellington unmasked fifty to sixty cannon all at once and fired. Napoleon 'understood the message'. He was certain now that the whole Anglo-Dutch-Hanoverian army was mustered there in front of him. In a sense, it was just as at Ligny. Success had rewarded Napoleon's familiar tactics: concentrate the maxi-

mum of his available forces, attack the enemy frontally, advance and pursue strongly if the adversary retreated, and destroy him in major battle if he stood his ground.

It was 6.30 p.m. Napoleon estimated that he needed two hours more to press the pursuit to a final conclusion. This would have opened up to him the road to Brussels, where he now confidently expected to arrive triumphantly with his army by dawn on 18 June after an overnight advance. However heavy clouds, about to burst again in torrential rain, were darkening the early summer evening.[26] Both armies paused, drenched and filthy, to bivouac and cook as best they could in the mud, separated by a distance of less than a mile: the Anglo-Dutch on the northern plateau of Mont St Jean, the French above the southern side of a rye field which formed an undulating valley between the two elevated positions. Napoleon felt as cheated by the weather as he had been disappointed by Ney's slackness and delays at Quatre-Bras.

Still, having established his headquarters at the farm of Caillou, about 2,500 yards behind La Belle Alliance, that evening, Napoleon felt that he had the situation well in hand. In the three days since the beginning of hostilities, after a brilliant concentration manoeuvre, he had surprised combined enemy forces twice the size of his own (see Appendix III), attacked and separated them, inflicted considerable casualties on both and gained a great victory over the Prussians. Now his Anglo-Dutch prey was here at his mercy. Grouchy, with some 33,000 infantry and cavalry with 102 cannon should be well able to prevent Blücher, whichever the direction of his retreat, from joining up with Wellington at Mont St Jean, at any rate before a French victory over the English (see Grouchy's movements on 17 June, page 44).

As for Wellington, Napoleon did not believe that he would be so foolish or so bold as to choose this ground and these circumstances to make a stand against the French army. He had behind him the narrow paths of the Forest of Soignes and if he were in dire straits during the battle, or if he were beaten, no retreat would be possible for his troops. Besides, as commander-in-chief of the Prussian as well as of the Anglo-Dutch army, Wellington's own agreed plan with Blücher, emphasized by the lessons of the previous three days of fighting, was to engage the French army only as a combined operation so as to ensure overwhelming superiority.

On the other hand, if Wellington took advantage of the night (17th–18th) to cross the Forest of Soignes on which he was backing up (as Napoleon thought he would do, most likely before 9 a.m.) in order eventually to unite with Blücher behind it, between Mont St Jean and Brussels, then the French army's position would become extremely delicate. In that event, even if Grouchy had rejoined him at St Jean by then, it would be impossible for the French army to take the risk of crossing the forest in order to fight, when coming out of the clearings, forces which would be more than double its own in strength, ready in position and in formation, and reinforced by the whole of their rearguards and reserves. Moreover, in a few weeks' time the considerable Russian, Austrian and Bavarian armies (at least 300,000 men in all) would be crossing the Rhine. The two armies of Rapp and Suchet covering Alsace and Chambéry with only 36,000 men (see Appendix III, Table 2) would be unable to stop them from advancing on the river Marne. This would take the war into France and cut off the French army in Belgium.

Napoleon's plan, therefore, was to resume the pursuit of Wellington's retreating army and to begin a movement designed to breach it, in spite of the darkness, as soon as the enemy started to move. He gave orders to prepare for this, and it was quite late before he went to sleep at Caillou, after dictating a few letters in answer to his mail from Paris reporting some worrying parliamentary agitation. Extremely preoccupied with this, as well as with the situation at hand, he did not sleep for long.

At about the time Napoleon was returning to Caillou, Grouchy was sitting down at Gembloux, some twenty miles from the army's headquarters, to write his report following his movements of that day (17 June). At midday, having been entrusted with his special mission by Napoleon (see page 41), Grouchy had ordered Vandamme and Gérard to proceed from St Amand and Ligny, respectively, to Gembloux. The first had to cover seven and a half miles, the second, eleven miles, to reach their common destination. Grouchy followed at a leisurely pace (less than two miles an hour), arriving at Gembloux with the two corps between 6 and 7 p.m.

On the way, Grouchy received a report from Exelmans (dated Gembloux 1.30 p.m. 17 June) saying that he was observing within cannon shot a Prussian army of some 20,000 men which was occupying that village and that he would shadow them if they moved. When Grouchy arrived at Gembloux, Exelmans had been occupying it since 3 p.m., having failed to see the Prussian corps (Thielemann, in fact) 'slip away' unnoticed an hour before.

Grouchy did not try to pursue the enemy there and then; it was raining hard, the roads were difficult to negotiate, the troops were tired, and they had started to cook. However, he sent Exelmans' scouts to reconnoitre. At 10 p.m., they reported to Grouchy that the Prussians were retreating towards Wavre. Grouchy then wrote this dispatch to Napoleon's Caillou headquarters: 'My information is that the Prussians are retreating towards Wavre. If the mass of their forces goes to Wavre, I shall follow *to prevent them from reaching Brussels and from rejoining Wellington*. If their principal forces retreat to Liège, I shall follow them there.'[27]

From various reports (Pajol, Teste) and from information gathered in Gembloux, Grouchy had known since 7 p.m. at least that a Prussian movement towards Wavre was taking place. He had done nothing about it. In spite of his assurances to Napoleon, all his marching orders to the corps under his command for the next day (18 June)

were clearly geared to a pursuit in the direction of Liège. At best, Grouchy was evidently putting Wavre and Liège on the same level of possibility, with a strong bias towards Liège. Yet he knew that any enemy movement on Wavre would be a threat to the French army's right flank, requiring immediate and vigorous action on his part, whereas any Prussian move towards Liège would simply put further distance between Blücher and Wellington, requiring only observation and pursuit. In Napoleon's orders to Grouchy, priority was un-

mistakably given to preventing a reunion between Blücher and Wellington. At a time when, unknown to Grouchy, and therefore to Napoleon, the four Prussian corps – Bülow, Pirch, Zieten and Thielemann – were already concentrated in and around Wavre, some seven miles away from Gembloux, Grouchy, having let them 'slip away', was still uncertain and undecided. In fact, he was expecting Napoleon from his headquarters in Caillou, to tell him specifically in which direction he should proceed from Gembloux.

At 1 a.m. (18 June) Napoleon came out on foot, accompanied only by Count Bertrand, to pace the line of the Guard.[28] The Forest of Soignes appeared to him lit by a thousand lights. From west to east, extending from Braine l'Alleud to the village of La Haye, the horizon sparkled with the fires of enemy bivouacs. There was complete silence. The Anglo-Dutch army was plunged in deep sleep after the exhaustion of the previous days. As he arrived near the woods of the castle of Hougoumont, Napoleon thought he heard the sound of a moving column. It was 2.30 a.m., the very time, he thought, the enemy's rearguard should have begun to leave its positions if it was retreating. But it was a short-lived illusion. The noise stopped. Several officers sent on reconnaissance, as well as scouts returning at 3.30 a.m., confirmed that the enemy were not moving at all.

At 4 a.m., dispatch riders brought to Napoleon a peasant who had been used as a guide by an English cavalry brigade which had gone to take up position to the east, at the village of Ohain. And two Belgian deserters who had just left their regiment reported to him that their army was preparing for battle, that no retrograde movement had taken place, and that 'Belgium was praying for the success of the Emperor since the English and the Prussians were equally hated by the population.'[29] The French troops were bivouacked in the mud. Their officers considered it impossible to give battle that day (18 June). The artillery and cavalry would be unable to manoeuvre on such soaked ground. They estimated that twelve hours of good weather would be necessary for the ground to dry up sufficiently.

As dawn broke, Napoleon returned to his headquarters at Caillou where he found Grouchy's dispatch dated Gembloux 10 p.m. 17 June (see page 44 and Appendix II) reporting that the Prussians seemed to be retreating in two columns, one to Liège, the other to Wavre, and that he would follow them accordingly. Napoleon went to sleep, satisfied that Wellington was making a great error of judgment in receiving battle at Mont St Jean, regretting only that he was himself being prevented by the bad weather from taking advantage of the situation. But already the weather was clearing. At 5 a.m., Napoleon awoke to the first pale rays of sunlight, knowing that the great battle would take place that day. He gave orders to prepare the attack for 9 a.m., confident that victory would crown with military success and with renewed imperial glory the lightning campaign which had brought him and his army to Mont St Jean.

2 THE ANGLO-DUTCH ARMY

William Seymour

It was around two o'clock on the afternoon of Saturday 17 June 1815. The Earl of Uxbridge, who commanded the Anglo-Dutch cavalry, was covering that army's withdrawal through the single narrow street of Genappe. Deepening storm clouds blotted out the sun, and the darkened Belgian countryside was lit by lurid flashes of lightning as the rain swept in a curtain drenching man and beast. The rain turned the ground into a quagmire, but it hindered the pursuers as much as the pursued, confining all to the paved road, and after the 7th Hussars and the Life Guards had fought back the French 1st Lancers, the moiled and weary heroes of Quatre-Bras went on their way unmolested.

Not that theirs was a beaten army; the Battle of Quatre-Bras, memorable in its own right although understandably dwarfed by the events of two days later, had been a stern struggle in which neither side could claim the victory – although Napoleon, himself not free from blame, was to censure Ney for a lost opportunity. However, the Prussians, under that gallant old warrior, Field-Marshal Blücher, had been given a hiding by the Emperor at Ligny and were withdrawing on Wavre. Wellington's army had therefore to comply, and, in a phrase to become so familiar to the descendants of these men a hundred and more years later, 'withdrew to a prepared position in rear'. The line upon which the Duke of Wellington had decided to stand and beat the French was some two miles south of the village of Waterloo, at Mont St Jean, where the Brussels–Charleroi road is crossed by the one between the villages of Ohain and Braine l'Alleud.

People have speculated as to whether Wellington chose this position in advance; should we perhaps believe Lord Fitzroy Somerset's assertion that his chief, who had sent Colonel de Lancey back from Quatre-Bras to reconnoitre a defensive line, was surprised that de Lancey did not choose the La Belle Alliance ridge? If the story of the Duke of Richmond's map at the famous Brussels ball is true then the Mont St Jean position had been pre-selected and Lord Fitzroy's memory was at fault.

One thing is quite certain: de Lancey knew Wellington well enough not to alter any selected position without orders. On the other hand, there is reason to believe that up to 15 June Wellington had formed no specific plan, for he had no idea which way Napoleon would move – indeed it was probably not until 3 a.m. on 18 June, when he heard from Blücher, that he finally decided to stand at Mont St Jean. However, knowing the Duke to have been a master of defensive tactics, it is difficult to believe that he was not personally responsible for the important decision as to where the battle should be fought.

What sort of an army was this? It had already lost some 4,500 men and now had to face, possibly unaided, a force of 72,000 French troops, many of them campaign veterans who looked upon their emperor as the god of modern war? It was a heterogeneous force that had been built up and hastily put together in the little time available. For the Battle of Waterloo Wellington put into the field a total of 67,661 men (of whom fewer than 24,000 were British), and 156 guns.[1] He had therefore almost 5,000 fewer troops than Napoleon and ninety fewer guns. But that is not the complete picture, for it has been reckoned that his whole force was equivalent to a British army of only 41,000 men,[2] and he was outgunned in calibre as well as in numbers of guns – although not in gunnery.

But the Anglo-Dutch army was brilliantly commanded. Wellington has sometimes been labelled a poor strategist, and he may not have been capable of the grand designs that were the hallmark of Napoleon in his prime, but he thoroughly understood all military problems, he was a master of timing, and throughout his Peninsular campaign he never allowed the possibility of a small tactical advantage to obscure the overall strategic prize. Not only in Portugal, but also in India, he had gained enormous experience in the handling of all arms; he had developed his own tactical ideas, and a series of victories had proved them sound. But there was nothing rigid in these ideas – he would change the infantry lines from two to four deep in the middle of a battle if occasion demanded; only certain principles designed to safeguard his men, or supplies, as far as possible were immutable – for although not over-cautious he understood the need to conserve.

When Wellington arrived in Brussels from the Congress of Vienna on 4 April 1815, two compelling matters engaged his immediate attention: the strengthening of his totally inadequate army, and the problem of the command and commanders. The British troops in Belgium at that time consisted of twenty-five battalions of infantry and six regiments of cavalry, some 14,000 men in all. Many of them were without battle experience, for of the superb fighting machine that Britain had built up for the Peninsular War most of the troops had either been demobilized or were in the process of

31 Right: Frederick William, Duke of Brunswick
32 Centre: Sir Thomas Picton; killed when a bullet pierced his famous top hat
33 Far right: Lord Fitzroy Somerset, Wellington's military secretary

being transported back from a senseless expedition to America. It was not until the beginning of May that the government overcame their reluctance to call out the militia – for the law prevented their embodiment unless the country was at war, which it was not – and were thus enabled to send a few thousand more troops to Belgium.

As far as the foreign half of the army was concerned, Wellington had even more reason to be apprehensive. At Waterloo it numbered 43,670 men, but of these only the King's German Legion[3] could be considered thoroughly reliable troops. There were almost 6,000 Brunswickers eager to avenge the death of their duke at Quatre-Bras, and 11,000 Hanoverians about whom little was known except that although the officers were good the troops they commanded were mostly untried in battle. The same applied to many of the 17,800 Dutch–Belgians, but with them there was the added danger that at best they would show little inclination to fight, and that at worst they might desert to the enemy, with whom some of them had been comrades in arms before the creation of the new Netherlands state, which in itself was resented by most Belgians. Wellington might grumble about his British soldiery, and occasionally refer to them with an abusive epithet, but with his unfailing sagacity he knew their worth, and realised that they and his King's German Legion troops were the crucible from which the victory would be achieved.

At the same time as setting to work on the British government over his lack of troops, Wellington was busily exerting all his tact – a quality with which he was not over-endowed – trying to persuade the somewhat prickly William I of the Netherlands to appoint him commander-in-chief of the Dutch–Belgian troops; these were, at the time of his arrival in Brussels, under William's eldest son, the Prince of Orange. He eventually achieved this at the beginning of May, much to everyone's relief, for Slender Billy (a nickname derived from the length of his neck), although capable of showing considerable charm and even more courage, was in no way fit to command an army. Indeed at only twenty-three, and with no more than two years' experience of war on Wellington's staff behind him, this was hardly surprising. Moreover, he had an exaggerated idea of his own importance, which at times manifested itself in an urge to invade France with his quite inadequate army.

The stream of letters with which the Duke assailed Lord Bathurst, the Minister for War, and Colonel Torrens at the Horse Guards, was not confined to the weakness of the army, however, but contained constant complaints at not being allowed the regimental and staff officers of his choice. Wellington had no use for a second-in-command; he preferred to keep all essentials in his own hands and seldom encouraged initiative on the part of his subordinates. He expected his commanders to obey his orders without question and leave the conduct of the battle to him. For this reason very few of his generals were distinguished for much else than personal valour, although there were some – Lord Hill for one – who had they been raised under a less formidable shadow might themselves have become great commanders. But it was for officers, close-knit by active service and tempered by discipline and loyalty, that he now clamoured so strongly – and to a great extent would eventually get.

The most important member of the headquarters staff was the quartermaster-general, whose task it was to deal with all matters relating to equipment, quartering, embarkation, disembarkation and the movement of divisions, and with his deputy-assistants to prepare topographical surveys and reports on bridges, roads, etc. In the Peninsular campaign Sir George Murray had filled this post with distinction, but now he was in Canada and the Horse Guards had sent Sir Hudson Lowe. Wellington very soon made it clear that Lowe would not do for him, and Sir William de Lancey,

a Peninsular veteran and a much more suitable choice, replaced him.

The adjutant-general, whose duties chiefly concerned discipline and statistics, was Sir Edward Barnes, an excellent man, who had been with Wellington in 1813 and 1814. Wellington's military secretary was Lord Fitzroy Somerset (later Lord Raglan), and nine aides-de-camp were included in a total headquarters staff of about seventy. Of the general officers of the allied powers that were represented at Wellington's headquarters the most important was the Prussian Baron von Müffling, a man of charm and competence, who made it his business to be helpful and understanding. It might not be too much to say that after Wellington, Müffling contributed more than any other individual towards the victory. Without his patient handling of the deeply suspicious Gneisenau, and his firmness with Zieten, Blücher and his Prussians might never have reached the field of battle in time.

The commander of the cavalry was the Earl of Uxbridge, who had arrived in Brussels at the end of April. Wellington had wanted Lord Combermere who, as Stapleton Cotton, had been with him in India and the Peninsula, but Uxbridge – who had also been in the Peninsula until his amatory exploits with Wellington's sister-in-law had interfered with his further employment there – was the Horse Guards' (or perhaps the Prince

Regent's) choice. He was a fine-looking man, an excellent officer who had distinguished himself with Sir John Moore at Corunna, and Wellington was well satisfied with his appointment. He had under his command 12,400 sabres, of which the seven brigades of British and King's German Legion cavalry formed the greater part. These men were superbly mounted, as indeed were the Horse Gunners, but with the exception of the King's German Legion and one or two British regiments, such as the 23rd Light Dragoons, had no battle experience. Many of the officers had joined for the social prestige and were better acquainted with the hunting field than the cavalry drill book; they had plenty of courage, very little expertise and rather too much *élan*. The sabre, pistol and short carbines were the cavalryman's weapons; the light cavalry carried a curved sword for cutting, while the heavy cavalry were usually armed with a longer and straighter weapon meant for thrusting.

The Royal Artillery was commanded by Sir George Wood, who had under him eight troops from what was known at that time as the Royal Horse Brigade, and five British field brigades, each of which was a unit of six pieces; in addition there were two troops of King's German Legion horse artillery, and three Dutch-Belgian, one Hanoverian and eight other foreign field brigades. The field brigades fired either 6- or 9-pounders. Colonel Sir

Augustus Frazer commanded the British Horse Gunners, and it was due to his foresight that at Waterloo three of his troops had 9-pounders instead of the normal 6-pounders, one was armed with 5½-inch heavy howitzers and another with rockets. The guns fired grape, round shot, shell, shrapnel and case;[4] the howitzers did not fire round shot, but included in their armament was an incendiary device within a shell for setting fire to a target, called a carcass; Major Whinyates' rockets were distinctively whimsical, but at times effective. It is sometimes argued that the proportion of British field brigades to horse artillery should have been reversed, but the mobility of the latter was to be a telling factor, and in the event Wellington was excellently served by both branches of his artillery – perhaps inspired by the proximity of the world's greatest master gunner.

The Anglo-Dutch army was divided into two corps and a reserve – although much of the reserve was to fight in the front line. The Prince of Orange commanded I Corps and General Lord Hill II Corps. The reserve remained under the overall control of the Duke. Orange's appointment was, of course, political, and his courage was little compensation for his dangerous incompetence. However, in Baron Jean de Constant Rebecque, he had an excellent chief of staff. Hill, on the other hand, was a much trusted and thoroughly efficient commander, a kindly man well liked by his troops, who in 1827 was to become commander-in-chief of the British army.

Orange's divisional commanders were General Cooke, who had the two Guards brigades under Maitland and Byng in his division; the veteran Sir Charles Count von Alten, whose brigade commanders were Sir Colin Halkett – as fierce a fighter as could be found on either side – Baron von Ompteda of the King's German Legion and the Hanoverian Count Kielmansegge; and Baron von Perponcher and Baron Chassé, who commanded the 2nd and 3rd Dutch–Belgian Divisions respectively. Prince Bernhard of Saxe-Weimar's Nassauers, who formed a brigade in Perponcher's division, were the first troops to be engaged at Quatre-Bras and had been handled with distinction.

Lord Hill had Generals Clinton and Colville as his divisional commanders and a mixed force under Prince Frederick of the Netherlands (Orange's eighteen-year-old brother), which included the 1st Dutch–Belgian Division. Only Mitchell's brigade in Colville's 4th Division saw action at Waterloo; the remainder of the division and Prince Frederick's troops spent the day at Hal some eight miles from the battlefield. Welling-

ton felt certain up to the last moment that Napoleon would come round his right flank and try to cut him off from the sea. The arguments for and against this thinking are numerous and do not form any part of the account of the actual fighting, but in order to meet this threat Wellington allowed 17,000 soldiers, whom he would badly need, to take no part in the battle.

The 5th and 6th British Divisions were the mainstay of the reserve; the 6th should have been commanded by General Sir Lowry Cole, but he had been granted leave to get married and missed the battle. His senior brigade commander, Sir John Lambert, who had on his staff that remarkable and romantic officer Harry Smith, brought his brigade almost literally straight from America to the battlefield. The commander of the 5th Division, Sir Thomas Picton, was perhaps the greatest character of all Wellington's generals. A rough-tongued Welshman, whose manners were more suited to the stable than the drawing-room, he was nevertheless a fine soldier with unbounded courage, and although a severe disciplinarian he was trusted and even liked by his men. Wellington, who knew his worth, but did not much like the man, had especially asked for him, and he arrived just in time to lead his division to Quatre-Bras dressed, as his A.D.C. Captain Gronow tells us, in a 'blue frock-coat, very tightly buttoned up to the throat; a very large black silk neckcloth, showing little or no shirt collar, dark trousers, boots and a round hat'.[5] In that battle he received a wound, which he refused to disclose, that might itself have proved mortal had he not been reserved for a hero's death two days later.

Wellington was as quick to censure as he was slow to praise – although he was not an entirely ungenerous man, and his commendations when they did come were all the more welcome for being sincere. His complaints to Lord Bathurst and others in the weeks preceding the battle were expressions of regret. In the Peninsula he had created a magnificent fighting machine, and when that war was over he had witnessed its dismemberment without undue dismay; now, like a petulant child, he was annoyed that the pieces could not be put together again. But he was a master of his art who knew very well the true quality of his officers and men; nor had the Horse Guards been entirely disobliging, and many of his brigadiers – such as Kempt, Pack, Halkett, Byng, Barnard, Ponsonby and Vandeleur – were among the great names of the Peninsula. All in all it was not really 'an infamous army'; the main trouble lay in the scarcity of its most important component – the British

infantry. For this reason Wellington made certain that the meagre 15,000 he had were distributed as widely as possible throughout the line. These men, rather more than half of whom were battle veterans, were stolid and fairly unimaginative; no toil was too hard for them, no hours of marching and fighting, often under appalling conditions, too long; no danger could shatter their unruffled calm.

At the beginning of the nineteenth century the British infantryman was armed with one of three different types of musket or rifle; he carried sixty rounds of ammunition, a variety of accoutrements, such as mess tin and camp kettle, and a pack containing blankets, greatcoat, other clothing and three days' biscuit. In all he humped a weight of some 60 lb. The musket in common use was familiarly known as Brown Bess; it had a 39-inch barrel, a .75 inch bore and weighed 11 lb., 4 oz. with bayonet. Beyond about seventy-five yards it was an inaccurate weapon, although its ball would carry to 400 yards. The light infantry musket, carried by the 43rd (who were not at Waterloo) and 52nd Foot, had a better grip, a notched V-block backsight and a semi-waterproof priming pan. The Baker rifle had a bore of .625 inches and weighed $10\frac{1}{2}$ lb. with sword-bayonet fixed; it was used by the 95th (Rifle) Regiment and the King's German Legion light battalions and companies. Although the Baker rifle could be fired with accuracy up to almost 200 yards, its rate of fire in practised hands of one aimed round a minute compared unfavourably with the three volleys that a skilled man could discharge in the same time from a Brown Bess. The British infantryman handled his musket more efficiently than his French opposite number, and the massive formations in which the French infantry came to the attack put them at an added disadvantage. Every man in both ranks of a British battalion in lines two deep could load and fire with ease, whereas in the French columns only about one-fifth of the men could fire at any one time.

Such was the army that gradually assembled on the rain-soaked plateau of Mont St Jean in the gathering dusk of Saturday 17 June. Officers of the quartermaster-general's staff were busy directing commanders to positions in the line. Darkness came and left much still to be done on the morrow. Meanwhile, bedraggled and bewildered men tramped the sodden ground intent only on getting what shelter a blanket, or for some lucky ones a bivouac, might provide and scrounging what food they could. Time in the morning to take stock of the ground that Old Nosey had given them to defend.

G THE PRUSSIANS

Colonel E. Kaulbach

'My army is in the best of shape and their morale is all that can be wished for,' wrote Field-Marshal Prince Blücher von Wahlstadt to the Prussian Prime Minister, Prince Hardenberg, on 2 June 1815.[1]

What was this army really like, which had been deployed along the Rhine as part of the second mobilization against Napoleon in the spring of 1815? What were its strengths and weaknesses, and how was its battle fitness achieved?

The 'Army of the Lower Rhine' which, under the command of Field-Marshal Prince Blücher, was assigned to cover the Prussian sector between the Maas and the Mosel, consisted of four army corps. The bringing of this army up to its intended total strength of 130,000 to 150,000 men took place under very difficult conditions. In the first place, the necessary manpower was not immediately available, since the Prussian army, in the winter of 1814–15, was in the process of a reorganization from wartime to peacetime strength; its organization was to conform to the new Prussian state which had been reconstituted in Vienna.[2] Both the militia and the volunteer units, which had made up a major part of the wartime army of 1813–14, were being gradually disbanded and parts of the regular line regiments had returned to their home provinces, where they were either reorganized or newly constituted and renamed. The rapid reinforcement of units to a wartime strength presented considerable complications.

The second great difficulty lay in the fact that both the state and the people of Prussia were impoverished, owing to the long years of French occupation, to the heavy contributions demanded by the occupying forces, and to the great loss of territory inflicted upon Prussia. To this were added the cost and effort of the war years of 1813–14, which could only have been sustained by the determination of the entire Prussian people. Both in 1813 and in 1815, it was the imposition of compulsory military service which made it possible for Prussia to create a mobile field army. Compulsory military service, provisionally introduced by Scharnhorst in 1812–13 for the duration of the war, was now incorporated by law as the basis of the military establishment.[3]

Although these circumstances had no more than an indirect effect on the Battle of Waterloo, they must be recognized if we are to understand the character and behaviour of Blücher's army, and to measure its achievements against those of the other armies taking part in the battle.

The basis of the Prussian field army, which was to be set up on the lower Rhine, was created from the former Prussian I, II and III Corps. These corps, acting ostensibly as the Prussian security force, with a strength of about 30,000 to 50,000 men, under the command of General von Kleist, had remained on the Rhine between Wesel and Koblenz. A fourth army corps was to be set up at home and brought up to the Rhine. Until the arrival of Field-Marshal Prince von Blücher who had recently been named commander-in-chief by King Frederick William III, Lieutenant-General Count von Gneisenau, appointed a new chief of the general staff of the army, had been instructed by the King to carry out all necessary organization of the army and its movements and to deputize fully for Blücher. The Order-in-Cabinet of 29 March 1815 states: '. . . I cannot, in view of the distance from the area of operation, give you any definite orders as to how you should act in the case of unforeseen events but I must leave it to you to make such arrangements with the Duke of Wellington as suit the circumstances and to act in agreement with him in all things. While I empower you to do so and assure you of my fullest confidence in you, I also make you responsible for acting with all prudence and the most careful consideration in every matter affecting the future of Europe.'[4]

In his account of the campaign, General von Ollech says:

Gneisenau had, then, been given unrestricted power and put into a position for which, by his intellectual genius, his shrewd judgement and the energy of his noble character, he was ideally suited.[5]

Indeed, this order indicates not only the Prussian king's faith in Gneisenau but also his very clear assessment of the situation and the unmistakable order to co-operate with Wellington; last but not least, it shows the weight of responsibility that could be placed at that time on a chief of the general staff in the Prussian army.

The mobilization of the entire Prussian field army, as well as their intended order of battle and the respective appointments, had already been ordered by the King on 23 March 1815.[6] This order stated that, in all, seven mobile army corps were to be set up, of which I, II, III and IV Corps were to receive priority as the front-line army on the Lower Rhine and V, VI and VII Corps were to form the reserve at home. The corps were homogenously organized under their permanent commanders, and comprised the then customary three main fighting services, infantry, cavalry and artillery. In addition they contained the necessary auxiliaries such as pioneers and supply columns. In this way, each individual corps was fully mobile and capable of independent operation. This progressive organization was the fruit of the experience of heavy fighting against Napoleon and of the opportunism of his generalship.

The infantry of each corps was made up of four brigades of three regiments, each with three battalions; this total of twelve infantry regiments with 2,500 men to a regiment constituted a very powerful fighting unit. The cavalry was equally strong; each corps had plans for at least two brigades of three to five regiments each. Two of these regiments were to be used in the field as reconnaissance and liaison units, permanently attached to the infantry; the remainder were to be the cavalry reserve in actual battle. Lastly each corps was allocated twelve artillery batteries, all with eight 6–12-pounder guns, either limbered or mounted – a total of ninety-six guns.[7] Of these, each infantry and cavalry brigade was to have one of the 6-pounder batteries. This organization made the infantry brigades tactically independent units, comparable to the divisions of later years.

The setting up of these corps took time. Although the reinforcement of the individual units with militia and replacement personnel started immediately, it dragged on for the next few months. On the very eve of the battle, units were still arriving to join their commands, and the last of the formations followed the army into France. As the line regiments were quite insufficient to bring the various brigades up to their planned strengths, the entire militia had been called up; additional troops and replacements were summoned from those provinces in Western Germany which, at the Congress of Vienna, had just been given back to Prussia, even though some had been under French dominion for as long as twenty years. At the same time, for the sake of the uniformity of the future army, the consecutive denomination and the new disposition of the units were pushed through, despite the imminent danger of war. Von Ollech is very reserved in his comments:

At this time the King had already issued orders concerning the composition of the field army, the execution of which was doubtless dictated by necessity, but which even today, under the same circumstances, we would not contemplate without grave misgivings. In the face of the enemy, whose attack was thought to be imminent, the idea was partially to split up all the army corps and by an exchange of regiments to weld them into new corps designated by different numbers. Such was the intention, to mix experienced and inexperienced regiments, regular and militia personnel. It was clear that the entire militia should be called up and that the

regiments from the old provinces under new commanders would have to hurry to the Rhine; but, as they had to move on foot, it would take some time for them to arrive. The simultaneous creation of fourteen new cavalry regiments, partly by detaching one squadron from each old regiment, together with their best officers, reduced the strength of both the old and the new regiments, temporarily, to three squadrons. . . .[8]

Considering the circumstances, it is remarkable that by 20 April 1815 sufficient reinforcements had arrived at the Rhine to enable the skeleton corps to take up their new names and organization. These were now as follows:[9]

The new I Corps was commanded by Lieutenant-General von Zieten with Infantry Brigades 1–4 from the former II Corps.

The new II Corps commanded by Lieutenant-General von Borstell,[10] with Infantry Brigades 5–8 from the former III Corps.

The new III Corps was commanded by Lieutenant-General von Thielemann, with Infantry Brigades 9–12 from the former I Corps.

The new IV Corps was commanded by General von Bülow, at first at home and later in quarters deployed around Koblenz with Infantry Brigades 13–16.

This clear and unified organization of the army certainly provided what the forthcoming battle demanded: mobility and strength. But it also provided what the internal demands of a conscript army required, an army of men from all sections of the people and supported by all sections; it had to be held together not so much by punishment and commendation as by a common resolve, by good will and by enthusiasm[11] – characteristics which were regarded by the allied monarchies as decidedly revolutionary and therefore suspect.

The prerequisites for success for such an army, however, were homogeneity and, above all, mutual confidence between leaders and led. And it was here that there were inevitable weaknesses brought about by the speed with which the units had had to be assembled and the delays in the arrival of some of them or of their commanding officers. Bearing in mind the troops' varying standards of training and varying experience of actual fighting, the initial mobilization order demanded that any given formation should be made up of mixed units. Thus, every infantry brigade was to consist of at least one line regiment, one militia regiment and, where necessary, one replacement regiment or unit from an area formerly not Prussian. The army, especially the higher command posts, was officered almost entirely by Prussians. The Prussian line regiments with their exceptionally high training and discipline were intended to form the adamantine rock within the brigades and to serve as distinguished examples to the rest. The rest had a similarly planned mixture; in this way at least a third, and up to two-thirds, of all the army corps consisted of insufficiently trained soldiers.

For the high command of the army and its army corps, with their units independent down to the brigades, a correspondingly homogeneous character was essential with regard to the conduct of operations. This was achieved through the organization of the general staff which had been laid down by Scharnhorst for the Prussian armed forces, which had been tried and polished during the campaigns of 1813–14, and which ran parallel to the normal adjutancy services in common use; general staff duties were concerned with operational active service. The army command as well as each corps command had a chief of staff assisted by a number of auxiliary staff services, and every infantry brigade and reserve cavalry command of each army corps had trained general staff officers.[12] General Gneisenau, chief of the general staff, had

under him a number of older general staff officers responsible for individual areas of command and this gave him novel expertise in matters of command. Certainly, it was not only the good morale of the troops and the energy of their commanders but also this new kind of staff support which enabled the barely trained units of the Prussian army to carry out the orderly withdrawal over unknown roads after the difficult evening at Ligny, and, what is more, to regroup rapidly and, on the following day, to be brought into action at Waterloo over extremely difficult territory and by separate routes.

When Gneisenau arrived at the Rhine early in April 1815, the grouping and reorganization of the Prussian 'Army of the Lower Rhine' was well under way. By the time Field-Marshal Blücher arrived on 21 April, this was nearly completed, but the individual corps were not yet up to full strength. For example, General von Zieten reported on 28 April that his I Corps still lacked three infantry regiments, two cavalry regiments,

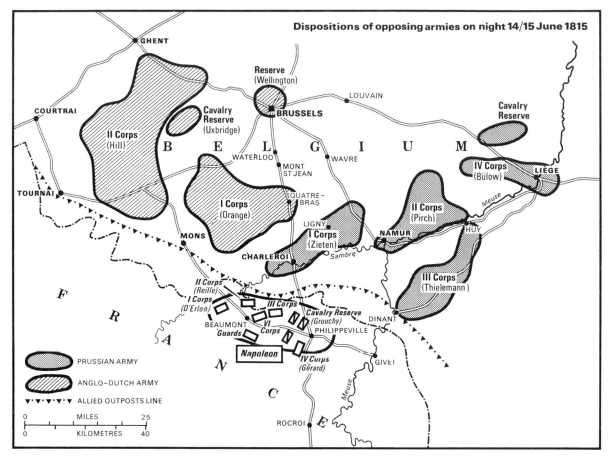

Dispositions of opposing armies on night 14/15 June 1815

PRUSSIAN ARMY

ANGLO-DUTCH ARMY

ALLIED OUTPOSTS LINE

two pioneer companies and four batteries.[13] Particular difficulties were caused by the setting up of the required number of batteries at home. As a result, Blücher's army had to march into battle on 16 June with only thirty-nine of the planned forty-eight batteries. The rest of the artillery did not reach their units until they were in France.

Nevertheless, a report of the general staff states:

Towards the end of May, the mobilization of the army could be said to be completed even though various Corps had not yet reached their full complement of units. . . . The combination of militia with regular troops within the brigades still had to prove itself, for the infantry of I and II Corps were one third militia, that of III Corps was half, and that of IV Corps two-thirds . . . The arms, clothing and equipment of the entire army were more or less operational but very uneven and, in the case of the militia, barely serviceable. The same applies to the number of horses. Everywhere there was a shortage of money,[14] so that, as in 1812–13, the soldiers could not always be paid. Blücher was able to get a loan of 100,000 Taler from England,[15] with difficulty, in order to pay for the most urgent requirements. . . .

The conclusion of this semi-official report is incontestable:

It must be taken as a very considerable achievement that by the end of May the Prussian Field Army of the Lower Rhine was able to report to its commander with some 113,000 men in 136 battalions, 135 squadrons and 288 pieces of artillery.[16]

Prussia's serious economic situation, already touched upon, did not only affect the formation of an army fit for battle. Its effects became even more noticeable once the Prussian units had to leave their home territory, and they were to have direct operational consequences. Gneisenau had made contact with the Duke of Wellington after his arrival at Liège in the beginning of April in order to discuss their future co-operation, as instructed by the Prussian king. The resulting request by the Duke[17] that he should advance the Prussian army corps into the area of the Sambre-Maas, that is to say on to Belgian territory, was based on the assumption that the Netherlands government would take over supplying the Prussian troops completely.[18] The Prussian authorities, as a result of the material difficulties already mentioned, were not in a position to carry out the necessary supply, nor had they the money to pay in cash for quartering the troops.[19] During the course of April and May the army reached its definitive cantonment and security areas:

> I Corps; district around Charleroi.
> II Corps; district of Namur-Huy.
> III Corps; district of Dinant-Ciney.
> IV Corps; further back towards Liège and district.

The troops had to be quartered in well-scattered areas so as not to prove too great a burden on the inhabitants. Nevertheless, the longer the occupation lasted, the more difficult the supply situation became for the army. The command had to face the impossible situation – the result of inefficient administrative measures by the Dutch authorities – of trying to concentrate its units in a confined area in expectation of a given critical situation, where there were no storage areas or depots available and any orderly supply of the Prussian troops after their concentration was, in practice, impossible. As early as 8 May, Gneisenau wrote apprehensively to the Prussian Minister for War, von Boyen: 'The problem of food supplies in this devastated country between the Maas, the Moselle and the Rhine is daily causing me greater anxiety. I consider we have reached the point at which we should quit this area and look for somewhere else where we may find the wherewithal to sustain ourselves.'[20]

Two occurrences deserve mention in any assessment of the fighting value of this rapidly conscripted army which was neither properly trained nor professional. First, the trouble with the Saxons at Liège at the beginning of May. Here were billetted the former Royal Saxon troops, who had been under French command until 1813, but had afterwards taken part, on the allied side, in the campaign of 1814, and were now again destined to fight with the allies. As a sign of the Prussians' confidence in the Saxon army, the Prussian army general headquarters had been established in Liège. When the Saxon regiments, in accordance with the arrangements made in Vienna, were divided up into those whose territories had been ceded to Prussia and those left to Saxony, they mutinied and threatened the army general headquarters. After punishing the ringleaders, Field-Marshal Blücher decided that the whole Saxon contingent should return to Germany. Although they would have formed a very valuable reinforce-

ment, both in quantity and in quality, with their strength of nearly 14,000 troops, it seemed wiser to limit the number of troops rather than use unreliable men in the Prussian army, which was entirely dependent upon close coherence and mutual support.

The second occurrence was the desertion of between 6,000 and 8,000 soldiers after the Battle of Ligny.[21] The troops concerned were all from the newly acquired western areas; many of these men had previously served under Napoleon and hardly fitted into the Prussian army under the prevailing circumstances. Their loss certainly represented a further diminution in numbers but it was definitely a gain for the army's fighting strength.

Taking all these factors into account – the uninterrupted arrival of new units right up to the moment of the fighting; the constant exchange of personnel and units; the impossibility of systematic training and preparation; the material and financial difficulties – the verdict reported by Lettow-Vorbeck is understandable: 'By any sensible calculation, this army was bound to be defeated.' But what he goes on to say is also undeniable: 'The fact that despite everything it was victorious and was able, as early as the second day and after a defeat, to surmount the greatest difficulties and make the decisive onslaught at Belle-Alliance, pushing home success with a pursuit unparalleled in military history, proves that the spirit of this army must have been excellent.'

Although the spontaneous enthusiasm of 1813 had evaporated, owing to the sobering effects of the negotiations in Vienna,

. . . yet the fear of French domination was still so vivid in the minds of the people that the resurgence of Napoleon provoked a general apprehension that all the oppression associated with him might now return. This was reinforced by the demand that France should be made to pay for the wrongs that had been suffered. . . . In many quarters this feeling hardened into hatred of Napoleon and of the whole French nation. The liveliest expression of this feeling came from their universally admired commander, who readily took every opportunity of declaring openly: 'This time Bonaparte and the French are going to suffer for it!'[22]

One can, nevertheless, conclude that the Prussian army, at the outset of hostilities, was not the equal of the last great Napoleonic army that they were going to have to face, either in training, equipment and fitness for battle, or in military ability, routine and experience. Yet, in willingness to endure hardship and fatigue, readiness and determination to conquer, they were their equal.[23] It is probable that upon these last characteristics, Blücher's confidence in his army rested.

General von Müffling, who was appointed by the Prussian King in May 1815 as liaison officer with Wellington, and who was present throughout the campaign, described in his memoirs the qualities of the two allied armies – the British under the Duke of Wellington, and the Prussian under Field-Marshal Prince Blücher – as follows:

. . . so these two armies stand side by side: the one stern as the rigour of the law in obedience to the dictates of duty, composed and calm; the other ambitious for honour, stimulated by the great urge of patriotism, restless yet full of generosity and, at an encouraging word, ready to make any sacrifice. A soldier need hardly be told that one is a magnificent, model army, well-nigh unrivalled in defensive warfare, whereas the other is most dangerous in attack and murderous in pursuit?[24]

The commander-in-chief of this army was the seventy-year-old Prussian, Field-Marshal Prince Blücher von Wahlstadt, a soldier whose military reputation was known far beyond the frontiers of Prussia. To the Prussians he was unique: his authority was unquestioned, the respect and love shown by his troops extraordinary, and his performance, despite an occasional sign of his age, amazing. It would not have been surprising if his behaviour as commander had been as authoritarian as that of Wellington, who planned, decided and led alone[25] – not to mention Napoleon who, as emperor and superlative soldier, was always isolated. But in this, Blücher was different: under him, and to a certain extent beside him, was General Count von Gneisenau, chief of the general staff of the army, adviser, assistant, and when necessary, deputy. These two men, utterly different in character, had worked together so excellently in the campaigns of 1813–14 that King Frederick William III insisted on a renewal of this co-operation in the new crisis. At the head of the Prussian army, therefore, was not only an exceptional commander of great personal magnetism, but also a chief of the general staff with the same attitudes and aims who could therefore act, if necessary, as the perfect deputy.

Blücher's success, reputation and popularity were due partly to his contagious drive and undiminished confidence, and also to his somewhat harsh hussar's manner, which some might well have found offensive.[26] Although these factors certainly played their part, there must have been something more to explain his personal effect on events. Blücher had a rapid and sure judgment in operational and tactical matters, as well as a sound knowledge of people and the art of handling them –

he had been able to lead even such difficult generals as Count Yorck von Wartenburg in the campaigns of 1813–14.[27] It was his aptitude that also enabled him to recognize the very different genius of Gneisenau.

Gneisenau was too different from Blücher for there to be any real intellectual harmony. The highly educated, gifted Gneisenau had little in common with the robust, shrewd Blücher. But Gneisenau revered Blücher for his enormous courage, his practical acumen and his human integrity. ... He also recognized that as a popular leader Blücher was irreplaceable and that it was precisely the association of the two of them that gave them such power.[28]

And Blücher on his side loved and treasured his chief of staff,[29] whose qualities he knew well. He trusted him completely, accepted his suggestions, and expressed annoyance if others tried to persuade him to the contrary or in any way interfere between them. Nor did Blücher ever feel any resentment at his colleague's intellectual superiority. He had no need to. His authority, based on his own personality, stood so unshakably firm that the well-known fact that he took Gneisenau's advice did his standing no harm.

In this way there developed from these two diametrically opposed characters – and any weaker personality would have been crushed to the wall by Blücher's robust egoism – the fundamental peculiarity of the chief of the general's staff's position, which was to become traditional in the Prussian general staff. During the campaign years of 1813–14, Gneisenau's position had become far more than that of a mere executive; he was the planner, the adviser, the one to utter warnings; the assistant directly responsible to the commander and also his colleague – though without in any way impugning the final authority of the commander-in-chief and his responsibility to the monarch. Gneisenau himself would have preferred a field command, carrying responsibility for his own orders and leadership. But he bowed to the will of the King for the sake of success. 'I am glad', he wrote, 'to sacrifice my small gesture of conceit to my sense of duty'.[30]

The result was a strong leadership which radiated calmness and confidence and a total will to victory. General Count Langeron, who had commanded a Russian corps under Blücher in 1813–14 and was certainly no admirer of him, wrote:

Blücher was over seventy, but his intellect and physique had lost nothing of their power. ... His zest for action verged upon the superhuman. ... Fearless in battle, fervent in his patriotism, generous and loyal, of soldierly appearance, with the bearing of a Grenadier, he knew

how to inspire his troops with the fullest confidence and win the affection of his men. It was not long before he was idolized by Russians as well as Prussians.[31]

The British Colonel Hudson Lowe, who was with Blücher's army in 1814, wrote after the heavy defeat of the Prussian army at Etoges:

Words fail me to describe my amazement at the fearlessness and discipline of these troops. The example of Field-Marshal Blücher himself who was to be found everywhere and in the most dangerous positions, ... of General Gneisenau who controlled the army's movements from the roadside, of General Zieten and of Prince August of Prussia who, always at the head of his Brigade, fired them to the most heroic achievements – all this inspired the troops with a fearlessness which struck even the enemy with wonder and amazement.[32]

Gneisenau himself wrote to Clausewitz of the situation in Etoges: '... we behaved as if we had not been beaten and, on the fifth day, we attacked again.'[33]

In the early morning of 17 June, the Prussian army with I, II and III Corps were withdrawing from the battlefield of Ligny towards Wavre. The enemy was not following. The IV Corps which, as a result of its late departure from Liège, could not take part in the battle, had also been ordered to Wavre. By the evening of the 17th, Blücher's army, with all four corps, was on both banks of the Dyle in the area around Wavre.

If we are to understand why the opening of the fight against Napoleon should have been so uncertain – a fight the eventual outcome of which, by reason of the superiority of the English and Prussian armies, could have been confidently predicted -- we must look back to the days immediately preceding.

The attack of the French *Armée du Nord* on Charleroi on the 15th did not come as a surprise, in the strategic sense, to the Prussian staff. But they were surprised at the timing and the place.[34] For some time, it had been known that the French troops were concentrating in the area to the south of the river Sambre.[35] But two previous false alarms had had the effect of a brake, and, in addition, the very difficult supply situation had delayed the decision of the Prussian headquarters to concentrate units. Furthermore, it was the opinion of both commands, the Anglo-Dutch as well as the Prussian, that, in view of the great numerical superiority of their combined armies, an attack by Napoleon at the moment when they had reached this strength was not likely.[36] They still thought so when it became known that the French corps had

been brought up from Lille and Valenciennes into the area of Maubeuge and also that the French IV Corps was marching north-west from Metz. Clausewitz, reviewing the situation, says: 'From this moment on one could no longer count with any certainty on receiving a second warning before the outbreak of hostilities and it was therefore high time to gather forces in greater strength and to dispose them in such a manner that every corps could reach the field of battle in twenty-four hours at the outside.'[37] In actual fact it was the definite reports from French deserters on the evening of 14 June, that an attack was to take place the following morning, which gave the final impetus to concentrate the Prussian corps. By midnight of 14–15 June the necessary orders had gone out. They resulted in II and III Corps actually reaching the required rendezvous at Sombreffe by midday on the 16th. In the case of IV Corps, which lay furthest away, near Liège, one misunderstanding was to have momentous consequences. As a result of a misinterpretation of an order from the chief of the general staff, the corps was seriously late in marching off; consequently, two further orders failed to reach General von Bülow in time. The resulting delay of the corps could no longer be made up, even by forced marches. By the evening of the 16th IV Corps had advanced no further than an area to the east of Gembloux and was therefore unable to take its planned part in the Battle of Ligny.[39]

At the last moment, then, it was possible, more or less, for the staff to save their army from a real surprise.[40] Von Ollech writes: 'So Gneisenau did succeed in preparing the army for an attack at the last moment, at midnight. A strategic surprise, on which Napoleon had certainly counted, was no longer possible.'[41]

At ten o'clock on the night of the 14th, Colonel Hardinge, British liaison officer with the Prussian general headquarters, sent a message to the Duke, informing him of the Prussian intentions. Giving the Prussian assessment of the situation, he wrote: 'The prevalent opinion here seems to be that Bonaparte intends to commence offensive operations.'[42]

The attack by the French army early on the 15th hit the advance guard of the Prussian I Corps, who were located along a broad front to the south of the Sambre, not far from the frontier. They had been warned, but being composed in part of militia lacking experience of battle, they retreated, in the face of a superior enemy, suffering serious casualties, up to and over the Sambre. Further resistance was offered at the river but without

great effect, as the French were soon advancing on both banks. The bridges over the Sambre had not been destroyed. Bernhardi comments: 'The French got over the river more easily than they had the right to, because, as an inopportune measure to spare the country, the bridges had not been blown.'[43]

As far as the lack of resistance by the very widely dispersed parts of the Prussian I Corps is concerned, it must be remembered that the earlier instructions of the army command, in this connection based on very different assumptions, were that in the case of a French attack, the Prussian army should be deployed for battle in positions in front of Sombreffe, in contact with Wellington's army. This is exactly what the surprise attack by Napoleon prevented.

The French army was able to cross the Sambre on both sides of Charleroi with most of their troops by the evening of 15 June, without being met by either of the two enemy armies deployed in battle formation. What is more, the Prussian army corps had to take up their positions on the morning of the 16th at Sombreffe in view of the French army, which was already drawn up for the attack. Their positions were no longer those originally chosen as good defensive positions on either side of Sombreffe; these would have stopped the enemy advancing in an easterly direction. But in actual fact, the Prussian high command, in order not to be separated from Wellington's army, deployed their right wing far to the west, along the road to Quatre-Bras. This was where it was assumed the allies would concentrate. As only three Prussian army corps were present to occupy this position they were very stretched. Furthermore, the ground was not ideal, with slopes running downhill towards the enemy, while the larger villages in the bottom of the valley, St Amand and Ligny, were far from the front; they were intended to be part of the defences but there had not been time or opportunity to prepare them fully for a defensive role.[44] The trained eye of Wellington recognized this immediately when he arrived at midday on the 16th to visit Blücher in order to discuss with him the question of the co-operation of the two armies.[45]

The Prussian high command decided to give battle, and under the circumstances they hardly had any choice.[46] A move towards the English, that is to say in the direction of Quatre-Bras, seemed too risky; a side-step to the north which in the end actually took place, was equally problematical, as it would have meant giving up their own supply line. To retreat in the direction of

Liège ran contrary to everything that had been intended in the first place, namely to work with Wellington's army and not to allow themselves to be separated from it under any circumstances. Lastly, it is probable that both Blücher and Gneisenau were convinced that even with no more than the 80,000 men who were actually in position on the 16th they would be able to survive the battle – at least until their IV Corps arrived and the expected support of the English became effective.[47]

So it came to the first great battle, at Ligny, which, as a defensive battle, without the originally planned overwhelming strength, was beyond the capabilities of the inexperienced and largely untrained army at this early date. General von Müffling comments: 'Chance would have it that, on the 16th June, the Prussian Army stood on the defensive while the English was disposed for attack. Officers of any discernment could all have wished it the other way round, but nothing could be done about that.'[48]

The French attack which started on 16 June between two and three in the afternoon was directed at the Prussians' right flank and centre, that is to say, mainly against the straggling villages of St Amand and Ligny. These had been occupied by the I Corps in the morning, while II Corps, from the time of its arrival until noon, was deployed as a reserve near Brye. III Corps arrived in the afternoon. It formed the left flank and occupied the heights between Sombreffe and Balatre. Right up to the evening it only experienced the demonstrations of strength from the French cavalry, so that III Corps was hardly brought into action at all. The French III Corps of General Vandamme, reinforced by a division, attacked the village of St Amand on the left repeatedly; the French IV Corps of General Gérard attacked Ligny on the right. The battle became a bloody street and house fight which did not permit a defence by closed formations. The fight for the villages continued until evening when, in part at least, they were still held by the Prussians. This fighting took its toll of the Prussian I Corps and, bit by bit, also of II Corps as the reserves were gradually committed by Blücher as support and for counterattacks on the right flank. The French corps also suffered heavy losses.[49]

But late in the evening, when Napoleon committed his Old Guard against the centre of the Prussian front to attack Ligny, these excellent troops were able to break through the Prussian positions in a massed attack. The few reserves left to the defence were unable to throw back the French troops, but they were able to stop them penetrating further. The flanks of Brye and Sombreffe remained in the hands of the defenders, as did the road from Sombreffe to Quatre-Bras.[50] Houssaye comments:

Even though they [the French] had made a hole in the centre, the enemy held their position on the two wings ... The Prussians, massed around La Haye, regained, step by step, the last summits of the little hills and stopped, by counter-attack, the infantry of Vandamme when they pressed too close. Their rearguard held on at Brye until daybreak.[51]

Field-Marshal Blücher himself, leading one of the cavalry attacks against the enemy as they were pressing on Ligny, had suffered a fall, and his whereabouts were unknown. The fighting units of the Prussian I and II Corps had, during six un-interrupted hours of street fighting where no quarter was given, suffered very heavy losses. More than 12,000 men, mainly from I Corps, had been killed or wounded, which meant, in effect, the loss of a major part of that corps' infantry.[52] It was these two corps alone that bore the brunt of the attack of the strengthened French III and IV Corps as well as that of the Old Guard.

Worry and anger at these sacrifices and at the outcome of the battle may well have moved the commanders of the Prussian army, and some reflection on the causes was quite natural. Doubt-less, in the heat of the moment, there was bitterness at the apparent absence of the support which might have been expected from the English.[53] Added to this was the inexplicable failure of IV Corps to arrive. It is also quite obvious that the tactical errors of the Prussian staff, in face of the in-itially superior generalship displayed by Napoleon had played a part;[54] the unsatisfactory position;

the move of the reserves to the right wing rather than to the threatened centre; the belatedness of the attempt to bring in the strength of III Corps as support for the heavy fighting on the front;[55] and, lastly, the tendency to attack rather than to conserve strength. Clausewitz remarks sarcastically: 'Our generals are too much of the opinion that advancing is better than standing and firing. Each has its place.'[56]

But this bitter day's fighting can be seen to have had another, very different effect; this new army, which at this early date was hardly ready for a great battle against an adversary such as Napoleon, had been, so to speak, thrown in at the deep end; they had experienced the shock and had survived. The units were now more under the control of their commanders than before, and they were soon to prove their new capabilities. After the heavy defeat at Etoges in 1814, Blücher's army had attacked again after five days; this time it was not to be so long.

Withdrawal of the Prussian Army after Ligny, 17 June 1815

The first great battle against Napoleon had been fought, but not won, as had been hoped. The question of what to do next demanded an im-mediate and comprehensive answer. It was in this difficult situation that Gneisenau made a decision, the consequences of which were to lead directly to Waterloo.

One thing was clear to the Prussian army com-mand in the midst of all the confusion of the night: the army had to be withdrawn from contact with the enemy in order to regroup and become a fight-ing force once more. But in which direction should it withdraw? To break through to Wellington was, in view of the wide dispersion of the army and the confusion resulting from the street fighting, im-possible. It would have been sacrilege to sidestep in the direction of IV Corps, towards Liège, al-though this was the simplest solution and the one Napoleon counted upon. For this would have meant the end of co-operation with Wellington's army. All that remained was to go north, and that meant poor, unknown roads and the abandon-ment of operational lines. Yet this was the only direction which did not leave them separated from the English and which also held the promise of rejoining their own IV Corps. Chesney comments on this decision:

The Allied mistakes were at once redeemed by the bold order which Gneisenau gave for the retreat on Wavre; for in this giving up the proper line of communication of the Prussians through Namur and Liège, at the risk of present inconvenience, he kept moving parallel to the road by which Wellington must retire, and so gave the armies that precious opportunity of aiding each other in battle which they had missed on the plains of Fleurus.[57]

This noble risk robbed Napoleon, at a stroke, of the fruits of his victory; the danger which had shown itself for a few hours at Ligny now hung over him.

Field-Marshal Blücher had vanished; the entire responsibility rested on the chief of staff, General Gneisenau. The story of the giving of the order for withdrawal at the burning mill of Bussy has often been told most dramatically. Actually, the event had little drama about it. The order was given at last light and, in view of the retreat out of Ligny, probably consisted of the simple words 'withdraw to Tilly' – though it is possible that, in answer to some of the officers' questions, the name of the larger place, Wavre, was given, as it would have been easier to find on the map. One can suppose that this was the order given to everyone who asked for instructions during the course of that confused night. And it was the activity of all the lower echelons that finally helped to restore some kind of orderliness, and to bring about a move in the right direction. Certainly the situation was too confused for Gneisenau to have examined all the consequences of the initial order for withdrawal: the concentration of the army at Wavre; and the fighting of the second battle, together with their allies. He probably had considered, during the battle itself, just what he would suggest to Blücher in the event of their losing the Battle of Ligny. This important decision – Tilly–Wavre – was certainly spontaneous but not wholly unconsidered; and it must have been a bitter one for Gneisenau to make, for it meant a step into the unknown, the denial of any cover for his rear, and the abandonment of the care and circumspection on which the King, in his Cabinet order of 29 March, had laid so much stress. Dominating his thoughts must have been the desire to withdraw his army from further attacks by Napoleon – for what would happen if the enemy followed up their victory, as must have been expected? There was no definite news from Wellington; the probability that he would withdraw in the direction of Brussels, to the north, and the necessity of remaining in effective contact with him, must have been the decisive consideration for Gneisenau in making up his own mind.[58]

Officers were posted along the road and in Sombreffe in order to stem any movement by units towards the east, and to give them their instructions and thus achieve some orderliness. Thanks to the discipline of the troops, the retreating flood became an orderly withdrawal, and the units gradually reformed at each halt throughout the night. The units of I and II Corps had withdrawn from the fighting of Ligny, and later from St Amand, towards the north and the heights by Brye. From here they were ordered on and flowed via Tilly–Mellery and Gentinnes in the general direction of Mont St Guibert. Parts of I Corps who stayed in Brye as rearguard later joined III Corps, which was holding Sombreffe. They assembled at midnight at Point du Jour and marched at daybreak on the 17th to Gembloux, which they reached between six and seven in the morning. The advance units of IV Corps, which was approaching by forced march from Liège, had arrived at Baudecet (north-east of Gembloux) by nightfall on the 16th. In view of the impossibility of their still taking part in the battle, General von Bülow ordered them to halt there and bivouacked the brigades, one behind the other, along the Roman road. This he reported to the army.

For the three army corps that had taken part in the battle darkness brought no rest. Siborne comments on the French and Prussian armies that evening:

The contrast between the circumstances of the two armies during the night was very striking; for whilst the victors were indulging in perfect repose, the vanquished were completely on the alert, seizing every possible advantage which the extraordinary inactivity of their enemies afforded during the precious hours of darkness; and never, perhaps, did a defeated army extricate itself from its difficulties with so much adroitness and order, or retire from a hard-fought field with so little diminution of its moral force. The Prussian commander, completely *hors de combat*, was carried to Gentinnes, about six miles in rear of Ligny, but from the moment his fall became known, his chief of the staff, Count Gneisenau, undertook the direction of affairs.[59]

Gneisenau had set up the army headquarters in Mellery as soon as it was certain that the rearguard of I and II Corps at Brye, as well as III Corps in Sombreffe, were covering the army's move northwards. It was here that he learned with relief that Field-Marshal Blücher was neither dead nor captured. Shortly after midnight Gneisenau and Grolmann found Blücher severely shaken but completely confident. He is said to have greeted them with the words, 'We have taken a few knocks and we shall have to hammer out the dents'.[60]

It would have been here, in the familiar command circle, that there took place a discussion of all the urgent questions, which until now time and circumstance had not allowed. Where to go with the army? How to join up as quickly as possible?

Problems of supply, and munitions; communication with Wellington. It had not yet been possible to inform the Duke about the outcome of the battle. This is an omission which can be explained only by the hectic circumstances.[61] But it is still strange; neither Wellington nor the Prussian liaison officer, General von Müffling, had, by the evening of the 16th, despite the much easier situation at Quatre-Bras, informed the Prussian command of the situation and of their own intentions. It was not until the morning of the 17th that the two commands resumed contact.

The situation was still, on the night of the 16th–17th, far too unclear for any far-reaching decisions to be made by the army command. Their first concern would have been to secure the army's disengagement, its re-unification, and the reforming of I and II Corps into a fighting force capable of continuing the battle at a later date.

Large parts of I and II Corps remained on the move during the night, in a northerly direction. In view of the continuing stream of straggling units moving through Mellery, General von Grolmann gave Lieutenant von Wussow, who was at the army headquarters, the order to place himself at the head of these marching troops and produce some kind of order of march that same night. Von Wussow reported that he had reached the head of the column of marching troops near L'Auzelle (three miles south of Wavre) by daybreak and had stopped them. They were now in the process of sorting themselves out. He asked for orders from the army high command as to which areas they were to disperse into, so as to speed up the crossing of the Dyle sector. His report concluded: 'Colonel Röhl asks, Sir, where the guns should be sent for repair. There is no food whatsoever'. He received, 'after some time', a handwritten answer from General von Grolmann: 'I Corps to bivouac at Bierges; II Corps near Wavre at St Anne; III Corps at La Bavette; IV Corps at Dion le Mont; the guns for repair to Maastricht.'[62]

This brief order makes it clear that by daybreak the army command had decided that the army should assemble in Wavre. It is quite certain that Blücher was in agreement with the withdrawal order given by Count Gneisenau. And it will have been on the basis of this decision that further plans were developed and clarified. It seems probable that Blücher's determination to carry on the campaign with Wellington played as great a part as Gneisenau's understandable determination to regroup the army into a fighting unit. It also

seems probable that Blücher's unflagging energy and Gneisenau's analysis were first collated and co-ordinated during these hours of darkness. There can be no disputing Chandler's verdict: 'Thus, from two circumstances, Gneisenau's ... selection of Wavre and Blücher's determined loyalty to his ally, there sprang the decision to support Wellington at Mont St Jean.'[63]

The necessary orders were issued to the corps in the early hours of the morning.[64] I Corps moved at daybreak over Gentinnes and Mont St Guibert to Wavre and went into bivouac around midday near Bierges. II Corps followed, but left a brigade as rearguard at Mont St Guibert and bivouacked at Aisémont (on the near side of Wavre). The commander of the 2nd Cavalry Brigade of II Corps, Lieutenant-Colonel von Sohr, received orders to take up positions with his strengthened brigade in the Tilly–Gentinnes area and to observe the enemy at Sombreffe and Brye. In the event of superior enemy advancing, he was to withdraw to the rearguard positions near Mont St Guibert. Major von Weyrach was sent to III and IV Corps with orders to march to the area of Wavre. In addition, IV Corps was instructed to detach, on the march, a strengthened brigade as rearguard and with this unit to relieve the outposts of II Corps at Mont St Guibert.[65] III and IV Corps had already made contact in the early hours of the 17th, and had arranged to march together in the direction of Wavre. The army order confirmed this decision. General von Bülow wrote to General von Thielemann, when he received these orders at 10.30 that morning, that he would move off with his corps immediately. He warned Thielemann to be wary of straggling. Nevertheless III Corps remained near Gembloux until about two in the afternoon and ran the danger of being overrun while on their own. French cavalry had observed the corps and reported them.[66] However, with great good luck they were able to withdraw to the north without the enemy following them.

Blücher moved his headquarters from Gentinnes to Wavre on the morning of 17 June. His ride past the marching troops with his entourage must have been a great encouragement to Blücher, confirming his own confidence despite the considerable pain he was still suffering from his fall. The units of I and II Corps greeted their beloved leader with cheerful shouts as he passed. Losses, exhaustion and hunger had obviously not affected the morale and behaviour of these men, who had been in action for two days and two nights. Von Ollech writes: 'Their spirit was unbroken, unvanquished, and betokened further courageous deeds in the

future.'[67] Before they moved off, Gneisenau had arranged for liaison with the Duke of Wellington to be re-established. Lieutenant von Massow of the general staff was sent to inform Wellington of the withdrawal of the Prussian army to Wavre, of the intention to concentrate the army there, and of the move of the army headquarters to that town. He had Blücher's authority to enquire whether the Duke was still willing to attack Napoleon's forces, in conjunction with the Prussians. Further decisions of the army headquarters depended upon the answers to these questions. They also affected the Duke's reaction to the Prussian will to continue their mutual co-operation.

Wellington, on his part, having had no news from Blücher by the morning of the 17th, sent his adjutant, Colonel Gordon, together with a cavalry reconnaissance unit, in the direction of Sombreffe.[68] Gordon came across some Prussian troops near Tilly and was informed both of the withdrawal to Wavre and of the move of the army headquarters. After Gordon's return and report, Müffling's adjutant, Lieutenant Wucherer, was sent to Wavre to Blücher. His mission crossed with that of Lieutenant von Massow, who had arrived in Quatre-Bras at about 8 a.m. Wellington's answer to von Massow was what the Prussian command expected. Von Ollech gives the contents of this verbal message in the following words:

I continue to adhere to the original intention of launching a joint offensive against the French army. However, I must move back into position at Mont St Jean where I want to take up the battle against Napoleon if I am to be supported by at least one Prussian army corps. After the battle I hope to go over to the offensive together with the Prince. However, without Prussian support, I would have to make an exclusive movement towards Brussels.[69]

The answer that Lieutenant Wucherer brought in, almost simultaneously, agreed throughout. It also contained the message that Blücher would not be ready to attack on the 17th but that he would come tomorrow, 'with the fresh corps and the others'.[70]

With that, communication between the two armies was re-established, and, more than that, the *first, practical agreement on objectives was reached*. Lettow-Vorbeck comments: 'The intention on both sides was to act together. Blücher was ready for anything, but first he had to reassemble his army; and, once again, *the covering of Ghent and Brussels* was a prior condition for Wellington's scheme.'[71] Chesney says: 'The next day would show whether the confidence of the Allies and their unshaken resolve to join as soon as possible in a decisive blow were to redeem the errors made at the outset of the campaign.'[72]

'The position in which the Prussian army command in Wavre found itself on the morning of the 17th was anything but favourable,' according to Lettow-Vorbeck.[73] In fact the army was divided into two halves, which were separated from each other; I and II Corps were already in Wavre; III and IV Corps, the two intact corps, were in Gembloux; they had received orders to move up, but it was not known whether their march would succeed or whether the enemy would delay them. I and II Corps were in urgent need of rest; they had lost more than 10,000 men at Ligny and their units needed to be regrouped. In addition, they were completely out of ammunition and it was not known where the ammunition trains were. 'Without ammunition,' writes Lettow-Vorbeck, 'these troops were as useless at Wavre as they would have been in support of their ally.'[74] The fact that the enemy had not started in pursuit of them left room to suppose that the French had also suffered heavily at Ligny. But that Napoleon would pursue had to be assumed.

The preparation of plans for future battles was, at this time, as problematical as was firm assurance of support.[75] This was the mood in which Gneisenau wrote a report at midday on the 17th, presumably addressed to General von Knesebeck, the military adviser to the King of Prussia:

The IV Corps has now been ordered here and will, perhaps, not arrive until tomorrow . . . it is rumoured that the Duke of Wellington's left wing was attacked early this morning but this has not been confirmed; he wants to accept battle at Waterloo, near the entrance to the wood of Soignes, if we can give him two corps. This we would like to do if we had the ammunition. But we have no information about the ammunition of two corps. If information comes we will accept the Duke's request, let Bülow's corps join him together with the still complete battalions of the other army corps, and consider what to do with the rest.[76]

These words reflect the anxiety with which Gneisenau was burdened and all his uncertainties as to how much support they would be able to give Wellington.

This tense situation, however, developed surprisingly advantageously during the course of the afternoon and evening. The enemy did not follow, but a constant stream of information about them came in from the area of Tilly, from Major Count Groeben, the general staff officer with the reconnaissance group of Lieutenant-Colonel von Sohr.[77] Until midday all was quiet in the Brye–Sombreffe area; but around midday columns were seen moving in the direction of Marbais and Quatre-Bras; it appeared that Napoleon was moving towards Wellington. The fear that French forces would move into the area on the west bank of the Dyle and so come between Blücher's and Wellington's army caused Gneisenau to give I Corps orders to cover this eventuality. The order to General von Zieten states 'Your Excellency will therefore give such orders as to ensure that the area on the left bank of the Dyle is under constant observation for all enemy movements and that communication is maintained with the Duke of Wellington.'[78] In obedience to these orders, I Corps undertook the necessary reconnaissance, and communications with Wellington's army were maintained by means of the cavalry.

By five that evening the desperately needed ammunition columns of the army corps reported in; I and II Corps were supplied with ammunition that same evening and were once again battle-worthy. The lucky arrival of the ammunition columns was largely due to the initiative of the artillery commander of II Corps, Lieutenant-Colonel von Röhl; he had started the columns, which had halted on the Sombreffe–Namur road, towards Gembloux on the evening of the Battle of Ligny, as soon as he learned of the withdrawal towards Wavre.[79] Finally, the marching groups of IV Corps began to arrive at Dion le Mont in the afternoon; by ten that night, General von Bülow reported that his whole corps had assembled with the exception of the still missing 13th Brigade; further, he reported setting up the 14th Brigade as rearguard at Vieux Sart and Mont St Guibert. By light in the evening the bulk of III Corps had also reached Wavre, crossed the Dyle and taken up bivouac positions, as ordered, near La Bavette. Only the 9th Brigade, which arrived later, remained on the other side of the Dyle.

This resulted in a development in the situation of the Prussian army, which, even on the morning of the 17th, could not have been foreseen. Twenty-four hours after the retreat from Ligny, the army was reassembled with all four corps at Wavre, fifteen miles from the battlefield of Ligny and in contact with their allies. The units could be regrouped and supplied – though the troops were exhausted and hungry after their great efforts, for food supplies throughout were insufficient. 'But the *morale* of the great mass of the Prussian army continued undiminished,' writes Siborne. 'The spirit of the troops was neither tamed nor broken.'[80] The army was ready for a new engagement.

This meant that it was now possible to give the Duke of Wellington further and firmer assurances for the next day. In the late evening information was received from General von Müffling that the Duke intended to start a defensive battle on the 18th, based on the positions taken up by him at Mont St Jean. Blücher's answer, which left at about midnight and was received at around 2 a.m., said:

I have the honour to report to Your Excellency that, following upon information I have received that the Duke of Wellington intends tomorrow to meet an attack in his positions from Braine L'Alleud to La Haye, I have arranged to dispose my troops as follows: von Bülow's Corps will march tomorrow at daybreak from Dion-le-Mont, through Wavre towards St Lambert, in order to attack the enemy right flank. II Corps will follow him immediately, while I and II will hold themselves in readiness to follow up this movement. The exhaustion of the troops, some of whom have not yet arrived [i.e. the last of IV Corps – ed.], makes it impossible to move any earlier. I beg your Excellency, however, to let me know in good time when and how the Duke is being attacked so that I may make my dispositions accordingly.[81]

At midnight the necessary orders went to IV Corps:

Wavre, the 17th June, 12 midnight. According to information just received from the Duke of Wellington, he has positioned himself as follows: his right wing extends to Braine L'Alleud, the centre is at Mont St Jean, his left wing is at La Haye. The enemy is facing him and the Duke is expecting the attack and has asked us for our co-operation. Your Excellency will,

therefore, with IV Corps under your command, move off from Dion le Mont at daybreak, march through Wavre and move towards Chapelle St Lambert where, if the enemy is not heavily engaged with Wellington, you will take up positions under cover. Otherwise you are to throw yourself at the right flank of the enemy with the utmost vigour. II Corps will follow immediately to the rear of your Excellency to lend support. I and III Corps will likewise hold themselves in readiness to follow in support, should the need arise. Your Excellency will leave an observation detachment in Mont St Guibert which, if pressed, is to withdraw slowly to Wavre. All baggage trains, and everything else not essential to the battle must be sent to Louvain.[82]

General von Pirch in Aisémont received orders at the same time to follow IV Corps with his II Corps. The other two corps received confirmation of the orders issued, and were instructed to cook early and to hold themselves in readiness.

The information passed to Wellington on the evening of the 17th makes it clear that at this time support by only two corps was promised, while the other corps were to 'hold themselves in readiness'. The situation of the Prussian army command in Wavre was unusual in view of a number of incalculable factors: the condition of their own army, the potential of their allies, and, lastly, information regarding the strength and intentions of the enemy in pursuit. Admittedly, the enemy had not yet interfered with the Prussian army, but it remained uncertain just what the units engaged in the pursuit would do. It would have been surprising under these circumstances, if, in the twenty-four hours at Wavre, there had not been serious wrestling between the temperamental commander-in-chief, who was pressing for an attack, and the chief of staff, who also wanted to attack but had to weigh up and explain the basis of operations, in order to arrive at the 'optimal solution' for the disposition of the Prussian forces. What, in the case of Wellington and Napoleon under similar circumstances, took place within themselves, had here to be played out between commander and chief of staff in the course of a common testing of ideas – until finally the decision had to be made by the commander. The few eye-witnesses of these discussions are not unanimous; Gneisenau's caution at this time has led to conflicting assessments. It is, therefore, worth considering exactly what were the absolutely firm facts of the difficult situation facing the commander and his chief adviser.

Both Blücher and Gneisenau were absolutely determined to defeat Napoleon. Added to this there was anger over the defeat at Ligny – and there may still have been some bitterness over Wellington's failure to give sufficient support in this first battle. Both had an unshakeable desire to recover and control the situation despite the reverse they had suffered – and it was quite clear that this could only be achieved with the full support of their allies. Any abandonment of such co-operation, or the missing of the first opportunity that presented itself, would mean not only a further retreat by Wellington, but also the capture of Brussels and, above all, the first great political success by Napoleon in the Netherlands. Moreover, this would also amount to a second defeat for the Prussians – an idea totally unacceptable both to Blücher and to Gneisenau. *The aim of both was therefore clear – to fight.* For Blücher this would have meant, from the beginning, a firm determination to support Wellington with every unit that was available and able to fight. But, though his aims were the same, the chief of staff had to think of the real difficulties that faced the Prussian army. He could not avoid the problem of what was actually possible and when. He had also to sort out the operational situation: the more obvious it became that Napoleon did not intend to pursue the Prussian army, the more certain it was that he would turn the greater part of his army against Wellington. This made the support of the Prussians even more imperative. But could the Duke resist an attack by Napoleon long enough for the Prussian army to reach him? What Prussian forces would have to remain on the Dyle to cover the flanking march of their own attack corps until they arrived at the battlefield and began their action against Napoleon? Holland Rose comments on Gneisenau's problems in these difficult hours: 'Gneisenau's only doubts seem to have been whether Wellington would fight and whether his own ammunition would be to hand in time. Until he was sure on these two points, caution was certainly necessary.'[83]

Although one is usually struck by the daring character of the operational proposals put forward by Gneisenau and the subsequent decisions taken by Blücher concerning the commitment of his army, the warnings of Gneisenau in these worrying circumstances may well have delayed the commander's final decision.[84]

The decision to move towards Wellington with the mass of the army was not made until the morning of the 18th. At 9.30 Blücher dictated to his adjutant, Count Nostitz, the following instructions to General von Müffling:

I request Your Lordship to tell the Duke of Wellington, in my name, that, ill as I am, I intend to put myself at

the head of my troops and attack the right flank of the enemy immediately Napoleon makes any move against the Duke. If, however, today should pass without any enemy action, then I believe that we should make a combined attack upon the French army tomorrow. I urge you to tell the Duke that I am deeply convinced of this, and to put it to him that I regard this proposal as the best and most practical in our present situation.[85]

'This decision of Blücher indisputably merits the highest praise', writes Clausewitz.

Against all the possible causes of action prescribed for such circumstances by traditional precepts and false reasoning, he followed the dictates of plain common-sense and determined to join Wellington on the 18th and, in a sense, to quit his sphere of action rather than to do things by halves. The battle which he had lost was no defeat; it had reduced his strength by only about one-sixth, and with nearly 100,000 men he could turn the battle facing Wellington into an undoubted victory. In addition, there was the desire to wipe away the blemish which his military honour had suffered on the 16th and to win the prestige of standing by an ally who, against all the odds, had been unable to support him the previous day, and of standing by him to an extent which surpassed all expectations. No more admirable motives, appealing to both heart and mind, could possibly be conceived.[86]

Count Nostitz showed Blücher's letter to General Gneisenau,

The latter was in complete agreement and at once gave his approval that I should take the step of writing privately to General Müffling, asking him to make absolutely sure to his own satisfaction that the Duke of Wellington was firm in his determination to do battle in his present positions. ... I wrote to the General as follows: 'General Gneisenau is aware and approves of the contents of the letter. He requests you to ascertain beyond doubt whether the Duke is firmly resolved to do battle in his present positions or whether he is merely engaging in a show which can only be of the gravest disadvantage to our army. Would you please let me have your views on the matter, as it is of the greatest importance that we should be accurately informed of the Duke's intentions, so that our own movements may be directed accordingly.'[87]

The position of the Prussian army and the decision to come to the aid of the Duke with all available strength confirmed what Gneisenau had written to the Duke on 13 April: 'We are firmly resolved to throw in our lot with the army which is under Your Excellency's command'.[88] But the situation remained uncertain enough. Much as Gneisenau might hope for action, it was not until he heard the thunder of cannon from Mont St Jean, which sounded the beginning of the great battle in the late morning of the 18th, that he could breathe more easily.

4 WELLINGTON'S DISPOSITIONS

William Seymour

Waterloo gave its name to the battle principally because it was in its village inn that the Duke of Wellington had his headquarters immediately before and after the battle, and from there that he headed his Waterloo dispatch. Field-Marshal Blücher suggested the name of La Belle Alliance, for it was there that the two commanders met at the end of the day when the victory had been won. However, Wellington, not through any sense of his own importance, for he was a model of unassuming behaviour, but mindful of the important role that his countrymen had played and no doubt possessing a lively comprehension of the capabilities of the English tongue, recognized the merit of Waterloo over La Belle Alliance or Mont St Jean.

Mont St Jean is some two miles south of Waterloo, and south of the village is Mont St Jean Farm. Here an east-west ridge of low heights crosses the Brussels–Charleroi road at right angles, and almost on the crest of this ridge the fairly wide *chaussée* was crossed by a smaller, unpaved country road leading from Ohain and Wavre in the east to the Brussels–Nivelles road three-quarters of a mile away to the west. The greater part of the Anglo-Dutch army was drawn up along and immediately to the north of the country road, as it were in a crescent with the right horn curling forward at Hougoumont and the left on the slightly less protruding farm buildings of Papelotte and Ter La Haye. Immediately to the east of the main *chaussée* the country road, which although unpaved was in good condition, was lined by two banked up holly hedges, and in parts it was deeply sunk, and these features together with the fairly gentle undulation on the north side of the ridge, gave good protection to troops on the reverse slope and considerably facilitated lateral communication.

The crossroads immediately south of Mont St Jean Farm was almost the centre of the Anglo-Dutch line, and in the south-west angle of the cross stood an elm tree beside which Wellington could often be found during the battle. The southern slope of the ridge presented in parts a fairly steep glacis, especially where the road leading south towards Charleroi passed through a cutting before reaching La Haye Sainte. This farm abuts the west side of the *chaussée* and is some 200 yards from the crest of the Mont St Jean ridge; from here the road, which bisected the battlefield, continues along an undulating, shallow valley until it reaches another ridge that crosses it from east to west and forms a plateau almost parallel to the one at Mont St Jean. On this ridge, to the east of the road, stands what was the farmhouse of La Belle Alliance, near which Napoleon had his headquarters during

part of the battle. These two ridges, upon which the rival armies were assembled, are separated by about 1,500 yards of open, undulating plain, upon which grew crops of rye, wheat and barley which, where the rain or soldiers had not flattened them, stood very high.

The two farms of La Haye Sainte and Hougoumont formed vital bastions of the defence, although it would seem, from the small number of troops allotted to defend it, that the importance of the former was not at first recognized by Wellington. La Haye Sainte was the key to any frontal attack, for so long as it remained untaken its garrison could pour a destructive enfilading fire on to any advancing column. The buildings formed a quadrangle and were of strong stone. To the north of the house and stables was a garden, at the southern end of the quadrant stood a large barn near a pond, and beyond the buildings to the south a long narrow orchard flanked the *chaussée*. The main entrance was from the road, but a side entrance led from the fields to the west of the buildings; Wellington in his dispatch infers that there was no access from the north, but the present occupier of the farm assured the writer that in 1815 there were two back doors to the farmhouse. It seems, therefore, that the failure to replenish the garrison's ammunition may have been due to their using the less common Baker rifle. A little to the north of the farm and to the east of the road was a sandpit, which was not so much a pit as a hollowed out semi-circle fronting the road with a hedge and mound on its north side.

Hougoumont, or to give it its correct name the Château de Goumont (although Victor Hugo would not agree), was at the time of the battle the pleasant country home of a Monsieur de Luneville. It consisted of the château, a square brick building, to which was attached a little chapel, a farmhouse that stood to the north-east of the château, a large and a small barn on the west side of the enclosure and a gardener's house to the south. There were two yards; the one opening out from the main north gate (which was reached from a tree-lined avenue leading off the Nivelles road) was a farmyard with a well in the middle of it, and leading from this was the courtyard. Besides the large and solid wooden gate at the north end of the enclosure, the high-walled buildings could be entered by another gate on the south side and by a small door that opened on to a lane running along the west side.

The garden, laid out in the formal Flemish style, was bounded on the south and east by a high brick wall, and on the north side by a hedge. There were two orchards; a large one to the east of the garden and a smaller one to the north. The southern boundary of the large orchard was formed by an extremely thick hedge, which had a gap in it at the angle where it was joined by a copse that stretched away to the south for about 300 yards. The hedge completely concealed the garden wall from the French, and was of considerable value to the defenders. Immediately to the north of the enclosure there was a 'Hollow Way' formed by a lane and double hedge, which played an important part in the battle.

A valley, which begins near La Belle Alliance, runs round the west of Hougoumont towards Merbe Braine; it is concealed from the Mont St Jean ridge, so if the Anglo-Dutch army had not held Hougoumont Napoleon would have had a covered approach along which to mount a left hook to outflank their position. Hence the importance of Hougoumont – for the position that Wellington had selected to defend was a strong one so long as the threat to his right flank, which was always uppermost in his mind, could be safeguarded. Hougoumont and Lord Hill's troops, some of whom occupied the shoulder of the ridge *en potence*, and also the high ground above Braine l'Alleud, took care of this.

The Duke's position from flank to flank covered some three and a half miles, but not much more than two miles was held in depth. At this time it was reckoned that to occupy a position strongly 20,000 troops were needed for each mile of front – this allowed for a quarter of the infantry, all the cavalry and a part of the artillery to be in reserve. Thus 50,000 men were sufficient for a two and a half-mile front, and Wellington had more than this at his disposal even without the troops at Hal. The left of the line, with its buildings, trees and enclosures, was strong by nature, and the guns on the hill behind Papelotte had an excellent field of fire; in the centre the ridge afforded protection from view, and to some extent from fire, for those troops on the reverse slope, and allowed for maximum manoeuvrability, while the strongpoints of Hougoumont and La Haye Sainte, and to a lesser degree the sandpit, exposed the centre and flanks of an attacking army to an avalanche of fire and steel. Also the condition of the ground favoured the defence. The heavy rain had made the going difficult, the movement of guns was not easy, French cavalry advancing up the fairly steep southern slope could less easily resist the downhill charge of the heavier British animals, and if the standing corn gave advantage to either side it was to the defenders.

On the whole it was a good position, and certainly the best that could be found for the defence of Brussels; apart from Napoleon, endeavouring at St Helena to restore his own military reputation at the expense of his conqueror's, only one senior officer is known to have criticized it, and Sir Thomas Picton, although a fearless and resolute fighter, was not a notable tactician.

Before both armies settled down to the miseries of the night there was a brief cannonade. The French started it as a means of discovering what had become of their enemy, and to the annoyance of the Duke his gunners replied, thus giving the French the information they required. Not that it made much difference, for the Anglo-Dutch army was deployed for battle on the Sunday morning in a manner that was to keep the French guessing until they were almost impaled by gleaming bayonets and swords.

For convenience of command, and to give the commander-in-chief greater freedom of action, the line was divided into three principal sectors. Lord Hill had charge of the troops to the west of the Nivelles road, the Prince of Orange was entrusted with the centre section, between the Nivelles and Charleroi roads, and Picton was made responsible for the eastern sector of the line. In doing this the Duke scrapped his corps organization, and as can be seen from a look at the detailed dispositions he also separated some of the divisional units. This was presumably part of his plan to stiffen the whole line with a sprinkling of his best troops, and in particular to give additional strength to the right flank.

We have seen the importance that Wellington, quite rightly, attached to this right flank, and it is appropriate, therefore, to look first at the troops whose task it was to hold this sector of the line. At Braine l'Alleud, which is some 1,300 yards to the north-west of Hougoumont and in the event was outside the battle area, Lieutenant-General Chassé's 3rd Dutch–Belgian Division was posted; its initial task was to secure the extreme right and to act as a bridge between the main army and Prince Frederick's and General Colville's troops at Hal. At the right end of the actual battle line, where the Mont St Jean ridge falls away to the valley that passes west of Hougoumont, was General Clinton's fine 2nd British Division, placed *en potence* as a further safeguard against a flank attack, or, should that not develop, as a tactical reserve. The left bridge (du Plat's King's German Legion) rested on the Nivelles road, then came Adam's 3rd British (Light) Brigade, and the 3rd Hanoverian Brigade under Colonel Hew Halkett formed the right of the division just to the south of Merbe Braine. The Brunswick Corps (commanded by Colonel Olfermann since their duke's death at Quatre-Bras) was also near Merbe Braine. Along the avenue leading from Hougoumont to the Nivelles road, and across it towards Braine l'Alleud, was Mitchell's 4th British Brigade (detached from Colville's 4th Division at Hal), which was supported by a squadron of the 15th Hussars.

The importance of Hougoumont was immediately apparent to Wellington's perceptive eye, and on the evening of the 17th he ordered the light companies of the 1st Guards Brigade (General Maitland) under Lord Saltoun, together with those of the 3rd Guards and the 2nd Battalion Coldstream Guards (both of which belonged to Byng's 2nd Guards Brigade) under Colonel Macdonell, to go there.[1] Lord Saltoun's men were to hold the orchard and

Macdonell's the chateau and buildings, which they fortified as best they could during the night. These troops arrived only just in time, for they had immediately to drive off a French force which was hoping to gain this important tactical position. On the morning of the 18th, after a visit by the Duke, the Hougoumont garrison was reinforced by the 1st Battalion of the 2nd Brigade of Prince Bernhard of Saxe-Weimar's Nassauers, a company of Hanoverian riflemen and 100 of Count Kielmansegge's 1st Hanoverian Brigade; all these reinforcements were positioned in the wood. One wonders why the Nassauers were so far separated from their main body on the extreme left of the line; it is possible that this battalion had become unreliable after Quatre-Bras – indeed at one stage they turned their fire in the direction of the commander-in-chief, but fortunately their aim was as unsteady as

their nerves. Immediately to the north of Hougoumont was the remainder of General Cooke's 1st
Guards Division; Byng's brigade was in close
support of the château troops, and because
Wellington knew that to be effective supporting
troops had to be close at hand the brigade was
positioned somewhat to the south of the ridge, with
Maitland's brigade on its left and higher up.

The front line of the army's right was thus made
as secure as possible by the wise deployment of
some of the best troops available. Most of this
wing was under the command of Lord Hill – and
though the sector in which the Guards stood was
nominally the responsibility of the Prince of
Orange, Wellington himself was there during the
early hours of the battle when the action was at
its most critical.

The troops on the right had to be positioned to
conform with the differing features of the ground,
in which ridge and valley, roads, woods and
buildings played their part, but the centre could be
strengthened according to Wellington's practice of
putting all his troops, less some of the guns and
skirmishers, on the reverse slope of the ridge.
Wellington had come to prefer lines four, rather
than two, deep, and formations would be staggered
in order to allow for room to form square from
line and back into line again as the course of the
battle demanded, and to present the smallest
possible target for the enemy's artillery. The
skirmishers and riflemen stationed on the forward
slope were to a great extent protected by the
standing corn.

General Sir Charles Alten's 3rd British Division
held the line from General Cooke's left up to the
crossroads. He had three brigades in the front line,
from right to left Halkett's 5th British, Kielmansegge's 1st Hanoverian and Colonel Ompteda's
2nd King's German Legion; the first two had
fought at Quatre-Bras, the Hanoverians with some
distinction. Attached to this division and in close
support were General von Kruse's Nassauers,
originally allotted to the reserve.

Immediately to the east of the crossroads came
the men of Picton's 5th British Division, which had
been very severely mauled at Quatre-Bras. The
division had four brigades up, from right to left
Kempt's 8th British, Pack's 9th British (or more
accurately Scots), Best's 4th Hanoverian and
Vincke's 5th Hanoverian. Best's brigade, whose
right rested on a very prominent knoll, was really
part of the 6th Division, but it had fought well at
Quatre-Bras under Picton and was kept with his
division. In front of the 5th Division, overlapping
part of Kempt's and Pack's brigades, was General

Bylandt's Dutch–Belgian brigade. The positioning
of this brigade is curious. Although at this point
the country road road ran slightly in front of the
crest, the rest of the troops contrived to protect
themselves fairly adequately. The morale of this
brigade, which formed part of General Perponcher's 2nd Dutch–Belgian Division, was in
doubt, yet here they were on the forward slope
and a sitting target for the worst that the French
gunners could do. It has always been assumed that
Bylandt, or his battalion commanders, refused the
offer of a safer billet, being more accustomed to
exposing themselves to the enemy. As it turned out
their exposure was of the briefest duration.

The extreme left of the allied line was entrusted
to General Vivian's 6th Cavalry Brigade (hussars)
and General Vandeleur's 4th Cavalry Brigade
(light dragoons); their role was to patrol the left
flank until the Prussians came up, and in front of
them, based on Papelotte and Ter La Haye, was
Prince Bernhard's 2nd Brigade of Nassauers, less
the battalion at Hougoumont. Protruding from
the centre of the long line were the strongpoints of
La Haye Sainte and the sandpit. La Haye Sainte
was occupied by Major Baring's 2nd Light
Battalion of Ompteda's brigade – only some 360
men, an insufficient number for so important a
post, and one that could have held double the
number – and in the sandpit were placed two
companies of the 95th (Rifles) from Kempt's
brigade. A third company occupied the mound
and hedge immediately adjoining the sandpit,
and they erected an abatis on the *chaussée* above
and below La Haye Sainte. The only other infantry
brigade, Lambert's 10th British, did not arrive on
the field until 11 a.m. and was then positioned at
the Mont St Jean crossroads.

The whole of the cavalry, except for those
regiments on the extreme flanks of the line, was
massed behind the infantry, most of them in the
triangle formed by the Nivelles and Charleroi
roads and the country lane. Lord Uxbridge took
personal command of the 1st or Household Brigade
(Lord Edward Somerset) and the 2nd or Union
Brigade of heavy cavalry (Sir William Ponsonby),
the former being stationed behind Alten's division
just to the west of the Brussels–Charleroi road and
the latter across the *chaussée* to its east. Also in the
triangle, and positioned in the hollow of the
reverse slope, were Grant's 5th Brigade (hussars
and light dragoons), which were behind Cooke's
division, and on their left Dornberg's 3rd and
Arentschildt's 7th King's German Legion Brigades.
In rear of the main cavalry line and behind
Grant's brigade were the Cumberland Hanoverian

Hussars (Colonel Hake), and still further in rear and astride the *chaussée* was General Collaert's Dutch–Belgian division comprising three brigades under Generals Merlen, Trip and de Ghigney. The Brunswick cavalry were stationed with their infantry on the extreme right near Merbe Braine.

Of the horse artillery six of the British troops were in theory attached to cavalry brigades; but in the confusion that marked the arrival of the army at Mont St Jean units tucked themselves away for the night as best they could. Captain Mercer's troop was at Mont St Jean Farm (not La Haye Sainte as is sometimes said), and Mercer tells us that Ramsay's and Bean's troops were also there. In the morning Mercer and his men were for some time forgotten, but they were eventually told to take up a position on the right of the line. Colonel Ross's Chestnut Troop fought from the high ground above La Haye Sainte, and the foreign troops mostly remained with their respective formations

Wellington's handling of his field brigades is sometimes criticized because of the punishment they received from the enemy artillery; there is some substance in this criticism, but the fact remains that neither at Waterloo, nor anywhere else, did he ever lose a gun. His method at Waterloo was to position most of his field pieces throughout the line, just forward of his infantry, where they could fire on the advancing infantry and cavalry, but he forbade the practice of firing on enemy batteries, for the results did not justify the expenditure of ammunition. In one phase of the battle that lay ahead the enemy was to attack with unsupported cavalry; in this case the gunners had orders to man their guns until the last minute and then dive for shelter into the nearest square, being ready to advance on their guns again as soon as the tide of horsemen ebbed. It worked surprisingly well, but must have been a nerve-shattering exercise.

The main features of this great defensive position were the weight of fire that could be brought to bear upon the attackers and the disproportionate strength of the right wing. Wellington had so arranged his line that before the French could get to grips with their foe they had to survive the accurate markmanship of the skirmishers, the grape, round shot and case (often double charged) of the artillery and then, when they least expected it, two feet of cold steel and successive volleys from Brown Bess. The excessive strengthening which Wellington gave to his right is not so strange as it may at first seem. Apart from the fact that until quite late in the day he still expected the enemy to mount a strong left hook, he had received information in the early hours of the morning that the Prussians would come up on his left; even more important, the ground on the right of the line offered a safer and tactically better harbourage from which he could draw off troops to reinforce weakness or strength, as required.

Thus was the stage set, on the British side, for one of those great conflicts whose majestic splendour has invested the grim and grisly business of war with glamour. Every man in this heterogeneous army would soon be called upon to perform incredible feats of endurance and courage; all knew that the struggle would be stern, the risks appalling, the losses cruel, and the outcome uncertain. But the destiny of nations marched with these valiant soldiers and their great commander.

5 PRELIMINARIES & FIRST BLOWS

Jacques Champagne

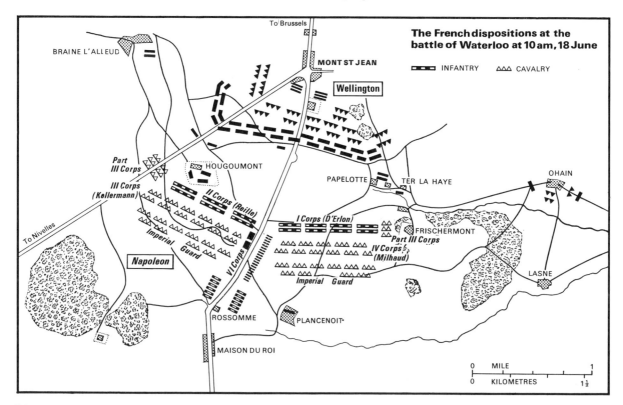

The French dispositions at the battle of Waterloo at 10 am, 18 June

INFANTRY   CAVALRY

To Brussels

BRAINE L'ALLEUD

MONT ST JEAN

Wellington

Part III Corps

HOUGOUMONT

III Corps (Kellermann)

II Corps (Reille)

PAPELOTTE   TER LA HAYE

OHAIN

I Corps (D'Erlon)

FRISCHERMONT

To Nivelles

Imperial Guard

Part III Corps

IV Corps (Milhaud)

LASNE

Napoleon

VI Corps

Imperial Guard

ROSSOMME

PLANCENOIT

MAISON DU ROI

| 0 | MILE | 1 |
| 0 | KILOMETRES | 1½ |

At 8 a.m. on 18 June, to the distant sound of
Plancenoit's church bells, Napoleon sat down at
breakfast at Caillou with Soult and several high-
ranking generals. After the meal, as maps were
being unfolded on the table, Napoleon declared:
'The enemy army is numerically superior to ours
by almost a quarter; yet, we have no less than 90
per cent of the chances in our favour, and not 10
against us.' Ney, who was just entering the room,
interjected: 'Quite so. That is if the Duke of
Wellington should be so simple as to wait for Your
Majesty. But I have come to tell you that already
his columns are in full retreat and are disappearing
into the forest.' 'You have not looked properly,'
replied Napoleon, 'it is too late for that. He would
expose himself to certain defeat. He has thrown
the dice and they have turned up for us.'[1]

Soult felt uneasy. He knew the plateau of Mont
St Jean, from which he himself had expelled the
allied armies in a frontal assault in 1794. He
regretted that one-third of the army was away
with Grouchy chasing the Prussians when battle
was about to begin against the English infantry,
who were famed for their stubbornness, their
accurate fire and their defensive tactics. Reille, a
veteran of Spain, coming into the room with
Prince Jérôme,[2] confirmed the costliness and
dangers of attacking English infantry frontally
and suggested that manoeuvring was the better
tactic. Jérôme, who had dined in a hotel in
Genappe the previous evening, told Napoleon that,
according to a Belgian waiter there, one of Wellington's aides-de-camp had said that the English and
Prussians had decided to join up in front of the
Forest of Soignes and that the Prussians would be
arriving from Wavre.

While dismissing Soult's and Reille's advice
regarding tactical manoeuvre, Napoleon was
sufficiently impressed by Jérôme's information to
take some precautions on the army's right flank.
He ordered the 7th Hussars to take up position
behind Frischermont with detachments in Lasne,
and he decided to write a new dispatch warning
Grouchy as soon as the army was in position on
the battlefield.

Napoleon expected his forces to be ready for the
attack at 9 a.m. But the troops, many of whom had
bivouacked as far away as Genappe during the
night, were only just beginning to assemble. In
any case, artillery officers who had surveyed the
plain were reporting that, owing to the state of the
ground, it would be another hour before the cannon
could be manoeuvred without too much difficulty.
Napoleon ordered General Haxo (engineers) to
get as close as possible to Wellington's left flank,

opposite the village of La Haye, and to ascertain
whether or not the enemy had built redoubts or
retrenchments there. Haxo's answer was in the
negative.

At 10 a.m., Napoleon dictated to Soult a letter
for Grouchy in answer to Grouchy's own dispatch
dated Gembloux 10 p.m. 17 June (see page 44).
Napoleon informed Grouchy that he was about to
attack Wellington at Waterloo and that, according
to new reports, a third Prussian column (Grouchy
had mentioned only two in his dispatch) was on
its way to Wavre, 'where you should proceed as
soon as possible in order to come closer to us and to
establish operational liaison with us whilst pressing
the enemy before you' (see Appendix II). Napoleon
then took up position on a hillock near the farm of
Rossomme, about a mile forward of Caillou, and
from there he surveyed Wellington's forces.

The Anglo-Dutch army had begun to assemble
at 6 a.m. (which accounted for Ney's impression
that the enemy was retreating) and was already in
battle position as follows:

In front line
(2 lines deep) between Braine l'Alleud and Nivelles
roads
Extreme right flank: Dutch–Belgian Division (Chassé) at
Braine l'Alleud. 2 batteries.
Right wing: English brigades (Adam and Mitchell),
Hanoverian brigade (Halkett), Anglo-German brigade
(Du Plat), perpendicular to the front line. 2 batteries.
Between the Nivelles road and the Charleroi road
Centre right: Guards brigades (Byng and Maitland)
leaning on the Nivelles road, Hanoverian brigade
(Kielmansegge) and Anglo-German brigade (Ompteda)
leaning on the Charleroi road. 4 batteries.
Forward position: 1st, 2nd (Coldstream) and 3rd Guards,
1 Hanoverian company and 1 Nassauer battalion at
Hougoumont.
Between Charleroi road and La Haye
Centre left: English brigades (Kempt and Pack) of
Picton division, Dutch–Belgian brigade (Bylandt), Han-
overian brigade (Best) leaning right on Charleroi road.
4 batteries.
Left wing: Orange–Nassauer brigade (Prince Bernhard
of Saxe-Weimar) and Hanoverian brigade (Vincke)
north of Papelotte and La Haye.
Forward position: 5 companies King's German Legion
and 1 battalion of the 95th at Papelotte and La Haye
Sainte detached from Prince Bernhard's forces.
In second line
Reserve in 2 lines deep
Extreme left flank: English cavalry (Vandeleur and
Vivian) at Ohain.
Behind centre right: Nassauer brigade (Kruse), Brunswick
Corps (infantry and cavalry), Anglo-German cavalry
brigades (Grant, Dornberg, Arentschildt), Guards
brigade (Somerset cavalry), Hussars brigade and Dutch–
Belgian cavalry (Trip and Van Merlen).

48 Left: La Haye Sainte after the battle, looking towards Waterloo, with Wellington's tree to the right of the farmhouse

49 Below left: Napoleon on the morning of the battle, giving an aide-de-camp a dispatch for Marshal Grouchy. Napoleon had taken up his position on a hillock near the farm of Rossomme, opposite the hill of La Belle Alliance

Behind centre left: English brigade (Lambert), English dragoons brigade (Ponsonby), Dutch–Belgian dragoon brigade (de Ghigney). 2 infantry battalions, 7 horse artillery, 3 batteries in reserve near the farm of Mont St Jean.

The French army was now deploying in eleven columns to take up their appointed battle positions on the heights of La Belle Alliance, where Napoleon was to review the troops. They looked like a great multicoloured mass, flags flying, drums beating and fanfares playing regimental marches, moving across the battlefield now bathed in sunshine. Shouting '*Vive l'Empereur!*' above the din, the cavalry brandishing their sabres, the infantry waving their shakos and bonnets on top of their raised bayonets, the army deployed in the following positions:

In front line
200 yards behind third line

Between Nivelles and Charleroi roads
Left wing: II Corps (Reille), 1 division light cavalry (Piré) 3 lines deep, straddling the Nivelles road level with Hougoumont. 46 cannon on the road.
Centre left: 3 infantry divisions 2 lines deep 60 yards apart (Jérôme, Foy, Bachelu) facing Hougoumont, leaning on Charleroi road left of La Belle Alliance.

Between Charleroi road and Frischermont
Centre right: I Corps (d'Erlon). 46 cannon. 4 infantry divisions (Allix, Donzelot, Marcognet, Durutte) 2 lines deep (as Reille) right of La Belle Alliance.
Right wing: 1 light cavalry division (Jacquinot), 3 lines deep (as Piré) facing La Haye Sainte left of Frischermont, light artillery on the right.
Extreme right flank: 7th Hussars behind Frischermont with detachments in Lasne, towards St Lambert and Wavre.

In second line
200 yards behind front line
Behind centre left Kellermann's cuirassiers (24 squadrons) 60 yards apart 2 lines deep checkerwise on $1\frac{1}{4}$-mile front, 1 battery of 8 cannon on each side.

100 yards behind front line on Kellermann's right Lobau's VI Corps. 2 infantry divisions (Simmer, Jeanin) in tight formation 200 yards deep leaning on Charleroi road, left of La Belle Alliance. 38 cannon in front, service corps behind.

100 yards behind front line
Behind centre right: 24 squadrons light cavalry (Domon, Subervie) in tight squadron formation 500 yards deep leaning on the Charleroi road behind La Belle Alliance. On their right, 24 squadrons of Milhaud's cuirassiers 2 lines deep (as Kellermann). Artillery on their left and centre left.

In third line reserve
200 yards behind second line, 2 lines deep
Behind centre left: 20 squadrons Grenadier Guards and dragoons (Guyot).
Behind centre right: 20 squadrons Guard chasseurs and lancers (Lefèvre-Desnouettes).

Guard infantry reserve
200 yards behind third line
8 infantry battalions of Young (Duhesme), Middle (Morand) and Grenadier Guards (Friant) of which there were 4 battalions on each side of the Charleroi road, each 6 lines deep, slightly in front of Rossomme. Artillery on the left and right flank of each regiment. Field and horse artillery reserve behind the lines.

Thus, in front line, from west to east, the French army was facing the Anglo-Dutch army respectively as follows:

> Piré – Adam and Mitchell
> Jérôme – Guards, Nassauers and Hanoverians at Hougoumont
> Reille – Byng, Maitland, Kielmansegge and Ompteda
> D'Erlon – Picton division, Bylandt and Best
> Jacquinot – Prince Bernhard of Saxe-Weimar and Vincke
> 7th Hussars – Vandeleur and Vivian.

The battle front was less than two miles long and the two armies' front lines were no more than a mile apart, although the French front was slightly concave opposite an almost straight Anglo-Dutch front: not much room for manoeuvre for a French army of some 70,000 men and 250 cannon facing an enemy estimated at some 90,000 men and 250 cannon (see Appendix III).

Mont St Jean was a good defensive position. From Rossomme, Napoleon could see clearly the enemy artillery on the crests and the infantry and cavalry on the plateau. What he could not see was a good deal of enemy infantry massed twenty, fifty and even 100 yards behind the ridge of the narrow road to Ohain, ideally situated all along the Anglo-Dutch front line for Wellington to apply his familiar defensive tactics. Nor did Napoleon know at this stage that Wellington had detached some 17,000 infantry and cavalry with thirty cannon to Hal, almost ten miles away, to protect his right flank against a totally illusory threat from Napoleon in this direction. Napoleon could not possibly have envisaged a main attack on Wellington's right (which was still by far his strongest point), since this would have been of no strategic or tactical value to the French. Wellington's left flank was Napoleon's obvious target for his usual frontal attack: not only was it the enemy's weakest point; it was also the only point from which to expect a possible Prussian arrival on the battlefield (if it were not foiled by Grouchy's intervention).

It was now almost 11 a.m. Napoleon dictated to Soult a battle order which left no doubt about his intentions: he did not expect now to attack before 1 p.m. Preceded by a devastating bombardment, it would be a frontal attack to pierce the enemy centre and to throw Wellington and his forces beyond Mont St Jean. Once master of this plateau, Napoleon would easily clinch the victory and destroy the enemy, who had no means of retreat (see Appendix II).

No sooner had Napoleon dictated his order of battle than a dispatch from Grouchy dated Gembloux 6 a.m. (see Appendix II) arrived at headquarters. It was more worrying than the previous one: instead of two Prussian corps retreating, one on Liège, the other on Wavre, Grouchy now announced that two enemy columns were *converging* on Brussels with the probable intention of *joining* Wellington. Nor was Grouchy talking any longer of 'preventing' this by marching on Wavre, since when he wrote his dispatch (6 a.m. 18 June) he had not even left Gembloux (see Appendix II).

But if Napoleon felt uneasy, he had other, more immediate matters to attend to. His attack on the enemy had already been considerably delayed, and he decided to probe Wellington with a diversionary action so as to induce him to draw some of his forces away from his centre. Napoleon ordered Reille to occupy the approaches to the castle of Hougoumont.

It was 11.30 a.m. Reille opened up with his batteries, drawing some response from English artillery. He entrusted Prince Jérôme with the attack on the woods of Hougoumont, supported by Piré's lancers. General Bauduin was killed outright in the first assault. After an hour of fierce fighting against the Nassauer and Hanoverian troops supported by the Guards, the French came out of the wood thirty yards from the castle and assailed it. They were caught in crossfire coming from all sides, from all the buildings, as they tried to climb the wall surrounding the park and to burst open the main door of the castle itself. They retreated with heavy losses to the cover of the wood.

But against the advice of his chief-of-staff (General Guilleminot), Prince Jérôme still intended to take Hougoumont. Calling on his second brigade (Soye), he advanced 600 yards under artillery fire to reach the northern face of the castle, there to lead the assault upon it. As Colonel de Cubières fell seriously wounded from his horse, Lieutenant Legros (1st Light), a giant of a man nicknamed *l'Enfonceur* (the Smasher), seized a sapper's axe, breached one panel of the castle door, and rushed into the courtyard with a handful of soldiers. They were all killed by enemy rifle fire or

in hand-to-hand fighting, while the Coldstream Guards, sent as reinforcements by Wellington, fell upon the whole French column, catching it in their crossfire. General Letort fell mortally wounded in this counter-attack and Prince Jérôme's forces withdrew, decimated, partly into the wood, partly towards the Nivelles road.

While the fighting was in progress at Hougoumont, preparations had been going on for Napoleon's main attack on Wellington. A formidable battery of ninety cannon had been assembled in front and

on the right of La Belle Alliance. Ney sent word that he was ready. It was 1 p.m.

Before giving his final order to attack, Napoleon surveyed once more the whole battlefield. His experienced eye noticed a distant cloud to the east in the direction of St Lambert, but could not quite make out exactly what was causing it. All staff officers trained their field telescopes on that point and came out with differing opinions. Some thought that there were troops at a halt there; others, that they were troops on the move; others, yet again, that there were no troops at all, just clusters of trees. The explanation came soon

enough. A cavalry detachment was being sent to reconnoitre, when French hussars posted at Lasne brought to Napoleon a non-commissioned hussar from the 2nd Regiment of Silesia whom they had just taken prisoner. He was carrying a letter from Bülow to Wellington announcing the arrival of his IV Prussian Corps at St Lambert and asking for instructions. The prisoner spoke French and told all he knew: 'The troops you see are General von Bülow's vanguard. Our whole army spent the night in Wavre. We saw no French troops and we suppose that they have marched on Plancenoit.'[3]

In view of Grouchy's last dispatch (see page 82), Napoleon was not unduly disconcerted by this development. He continued to hope that the main body of the Prussian army was still near Wavre and that it would march on direct to Brussels. But it was possible, of course, that the Prussians might try to join Wellington by a flanking movement reinforcing Bülow's corps, which was already in St Lambert. Napoleon therefore immediately dictated to Soult another dispatch for Grouchy. This time he was very specific: Grouchy was to come closer to the army so as 'to *join it before any corps can come between us*'. The Marshal was to decide himself the best way to do this in close operational liaison with the army and he was to 'always be in a position to *fall upon and crush* any enemy troops who would try to worry our right flank'. The dispatch ended: 'At this very moment, the battle is engaged on the line of Waterloo.' Soult added the words: 'In front of the Forest of Soignes. The enemy centre is at Mont St Jean. Do manoeuvre to join our right.' Moreover, just before the letter was dispatched to Grouchy, Napoleon, having finished interrogating the Prussian hussar and realizing what the 'distant cloud' at St Lambert was, had this post-script added by Soult: 'A letter just intercepted indicates that General Bülow is going to attack our right flank. We think that we can see this corps on the heights of St Lambert. Do not lose one moment, therefore, in coming closer to us, in joining us and in crushing Bülow, whom you will catch red-handed' (see Appendix II).[4]

Finally, Napoleon took additional precautionary measures to protect his right flank. The light cavalry divisions of Domon and Subervie were detached eastwards to observe the enemy, to occupy all the exits from St Lambert and to combine with Grouchy's head of columns as soon as they appeared. Count Lobau was ordered to bring his VI (infantry) Corps into a good intermediary position, perpendicular to the right flank of the army, where he could contain the Prussians between Ohain and Lasne.

6 THE DEFENCE OF HOUGOUMONT
11.30 am-1.30 pm
William Seymour

The decision to stand and fight at Mont St Jean had only been taken a few hours before the Duke of Wellington and his staff left the inn at Waterloo to ride the two miles to the battlefield. In sombre contrast to the scarlet and gold that adorned the tunics of his staff, Wellington was plainly, but immaculately, dressed in a blue civilian coat, white buckskins, hessian boots, a white cravat and a blue cloak, which he made full use of whenever there was a shower. His cocked hat carried no plume, but four cockades – the insignia of England, Spain, Portugal and the Netherlands. As he rode along the line, some two hours before Napoleon started the battle, he looked – and was – completely relaxed. He had a word for many of his soldiers, and at the crossroads he stopped for a mug of tea brewed by Captain Kincaid's riflemen. The men did not cheer him, for it was generally known that he disliked any overt emotional display, and anyway he was not a man the soldiers would have been likely to cheer. They had no love for him, nor he for them, but there was mutual respect and understanding; the British army trusted and admired him; and more important to them than his love was the sense of calm and strength he gave them.

Very different was the scene a thousand or so yards to the south, as Napoleon, contrary to his usual practice, reviewed his army as it marched past to deploy along the ridge of La Belle Alliance. Lancers, dragoons, cuirassiers and chasseurs rode past in magnificent array; theirs was an army that had for many years held the professional primacy of Europe, and with which the Emperor was confidently preparing for what he contemptuously thought would be 'little more than a picnic'.

The thunderous cheers and shouts of '*Vive l'Empereur!*' that echoed across the valley may have sent a chill of horror up the spine of many a Johnny Newcome, but the old soldiers had heard it all before. As Wellington and his staff watched with interest and tried to make some calculation as to the numbers that would be unleashed against them, the army continued with its preparations. Guns were dragged across muddy fields into their final positions, and the constant popping of muskets indicated the simplest way of clearing damp charges. When all was done the men settled down to wait, to talk quietly among themselves, the veterans to reminisce, and perhaps all to fret a little at the inexplicable delay by the French in making their move – for when men are keyed up for battle, suspense can fray the nerves badly.

There was a divergence of opinion among some of those who took part as to exactly what time the Battle of Waterloo started. The Duke wrote in his dispatch, 'at about ten o'clock he [Napoleon] commenced a furious attack upon our post at Hougoumont', but he was undoubtedly mistaken. Lord Hill said that it was 11.50 a.m. by his watch, and Lord Edward Somerset agreed with him, while an officer of the 52nd made it noon. All we can say with certainty is that it was between 11.30 and noon when the French cannon opened up with a mighty roar all along the allied line, though with the weight of their attack directed at the right flank.

Wellington, with his intuitive battle sense, had always expected the first assault to be aimed at his right; it was, therefore, no surprise to find him at this time on the high ground just above Hougoumont, sitting calmly on his horse Copenhagen and apparently quite unconcerned at the amount of lead that was either whistling through the air or churning up the mud all around him. The men were told to lie down to minimize the effect of shell and shot, which was already beginning to have a devastating effect. Meanwhile the British artillery came into action – it was about this time that Captain Mercer received his orders to limber up and bring his guns over to the right close to the 14th Foot – and directed their fire (contrary to the Duke's orders, as he himself admitted) against those batteries from Reille's II Corps that were coming into action in support of Prince Jérôme's division. These troops, accompanied on their left flank by General Piré's 2nd Cavalry Division and preceded by a swarm of skirmishers, were advancing upon the south and south-western end of the small wood that lay to the south of Hougoumont.

This opening phase of the Battle of Waterloo was conducted by both sides with the same savage fury that was to last throughout the long day. At first the Nassauers and Hanoverians managed to repulse Jérôme's men, and it may have been in the very earliest minutes of the attack that General Bauduin, the commander of the leading French brigade, was killed. But gradually, fighting from tree to tree, the Germans were driven back, although the French were hard pressed both by infantry and artillery. Wellington had ordered Sir Augustus Frazer to bring up Major Bull's howitzers, and having warned Frazer that he was about 'to do a delicate thing' watched the battery fire shrapnel over the heads of the allied troops and into the enemy; it was indeed a delicate task, and admirably performed, but it could not stop the French driving the Germans out of the wood.

At this time Lord Saltoun's light companies were in the orchard; the light company of the 2nd

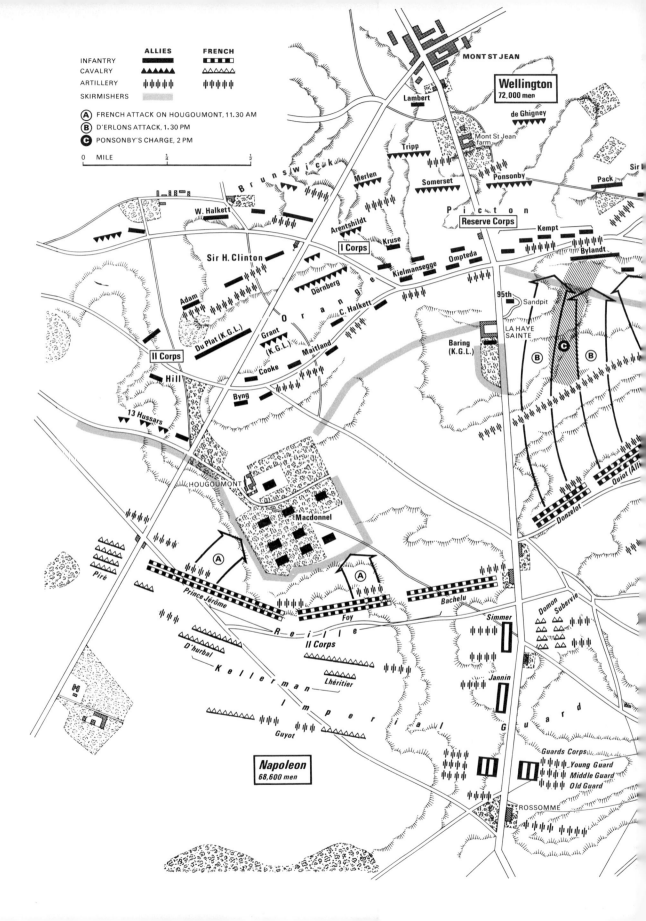

ALLIES   **FRENCH**

INFANTRY ▮▮▮▮   ▤▤▤▤

CAVALRY ▲▲▲▲▲   △△△△△

ARTILLERY ⑂⑂⑂⑂⑂   ⑂⑂⑂⑂⑂

SKIRMISHERS ▬▬▬▬

Ⓐ FRENCH ATTACK ON HOUGOUMONT, 11.30 AM

Ⓑ D'ERLONS ATTACK, 1.30 PM

Ⓒ PONSONBY'S CHARGE, 2 PM

0   MILE   ¼   ½

MONT ST JEAN

Lambert

Wellington
72,000 men

de Ghigney

Mont St Jean
farm

Tripp

Merlen

Somerset

Ponsonby

Pack

Sir

B r u n s w i c k

P i c t o n

W. Halkett

Arentshildt

I Corps

Kruse

Reserve Corps

Kempt

Bylandt

Sir H. Clinton

Kielmansegge

Ompteda

95th ← Sandpit

LA HAYE
SAINTE

Adam

Dörnberg

O r a n g e

C. Halkett

Ⓑ   Ⓒ   Ⓑ

Du Plat (K.G.L.)

Grant
(K.G.L.)

Maitland

Baring
(K.G.L.)

II Corps

Cooke

Hill

Byng

Ouiot (Alli

13 Hussars

Donzelot

HOUGOUMONT

Macdonnel

Ⓐ

Ⓐ

Bachelu

Simmer

Domon   Subervie

Piré   Prince Jérôme

Foy

R e i l l e

II Corps

Jannin

D'hurbal

Lhéritier

K e l l e r m a n

I m p e r i a l   G u a r d

Guyot

Napoleon
68,600 men

Guards Corps

Young Guard
Middle Guard
Old Guard

ROSSOMME

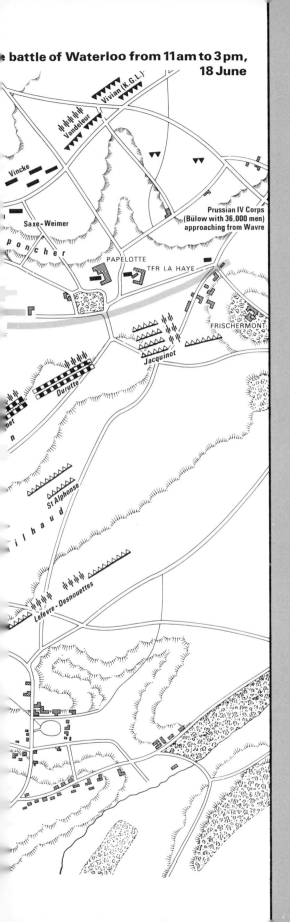

The battle of Waterloo from 11am to 3pm, 18 June

Vivian (K.G.L.)

Vandeleur

Vincke

Saxe-Weimer

poncher

Prussian IV Corps
(Bülow with 36,000 men)
approaching from Wavre

PAPELOTTE

TER LA HAYE

FRISCHERMONT

Jacquinot

Durutte

net

n

St Alphonse

ilhaud

Lefevre-Desnouettes

Coldstream held the southern wall of the garden, with its right in the main building, while the light company of the 3rd Guards held the lane to the west of the enclosure. A counter-attack by the light companies in the orchard and the lane, together with the Germans, was only partially successful, for Prince Jérôme had reinforced his attack with a part of Foy's division, who advanced frontally down the side of the wood, and Soye's brigade which came in from the west flank closely supported by Piré's horse battery. The weight of this attack gradually drove the defenders out of the wood and back to their original positions in orchard and lane. But the French, thinking the thick hedge that bounded the wood was the last obstacle before they reached the garden, were amazed to find themselves being hideously mauled by the murderous fire of the Coldstreamers from the loopholed garden wall and buildings as they rushed the fifty yards of open field that separated the hedge from their goal. They came on with much courage, and some even attempted to scale the wall, but the attempt was in vain; by the time the survivors were back in the comparative safety of the wood many lay dead in that narrow strip of field.

It was now shortly after twelve. The Nassauers had been withdrawn, but the Hanoverians were left with Saltoun's companies in the orchard. The situation on the right flank had become critical; the 3rd Guards in the lane, with a blazing haystack at the south end and Soye's troops coming at them from the west, were being forced back towards the main gate. Bull's guns, now enfiladed by those of Piré on the Nivelles road, were unable to give much support, and the race for the gate was on. It was the only gate left open, and the outflanking French troops had seen it; if they could seize the gateway and hold it Hougoumont would be lost.

The 3rd Guards succeeded in falling back into the yard to join the Coldstreamers, and the gate was closed. But the French were close behind them, led by the 1st Light Regiment, which in turn was led by a giant of a man, Sous-Lieutenant Legros – aptly nicknamed *L'Enfonceur* – who, wielding a heavy axe, managed to force the gate and charge into the farmyard at the head of a small party. There now ensued a tremendous fight; Colonel Macdonnell, himself no lightweight, seeing what was afoot and helped by two burly sergeants (Graham of the Coldstream and McGregor of the 3rd Guards), rushed from the garden towards the gates that had been forced open and managed to shut them once more by fixing the heavy cross-bar that secured the doors. The gallant French storming party (less one unarmed drummer boy) were

all killed or wounded. *L'Enfonceur*, the axe still grasped in his hand, died at the door of the chapel. His comrades continued to hack and batter at the gate from without, with a fury that was only abated by the fire of the defenders, which took a terrible toll, and the arrival of fresh companies of Coldstreamers.

The commander of the 2nd Guards Brigade had been watching the progress of the battle with some anxiety, and at about 12.30 he ordered Colonel Woodford to go forward with his Coldstream battalion – less the Colours and two companies – to relieve the pressure brought about by Soye's attack, for at this moment the enclosure and surrounding fields were lapped about by the enemy. Woodford's men drove in the French skirmishers, who fell back on those still trying to force the gate, but after a brief action these French troops were driven off and Woodford's troops entered the enclosure by the small gate on its west side. Now Hougoumont could be more strongly manned, particularly the east wall of the garden, which was soon to be of great importance, for Foy was about to send in his last brigade (Gautier's) in a frontal and flanking attack on the orchard.

Gautier's men charged through the gap in the thick hedge at the point where the orchard meets the coppice, and at the same time skirmishers worked their way round Saltoun's left flank. Thus threatened he withdrew his troops back to the safety of the Hollow Way. General Alten, seeing this dangerous outflanking movement, prepared to send in the light companies of his 3rd Division, but either the Duke, or the commanding officer of the 3rd Guards on his own initiative, anticipated him with the grenadier and one other company of that regiment, who under Lieutenant-Colonel Home outflanked the outflankers and with the aid of the Coldstream men firing from the east wall of the garden drove them from the orchard. Lord Saltoun then re-established his position along the south hedge.

The fight for Hougoumont had been in progress for almost an hour and a half; there had been little respite from intensive fire and the slaughter had been heavy. The French still held the wood in strength, and now sent a howitzer forward to shell the buildings. Saltoun's battle-weary men, together with Home's fresh grenadier company, made a determined effort to destroy this nuisance, but as they were opposed by almost three French brigades it was hardly surprising that their attack failed, and Saltoun found himself back in the Hollow Way. The light companies of the 1st Guards Brigade had done a magnificent job, and it was

52 Above: Closing the south gate at Hougoumont. Colonel Macdonnell is shown holding the left gate (with sword).
53 Left: An aerial view of Hougoumont as it is today, showing the courtyard and the chapel

time for them to be relieved; a little after 1 p.m. Colonel Hepburn brought the remaining seven companies of his 2nd Battalion 3rd Guards into the Hollow Way, and Lord Saltoun's men joined their battalions on the main position.

Shortly after this Hepburn assumed command of the 2nd Guards Brigade, because General Cooke had been severely wounded and his place as divisional commander had been taken by General Byng. The new brigade commander had his whole brigade, less the two Coldstream companies, in or around Hougoumont. The 2nd Coldstream occupied the château buildings and garden, while the 3rd Guards (less their light company, which was in the enclosure) and what remained of the Hanoverians lined the Hollow Way. The orchard was occupied by the enemy, and it was Hepburn's intention to remove them from it.

But by 1.30 the pressure was to some extent lifted from these 2,000 Guardsmen and Hanoverians, who had denied 10,000 of some of Napoleon's best troops the prize that they had striven for two hours to win. The great thrust against the allied centre and left wing, which Ney had been preparing while Hougoumont was under attack and which he, at any rate, felt sure would be decisive, was about to begin. Even though he could not know that Napoleon would shortly have to detach 11,000 men and thirty-two guns to meet the still distant Prussian menace, Wellington had reason to be well pleased with the way embattled Hougoumont had held out. One prong of the French attack had already been blunted, and the fight around the château would continue to occupy many enemy formations during the rest of the day and to deny the French the space vitally needed if their massive assaults were to be successful.

Talking to Thomas Creevey a short while after the battle, Wellington commented, 'You may depend upon it, that no troops but the British could have held Hougoumont, and only the best of them at that!'

7 THE PRUSSIAN ADVANCE
Daybreak-Midday
Colonel E. Kaulbach

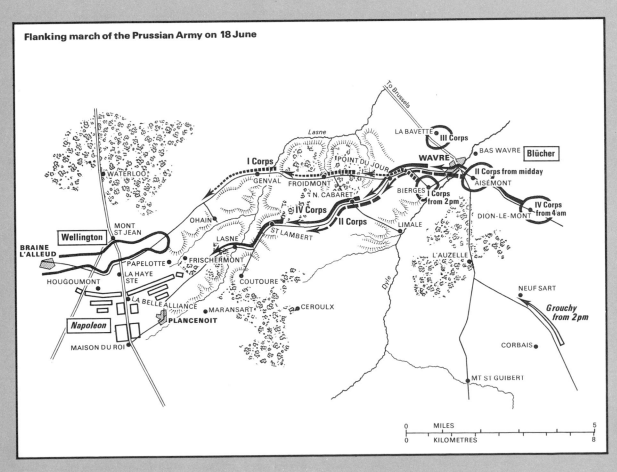

Flanking march of the Prussian Army on 18 June

The advance of the Prussian army was planned so that the bulk of the army, two to three corps, should move against Napoleon's right flank and, if necessary, one of these corps would move to Wellington's left wing. One last corps should remain in Wavre as rearguard for as long as there was any danger that the enemy pursuit units might approach and attack. IV Corps was planned for the first attack on the French right flank, with II Corps in close support. IV Corps was to move off at daybreak in order to reach the battlefield in good time. The defeat of Napoleon was entirely dependent upon their timely arrival and their joining battle in support of Wellington's army.

But two circumstances, the final consequences of which could not possibly have been foreseen on the 17th, produced delays in the advance of the Prussian corps – true 'frictions' in the Clausewitz sense; first, the extremely difficult conditions of the roads and the ground between the Dyle and the Brussels road caused by the weather, and second, the complications caused by the massing of the entire Prussian army in the area of Wavre.

Even a visit to the battlefield today, approaching Mont St Jean from the direction of Wavre, can, despite the much changed landscape, give some idea of the difficulties of the terrain; the wooded hillocks, the deeply cut streams, the tortuous paths whose steep sides made any evasive movement difficult. A hundred and fifty years ago there were no roads and no firm paths here, only field paths which wound their way over the hills and down into the valleys. Even in good weather, when it was dry underfoot, the army's advance would have been difficult. But from midday on the 17th until the morning of the 18th it rained torrentially and without ceasing; the paths became bottomless, the low ground a morass. This applied particularly to the valley of the Lasne, which had to be crossed by two army corps. All calculations of time were thrown out and any talk of 'normal progress' on the 18th became meaningless. The troops had to move through deep mud. It must be remembered what difficulties the French army experienced, despite having a wide, paved road to use; Napoleon's attack on the morning of the 18th had to be postponed because the artillery could not take up positions off the roads any earlier.

The Prussian corps were already under way at the time that the French attack was postponed and had to cover some ten to twelve miles under the most difficult conditions. That the Prussian army, especially the artillery, was brought through and still arrived in time for the battle can now be seen as little short of miraculous.[1] It could not have

happened without the drive of Blücher and all the other commanders, as well as the good will of all the men.

A further difficulty resulted from the concentration, luckily achieved, of the entire Prussian army in the area of Wavre. Once again, it must be remembered what this area looked like in those days – the deep narrow valley of the Dyle, the soft paths and boggy low ground, the few villages. Here 90,000 men, with the whole of their transport and baggage trains, and the entire artillery and cavalry, were all pressed together. The innumerable carts could not leave the paths, on account of the rain, and when the corps started to move in the morning, the result must have been an unimaginable traffic jam.[2]

Virtually all commentators have found it impossible to account for the order in which the Prussian command brought forward the various corps for battle on the 18th. While they have all approved Blücher's courageous decision they have viewed its practical execution by the army command as partly or wholly faulty and the principal reason for the late arrival of the Prussian army on the battlefield.[3] The most distant unit, IV Corps, was designated to point the attack, to get into position it had to cross the Dyle and, with 30,000 men, pass through the bottle-neck of Wavre. One critical observer, the Prussian General von Caemmerer, comments '. . . Gneisenau had, mistakenly, taken the most easterly corps, that of Bülow, to the head of the movement. . . .'[4] Today these orders are still puzzling. In a situation, in which everything depended upon the timely arrival of the troops on the battlefield, the two nearest corps should surely have been in the lead – III Corps in the direction of Mont St Jean, I Corps on St Lambert. Moving off at the same time II Corps could have followed I Corps to St Lambert, while IV Corps could have stayed as rearguard after crossing the Dyle and have followed up, wholly or partly, as the situation developed. In this way all four corps could have started simultaneously and a crossing of routes would have been avoided.

That is how it looks today. And yet this view does not satisfy, since it is a judgment *a posteriori*. Lettow-Vorbeck, in his very critical examination, comes to the conclusion that it will never be entirely possible to put oneself in Blücher's position at the time he made his decisions.[5] Above all, the present-day observer must ask himself whether generals with such experience of war as Blücher, Gneisenau and Grolmann would, in so urgent a situation, where everything hung on a thread, have ordered their army as they did without very real reasons and considerations. The order of march *had* to be sanctioned by Blücher. Gneisenau may well have made the initial suggestions but it was Blücher who took the authoritative decision – and never more so than when the decision involved committing the entire army to battle, or the actual conduct of the battle. Even the course of action at Ligny shows Blücher's leadership. For the advance to Waterloo it was certainly Blücher's desire to have the 'intact' IV Corps in the van; as early as the morning of the 17th he made this clear in his first agreement with Wellington. The others corps, especially I Corps' were so weakened by Ligny that Blücher's feeling was understandable. In particular I Corps, resting in Bierges on the left flank, was to remain stationary as flank guard for as long as there was the possibility that the enemy might advance on the west of the Dyle.[6]

From Pertz's account it is clear that concern about a late arrival on the battlefield, when the orders for the advance were given on the evening of the 17th, had not at the time the significance which it was later to assume. I Army Corps was stationed not more than $1\frac{1}{2}$ miles away from where the next day's engagement was to be fought; nothing therefore was further from their thought than any fear of arriving late. Orders were given for the advance in the most correct and methodical fashion without considering that this could mean some hours' delay.[7] Whether all other 'frictions' could have been foreseen in time is immaterial; army orders for a complicated movement cannot be rapidly changed without producing confusion.

So our verdict today must be that contemporary circumstances carried their own weight, even if the results may later be found incomprehensible. One can, however, join Clausewitz in his measured criticism based on the success of the final outcome:

There were apparently, then, some 20,000 men for the immediate support of the English left flank besides 70,000 on the right flank and to the rear of the enemy. Things could not have been arranged in a simpler, more natural or more practical manner. At most one might criticise the action of not sending I Corps, which was in bivouac at Bierges, with the others to St Lambert, while sending II Corps, which had first to cross the Dyle, to Ohain. This caused the two columns to cross, and resulted in delays.[8]

Chesney is also critical, but has this to say about Clausewitz's views: 'On the other hand there are few who will not agree with his remark upon the march, that "its general design, to support the English left with 20,000 men and throw the other 70,000 upon Napoleon's right, could not have been more simple, more practical, or more effective".'[9]

The advance of the Prussian army on the 18th from Wavre to the battle took place under circumstances that asked the utmost of the troops.[10] IV Corps started at four o'clock in the morning. General von Bülow had placed the strengthened 15th Brigade in the van, behind them the bulk of the 16th and 13th Brigades followed by the reserve artillery, and the reserve cavalry of the corps rearguard was the 14th Brigade. The entire baggage train was moved off towards Louvain. The corps orders stated expressly: 'No carts will be allowed in the columns.'[11]

Bülow's advance guard marched through Wavre between five and six in the morning and reached its first objective, St Lambert, between nine and eleven.[12] The main body following was held up in Wavre owing to a fire, so that it did not arrive at St Lambert until midday – some considerable distance behind. The last brigade did not arrive until three in the afternoon. The paths were in an appalling state and became worse with the passage of each marching unit. II Corps had been ready at Aisémont since early morning; however, because of the delay in the advance of IV Corps it could not move off until about midday. I and III Corps waited in their bivouac positions during the morning.

Field-Marshal Blücher moved out of Wavre with his army headquarters to join IV Corps at the head of the army at about eleven o'clock. Before riding off he had arranged for orders to be sent to I Corps to join Wellington's left flank at Mont St Jean via Froidmont. The orders were transmitted verbally and reached I Corps between eleven and twelve. But their departure also was delayed, until about two in the afternoon, because units of II Corps were still occupying the route.

The position around midday on 18 June was as follows: IV Corps was at Chapelle St Lambert; II Corps was leaving Aisémont through Wavre to follow IV Corps; I Corps was about to break up in the area of Bierges; III Corps stood at La Bavette, though without the 9th Brigade which had remained on the east side of the Dyle.

8 ATTACK AND COUNTER-ATTACK
D'Erlon & Uxbridge
1.30pm-3pm
William Seymour & Jacques Champagne

55 The defence of La Haye Sainte by the King's German Legion. These men suffered the brunt of the attack by d'Erlon's I Corps

The English View

While the attack on Hougoumont was in progress Wellington was keeping a sharp watch on what Napoleon was doing along the rest of his front. The move forward of artillery to cover the allied line from the right of Alten's division to Wellington's extreme left around Papelotte and Ter La Haye indicated very clearly that a powerful thrust was being prepared against his left and centre. Almost equidistant between the rival armies there was a minor intermediary ridge, and it was on to this ridge – particularly that part of it east of the Brussels road – that Napoleon was bringing forward a good proportion of the seventy-eight guns which were to support the 17,000 or so men of General d'Erlon's I Corps.

Soon after 1 p.m. these guns, some of them firing at a range of only 500 yards, thundered into action, developing, along a two-mile front, a fire so intense and destructive that even the veterans, for all their bravado, could not recall anything like it. Shot and shell screamed through the air taking a terrible toll of man and horse. It was all the harder to bear for Wellington's refusal to allow the allied artillery to waste powder and shot in futile retaliation. It was the prelude to the sort of set-attack in the grand manner that had so often first demoralized and then destroyed continental armies; Napoleon knew, no one better, the powerful effect of a massive bombardment. Men were not just killed, they were horribly mutilated. There is no doubt that this artillery barrage blasted the courage from Bylandt's Dutch–Belgian brigade, which had been severely tested at Quatre-Bras; but there is some doubt as to exactly where they were when the guns opened up. They had certainly come into line with Picton's forward troops before the infantry attacked, and it seems probable that they had done so before the bombardment, because although badly shaken they withstood this pounding.

At about 1.45, to the cheers of '*Vive l'Empereur*!' and the sound of the drums beating out the *pas de charge*, d'Erlon's men advanced; although partially concealed by the thick smoke that now filled the valley, they were still supported by their guns until it was no longer safe for them to do so. This great mass of infantry came on in four divisions, echeloned from just west of the Brussels road to the extreme left of Wellington's line. The infantry was covered by cavalry on both flanks, and light field guns were brought up with it. On d'Erlon's left Bachelu's division was in support, while Prince Jérôme renewed his attack on Hougoumont. D'Erlon's divisional commanders were Allix (or

Quiot, the command changed at some stage of the campaign), Donzelot, Marcognet and Durutte; they probably advanced from left to right in that order, although to the British soldiers anxiously manning the crest this was of little importance. What did matter was the formation in which the leading battalions attacked; although the French usually advanced in massed close column of battalions, which presented a clumsy formation incapable of developing effective fire power, d'Erlon made some attempt to avoid this.

The left division advanced initially on a two-brigade front (one each side of the main road), with the battalions in line three deep; the brigades of the two centre divisions marched one behind the other but with both battalions in line, while the right-hand division seems to have marched in the more usual formation of column of battalions each with a two-company front. A battalion advancing in three lines would have had perhaps 175 men in each rank, and in theory all three ranks of the leading battalion were trained to fire simultaneously. Again in theory, brigades thus formed could deploy their battalions to a flank quite quickly – and indeed this worked well during the attack on La Haye Sainte – but if the battalions were allowed to close up and form one great mass, as was inclined to happen, then the whole formation became hopelessly unwieldy and an easy prey to cannon. As this massive onslaught rolled forward, seemingly irresistibly strong, it must have been an awesome sight, especially to those men in the outposts – the King's German Legion in La Haye Sainte and the 95th in the sandpit – who would have to bear the initial brunt of the attack.

It was not long before the skirmishers of both armies were in action, and at about the same time Wellington gave the order for the allied artillery to open up on the advancing columns. Considerable damage was done to the enemy as the shot and canister ripped through the closely packed ranks, but the check was scarcely noticeable, and soon La Haye Sainte and the sandpit were encased by hordes of fiercely determined men. La Haye Sainte had not been properly prepared; worse than that, one of its massive wooden gates had been dismantled the previous evening for firewood. But Baring's 2nd King's German Legion were great fighters, and though driven out of the orchard they fell back to a line just west of the building with their left resting on the open gate. Reinforced by a battalion of Kielmansegge's Han-

overians, Baring attempted to counter-attack the troops that had driven him from the orchard. But the appearance – seemingly from nowhere, for they had been concealed by a fold in the ground – of a regiment of cuirassiers played havoc with the Hanoverians. Pressed back into the buildings, Baring and his Germans held on, isolated, but not defeated.

The position around the sandpit and on the extreme left of the line was even less enviable. Wellington had ordered the 1st Light Battalion from Ompteda's brigade to cross the *chaussée* in support of the 95th companies in the sandpit; then, leaving Picton, whose 5th Division though light on the ground was absolutely dependable, to cope as best he could, he hurried on towards Papelotte. But Prince Bernhard's Nassauers had been driven out of this advanced post by the men of Durutte's division. Back at the sandpit the weight of the attack had become too great for this unprotected position to be retained and the men of the 95th fell back through the hedge on to their battalion, having previously taken great toll of the enemy with their frontal and enfilading fire. It is difficult to be certain exactly when Bylandt's brigade beat its hasty retreat to the rear, where it stayed for the rest of the battle. It was probably just before the 95th companies were outflanked and forced to retire, and although the disappearence of this badly shaken brigade gave the French a momentary illusion of success, it had no moral or physical repercussions on Picton's thin line, which quickly closed up and was indeed better off without such troops.

The situation on this part of the front had become very critical. Through the standing corn, over ground already soaked by the rain, now churned to mud and reddened by the blood of fallen comrades, the French infantry came doggedly on and gained the crest of the ridge; there seemed to be little between them and Brussels. But Picton's two brigades, though sorely battered by the fighting at Quatre-Bras, were still capable of giving a very good account of themselves. There now developed some of the fiercest fighting of this very fierce day.

As they neared the Ohain road the two left-hand French divisions started to deploy, but Marcognet's men, deeming this too risky an operation, struggled through the hedge still in column. The allied gunners had been taking a terrible toll at almost point-blank range, but suddenly some of them seem to have become confused or discomfited and to have abandoned their pieces (one sergeant even spiked a gun), contrary to specific orders, and disappeared to the rear. Eight thousand Frenchmen were now almost on top of Kempt's and Pack's much attenuated brigades; it seemed that nothing could stop them. But, arrayed in line two deep, the British soldiers were ready for Picton's word of command to advance and fire; at a range of less than fifty yards, 3,000 muskets poured a hail of lead into the oncoming French and the air around crackled with the whiplash sound of close-range ball as firing continued by half-company volleys. But such were their numbers that this only served as a momentary check on the enemy hordes; the great voice of Picton was heard for the last time, 'Charge, charge, hurrah' and, turning to Kempt, 'Rally the Highlanders'. As this brave soldier fell with a bullet through the temple, Scots and English were desperately thrusting and parrying in a bayonet mêlée with the leading French battalion.

While this important action was taking place to the east of the Brussels road, the situation was every bit as critical on the other side. Here Allix's left brigade had not been halted, and the cuirassiers that had inflicted such damage on the Hanoverians were in close support. Wellington ordered the German brigades in front of these oncoming horsemen to form square, for all along the line his infantry was bending and cavalry could have ridden through it. But help was at hand.

Another one of those interesting, partly unsolved issues concerning this great battle is who ordered the heavy cavalry to charge at this most fortuitous moment? The Earl of Uxbridge, writing some years afterwards, said that it was he who first ordered Sir William Ponsonby's Union Brigade (the Royals, Scots Greys and Inniskillings – 900 sabres in all) to wheel into action with the Household Brigade (squadrons from the 1st and 2nd Life Guards, the Royal Horse Guards and the King's Dragoon Guards – 1,220 sabres) and that he then galloped back to the Union Brigade and put the whole into action. History has given him the credit for personally initiating this epic charge; but as Wellington is known to have been near the crossroads at the time it seems more likely that Uxbridge first received orders from him. But what mattered was not who gave the order, but how it was carried out and how – at great cost – it saved a most dangerous situation.

The Household Brigade quickly launched into the cuirassiers, just as they were scrambling in and out of the sunken road immediately to the west of the crossroads. Taken at a disadvantage and borne down upon by the sheer weight of the heavier horses, they were soon scattering, some to their left, others on to the Brussels road and over or round the abatis by the sandpit; furthermore, in their headlong rush, closely followed by the Life Guards and King's Dragoon Guards (at this stage the Blues were in reserve), they rode down their own infantry. Other squadrons from the Household Brigade caught some of the battalions of the French left division still deploying and threw them into utter confusion. Meanwhile, on the left, the Union Brigade tore into the mass of Donzelot's and Marcognet's infantry. Taken completely by surprise, and in a formation totally unsuited to resisting cavalry, the carnage was fearful before they managed to disengage themselves from their tightly packed ranks and scamper down the hill. More than 2,000 prisoners and two Eagles (that of the 45th Regiment by Sergeant Ewart of the Greys, and that of the 105th by Captain Clark of the Royals) were taken.

The two cavalry brigades had now joined together, and having suffered very few losses themselves (some Life Guardsmen had been shot by flanking fire from men of Bachelu's division) they had the satisfaction of seeing the whole of d'Erlon's corps in full flight ahead of them. Seldom ever before had formed infantry been smashed so thoroughly and so quickly by cavalry. No wonder these men were exhilarated. Now, quite out of hand, they careered on with shouts of 'Scotland for ever!', as the Greys – earmarked as support troops – thrust their way into the forward line. Across the smoke-filled valley and right into the French positions they thundered, overturning guns and sabring the gun teams, and on up the slope of La Belle Alliance. But the going was heavy and their horses were becoming blown; retribution was at hand, for they now found themselves among 30,000 fresh French troops, including the Imperial Guard, and Napoleon was ready for this whirlwind of hostile cavalry that was rapidly becoming a spent force.

On the left of the British line the Scots Greys, and some of the Royals and Inniskillings, were playing havoc among Napoleon's great battery of seventy-eight guns when suddenly, and furiously, they were assailed by two regiments of lancers and badly cut up, losing their brigade commander, Sir William Ponsonby. Further to the right the 2nd Life Guards and King's Dragoon Guards, with whom Lord Uxbridge had charged, were in a similar difficulty with two regiments of cuirassiers. Both brigades might have been entirely annihilated had it not been for a vital rescue operation by Vandeleur's brigade of light dragoons. As it was, almost half of these magnificent brigades, with their

horses, were lost; barely 1200 men rode their tired animals back to safety.

Why did this tragedy occur? Apart from the almost too fine spirit of the British cavalry, already touched upon, there was no time before the charge to give proper orders – save to name the Blues and Greys as support troops – and there was no channel of command with Uxbridge riding in the van. Had he held back and allowed a divisional commander (one had never been appointed) to take charge of the van, Uxbridge might have been able to control the supporting squadrons, and anyway bring in Vandeleur's men more quickly, for they – with the exception of two squadrons of the 12th Light Dragoons, acting on their own initiative – had been a little tardy in attacking.

Nevertheless Wellington's hard-tried infantry had, for the time being, been granted a respite, for the French had been driven right back along the whole line; Durutte's division had not been caught up in the general destruction, but had found itself isolated and then fiercely attacked on its right flank by Colonel Ponsonby's 12th Light Dragoons. There now ensued a brief lull in the fighting, save for the continuing artillery bombardment, while both sides gathered up the pieces and prepared for the next round. The French had lost heavily; apart from the prisoners and two Eagles, already mentioned, some twenty-five guns had been disabled and three of d'Erlon's brigades had been so mauled and demoralized as to render their further use doubtful.

But the Anglo-Dutch army had not achieved this chastisement without considerable loss to themselves. The charge had torn the entrails out of the heavy cavalry; the 12th Light Dragoons had also suffered casualties, among them being their colonel who was left on the ground for dead;[1] the infantry had lost General Picton and many of their rank and file, while one whole brigade had withdrawn itself from the battle.

No sooner had the French been swept from personal contact than Wellington set about reorganizing and strengthening his line. The companies of the 95th went back to the sandpit; Prince Bernhard's men returned to the Papelotte area; some companies of his Nassauers that had been withdrawn from Hougoumont were sent to reinforce La Haye Sainte, and, with the threat of an outflanking movement obviously receding, troops originally positioned west of the Nivelles road could be brought across to form a close reserve. A battalion of Brunswickers, and parts of du Plat's and Hew Halkett's brigades, were moved to a position north and east of Hougoumont to take

57 An order from the Duke of Wellington concerning the defence of Hougoumont. These orders were written on specially prepared skin and were designed to be wiped clean, consequently few survive

the place of Byng's brigade, which had gone to reinforce the garrison; soon the whole division would be brought into the front line. At the left centre of the allied line Kempt had taken command of the 5th Division, and General Lambert's 10th British Brigade, consisting of three Peninsular battalions, had been brought up from Mont St Jean to be in reserve behind and to the west of Papelotte. Thus the Duke had close at hand, both on his right and centre, a fairly strong reserve that he could throw in where needed, while on the extreme left Best's and Vincke's Hanoverian brigades were still comparatively unscathed.

Throughout the bitter confrontation with d'Erlon the action at Hougoumont had continued unabated. When we left the situation there the enemy were in possession of the orchard while the 3rd Guards lined the Hollow Way. Colonel Hepburn always considered that his proper post was the south hedge of the orchard, and in a determined attack on the French tirailleurs, who were manning the orchard, drove them out with heavy loss and occupied the line of the south hedge. Two attempts from columns of General Bachelu's division to attack the position from a new angle (due west after they had been deflected from the centre) were broken up in confusion by fire from Captain Cleeves' King's German Legion battery. However, at 2.45 p.m. precisely, according to Sir Augustus Frazer's watch, the garrison was called upon to withstand the added terror of a fire in the farm buildings.

Napoleon had ordered a battery of howitzers into a position from which they could shoot 'carcass' projectiles on to the thatched roofs of the buildings. Very soon the great barn was alight, and the fire spread rapidly not only to the outbuildings but to the château itself, only stopping at the foot of the cross in the chapel. It failed completely, however, in its purpose of dislodging the garrison, who fought on, doing their best to comply with the Duke's hastily written message 'to keep your men in those parts which the fire does not reach' – although they were unable to comply fully with his 'Take care that no Men are lost by the falling in of the Roof or floors'. Sergeant Graham, hero of the fight at the gate, sought and obtained permission to rescue his brother, but the remainder of the garrison, shrouded in smoke and blackened by powder, had to endure the screams and groans of those of the wounded who were unable to move as they perished in the blazing barn; for throughout the period of this hideous inferno every man was needed at his post to ensure that not a single Frenchman entered the enclosure.

The French View

By now, it was already 1.30 p.m., and Napoleon at last gave Ney the order to attack Wellington. For the past quarter of an hour, the big battery of ninety French cannon had been pounding incessantly, with devastating impact and mighty noise, the enemy's left flank, whose batteries were responding vigorously. D'Erlon brought his whole infantry forward. The French big battery ceased fire for a while to let the troops go down into the valley. They marched in four echelons, each division 400 yards apart (Allix first, Donzelot second, Marcognet third, Durutte fourth) with Ney and d'Erlon leading them in very tight formation, with cannon shells from both sides criss-crossing over their heads. Shouting 'Vive l'Empereur!', Allix's leading brigade charged the orchard of the farm of La Haye Sainte under heavy fire from Major Baring's German companies; the Germans were dislodged and entrenched themselves in those farm buildings which had not been destroyed by the French artillery fire.

As at Hougoumont, the solid walls resisted all French attacks, while the assailants were shot at from all sides through windows and loopholes. But the French were surrounding the farm and, on Wellington's orders, Ompteda sent in a German battalion to succour Baring. As these reinforcements arrived at the orchard, a squadron of Milhaud's cuirassiers (led by General Travers) supporting d'Erlon's infantry smashed through them and, in the same sally, sabred Kielmansegge's skirmishers at the edge of the plateau.

Meanwhile, d'Erlon's other columns had climbed the muddy slopes under cannon and rifle fire from the 95th (English) and the Bylandt brigade deployed forward of the Ohain ridge. The first echelon (Bourgeois) dislodged the English skirmishers and the carabiniers and threw them back into the high hedges behind the ridge. The second echelon (Donzelot) and the third (Marcognet) similarly dealt with the Dutch–Belgians, who disrupted the ranks of the 28th (English) in their flight. Durutte expelled the Nassauer companies from the farm of Papelotte and was already threatening Best's Hanoverians. From Napoleon's headquarters, the situation looked good. The enemy was still entrenched in its forward positions

at Hougoumont and La Haye Sainte, but these posts were overrun and surrounded, and Wellington's centre left was seriously mauled and threatened. Travers' cuirassiers and d'Erlon's skirmishers seemed to dominate the plateau of Mont St Jean, with the massed columns of infantry following closely behind.

But the Picton division was lying (literally) in wait behind the hedges, 100 yards or so behind the Ohain ridge. Before the French infantry's tight columns chasing the Dutch had time to fan out, Picton shouted: 'Up! At them!' The Kempt brigade rose from the ground, the men jumping through the double row of hedges which had kept them hidden hitherto. They scattered the French skirmishers and opened rolling rifle fire at forty yards' range on the Donzelot column, which wavered under the onslaught. Picton seized the opportunity and bellowed: 'Charge! charge! hurrah!' And the English, still firing, rushed into a bayonet attack on the compact mass of Frenchmen. The French held their ground, however; they counter-attacked and were assailed again in close hand-to-hand combat. A French officer was

shot dead as he was taking the 32nd English regimental flag and Picton was killed outright by a bullet through the temple.

The Marcognet column, arriving level with the Donzelot echelon, overtook it, charged through the double hedges and came upon a Hanoverian battery. Pack's Scots brigade appeared in battalions deployed checkerwise in four ranks to the wailing sound of their bagpipes. The 92nd Highlanders opened fire at 200 yards, followed by the other regiments. The French could only fire once before charging with bayonets in ferocious hand-to-hand combat. And now the English cavalry was upon them as well.

As Travers' cuirassiers and d'Erlon's infantry were beginning to take a hold on the heights of Mont St Jean, Lord Uxbridge ordered his élite cavalry to charge. Somerset's Life Guards, Blues and dragoons and Travers' cuirassiers charged simultaneously to meet head on at full gallop. A French squadron was thrown into a ravine by the shock. The cuirassiers negotiated it at speed and came out level with the field only to find the Life Guards rushing straight at them. To avoid the inevitable crush, the French backed down into the ravine again, came out on the road near the elm where Wellington was watching the battle and re-assembled in a nearby sandpit. Before they could re-group, the Life Guards in pursuit were upon them again, followed by the rest of Somerset's cavalry. Overwhelmed by numbers and disadvantaged by the terrain, Travers' cuirassiers were thrown back down into the valley after close sabre fighting.

Simultaneously, Ponsonby's dragoons brigade had charged d'Erlon's infantry columns. The Royals scattered the Bourgeois brigade, the Inniskillings fell upon Donzelot and the Scots Greys, shouting 'Scotland for ever!', charged Marcognet. Fired upon in front by enemy infantry, charged on both flanks by English cavalry, the French, still in tight formation, were pressed close together; while the cavalry was sabring them ruthlessly they could hardly fire or use their bayonets effectively. Their columns were disrupted, cut to pieces and thrown down the slopes. The Bourgeois brigade retreated in disorder and the Quiot brigade abandoned its attack on La Haye Sainte. But near Papelotte Durutte's division, attacked on its right by Vandeleur's dragoons and de Ghigney's Dutch and Belgian hussars and dragoons, retired in good order and without heavy casualties. There were now no French troops left on the heights of Mont St Jean, though the slopes and plateau were covered with the dead and wounded of both armies.

Now, flushed with success and excitement, the English cavalry crossed the valley at speed, despite Uxbridge's recalling order, and climbed the slopes on the French side. Life Guards and dragoons were decimated by Bachelu's rifle fire as they reached the crests. The Scots Greys followed, threw over some French batteries, sabred their crews and attacked the big battery. A flank attack by Colonel Martigue's lancers wiped out most of the English cavalry, while Colonel Bro's lancers were breaking Vandeleur's dragoons' deadly grip on the Durutte division. During this mêlée, a French lancer named Urban unsaddled Ponsonby and, fearing to lose his prisoner to a few Scots Greys who were arriving to the rescue, pierced Ponsonby with a deadly thrust of his lance before turning and killing three of the approaching enemy dragoons. On Napoleon's order, the brilliant and successful lancers' charge was soon supported by two regiments of Milhaud's cuirassiers under General Delort. They galloped down the slopes of La Belle Alliance and swept the whole valley in pursuit of the Life Guards and dragoons right up to the slopes of Mont St Jean beyond La Haye Sainte. Vivian's and Merlen's light cavalry had thought it better not to intervene during Uxbridge's action, which they had watched from afar.

There was a lull while French and Anglo-Dutch returned to their respective positions.

One solitary cuirassier, leaving his regiment, galloped right through the deadly valley towards La Haye Sainte where the Germans, thinking he was a deserter, held their fire. Stopping dead, right against the farm's orchard, he raised his giant body straight on his stirrups, brandished his sabre and shouted 'Vive l'Empereur', before rejoining the French lines under a hail of bullets.[2]

At Hougoumont, the fighting continued, intensified as both assailants and defenders were reinforced: the French by two regiments of the Foy division, the enemy by three companies of Guards, one Brunswick battalion and one King's German Legion battalion (du Plat). The French had lost and retaken the wood and the orchard, but the Guards were still entrenched and firing from the garden of the farm. Napoleon ordered howitzer batteries to bombard the château. Soon fire broke out in an attic and spread to the farm and stables, engulfing the wounded who had not been evacuated from there, then to the château itself, where the burning beams and the roof fell on the defenders. Yet, the survivors managed to entrench themselves in the chapel and continued to hold it and to fire on the French assailants.

It was now 3.30 p.m. The battle at Mont St Jean had been raging for two hours along the whole front. Napoleon's first attack on Wellington had been repulsed. French infantry and cavalry had suffered serious casualties but the Anglo-Dutch had also been heavily mauled and their centre left had been so shaken and disrupted that, at Wellington's headquarters, there were fears of not being able to sustain a second French attack. Wellington was anxiously waiting for Bülow's corps (which had not been engaged at Ligny) to attack the French right flank from St Lambert, while Napoleon expected Grouchy's early arrival from that same direction on Bülow's rear. But whereas Bülow was present and ready so to intervene, Grouchy was at this very moment almost nine miles away, on his way, not westwards to Mont St Jean, but northwards to Wavre, where he should have been since the previous day (17 June).

He had left Gembloux this very morning (18 June), not at 6 a.m. as he had said in his last message to Napoleon (see page 82), but at 8.30 a.m., preceded by Gérard's and Vandamme's corps which had started late, at 7.30 a.m. At a leisurely pace, Grouchy arrived at Sart-a-Walhain at 10 a.m., with Vandamme's heads of columns. From there, at 11 a.m., Grouchy wrote to Napoleon that, according to his latest information, *the main body of the Prussian Army had left Wavre* by crossing the river Dyle and was now 'camping on the Chyse Plain' (about seven and a half miles *north-east of Wavre*) near the road from Namur to Louvain. Grouchy ended his dispatch with these words:

This evening [18th]. I shall be massed *in Wavre* and thus situated between Wellington, who I presume is retreating before Your Majesty, and the Prussian Army. The land between Wavre and the Chyse Plain is difficult, cut and partly marshy. I shall easily reach *Brussels* before anything which is now camping on the Chyse Plain . . . Deign, Sire, to transmit your orders to me; I can receive them before beginning my movements to-morrow. [19 June !!!]

Major La Fresnay, an ex-page of Napoleon, left immediately with this message and the Marshal sat down comfortably to lunch.

He was finishing with a plate of strawberries when Gérard entered the room with his chief-of-staff, who had heard a distant cannonade from the garden of the house. They all proceeded to the garden where General Baltus, commanding the artillery of IV Corps, General Valazé (engineers) and several other staff officers, were listening attentively to the distant rumbling sound of cannon. Gérard suggested that they should 'march to the guns'. Grouchy replied that it was probably just a rearguard action. But, as the ground was actually shaking and clouds of smoke were visible on the horizon, Gérard insisted: 'Such terrible fire cannot be a simple engagement. Monsieur le Maréchal, we must march on the guns. If we take to our left, we shall be on the battlefield within two hours.' Valazé supported Gérard when Grouchy's host, who owned the house, confirmed that the cannonade was coming from the Forest of Soignes, about eight miles away.

But Grouchy, vexed to hear his subordinates contradicting his own views so publicly, replied:

The Emperor told me yesterday that he intended to attack the English Army if Wellington accepted battle. I am therefore not at all surprised by the present engagement. Had the Emperor wished me to take part in it, he would not have kept me away from him at the very time he was marching against the English Army. Anyway, if I take my Army corps through bad cross country lanes, soaked by yesterday's and this morning's rain, I shall not arrive in time at the place of combat.

Baltus agreed that the artillery would negotiate the lanes with difficulty, but was countered by Valazé who said that his sappers could open the way for a three- to four-hour march to Soignes.

Gérard was getting angry: 'Monsieur le Maréchal, it is your duty to march to the guns . . .' he started. Grouchy cut him short, offended that Gérard should dare teach him his duty (see page 41) in front of about twenty other officers. He said sternly: 'My duty is to execute the Emperor's orders which prescribe that I should follow the Prussians. To comply with your advice would be to contravene his instructions.' At this moment, Major d'Estourmel (Exelmans' aide-de-camp) arrived to announce that, according to all reports, the Prussian army which had left Wavre during the night (the 17th–18th) and that morning (the 18th) was marching closer to the English army (i.e. westwards to St Jean, not northwards to Brussels). The major added that Exelmans was planning to follow the Prussians on the left bank of the Dyle. All this tallied with Gérard's advice, but Grouchy ignored it, saying drily that he himself would give direct orders to Exelmans. He then asked for his horses. As he was mounting, Gérard tried a last request: 'If you do not want to march on the Forest of Soignes with all your troops,' he said, 'at least allow me to make that move with my corps and General Vallin's cavalry. I am certain to arrive, and to arrive usefully in time.'

'No,' replied Grouchy. 'It would be an unforgiveable military fault to divide my troops and to have them acting on both banks of the Dyle. I would expose both fractions, which could not support each other, to be crushed by forces two or three times superior to them.' And Grouchy galloped away.[3]

He arrived before Wavre at 4 p.m. to find Napoleon's letter from Caillou dated 18 June 10 a.m. (see Appendix II) telling him of the impending attack on Wellington at Mont St Jean and warning him of a Prussian march towards Wavre, where Grouchy should proceed so as to come closer to the French army and to establish *operational* liaison with it (see page 79). The officer bearing this message had brought it through Genappe, Quatre-Bras, Sombreffe, Gembloux and Sart-a-Walhain, i.e., along the two sides of the 'operational' triangle instead of cutting diagonally across it. His had been a twenty-eight-mile ride and had taken six hours. Yet, to Grouchy's way of thinking, Napoleon's letter was simply confirming that his presence before Wavre at this time (4 p.m. 18 June) was correct, irrespective of what might have happened in the meantime or, indeed, of what might be happening at this very moment at Mont St Jean . . .[4]

9 A CLOUDBURST OF CAVALRY
3.30pm-6pm
Jacques Champagne & William Seymour

The French View

As soon as d'Erlon had re-assembled some of his battalions at about 3.30 p.m., Napoleon ordered Ney to renew the attack on La Haye Sainte.

Ney led the Quiot brigade, while one Donzelot brigade, fanned out this time, climbed the slopes east of the Charleroi road to fire at twenty yards' range on the English in ambush behind the hedges of the Ohain ridge. The first were decimated by Baring's rolling fire, the second were thrown back even before reaching the crest of the plateau. To support the attack, the great battery had interrupted its fire against the enemy centre left while Reille's artillery, reinforced by some of the Guard's 12-inch guns, was pounding the enemy centre right. It was the worst bombardment of the day. A few English front line battalions withdrew a hundred feet from the crest for protection. Groups of wounded, prisoner convoys and runaways began to fall back with empty ammunition wagons on the Forest of Soignes. Mistaking this for the beginning of an enemy retreat, Ney called on a brigade of cuirassiers to occupy the plateau. Delort, commanding the division, objected that this move was imprudent on such a muddy terrain. But Ney, dreaming of leading an all-out cavalry charge to hasten the English retreat, answered by ordering the whole of Milhaud's corps to move forward. The two cuirassiers' divisions started up at the trot, followed in their movement, perhaps instinctively (for they were not ordered to do so), by Lefèvre-Desnouettes' Red Lancers and the Guard's mounted chasseurs, all impatient for action. Ney rapidly assembled these 5,000 cavalrymen on the left side of the Charleroi road down in a hollow part of the valley (which, incidentally, Napoleon could not see from his new observation post near Rossomme) and led the charge against the Anglo-Dutch enemy.

Far from retreating, Wellington was reinforcing the whole of his front line with several second line and reserve brigades. Between the Nivelles and Charleroi roads, twenty English, Hanoverian, Brunswick and German battalions were formed checkerwise into squares in two lines. Artillery crews were ordered to fire until the last moment and then to abandon their guns and withdraw inside the squares.

Preceded by artillery fire, the French cavalry in squadron columns checkerwise, cuirassiers on the right, light cavalry on the left, started up towards the slopes of Mont St Jean in a somewhat oblique movement which made their flanks vulnerable to enemy artillery. The English cannon intensified their fire, their guns loaded with 'double charge'.

The horses were slow to climb in the muddy, heavily trodden down terrain and the columns' advance was stopped by each salvo, the last one of which sliced through half the first squadrons. The others hesitated, but at the sound of the bugles they charged furiously. The cuirassiers rushed to the cannon and captured all the crewless batteries one after another. Yet, no one bothered, or had the time, to spike the guns. Elsewhere, rifle fire rained on the cuirassiers and the lancers, who had little room for impetus as they charged the enemy squares, which presented four solid outer walls of steel – rifle butts on the ground and bayonets raised.

Wave after wave of French cavalry flooded the plateau. Cuirassiers, chasseurs and Red Lancers swarmed around the squares hammering at their sides at close range with sabre, lance and pistol and opening ghastly breaches which were immediately filled up again. Uxbridge launched all his fresh cavalry on these swarming masses of French squadrons. Altogether, 5,000 English and German dragoons and hussars, Brunswick Black Lancers and Dutch and Belgian carabiniers charged the French who, sabred, fired upon and overwhelmed, withdrew from the plateau. The enemy crews rejoined their guns and reopened fire from the crests all along the line. But, barely reformed in the valley, Milhaud's and Desnouettes' men attacked again, climbing the slopes under heavy fire. They captured the batteries on the crests, fanned out on the plateau and again murderously charged the enemy squares, but again they failed to break through them.

From La Belle Alliance, the spectacle looked magnificently encouraging to the French army and the general staff. Yet Napoleon was rather displeased to see so much of his cavalry engaged by Ney without his own specific orders. Turning to Soult, he said: 'This movement is premature and may yet have disastrous results on this day. It is one hour too early, but we must support what is done.'[1]

So, Kellermann was ordered to move forward. His first division started up almost before receiving the order, and were followed soon after by the second division, with Guyot's heavy cavalry (Guard's dragoons and grenadiers) joining in support on Napoleon's order. Kellermann, worried by this total cavalry commitment, formally ordered General Blancard to stay near the Château of Hougoumont with his group of 800 carabiniers and not to budge from there without his personal command. This force now formed the army's sole cavalry reserve.

The situation on the battlefield had reached a critical point, this time both for Wellington and for Napoleon. For the past two hours the Duke had been anxiously pressing Blücher in vain to attack on the Anglo-Dutch left flank, and the Emperor's right flank was now seriously threatened by Bülow coming in force from St Lambert. At 4.30 p.m. Blücher himself appeared with part of Bülow's corps near Lasne, where Domon's hussars had been posted since the morning (see page 83). The Emperor had compensated for this move by advancing the Foot Guard near La Belle Alliance and ordering Durutte to assail Papelotte and La Haye Sainte in order both to support Ney's big attack and to cut communications between Bülow's right and Wellington's left.

With his seasoned troops, Lobau attacked the Prussians forcefully. They fell back at first, but renewed their offensive as two more divisions (Ryssel and Hacke) arrived to support them. There were now some 30,000 Prussians against 10,000 French. Yet, Lobau's men gave such a fierce account of themselves that Blücher decided to turn his opponent's right towards Plancenoit. Lobau backed down to this village and occupied it with one brigade, which was soon expelled by the Prussians. Plancenoit was in their hands while Bülow, from his side of the front, was bombarding Lobau's other three brigades with eight batteries, whose shells were reaching as far as the Charleroi road, right in the middle of the French Guard's battalions, and even falling on Napoleon's headquarters. The Emperor was overrun and his line of retreat was seriously threatened. He therefore ordered Duhesme's Young Guard to recapture Plancenoit. The eight battalions, four voltigeurs and four tirailleurs, charged at the double and expelled the Prussians from the houses and from the cemetery where they had established a redoubt. The Prussians' attack on Napoleon's right flank had been repulsed by the French fighting one against three.

At 5.30 p.m., the Anglo-Dutch line was still holding. Kellermann's and Guyot's heavy cavalry appeared in the valley as Milhaud's men, repulsed by English dragoons, were coming down the slopes of Mont St Jean. Quickly reformed, they joined the three fresh cavalry divisions, and together more than sixty squadrons of cuirassiers, dragoons, chasseurs and grenadiers charged once again up the slopes, now littered with dead men and horses. Like a sea of steel helmets, sabres and breast-plates, the French covered the whole front, from Hougoumont to La Haye Sainte, in such numbers and in such tight formation that some of their horses were lifted up by the pressure. The enemy received them with the same tactics as before: their gunners fired on the cavalry and then retired inside the infantry squares, who opened rolling fire at thirty paces, bringing down whole ranks of their assailants and receiving the others on the triple row of their raised bayonets. Some of these enemy formations, which sustained up to thirteen French assaults, were partially breached, if not ruptured, and their casualties were appalling. Captain Klein de Kleinenberg (Guard's chasseurs) had his horse killed under him as he was capturing the flag of a German battalion. A non-commissioned officer of the 9th Cuirassiers captured an English flag, which was brought to Napoleon at La Belle Alliance.[2] But most of the squares remained impregnable, disappearing from time to time in the swarming floods of French cavalry and then reappearing through the smoke with their bayonet walls still raised to the sky.

Lhéritier's cuirassiers, charging under fire through the second line of squares, were struck down by enemy reserve batteries. A whole cavalry regiment galloped on to the Nivelles road, sabred Mitchell's skirmishers on the way, rushed around Hougoumont and reformed on the plateau of La Belle Alliance. The Guard's dragoons, giant men on giant horses, advancing in line at the trot, were butchered by two cannon salvos and decimated by the rifle fire of two Brunswick squares. General Jamin, colonel of the Guard's dragoons, was shot dead and fell over the barrel of a gun. The survivors jumped over the batteries, which were littered with the corpses of men and horses, and joined up with the cuirassiers to charge again.

The atmosphere was red hot, the horses were out of breath, the combatants were tiring and the dead were piling up on the enemy's cannon and inside the squares. The charges began to falter. The whole plateau, the slopes and the valley were packed with dismounted cavalrymen walking heavily back to their lines; wounded men dragged themselves out of the fighting while riderless horses galloped wildly in all directions. Thirteen generals were wounded[3] and Ney, having had three horses killed under him during the action, was standing alone, lashing out angrily with the flat of his sword at the barrel of an enemy gun. Wellington, leaving the 73rd's square where he had stood at the peak of the fighting, launched his cavalry on the dismembered French squadrons who, for the third time, abandoned the plateau.

Yet, for a fourth time, the French cavalry charged up the slopes to attack the enemy, Ney leading them at the head of the carabiniers whom he had collected, despite Blancard's protests, where Kellermann had left them, by bellowing Napoleon's previous words at Ligny: 'The salvation of France is at stake!' Obstinate and impetuous, the Marshal was now enraged; his brave men were maddened and embittered, their charges, furious and desperate, were beginning to lack conviction. They tried again and again, but in the end they fell back, discouraged, into the valley, followed at a distance, rather than really pursued, by the equally exhausted English cavalry.

This massive cavalry onslaught upon the enemy could have been successful, had they been supported simultaneously by infantry. But in the heat of the action Ney had forgotten that, for several hours now, the French infantry had been waiting less than a mile away for his order to combine their action with that of the cavalry. 'Always first in the fire, Ney was forgetting the troops which were not immediately in his sights'.[4] And now Ney was calling on the Bachelu division and the Jamin brigade of the Foy division to second the attack of the exhausted cavalry. The 6,000 infantrymen moved in column echelons down the valley of death. But it was too late. They were decimated by enemy artillery and Wellington's infantry, extending its front into a curve towards Hougoumont, took them in crossfire. Some 1,500 Frenchmen were shot dead or wounded in a few seconds.

It was 6 p.m. At Hougoumont the fighting was still fierce, and at La Haye Sainte (Ney's original objective) Baring was holding out almost without ammunition. Wellington sent him two companies as reinforcement. Napoleon was rushing round the battle line under enemy artillery fire. At his side, General Devaux, commander-in-chief of the Guard's artillery, had been killed and his second in command, General Lallemand, together with General de Monthyon, his chief of staff, had been seriously wounded.

The English View

It was around 3.30 p.m. when the next phase of the battle began. There had been little let-up, along the whole front, of the intense artillery bombardment; the French 12-pounders pulsated furiously and under cover of their destructive fire the enemy launched another attack on La Haye Sainte. Marshal Ney had got together what men of d'Erlon's corps could again be mustered – elements of Allix's division, with skirmishers from Donzelot's protecting his right on the east side of the *chaussée* – and also troops from Bachelu's division of Reille's corps. But the attack was not pressed home with sufficient resolution to dislodge the reinforced garrison, although there was some fierce fighting around the open doorway on the west and the French managed to set fire to some of the buildings. However, the Nassauers were equipped with large metal cooking pots, and these served admirably to quench the flames. Major Baring and his men were never seriously in danger of being evicted, but this latest attack imposed a further strain on their ammunition reserves, and urgent appeals for replenishment went, for some reason, unheeded.

While this attack was in progress part of the French artillery was being realigned. Some batteries were moved to the west of the Brussels road and new ones were added, so that a greater weight of fire was now brought to bear on the right centre of Wellington's line. The terrible storm of iron that hurtled through the air and thudded around the allied line made what had gone before seem like little more than the murmur of musketry. It was on a scale that no one present had ever experienced; Captain Mercer remarked later that 'so thick was the hail of balls and bullets that it seemed dangerous to extend the arm lest it should be torn off'. The Duke ordered the infantry to retire a few paces and lie down to minimize the effect of this cascade of shot and shell. That this artillery pounding was a prelude to a renewed offensive was obvious to Wellington, his staff and regimental officers, but the form that that offensive was to take astounded every experienced commander in the allied army.

We know now that Ney was misled by the partial withdrawal of the allied infantry into thinking that he could accomplish a speedy victory through the use of heavy cavalry unsupported by infantry. But at the time Wellington could scarcely believe his eyes when he saw 5,000 horsemen, in some forty-three squadrons, advancing in perfect order in echelon from the right – slowly, majestically, and alone. It seemed to him incredible that Napoleon should attempt to defeat good infantry – and much of his was not only good but comparatively fresh – with unsupported cavalry. Yet it had been done before, and Ney was doubtless confident that it could be done again. Wellington gave the command to prepare to meet cavalry; it was an order that the allied army knew perfectly how to execute. Battalions formed square, and the squares were staggered so as to be in some degree self-supporting and to allow room for manoeuvre.

Properly trained battalions could form square from column or line in about half a minute; the average battalion at Waterloo was not much over 500 men.[5] The usual method was to form a square sixty feet on each side, but when squares were checkered, as at present, the front and rear ends were the most important and probably comprised three companies each to two at the sides. General Alten's 3rd British Division was most effectively organized by Captain Kennedy into oblongs or rectangles, with four companies back and front and only one on each side; they therefore had considerably greater frontal fire power. The British square consisted of four ranks; the first knelt with muskets resting on the ground, so presenting a ring of steel; the bayonets of the second rank were held low and not far behind those of the first. These two ranks represented the *chevaux de frise* element, and it is doubtful if the front rank ever fired. But the strength of the square was two-fold; it lay not only in the bristling bayonets ready to impale enemy horses, but, even more important, in the fire power of the third and fourth ranks. These men may never have fixed their bayonets, as this would only have hindered their reloading; their method of firing varied with the different formations, but was usually by half-company volleys.

The gunners, as already related, were ordered to fire their guns up to the last moment and then to run for the shelter of the squares. That this order was precisely executed is a great tribute to the courage and discipline of the gunners; it could have proved disastrous. During the six or seven separate cavalry charges that the French made, there was no attempt to bring up men who could spike the guns, and every time the cavalry retreated the gunners, disdaining the obvious safety of the squares, bravely went forward to man their guns. The infantry had been slightly withdrawn, and the guns were therefore in some cases 100 yards to their front; this made the operation all the more hazardous for the gunners, who could hardly have removed a wheel (as is sometimes asserted), although they probably seized what implements they could manage in their scramble back to the squares. The extra distance would also have made it easier for the French to spike the guns had they thought to do so.

Thus was the first line made ready to receive the impending cloudburst of cavalry. But Wellington had more infantry and artillery and regiments of so far uncommitted cavalry in the rear. Moreover, Hougoumont and La Haye Sainte were still holding out, and besides being proof against cavalry attacks they very greatly restricted the area which the French horsemen had to manoeuvre in. The distance between these two outposts would have been about 1,000 yards, but to avoid the damaging effects of flanking fire the French would have needed to close up into an area hardly more than 800 yards across. It is not surprising to learn, therefore, that when the attacks were reinforced with still more squadrons the ranks were so tightly packed that some horses were literally lifted off the ground.

Just before the main attack began some lancers of General Piré's force appeared on Wellington's extreme right, and always anxious about this flank Wellington ordered Lord Uxbridge to detach General Grant with two of his regiments and one from Dornberg's King's German Legion brigade, which somewhat weakened his cavalry reserve. There were still fresh squadrons of foreign cavalry available, but the quality of their performance was uncertain.

Meanwhile, advancing obliquely towards the allied centre, was the pride of the French army – their magnificent cavalry arm. Murat, who had led them to so many victories, was missing, but the indomitable Michel Ney, Marshal of France, Prince of Moscow, with his mop of red hair and Irish blood, was at their head. They came on slowly at a measured trot, for although the ground had not yet been churned into a quagmire, the tightness of their formation forbade a greater speed, and anyway it was their wont to ride into battle unhurried. Milhaud's cuirassiers, the sun glinting on their breastplates and their steel helmets with horse-hair manes, led in the first line, followed by the light cavalry of the Guard – *Grenadiers à Cheval* in plain uniforms with broad belts and huge bearskin caps, the 'Red' Lancers with their tall white plumes, and *Chasseurs à Cheval* in green dolmans and black bearskin shakos. And the kaleidoscope of colour was completed by squadrons of hussars, dragoons with their striking tiger-skin headdresses, and carabiniers in immaculate white uniforms and tall, curiously designed helmets.

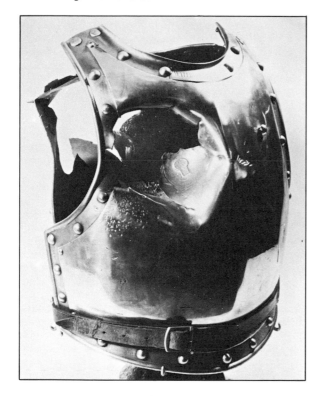

62 Below: The cuirass of Antoine Faveau, who was killed
at Waterloo. Even these breastplates, so impressive when
the sun shone on them, were no protection against enemy
cannon
63 Bottom: The Duke of Wellington's telescope, which he
used throughout the battle

It was a formidable and, to the inexperienced, a
terrifying sight; Captain Gronow, who was in a
1st Guards square, thought that 'nothing could
have resisted the shock of this terrible moving
mass'. But to those who knew the value of the
square and had faith in its collective strength, the
close approach of the cavalry was welcome for the
temporary respite it gave from the much more
damaging artillery barrage.

As the cavalry began their ascent to the top of
the ridge the skirmishers, who had accompanied
them thus far, dropped back and the great batteries
of guns fell silent. The usual noise of battle
suddenly gave way to the thundering of thousands
of hooves as they beat upon the ground; the pace
did not quicken, nor did the formations waver when
faced with the muzzles of the allied guns. Then,
when the horsemen were less than 100 yards away,
all hell was let loose; case and shot tore into the
solid mass, whole ranks were shorn away under
this metal flail; men and horses lay on the ground
in shapeless heaps, while others quickly closed the
gap that the tornado had created. But it seemed
that Gronow was right and that nothing could stop
them; the gunners sought protection among the
friendly squares.

All of them save Captain Mercer's troop. Sir
Augustus Frazer had ordered Mercer to limber up
and gallop into a new position more towards the
centre of the line, a manoeuvre which he carried
out quickly enough to earn a rare commendation
from the Duke, but he only arrived at his new post
a minute or two before the cavalry breasted the
ridge. He had behind him a square of Brunswickers, young boys for the most part, who had
already been badly dented by the bombardment.
Mercer knew them to be unsteady, and feared
that the sight of his men running back to their
square would completely destroy their morale –
indeed, had it not been for the splendid example
and efforts of their officers and N.C.O.s, they
would almost certainly have bolted anyway. So he
decided not to tell his men about the Duke's order,
and through his personal courage and leadership
held them to their guns throughout.

The sight of the abandoned guns and retreating
gunners undoubtedly relumed the spirit of the
battered squadrons, for although they did not
increase their pace – and there were those who
said that had they charged as cavalry should, not
counting the cost, they must have broken the
squares – they let out a great shout of triumph.
But their moment of elation was short-lived; almost
before they knew it they were upon the allied
infantry,[6] who, far from fleeing in the beaten,

111

disorganized mass that the Frenchmen expected, greeted them with a devastating volley aimed chiefly at the horses. The confusion was appalling; horses reared and screamed and came crashing down upon their riders, who groped about on the ground amid a tangle of flailing hooves, the less fortunate being thrown against the deadly line of bayonets. The din was by now terrific, and not least was the curious patter of musket balls against cuirasses – Gronow likened it to a hail-storm beating on windows – which did give some protection against glancing shots.

As the mass of cavalry swirled around the squares trying every means, short of a suicidal charge, to gain entrance, casualties were bound to occur among the allied infantry – although they were far less numerous than those inflicted by the artillery fire – but no sooner did a man in the front ranks fall than his place was taken by a comrade from behind. Nevertheless, the squares were to become alarmingly thin before Ney eventually owned defeat. If Captain Gronow's watch was correct, even by 4 p.m., while the first charge was still in progress, his square was a scene of carnage. 'A perfect hospital' is how he described it, 'being full of dead, dying and mutilated soldiers', with the survivors 'nearly suffocated by the smoke and smell from burnt cartridges'.

As the French horsemen milled around the allied squares, jabbing, thrusting and discharging their carbines here and there, their formations inevitably broke up, so that they no longer acted as a cohesive force. This made them vulnerable to attack by the allied cavalry. Wellington and Uxbridge had been watching their chance anxiously; the heavy cavalry had been sadly reduced, and the light could not be risked against the heavier French horse until the exhaustion and confusion of the latter rendered the moment propitious. The first of these moments came at about 4.15, when the hard-pressed infantry were delighted to see the remnants of the heavy cavalry, now joined into one brigade, and some regiments of light horse, charge into the enemy squadrons and drive them from the slope. No sooner had they begun to withdraw than the gunners were back at their guns to speed them on their way. The allied cavalry had strict orders not to pursue, but in the excitement of the moment Dornberg's 23rd British Light Dragoons and his 1st King's German Legion Light Dragoons could not resist the joys of chasing cuirassiers and lancers. When eventually the enemy rallied and turned on them they were able to withdraw without too much mishap, however, thanks to the timely and accurate fire of a

field battery positioned to the west of the Nivelles road with a field of fire between the squares.

Thus was Ney's first cavalry charge repulsed. It had achieved very little, and had left behind it a mass of dead and wounded men and horses strewn around over every yard of the ground. The younger soldiers of the Anglo-Dutch army had gained confidence in the safety of the squares and, like their elders, came to look upon a cavalry charge as a much lesser evil than the terrible pounding of artillery, which now began again. But not for long, for Ney was hastily reforming and leading his squadrons up the ridge and into the attack for the second time.

It was now a little after 4.30, and the distant sound of gunfire away to the east told Wellington that the Prussians were at last in action. Although they were still some way from giving him direct aid, with Napoleon committed to dealing with fresh troops on the allied left, Wellington could feel confident that there would be no attempt to outflank his right. An order was now sent to bring up Adam's fine brigade of the 52nd, 71st and 95th. The exact timing of the reorganization of units on the right flank is in some doubt. We have already noted that the Brunswickers and parts of Hew Halkett's and du Plat's brigades had come up to take the place of Byng's brigade behind Hougoumont, and it is possible that the whole of the 2nd Division (less Adam's brigade) came into the forward line during the brief lull before the first cavalry attack. Certainly Wellington waited until General Chassé's Dutch–Belgian division, which had been ordered up from Braine l'Alleud to form a reserve in the area of the Nivelles road, was approaching before bringing Adam's men forward, and the remainder of the division may have come up at the same time. At any rate by now the whole of the 2nd British Division was in the forward line, and the 1st Battalion of the 23rd Regiment from Mitchell's brigade had taken up a position among the Brunswickers to give additional strength to that sector.

The pattern of the second cavalry attack was very much the same as that of the first. An avalanche of men rode unflinchingly to swift destruction through a hell of whistling ball. Captain Mercer has left us a vivid description of how his troop greeted the first wave of horsemen.

Every man stood steadily at his post, the guns ready, loaded with a round-shot first and a case over it; the tubes were in the vents; the port-fires glared and sputtered behind the wheels . . . It was indeed a grand and imposing spectacle. . . . I allowed them to advance unmolested until the head of the column might have been about fifty or sixty yards from us, and then gave

'Never did I see such a pounding match...'

The Duke of Wellington, 2 July 1815

I   The French cavalry launching an attack on British squares, by Denis Dighton

II Below: The farm of La Belle Alliance after the battle, by
Denis Dighton

III Right: A distant view of La Belle Alliance, by Denis
Dighton

IV Bottom: La Belle Alliance as it is today, from the south

V Following pages: Allied Guardsmen fighting Prince
Jérôme's men of the 6th Division outside the Hougoumont
gate, by Denis Dighton

VI The battlefield seen from the Lion Hill, showing La Haye
Sainte (left) and La Belle Alliance (right)

VII The battlefield seen from the Lion Hill, looking North-east. The British line was to the north of the road; La Haye Sainte is to the right

VIII Below: The view from the French side towards the end of the battle of Waterloo, from a painting by Sir William Allan

IX and X Below: The Lion Hill, the Netherlands memorial
to the battle and (bottom) La Haye Sainte as it stands today

XI and XII The valley from Picton's ridge up which D'Erlon
led his cavalry charge and (bottom) the Château of Hougoumont
from the north gate, with the chapel on the left

XIII French cuirassiers charging Highlanders in a square, by Felix Philippoteaux

the word, 'Fire!' The effect was terrible. Nearly the whole leading rank fell at once; and the round-shot penetrating the column, carried confusion throughout its extent.

But sheer weight of numbers bore them on relentlessly towards the waiting squares, and once again they prowled around between the allied infantry, seeking in vain to break the ranks of those dour, determined men.

The one change that Ney did make was to detail some of his forty squadrons to be held in reserve for the purpose of engaging the allied cavalry. This they did, although Uxbridge's men did not wait to be engaged, and soon a furious cavalry battle was in progress amid the squares. The remnants of the Household and Union Brigades, the 23rd Light Dragoons, the 7th Hussars from Grant's brigade, squadrons of Brunswick hussars and lancers, and those of General Trip's Dutch–Belgian carabiniers who could be persuaded to join the fray, closed with the enemy in a desperate struggle. The French had not only to withstand the cut and thrust of the cavalrymen's sabres, but also the bullets poured into them from the squares, and before long they were driven off once more down the valley. This time, as their flight gathered momentum, they took with them the men of Allix's and Donzelot's divisions, who were still attempting to get into La Haye Sainte, and for a short while the whole allied centre was free of enemy soldiers.

Nobody could remember how many times the inexhaustible Ney led his cavalry up the slope and into the attack; desiring solely to stay alive and keep the foe at bay, no one had much time for counting. Least of all the commander-in-chief, whose calm and fearless behaviour, riding up and down the line and occasionally taking shelter in a square when the cavalry were almost upon him, inspired his rapidly thinning ranks and encouraged them to stand and stick it out. Some say there were as many as fifteen separate attacks in the space of two hours, but more likely it was about half the number. Somewhere around the third or fourth attack Ney received reinforcements; Kellermann's corps and Guyot's division of the Guard had been sent forward by Napoleon. Rather more than 9,000 horsemen, riding boot to boot and seemingly in a solid phalanx, struggled up what was by now a miry, slippery slope, strewn with the bodies of the fallen lying in tangled heaps among the trampled corn. Ney had four horses shot under him, but continued on foot until an empty saddle came his way. There was savagery on both sides; Mercer saw the Brunswickers break

square to finish off a wounded French colonel, and the French lancers seldom spared a wounded soldier as they rode around the squares.

Towards the end Ney did what he should have done far earlier; he attacked with infantry and some light field pieces in support. Moreover, he struck where the Brunswickers were stationed, perhaps the weakest part of the line. For a short while the situation was dangerous, but by now Grant had realized that Piré's cavalry (see page 110) was no more than a demonstration. He therefore brought the 15th Hussars and 13th Light Dragoons in a sweeping movement against the cuirassiers' left flank and, aided by artillery fire, drove them back on to their main body. Then his own men withdrew in an orderly fashion through the squares. Lord Uxbridge was again in the thick of it with other cavalry regiments, and narrowly escaped disaster when attempting to lead some of Trip's Dutch–Belgian men, who failed to follow him. There was, perhaps, some small excuse for these troops, who had no idea who he was, Uxbridge having been given command of them only that morning, but there was absolutely none for the behaviour of Colonel Hake and his Cumberland Hussars. This regiment not only refused to fight, but galloped off the field and into Brussels, where they spread a false rumour of defeat.

Ney's combined offensive had been left too late, for at last the strain was beginning to tell on the magnificent French horsemen. They had done more than could be expected of them, and now for the last time they began to surge back down the slope, taking the infantry with them and the flotsam and jetsam of battle in the shape of dismounted men and wounded riderless horses. During the last two hours Napoleon had achieved virtually nothing. The allied line, though sadly thinned, still held; valuable time had been bought, albeit at a terrible price, and the Prussians were drawing inexorably closer. And what of the French cavalry? Those splendid warriors, in all perhaps 15,000 of them, who had advanced so magnificently in charge and counter-charge, were no longer capable of any further sustained effort; they had been shattered and ruined in senseless, unsupported attacks.

But even while the French cavalrymen drifted away through the smoky valley the men on the ridge were to be called upon for further efforts of constancy and courage. This time there was to be no pause before the next onslaught; the French artillery were already preparing the way for the one positive success that came to Napoleon during the closing hours of the battle.

10 THE PRUSSIANS IN ACTION
Midday-6pm
Colonel E. Kaulbach

64 Previous pages: The Prussians and the French fighting at Plancenoit. The village of Plancenoit was a convenient point for the IV Corps to open the push against the deep flank of the French army. It was to become the centre of the Prussian attack

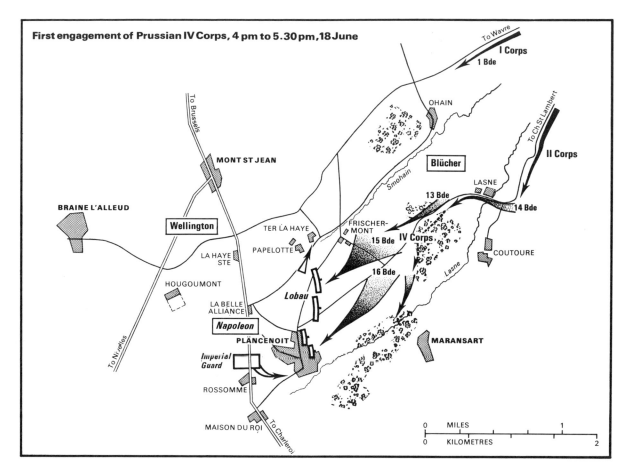

First engagement of Prussian IV Corps, 4 pm to 5.30 pm, 18 June

The part played by the Prussian army in the great battle was not restricted, as is commonly supposed, to the evening hours; their influence was in fact felt over a great part of the afternoon. This influence was the result of two distinct phases. During the first phase the Prussian army did not fight, except at Wavre, but by their very presence had a fundamental effect on both the planning and the outcome of the battle. On the one hand the knowledge of the Prussians' approach increased the confidence of their allies and helped them to withstand the heavy French attacks.[1] On the other hand, Napoleon was disturbed, confined and hurried by the same knowledge. It is known that he had discovered the Prussian columns near St Lambert at around one in the afternoon, and he was in any case fully informed of the presence of Blücher's army through captured letters and prisoners' statements.[2] His basic plan, to isolate Wellington's army and to destroy it, was now in question. At short notice he had to make other

plans – and without being able to dispose of his reserves with his former freedom.[3] This first phase lasted from 1.30 to 4.30 p.m.

During the second phase the Prussian troops, exhausted as they were from the difficult approach march, entered the battle. This started at 4.30 and continued throughout the night until daybreak on the 19th, when the pursuit was broken off in the area of Frasnes-Mallet, about twelve miles from the battlefield.

Looking at these events in a wider perspective, it can be seen that what occurred at Waterloo had taken place earlier at Ligny and Quatre-Bras, but with the roles reversed: that is, the attempt at co-operation by Wellington and Blücher.[4] At Ligny, Blücher accepted battle in the expectation of support from Wellington's army. The fact that no direct support came but only indirect help was inexplicable to the Prussian command; otherwise they would have husbanded their strength. At Waterloo, it was Wellington who provided the iron resistance against which the French attacks broke – and he succeeded in doing this in the assurance that support would come from his ally. And Blücher, in turn, while Grouchy was held off with a minimum of strength, led his army into a 'direct' attack against Napoleon's flank and thus helped to turn the French army's defeat into a rout. 'Wellington won the victory' writes Hooper; 'Blücher changed a terrible defeat into an irrecoverable disaster'.[5]

Field-Marshal Blücher had left Wavre with the army staff at around 11 a.m. When he arrived in Chapelle St Lambert at about midday he found IV Corps there with more than half of its troops; the 13th and 14th Brigades were still on the march. It was these halted columns which Napoleon's sharp eye discovered a little later, at a distance of four or five miles, as the crow flies, on the heights of St Lambert. The approach so far had been wearisome enough. But the worst part of the way, the broad boggy basin of the Lasne with its steep slopes on both sides, had still to be crossed. The Bois de Paris, on the far side, had to be reached as a jumping-off place for participation in the battle. General von Bülow had meanwhile sent out a strong cavalry reconnaissance force in order to avoid being surprised by the enemy while crossing this defile. The area between the Lasne and the Dyle was reported to be free of the enemy as far as Maransart and Céroux,[6] as were the entire Lasne sector and the Bois de Paris. For the Prussian command this seemed an unbelievable stroke of luck; their worry over this obstacle which, even with weak enemy opposition, could have caused great difficulties, had been considerable. Blücher sent two of his staff officers, Colonel von Pfuel and his adjutant, Count Nostitz, over the Lasne to confirm the report and also to get some picture of the battle towards which the thunder of guns was urging them. Both officers reached the south-west edge of the wood without meeting any of the enemy; from here they could see the entire battlefield, the French attacking columns and Napoleon's massive reserves.

Count Nostitz hurried back with his information. Blücher ordered IV Corps to cross the defile, urging them on with all his energy and himself riding with the leading troops to the edge of the wood. Count Nostitz describes the situation: 'The Prince, with the eye of a hawk, surveyed the entire battlefield, saw clearly the way the fighting was going, and devoted his main attention to the disposition of the English batteries.'[7]

Count Nostitz adds that he had expressed his concern to General Gneisenau that Napoleon, on recognizing the approach of strong Prussian forces, would use all available troops against this threat. But Gneisenau replied '. . . that, on the contrary, he was convinced that Napoleon would then use his entire strength and effort in an attempt to breach the English line of battle and would bring to bear upon us only such forces as were needed to hold us up long enough to allow him to deliver his decisive blow against the English.'[8] Gneisenau well knew Napoleon's determination in attack.

Now, before the engagement of the Prussian troops, in view of the battle, and knowing what advantageous attack positions they had succeeded in reaching, the assessment of the situation by Blücher and his entourage may, for the first time, have been completely confident. The successful assembly of the army at Wavre; the clearly successful, though very risky, flank march which could so easily have been prevented or hindered by a timely intervention by the enemy; the readiness of IV Corps, which would be completely in position as soon as the 13th and 14th Brigades had crossed the Lasne; II Corps close behind; I Corps on the way to Wellington's left flank – everything spelled 'revenge' for Ligny, and not only for Ligny but for so much more that Napoleon had inflicted on Prussia. Furthermore, in these circumstances it seemed possible to dispose of III Corps, still near Wavre; in view of the mass of troops which Napoleon was visibly committing to the battle, it seemed that he could hardly have left a major force behind the Prussians which could attack the easily defensible positions on the Dyle as far as Wavre. So Blücher arranged for III Corps to be ordered to follow the army, as the left flank group, to Couture, in so far as the situation at Wavre permitted this.[9] When, later, the sound of guns from Wavre indicated that fighting was going on there, and when this was confirmed by the message from III Corps, the idea of such support had to be abandoned. To compensate for this, the approaching II Corps was ordered to detach one of its brigades – the 7th was named – to advance via Couture to Maransart. Meanwhile Bülow's IV Corps had crossed the Lasne ground with all the forces that had arrived; by between 3 and 4 p.m. two brigades, the reserve cavalry and the reserve artillery stood in the Bois de Paris, at about the level of Beau Chêne. General von Bülow comments:

First two battalions and the Silesian Hussar Regiment were positioned under cover of this thick wood. They were followed by the 15th and 16th Brigades together with the reserve artillery and cavalry. These troops were posted in camouflaged positions along a broad front and in close order on both sides of the track through the wood.

The artillery was drawn up on the track itself, and everything was in readiness to break forth at the right moment towards the open heights of Frischermont opposite. The reserve cavalry stood in wait behind the wood, ready to follow the infantry immediately.[10]

Von Ollech describes the situation: 'The troops waiting in the wood in hushed and tense expectation had been on their feet since four that morning, that is to say for twelve hours; they had had no cooked meal, and little food of any kind, and now they had to go into action. The strain was great, and grew greater with the struggle, but all thought of hardship was banished by the thrill of victory'.[11]

The Prussian army command initially had no intention of attacking at half-strength.[12] Both Blücher and Gneisenau wanted to await the arrival of all their troops and then to undertake a full-strength flank attack against the enemy. But Napoleon's heavy attacks against Wellington's positions, the penetration of French mounted squadrons into the English lines, and the temporary silence of the batteries in the area shook not only the British defence but also the Prussian observers to the east of Frischermont. The fear that Wellington's front might break under this pressure made Blücher change his plans. When fresh French preparations for a new attack became visible, he decided to go ahead immediately with what was available: the 15th and 16th Brigades of IV Corps.

It now seemed just as important to strengthen the allied rear as to make Napoleon commit his reserves against the Prussians, and thus reduce the pressure on Wellington. Between 4 and 4.30 p.m., Count Nostitz brought to General von Bülow the order to attack.[13] Field-Marshal Blücher insisted on these orders being carried out, although Bülow pointed out that the still missing 13th and 14th Brigades were not far off. So began the Prussian entry into the great battle, not with a mighty thrust into Napoleon's right flank but with a demonstration of movement and fire power which was to develop into a full attack as the units, hurrying to join them, arrived.[14]

Napoleon had sent the two cavalry divisions, commanded by Dumont and Subervie, to cover his right flank, and somewhat later detached the stationary VI Corps of Count Lobau, which was positioned behind the centre of the main front, as a thrust reserve. When the Prussian IV Corps emerged from the Bois de Paris at about 4.30, it faced the French cavalry which had been stationed as observers on the heights south-west of Frischermont.

The French VI Corps had placed itself, with its two divisions behind each other, astride the road to Plancenoit, a powerful bulwark on the high ground to the south of Frischermont.[15] Bülow advanced his two brigades side by side,[16] Losthin's 15th Brigade on the right, to the west of the path to Plancenoit, von Hiller's 16th on the left, on the east side of the path. To cover their flanks, both these brigades sent out several battalions on either side; of their nine battalions there remained to the left brigade seven and to the right brigade six. This was not much; indeed von Ollech is of the opinion that General von Bülow had only the psychological effect of his appearance to count on: 'Tactical success could not be expected until the tail of his corps, the 14th Brigade, and at least the head of II Corps had passed through the Lasne defile and was likely to support IV Corps.'[17]

The leading batteries, steadily strengthened by the reserve artillery moving up behind them, had immediately opened fire on the enemy cavalry; they did this more to advise their allies that the Prussians were on the way than for tactical effect. While this bombardment was going on, the missing two brigades gradually came up between about 5 and 5.30 p.m.; von Hacke's 13th Brigade was deployed on the right, behind the 15th; von Ryssel's 14th Brigade on the left behind the 16th, which was where the reserve cavalry was also stationed.

Blücher ordered that the advance was to take place in the direction of Belle Alliance. At the same time he instructed IV Corps to move steadily to the left; it was obviously the intention of the army command to push against the deep flank of the French army. The village of Plancenoit, lying on low ground and at this time not yet strongly occupied by the French, was a convient point to start such a move and was therefore chosen as a first objective. The result was that the front of IV Corps gradually assumed a very extended and oblique line, with the left wing in the van. The fight with the French VI Corps was carried out by the 13th and 15th Brigades mainly on the right wing, while the left concentrated on the attack on Plancenoit. A further result was that IV Corps, with its many, untrained, militia, found itself involved in a bloody street fight – a form of battle experienced at Ligny by I and II

Corps and for which IV Corps was quite unprepared.

Count Lobau had advanced with his corps and
engaged the Prussians, and a violent battle ensued
on the heights to the south of Frischermont. The
French division had not been previously engaged
and consisted of first-rate line regiments. 'But
Lobau had regiments from the old formation,
solid as rocks. . . . With these magnificent troops
Lobau presented so bold a front that Blücher,
instead of sticking obstinately to his parallel attack,

sought by a manoeuvre to turn the right flank
of VI Corps . . . .'[18]

But, worried at the risk of being outflanked,
Lobau began to withdraw his corps on to the
heights of Plancenoit, leaving the village itself
occupied by one of his brigades.[19] This was the
beginning of the fight for Plancenoit, which became the centre of gravity of the Prussian flanking
attack. 'If only we had the damned village,'
Blücher is said to have exclaimed grimly.[20] He had
ordered the capture of Plancenoit as part of the

advance of IV Corps. Colonel von Hiller achieved this at about 6 p.m. with six battalions of his 16th Brigade, two battalions each from the right, the centre and the left. After heavy fighting the village was at last entered and held for a while. But only for a short while; a counter-attack by the entire Young Guard, eight battalions, sent by Napoleon for the defence of Plancenoit, together with a quantity of artillery to protect the flank of the French army, threw the exhausted Prussians back.[21] A further attack by the Prussians was also warded off by the Guards. The Prussian troops were then collected, regrouped and prepared for a new attack. Meanwhile the 14th Brigade had arrived and could be included.

At almost the same time as von Hiller's brigade attacked Plancenoit, a second message arrived from III Corps at Wavre. General von Thielemann reported that 'he was concerned that he might not be able to protect the Dyle crossings against the superior strength of the enemy'. Blücher was then concentrating entirely on the attack on Napoleon, and his answer to Thielemann, dictated by General Gneisenau to Lieutenant von Wussow, was unequivocal; he was to resist the enemy, step by step, with all his strength: victory over Napoleon would compensate for any loss, however great, suffered by the corps.[22]

━━━━━━━━━━━━━━━━━━━━━━━━━━━

The Prussian II Corps, which had been in readiness for the whole morning at Aisémont, owing to the delays in IV Corps advance, was unable to move off in the wake of the 14th Brigade until midday. When the greater part of the corps, the 5th and 6th Brigades, the reserve artillery and the reserve cavalry, had passed Wavre, the commanding officer, General von Pirch, received a message that enemy cavalry was approaching from the south.

To cover the movement of the corps, he ordered the 7th and 8th Brigades, as well as Lieutenant-Colonel von Sohr's cavalry brigade, to remain behind on the east bank of the Dyle, and placed the brigades under the command of General von Brause, who moved the 8th Brigade up, in the direction of L'Aucelle, and placed the 7th behind it. They were joined at the edge of the L'Aucelle wood by two battalions and a cavalry regiment of IV Corps under the command of Lieutenant-Colonel von Ledebur, which had been left behind as rearguard cover at Mont St Guibert.

As stronger enemy formations appeared, the Prussian forces retreated towards Wavre and, at a considerable distance, followed II Corps to St

Lambert. The 7th Brigade moved from there to Couture and Maransart, which they reached in the evening. Meanwhile the mass of II Corps continued their march. By 6 p.m. Tippelskirch's leading 5th Brigade was in front of Plancenoit, close behind the 14th Brigade.

━━━━━━━━━━━━━━━━━━━━━━━━━━━

General von Zieten had received orders at about twelve noon for his I Corps to march, via Froidmont, in the direction of Mont St Jean, to the left flank of the English defence positions. In the corps orders addressed to this unit, now operating outside the immediate area of action of the army, was the following comment:

IV, II and I Corps will march in two columns in such a manner as to support the Duke of Wellington, whose right flank is at Braine l'Alleud and his left at Mont St Jean, and to provide a diversion on Napoleon's right flank. IV and II Corps will make up the column on the left wing, marching via Neuf Cabaret and St Lambert. I Corps will form the right wing column and march via Froidmont towards Ohain.[23]

General von Zieten had placed von Steinmetz's 1st Brigade, strengthened by two batteries and the reserve cavalry, in the van; the main body, consisting of the 2nd, 3rd and 4th Brigades as well as the corps reserve artillery, was to follow. Typifying the determination as well as the feelings of pain and pride, which Ligny had left, General von Zieten's orders conclude: 'I will count it as one of the luckiest days of my life if the 18th of June shows the same Prussian bravery as the 16th, but greater success. With the command of such brigade commanders and senior officers as I have in I Corps, I am certain in advance of the success of my dearest wishes.'

The road to Froidmont crossed that to Neuf Cabaret. Gaps in the advancing II Corps had to be used for the advance of I Corps, so their departure could not begin before 2 p.m. The route presented the same difficulties as those encountered by IV and II Corps. Colonel von Reiche, chief of staff of I Corps, reported:

The march to the battlefield was extremely difficult. Bottomless paths, cut into deep defiles, had to be followed. The ground on both sides was almost all wooded, so that there could be no question of evasive action, and the march was very slow, particularly since at many places men and horses could move only in single file and the artillery could be brought up only with the greatest difficulty. As a result the columns became very stretched ... any attempt to keep them closed up had to be abandoned and we had to be content if only the brigades and regiments just remained together as units.[24]

General von Zieten also received reports from his rearmost 4th Brigade which was still in Bierges while the mass of the corps was already moving, that the enemy was approaching and attacking III Corps. He therefore ordered the 4th Brigade to provide a rearguard to remain behind for protection.[25] The corps itself continued its march to the left wing of the English army. 'Rifle fire behind them and the thunder of cannons heard from Ohain – all pushed forward with a supreme effort,' comments von Ollech.[26] But it moved slowly: by 6 p.m. the advance units were level with Ohain on the way to Mont St Jean, and in sight of the battlefield.

The afternoon of 18 June brought changes of orders, worrying decisions and difficult commitments also to III Corps, which lay, with the bulk of its troops, around La Bavette; Major-General von Borcke's 9th Brigade was still on the east bank of the Dyle by Aisémont. At about 1 p.m. before following the army staff to St Lambert, General von Grolmann had informed Colonel von Clausewitz, chief of staff of III Corps, to hold the sector of the Dyle by Wavre in the case of heavier enemy attacks and thus protect the army's rear or, if this eventuality should not arise, to follow the army as reserve.[27]

As everything remained quiet to begin with, General von Thielemann had the corps ready to move off, but an immediate move was not possible as the paths they were to follow were still occupied by part of II and III Corps. At about 3 p.m. orders were finally received to follow the army to Couture, as the left-hand column. Although, meanwhile, messages had been received that enemy cavalry was approaching and fighting could be heard to the south-east, General von Thielemann marched off with the bulk of his corps from La Bavette. Earlier he had instructed the 9th Brigade to follow to Couture via St Lambert, leaving a detachment in Wavre as rearguard for the corps. General von Borcke had consequently left Colonel von Zeppelin with three battalions to occupy Wavre. He himself, because the 7th and 8th Brigades of II Corps were moving back towards Wavre and over the bridges, had moved away with most of his 9th Brigade to Bas-Wavre, where he had left behind half a battalion and ordered the destruction of the bridge there; he had then continued his march in the direction of St Lambert.[28]

Meanwhile, General von Thielemann had moved off with III Corps but without the 9th Brigade.

However the fighting to the east of the Dyle had intensified to such a degree that he thought he ought, in accordance with his earlier instructions, to remain with his corps in Wavre to defend the Dyle sector.[29] At this time, between 3 and 4 p.m., the following units were along the Dyle in the area of Wavre: at Bierges Stengel's detachment of I Corps with one infantry regiment and one cavalry regiment; in Wavre, Colonel von Zeppelin with three battalions of the 9th Brigade; in Bas-Wavre the two companies of the 9th Brigade. General von Thielemann placed the artillery of III Corps on the commanding heights to the west and southwest of Wavre, his three brigades, ready to attack at Bierges and on the heights to the west and north of Wavre, and the riflemen of the brigades along the river bank between Bierges and Bas-Wavre.[30]

With the Prussian troops thus disposed the fight began with the constantly increasing enemy, Vandamme's III Corps and parts of General Gérard's IV Corps. By evening thirteen attempts by the enemy to capture the bridges of Bierges and Wavre and to force the crossing of the Dyle had been repulsed with much bloodshed. As a result of this heavy fighting, III Corps failed to cover the more southerly crossings of the Dyle at Limal and Limalette; this was to prove a serious omission.[31]

On 18 June at about 6 p.m., when the great battle was at its height, Blücher's men were either committed to the battle at Mont St Jean or the fighting at Wavre or were on the move. IV Corps was in battle with the French VI Corps and the Young Guards. Plancenoit had begun to make itself felt as a centre of gravity, and this required Napoleon's attention as much as the increasing commitment of his reserves – up to now almost half of what had been meant for a push against the English front. II Corps was on the march to Plancenoit with the 5th Brigade; the 6th Brigade was close behind, and the 7th and 8th Brigades were on the march from Wavre. The advanced units and cavalry of I Corps had moved past Ohain and were in sight of the English positions. III Corps had successfully warded off all the attacks of Grouchy's troops. The following is Becke's comment on the general situation at 6 p.m.: 'So far the Emperor had gained no tangible result at Belle Alliance, despite the desperate nature of the fight. Not only was his Cavalry ruined, but on the eastern horizon lowered ever-increasing masses of Prussian troops. At the end of this Third Phase, the growing seriousness of the situation was only too apparent.'[32]

11 LA HAYE SAINTE FALLS
6pm-7pm
William Seymour

It is possible that Wellington's obsession with the danger to his right flank may have been responsible for his apparent neglect of La Haye Sainte, a feature of great tactical importance. Hougoumont was to be held strongly from the first, and although there was an ammunition crisis during Bachelu's and Foy's attacks, while Ney was hammering at the centre with his cavalry, this was righted by the prompt action of Colonel Horace Seymour of the general staff. Hougoumont was adequately reinforced, and despite the fact that throughout the day the fighting in and around the orchard was of a see-saw nature, only once – during the brief scuffle at the gate – were the buildings in serious danger of being captured.

But with La Haye Sainte the situation was different. The buildings were only lightly garrisoned from the start, the comparatively junior officer in charge seems to have been given no positive instructions as to the need to strengthen this important outpost, and even when it became obvious that Napoleon had no intention of turning a flank but was bent on a thrust at the heart the garrison was only sketchily reinforced – although, admittedly, by that time reinforcements were not easily come by. Moreover, the most curious feature of the whole business, Major Baring's constant pleas for ammunition were disregarded; his men were armed with the Baker rifle, but so were those in the sandpit, and they never went short. A possible explanation is that a wagon-cart, which had been overturned further back on the Brussels road, contained supplies of rifle ammunition that should have gone to Baring. The unkindest cut of all came two months later when the Duke, writing from Paris (possibly to Sir Walter Scott), said of La Haye Sainte, 'This they got, I think at about two o'clock, and got it from a circumstance which is to be attributed to the neglect of the officer commanding on the spot.'[1] The truth was that Major Baring and his men fought most valiantly even after they had fired their last round.

After d'Erlon's attack Baring had been sent two companies of the 1st Light Battalion King's German Legion and some Nassauers. Now, after Ney's cavalry had spent itself, Wellington gave him the light company from the 5th Battalion King's German Legion and instructed him to hold the buildings at all costs, but to abandon the orchard. At the same time Lambert's brigade was moved from behind Papelotte to just east of the crossroads, because d'Erlon's shattered battalions had been partially revived as a potent fighting force. It was a little after 6 p.m. when once more the French advanced – infantry and cavalry, preceded by a whole swarm of tirailleurs – and Baring's Germans knew that their hour was at hand. From an initial, totally inadequate, sixty rounds per man, they were now down to no more than four – except for the Nassauers with their muskets. The men cursed and grumbled to Baring; and who can blame them, left isolated without the means to protect themselves? But they were troops of the very highest calibre, and told Baring, 'No man will desert you – we will fight and die with you.' And this they did, until the last pathetic remnants were ordered to retire.

As the French infantry neared the farm the absence of rifle fire must have led them to cheerful conclusions. But when they closed around the buildings, striving to gain an entrance and attempting to snatch enemy weapons from the windows and openings, they realized that the defenders, isolated, invested and inadequately armed as they were, were nevertheless fiercely determined men with a deep sense of duty. Soon seventeen Frenchmen lay dead in the western passage through the barn; but others forced their way in and once more set the barn alight. In this chaos of blood and fire the French and Germans fought hand to hand, but it was an unequal fight, and once the enemy got a lodgement on the roofs they were able to pick off the Germans at will and without any risk. As Baring's men retreated through the house the French were axing down the main gate on to the *chaussée*, and then, pouring into the yard, were quickly upon their heels. A sharp skirmish took place in the hall, but it was hopeless to fight on. Baring ordered the men to withdraw individually back to their battalions on the ridge.

Those who managed to get clear of the garden were protected by the covering fire from the rifles in the sandpit as they made their way up the slope. But Baring and another officer, a Scot called George Graeme (who was wounded and who later wrote an account of the episode), and a miserable total of forty-two out of 360 men were all that got back to the main position. One other officer survived, a young ensign called Franck, who when wounded took refuge under a bed in an upstairs room. Two other wounded men in the same room were bayoneted by the French, but Franck remained under the bed and undetected for the remainder of the battle.

The loss of La Haye Sainte quickly brought about a critical situation along the whole allied line. Ney was not slow to exploit this success; soon his skirmishers were firing almost from the ridge, and he brought forward light field pieces to the

entirely clear – possibly ignorance, possibly pique – peremptorily ordered Ompteda to deploy and advance. The gallant Peninsular veteran instantly obeyed; shouting to his second-in-command to take care of his nephews, who would have followed him, he drew his sword and, riding at the head of his two battalions, crossed the sunken road and went into the fray. The Germans soon had the enemy foot in disarray, but, as Ompteda knew full well would happen, the cuirassiers took his right-hand battalion (the 8th) in flank and cut it to pieces. Nearly every officer and man was killed, including Ompteda himself and the battalion commander, the ensign was wounded and the Colour was captured.[2] Utter disaster was only averted by the prompt action of Arendtschildt, who threw in his King's German Legion hussars to help the 5th Battalion regain the ridge.

At the time of this débâcle Wellington was on the right of the line with Maitland's brigade. Here, too, a mass of tirailleurs was pouring a most destructive fire into Maitland's squares and into Adam's square formed by the 95th Rifles. Wellington took personal charge, ordered Maitland's Guards into line four deep, and with one of his well-known, crisp commands, 'Drive those fellows away!', watched them do exactly that; but on being charged by a body of French cavalry they were quickly back into square. This ability to wheel into line to make their fire power more telling, and to reform square instantly, was a great feature of a well-disciplined battalion, and one that made a battalion proof against all assaults other than a closely combined infantry and cavalry attack, which the French resorted to only on a few occasions at Waterloo.

Alten's 3rd Division had almost reached the point of disintegration, and further to the east the brigades of Kempt, Pack and Lambert were under great stress – the 1st Battalion of the 27th Foot in Lambert's brigade had been virtually wiped out. Ompteda's broken brigade, Kruse's Nassauers and Kielmansegge's two squares of young Hanoverians comprised a very inadequate defence against the strong and persistent French attack on this sector. Morale was low and so was ammunition; Alten was off the field wounded and the command of the 3rd Division had devolved on Kielmansegge, who had his hands full steadying his own men against the almost unbearable weight of cannon and musketry fire. Captain Kennedy, seeing a dangerous gap springing up between Halkett's brigade and the Brussels road, and realizing that he was the most senior officer left on the divisional staff, galloped over to Wellington – who for once was

garden with which to bombard Kempt's and Lambert's brigades. The occupants of the sandpit and the mound had no alternative but to retire again on to their battalion, but their accurate rifle fire soon made the French artillery position in the garden untenable.

It was at about this time that the Prince of Orange demonstrated once more his unfitness for high command. General Alten, soon to be severely wounded, had observed the critical situation in and around La Haye Sainte, and had sent orders to Ompteda to advance his two remaining battalions – the 5th and 8th Line – to drive back the French infantry column then debouching from the farm area. Ompteda could see the cuirassiers to the west of the farm, who because of a fold in the ground were hidden from Alten's view, and naturally he demurred. But at that moment Orange galloped up, and for reasons that are not

not at the point of greatest danger – to tell him of this most critical situation. Kennedy has left us an account of this meeting. The Duke received the startling information with his habitual coolness, his firm but unhurried reply clearly showing his determination to halt this savage storm of skirmishers. 'I shall order Brunswick troops in reserve behind Maitland to the spot, and other troops besides,' Wellington told Kennedy. 'Go you and get all the German troops of the division to the spot that you can, and all guns that you can find.' He then ordered Vincke's Hanoverian brigade and Vivian's light cavalry to come across from the left, and himself brought up five young Brunswicker battalions.

Vivian had in fact anticipated the order, for by now (6.45 p.m.) the Prussians were close on his left and he could see how badly mauled the allied cavalry in the centre was. His vivid description of the scene on arriving there is all the more poignant as coming from one by now accustomed to the trials and tribulations of this day: '. . . and never did I witness anything so terrific; the ground actually covered with dead and dying, cannon shots and shells flying thicker than I ever heard even musketry before, and our troops – some of them – giving way.' He was just in time to prevent the Brunswickers (whose task here was as difficult and dangerous a one as could confront any young and untried troops) from breaking. But his cavalry deployed behind them, and the presence of their dauntless commander-in-chief to lead them, steeled their courage; Wellington was able to bring them up to form a fresh line that lent strength to Kruse's and Kielmansegge's hard-pressed soldiers. Even with this additional fire power the issue hung in the balance for several agonizing minutes, but with fresh cavalry also attacking them it was the French whose resolution broke first. Quite suddenly the tirailleurs retreated down the slope, and the allied gunners were then able to put pressure on the infantry columns, thus restoring the whole line to some semblance of stability.

But the cost had been dreadful. Alten's division was now no more than a weak brigade, the allied cavalry was terribly depleted, and many of the batteries had been silenced. All the officers of the 73rd Regiment had been killed, and the casualties among the staff were alarmingly high. The Prince of Orange, always courageous, had been shot in the shoulder leading a charge of Kruse's Nassauers; Lord Fitzroy Somerset had had his arm shot off while sitting on his horse alongside the Duke; de Lancey had received what proved to be a mortal wound; and Colonel Canning and Sir Alexander Gordon, two other members of Wellington's personal staff, had been killed and mortally wounded respectively. In all, three generals had been killed and five others had left the field wounded. Amid this delirium of death and killing, Johnny Kincaid of the 95th paused to wonder if there had ever been a battle in which everyone on both sides had been killed; he had never heard of one, but this seemed likely to be the exception.

And what of the extreme flanks of the allied line, seen only dimly from the centre through a yellow fog of powder smoke? Hougoumont had been under constant pressure throughout this phase of the battle, and here the French had made some use of cavalry in support of infantry; it was in one of these combined attacks that du Plat had been killed. The buildings were never in danger of being taken, but the orchard changed hands repeatedly, and for a moment the whole position became isolated when the French infantry pressed on to the top of the ridge beyond the farm. Adam's brigade swept them away, however, and what might have been a dangerous gap just to the right of Maitland's brigade was closed.

On the extreme left Prince Bernhard had displayed considerable tactical skill. Throughout this trying period, when Durutte's division attacked him fiercely, he had to yield some ground and may have had to relinquish isolated buildings, but he never appears to have lost the farms of Papelotte and Ter La Haye. Both Vivian's and Vandeleur's cavalry had been withdrawn, but the position was naturally a strong one and the Prince's Nassauers had had time to strengthen it. They were, therefore, able to resist Durutte's final offensive, which came at about 6.45, and thereafter Durutte was more concerned with the Prussians to his right.

As this, the most vital phase of the whole battle, drew to its close, Napoleon could count La Haye Sainte as a gain. Beyond that there was little to give him satisfaction. The battle had been raging for almost eight hours and not a single square had been broken – although the 27th defended theirs with their dead bodies – and the line had been shored up at its weakest points. But Wellington knew that the Emperor still held what he considered his trump card. So often in the past had the Guard advanced, after others had performed the terrible process of softening up, to put the finishing touches to victory. This time when they came, as come they must, the Duke felt confident that his sadly depleted ranks of tired soldiers were nevertheless still capable of striking hard and decisively to gain the victory through a last bloody punch.

12 THE PRUSSIANS CLOSE IN
6pm-7pm

Colonel E. Kaulbach

In the Prussian records of the Battle of Waterloo, as far as the tactical details of the Prussian participation in the battle are concerned, there is considerable inconsistency. This applies particularly to times and localities and also to most of the verbal orders. Even later, very careful investigations such as those of von Ollech and von Lettow-Vorbeck or of the historians Lehmann and von Pflugk-Harttung have not been able to clarify the facts. The reason for this is that the Prussian army was constantly on the move from 15 June and that the ceaseless pursuit to Paris followed the heavy fighting and movements of the army which took place between 16 and 18 June. All records had therefore to be retrospective and were made under difficult conditions; and the difficulties were accentuated by the fact that the supply columns and baggage trains were, for the most part, not present. Uncertainties regarding times and exact routes of advance are especially marked in the case of IV Corps, and everything concerning the arrival and commitment of I Corps is doubtful. Lettow-Vorbeck comments, 'All reports and statements regarding the commitment of I Corps are rather contradictory so that only the general lines can be taken for granted.'[1]

The following account is therefore restricted to showing the 'probable' sequence of events, based on a comparative examination of the most important publications.

Towards six in the evening, as the battle reached its decisive climax with the attack on La Haye Sainte and its capture by the French, the attack by IV Corps against the French flank had begun to falter.[2] The Prussian right wing, with the 15th and 13th Brigades, was in contact with the French VI Corps from Frischermont, across the heights to the south, in front of the Frischermont woods and right up to the path to Plancenoit.[3] The left wing, the 16th Brigade, and to the left behind them the 14th Brigade, which had meanwhile come up close to them, were on the south side of the path to Plancenoit, on the heights as far as the Bois de Virère; the units of the 16th Brigade were about to form up for a new attack on Plancenoit.

The spread of IV Corps between the valley of the Smohain brook and the deeply cut Lasne low ground, the echelon formation of the front and the various points of attack did not allow the numerical superiority of the corps to have its effect; it prevented the formation of a main attack centre, as was particularly necessary against Plancenoit. The position on the right wing, due to the obstinate resistance of the divisions of Count Lobau's VI Corps and the very active French right wing division of Durutte, was becoming critical. The right flank group of the 15th Brigade, consisting of about five battalions of both brigades, had advanced on Papelotte from Frischermont but had had to withdraw again. On the left wing the strength of the 16th Brigade had not been sufficient to take and keep Plancenoit. 'So far,' comments Becke on the situation at 6 p.m.,[4] 'Bülow's action had not turned the fate of the day and, if no other Prussian troops had arrived, Napoleon would have beaten Wellington and Bülow.'

In view of Blücher's impatience to advance and to contribute to the final decision, the hold-up must have been unbearable. Plancenoit had to be taken; this place, low-lying but close to the French line of retreat, must have been regarded by the Prussian command as of prime importance as a goal if they were to strike significantly at Napoleon and thus to influence the course of the battle.[5] But to take Plancenoit reinforcements were necessary. Where had I and II Corps got to? Was I Corps really necessary on Wellington's left wing? Would it not be of greater service to the English front if the Prussians advanced over Plancenoit, deep into the flank and rear of the enemy? Would it not be better to let I Corps turn off at Ohain and bring them up directly to the left wing of IV Corps rather than let them make the long detour across the English front? Blücher's desire to have I Corps at Plancenoit may well have arisen from such considerations; in any case the result was the order to I Corps to turn off towards the south and hurry across the Smohain brook in the direction of Frischermont. Captain von Scharnhorst is named as the bearer of this order.[6]

The order put I Corps in a difficult position. Between 6 and 6.30 that evening, I Corps was on the march to the English left wing, along the path which passes to the north of Ohain. The advanced units, the strengthened 1st Brigade and the corps reserve cavalry had passed Ohain and had arrived to the north of Cheval du Bois, that is to say about a mile north of Frischermont. The main body of the corps, with the 2nd Brigade leading, was probably level with Ohain. It was here that General von Zieten would have received Blücher's orders and then instructed the leading 2nd Brigade to move to the left.[7]

The chief of staff, Colonel von Reiche, had earlier ridden ahead of the advance guard in order to reconnoitre the position and to prepare for the commitment of the units on their arrival. There he met General von Müffling, who had been sent by

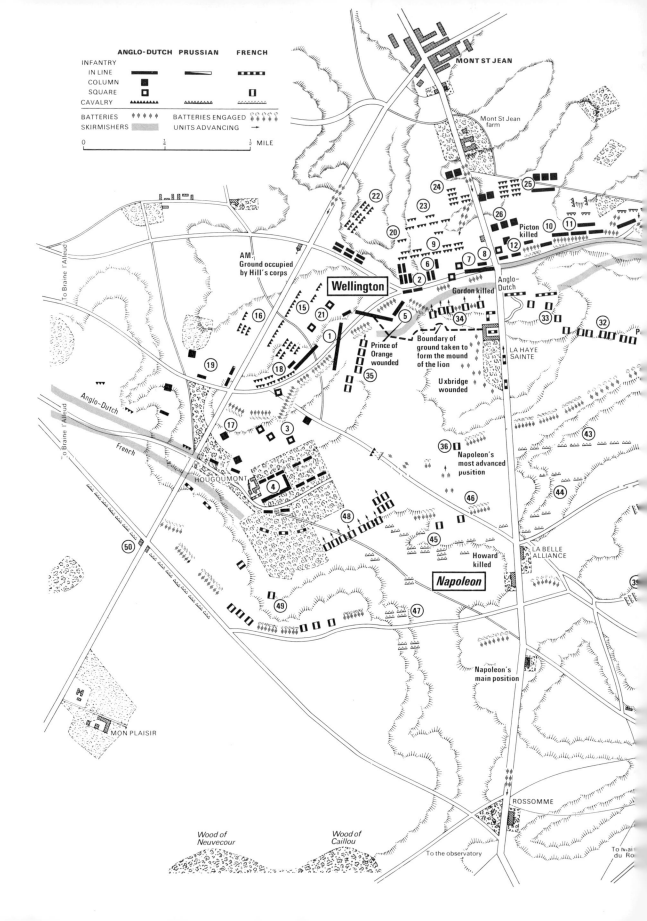

MONT ST JEAN

Mont St Jean farm

To Braine l'Alleud

AM.
Ground occupied
by Hill's corps

Wellington

Picton
killed

Anglo-
Dutch

Gordon killed

Boundary of
ground taken to
form the mound
of the lion

Prince of
Orange
wounded

LA HAYE
SAINTE

Uxbridge
wounded

To Braine l'Alleud

Anglo-Dutch

French

HOUGOUMONT

Napoleon's
most advanced
position

Napoleon

Howard
killed

LA BELLE
ALLIANCE

MON PLAISIR

Napoleon's
main position

ROSSOMME

Wood of
Neuvecour

Wood of
Caillou

To the observatory

To Mai
du Ro

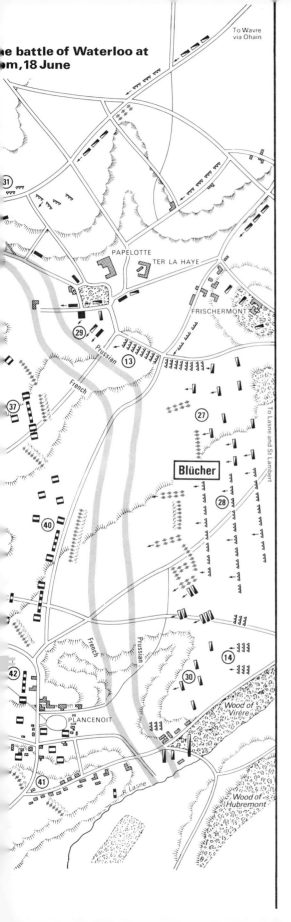

e battle of Waterloo at
m, 18 June

The Dispositions

Anglo-Dutch Army

In front line

Right wing Adam and Mitchell (English) **1**, Halkett (Hanoverian) **2**, Duplatt (Anglo-German) **3**, Byng (Guards) and First Nassauer battalion at Hougoumont **4**

Forward position Maitland **5**, Brunswick and Nassau brigades **6**, Kielmansegge (Hanoverian) **7**, Ompteda (Anglo-German) **8**, Vivian **9**

Centre left Kempt and Pack **10**, Best (Hanoverian) **11**, Lambert **12**

Left wing Prince William (cavalry) **13** and **14**

In second line

Behind centre right Vandeleur (dragoons) **15**, Brunswick corps (infantry and cavalry) **16-17**, Grant and Dornberg (Anglo-German cavalry) and Mitchell **18**, Coldstream Guards and Halkett (Hanoverian) in reserve **19**, Hussars **20**, and Tripp and Merlen (Dutch-Belgian cavalry) **21-22**

Behind centre left Remains of Somerset and Ponsonby brigades **23**, Merle, de Ghigney and Bylandt (Dutch-Belgian) **24-25**. Remains of Pack's brigade **26**

Prussian Army

Centre Hack and Losthin **27**, Jürgass **28**. Steinmetz and Prince of Saxe-Weimar **29**

Left Ryssel and Hiller at Plancenoit **30**

Right Röder (cavalry) **31**

French Army

In front line

Right wing Marcognet **32**

Centre right Allix **33**, and Donzelot **34**

Centre left First and second attacking column of Imperial guard **35-36**

In second line

Right wing Durutte **37**, Subervie **38**, Domont **39** and Jeannin **40**

At Plancenoit Young and old Imperial guard **41**, Simmer **42**

Centre Jaquinot **43**, Wathier and Delort (cuirassier) **44**

Left wing Rousel and remains of Imperial guard (cavalry) **45**, two battalions of Old guard (reserve) **46**, Lhéritier **47**, Bachelu **48**, Foy and Prince Jérôme **49**, Piré **50**

Wellington to the left wing to receive the Prussian corps.[8] After discussing the situation and the need for urgent help, von Reiche rode back. Meanwhile General von Müffling, who was expecting the Prussians, who were already close at hand, to arrive very soon, instructed the two cavalry brigades commanded by Vandeleur and Vivian, in accordance with Wellington's orders, to move from the left wing to relieve the centre.[9] According to Colonel von Reiche, he received Blücher's order to turn left from Captain von Scharnhorst when he reached the forward units.[10] As, however, the leading elements of these units had already passed the turning off point to Frischermont, he ordered them to march back to the fork in the road and there await General von Zieten's orders. General von Müffling saw this movement; galloping up, he learned for the first time of Blücher's orders. When he met von Zieten, who had also come up,[11] a decision had to be made about the further advance of I Corps. This was difficult; in front was the English left wing, visible and in difficulties; the leading troops of the French right wing had just captured Papelotte and La Haye, so it was high time to help. But Blücher's orders were categorical, and according to Captain von Scharnhorst things were far from well at Plancenoit. General von Müffling's urgent representations[12] – 'The battle is lost if the Corps does not keep on the move and immediately support the English Army' – together with the visible evidence of the fighting ahead, helped General von Zieten reach his decision, namely not to follow Field-Marshal Blücher's orders but, in accordance with the local situation, to keep to the original instructions and hurry with the corps to the help of the English left wing.[13]

There is no doubt that this decision was difficult, significant, and correct. It made it possible, despite the late hour, for at least the strengthened 1st Brigade and the cavalry of I Corps to take part in the final decisive phase of the battle, attack the French right wing and help to throw them back. If the corps had turned off, this would not have

been possible, and the whole corps would presumably have arrived too late to be of help at Plancenoit.

Some delay occurred as a result of the halting of I Corps but by about 7 p.m. the units of the 1st Brigade were approaching the English left wing as planned.

Some time between 5.30 and 6.30, Colonel von Hiller had tried to capture Plancenoit with the battalions of his 16th Brigade. The first attack succeeded in penetrating the village and, after severe fighting, in pushing out the units of the French VI Corps. But the village was quickly recaptured by the Young Guard, which had halted at Rossomme only a few hundred yards away and had hurried up on Napoleon's orders, with eight battalions and twenty-four guns; the Prussian troops were then thrown back as far as the heights to the east of Plancenoit. A second attack by the 16th Brigade was unsuccessful. Colonel von Hiller reported as follows:

... In the second assault two battalions of the 14th Brigade also took part, while I kept the 1st Silesian Militia Regiment in reserve. This attack was also repelled, but the troops did not lose their morale. Lieutenant-General Count Gneisenau was also here. With his influence and that of the officers of the 15th Regiment it was possible to lead up the columns for the third time and with great success.

It is worth remembering that, of the Prussian troops who took part in the fight for Plancenoit, more than half were militia; for them this bloody fighting at close quarters against French Imperial Guard was their very first engagement. Furthermore, IV Corps had been on the move almost without a break since the 15th; it had moved by forced march from Liège to Gembloux, and then to Dion le Mont, where it finally had a short rest, late on the evening of the 17th. On the 18th the troops were on the march from four in the morning; after surviving the atrocious paths and the Lasne low ground they had been committed to the

146

fighting at Plancenoit virtually without rest, and had immediately suffered serious casualties. Nevertheless, these units continued to attack the village for four hours; they captured Plancenoit twice and were thrown out twice before finally, late in the evening, capturing it for the last time. The losses suffered by the troops, particularly those of IV Corps, were disproportionately high.

Two battalions of von Ryssel's 14th Brigade had already taken part in the second attack on Plancenoit; meanwhile, the main body h. d arrived and a new attack was formed up, and carried out mainly by five battalions of the 14th Brigade, followed by two battalions of the 15th Regiment of the 16th Brigade. This attack was carried out by a number of columns attacking from different directions, and this time, after very heavy fighting, they succeeded in throwing out the Young Guards.[15] The time cannot be given exactly. However, this struggle may have taken place simultaneously with the conquest of La Haye Sainte by Marshal Ney, who afterwards asked the Emperor in vain for support. Houssaye describes the situation as follows:

But Napoleon, without a cavalry reserve, did not think he had a sufficient number of his 'busbies' to hold his position. The moment was no less critical for him than for Wellington. Under a third push by the whole von Bülow Corps, Lobau gave way and the Young Guards, after a stubborn defence, were forced to yield Plancenoit. Once again the cannonballs of the Prussian batteries churned up the ground near Belle Alliance. Napoleon, already overwhelmed on his flank, was threatened by a Prussian surge behind his battle line. He ordered eleven battalions of his Guards to form up in as many squares and placed them, facing Plancenoit, along the road to Brussels, from Belle Alliance as far as Rossomme. The [1st] Battalion of the 1st Chasseurs was kept at Caillou. General Morand received orders to re-take Plancenoit with the 2nd Battalion of the 2nd Grenadiers (Major Golzio) and the 1st of the 2nd Chasseurs (General Pelet).[16]

As can be seen, the threat to the French army resulting from the capture of Plancenoit had far-reaching effects. First, it caused Napoleon to commit his last reserves to safeguard his flank; second, he sent two battalions of the Old Guard to recapture Plancenoit. This put an end to the short-lived satisfaction of the Prussians at being in possession of this village where they suffered so many casualties. The attack by these two Guards battalions was brilliantly carried out; it is a classic example of what a magnificently trained, experienced, proud and disciplined force could do to an enemy, particularly an enemy so exhausted and surprised. The two Guards battalions crossed the short distance from Belle Alliance to Plancenoit 'at the double', penetrated in two columns into the village without a shot being fired, and in no time threw the Prussians out and back to their original positions. The Young Guards then took heart and re-occupied the village; so did Lobau's corps.[17]

All the efforts and sacrifices of the Prussians had apparently gone for nought; the thrust deep into the flank and rear of the French army seemed doomed to failure. And yet these attacks were not in vain; the disquieting of Napoleon and the immobilizing of his reserves had its effect. In addition, the speed with which Plancenoit was recaptured may have led Napoleon to think that the forces committed by him in the east were sufficient to cover his right flank – and this may have contributed to his decision to throw his remaining battalions against the English position in one last great attack.

By seven in the evening the Prussian army hardly seemed to have affected the course of the battle; but in fact it had. IV Corps, which had so far had to carry the main weight of the fighting, was still disposed along a broad front with all its strength, notably with its entire artillery between Frischermont and the Lasne valley, in contact with Lobau's VI Corps, against parts of the French right wing and against the Guards, who were holding Plancenoit with ten to eleven battalions. IV Corps had not had sufficient strength to break through to the rear of the enemy, but for hours the attacks by this army corps had tied down a great part of the French reserves, and as a result Napoleon was driven to decisions which were heroic but perilous. Even if no fresh Prussian troops had arrived, it seems doubtful, in view of the commitment of these forces and the defensive strength of the English, whether it would have been possible for Napoleon to have come out of this day victorious, as Becke thinks he might have.[18]

But meanwhile other Prussian units were ready to take part in the battle. Behind IV Corps, II Corps had approached with its leading brigades; Tippelskirch's 5th Brigade was about to join the 16th and 14th Brigades in front of Plancenoit, and the 6th Brigade was following closely; the 7th Brigade was on the march to Maransart. And on the right wing the leading 1st Brigade of I Corps, commanded by von Steinmetz, was preparing to attack from the heights against the villages of La Haye and Papelotte which were held by the enemy. The scales were about to tip in the allies' favour.

147

13 VICTORY THEN DEFEAT
6pm-11pm
Jacques Champagne

Ney was ordered to take La Haye Sainte at all costs. With two regiments (one infantry, one engineers), he attacked the farm, losing seventy men in the first assault, while sapper Lieutenant Vieux broke down the main gate with an axe to let the infantry into the courtyard, where the Germans fought it out in hand-to-hand combat. Only forty-two men (out of nine companies) escaped with Baring back to Mont St Jean. Ney then established a light battery on a hillock, and once again expelled the 95th (English) from the sandpit they were occupying. From these two positions, the French guns could fire at 300 yards' range, and the skirmishers from eighty yards, on Wellington's centre line. Under this cover, the remnants of Allix's, Donzelot's and Marcognet's divisions reached the Ohain ridge and attacked the enemy. Ompteda was killed when he counter-attacked with two battalions of the King's German Legion, while a squadron of cuirassiers destroyed one of the battalions, killing its colonel and capturing its flag. Only thirty men escaped from the French sabres. Napoleon's army now held La Haye Sainte.

Wellington's centre left (Kempt, Pack, Lambert, Best and Vincke) was still holding. But on the extreme left Durutte was once again dislodging the Nassauer troops from Papelotte, while the enemy's centre right, seriously shaken, was at the end of its tether. Ammunition was getting scarce, guns were dismantled or crewless. Behind the lines, there were many stragglers and runaways. A whole regiment of Cumberland Hussars cantered away on the Brussels road, headed by its colonel. There was even disorder in the Colin Halkett brigade. The ranks were thinning out. Many wounded were being taken away to the ambulances, accompanied by almost as many sound men. Wellington was getting anxious as night approached and effective Prussian support was not forthcoming. But in this critical situation for the second time in the day, he seemed determined to hold out to the last of his men.

Ney sensed that the Anglo-Dutch were faltering and, as his own men were tired, he asked Napoleon for some fresh infantry to break the enemy's last resistance. But the Emperor, deprived of all his cavalry reserve, answered that he had none to spare. He had eight Old Guard and six Middle Guard battalions to maintain his own position on the front and, under renewed pressure from Bülow's corps, Lobau was falling back and the Young Guard was being expelled from Plancenoit again.

Overrun on his right and threatened on his

rear by the Prussians, Napoleon ordered eleven Guard battalions to form squares and to deploy facing Plancenoit on the Charleroi road from La Belle Alliance to Rossomme. The 1st Battalion of the 1st Chasseurs remained at the farm of Caillou. Then, under Generals Morand and Pelet, the 1st Battalion (2nd Grenadiers) and the 1st Battalion (2nd Chasseurs), all seasoned veterans, charged at the double in tight columns. They overtook the Young Guard, which had been rallied by Duhesme, entered Plancenoit without firing a shot, threw over, crushed and pushed back the Prussians masses. The attack was so impetuous that the whole village was cleared of enemy in twenty minutes, the Guard pursuing the enemy for 600 yards on the opposite slopes, behind the Prussian batteries of von Hiller which were abandoned for a while. The Young Guard reoccupied Plancenoit in support, and Lobau, fighting the two Prussian divisions (Hacke and Losthin), regained ground. In one ramming thrust, Napoleon had stopped the Prussians, freed his right flank and regained his freedom of action on the battlefield.

It was 7 p.m. There were still two hours of daylight left. The sound of a cannonade coming from Limale was intensifying. It must be Grouchy falling upon the Prussians' rear at last. He would surely occupy them long enough to prevent them from joining Wellington on the battlefield. Bülow's forward corps could be contained by Lobau, Duhesme and the two battalions of the Old Guard. Durutte's division, holding Papelotte and La Haye Sainte, was climbing to the plateau. On the left, there was still fighting at Hougoumont, which was in flames. Jérôme was overrunning the position with an infantry brigade supported by Piré's lancers and was now beyond the Nivelles road. In the centre, Donzelot, Allix and Marcognet were on the crests, pressing hard on the English along the Ohain ridge. In the valley, six regiments of the Bachelu and Foy divisions were regrouping with the cavalry remnants. The enemy line seemed to be breached. This was the time for a decisive attack.

Napoleon ordered Drouot to move forward with nine Guards battalions out of the eleven formed into squares. The other two were to stay in Plancenoit and there were three more battalions remaining on the plateau of La Belle Alliance as a last reserve. At the head of the first square, the Emperor moved towards La Haye Sainte. This movement might have been decisive half an hour earlier when Ney had asked for some infantry. Now it was too late.

Wellington had reinforced his crumbling centre front from left and right. With this support, he was already repulsing Donzelot, Allix and Marcognet along the Ohain ridge and neutralizing Ney's batteries at La Haye Sainte. And as Napoleon and the Guard were approaching La Haye Sainte, Zieten's corps (not Grouchy) was arriving from Ohain to reinforce Bülow's forces, which were being held up by Lobau. Already, some French troops were falling back on the Guard under this powerful new irruption of the Prussians on to the battlefield. Napoleon checked the retreating troops and they advanced again with him. He then posted one Guard's battalion on a hillock between La Haye Sainte and Hougoumont and gave Ney command of the five others to attack the Anglo-Dutch centre right. The artillery was ordered to accelerate its fire, and d'Erlon and Reille, to support the Guard's movement with cavalry on their respective fronts. And, to counter the spreading news that a new Prussian corps had arrived on the battlefield, Napoleon ordered La Bédoyère and his other ordnance officers to ride all along

the French line to announce that Grouchy had arrived. The army thus regained its confidence and its enthusiasm.

Whether or not Wellington saw clearly Napoleon's dispositions and the Guard's movement through the thickening smoke that enveloped the battlefield, the fact is that a French traitor left him in no doubt about Napoleon's intentions. As Drouot was assembling the Guard, a captain of carabiniers galloped fast across the valley through the shells and the bullets and approached the skirmishers of the 52nd (English) with his arms raised and his sword in its sheath. Taken to the regiment's major, who was talking to Colonel Fraser, commanding the light artillery, this French officer shouted: 'Long live the King! Get ready! That b . . . of Napoleon will be upon you with the Guard before half an hour.' Fraser went immediately to tell Wellington, who rode all along the line between the Charleroi and the Nivelles roads to give his final orders: the gunners must stop answering the French batteries and con-

centrate all their fire on the assault columns.

With d'Erlon's, Reille's and Lobau's corps, and the cavalry and artillery in general support on their respective fronts, five battalions of the Middle Guard led by Ney in square formation advanced in echelons with two horse artillery 8-inch guns between each, against the Anglo-Dutch army. Drums beating, they marched under enemy fire, their rifles at the ready in superb parade order, officers in front. The enemy artillery, now deployed in a curve from the Nivelles road to Hougoumont, was vomiting death on the Guard at 200 yards' range. Each salvo opened up breaches in the squares, but the Guard marched on, closing the ranks and shouting, '*Vive l'Empereur!*'. Ney, thrown from the fifth horse killed under him on that day, got up and marched near Friant, sword in hand.

The right wing echelon (3rd Grenadiers) overthrew the Brunswick corps, captured crewless batteries and put the 30th and the 75th (English) to disorderly flight. Friant, wounded, had to leave the battlefield at this moment of success, just before

73 and 74 Left: Napoleon's flight after the battle at La Belle Alliance and (below) Napoleon viewing the attack on his Imperial Guard from La Belle Alliance

75 Following pages: Wellington on the plateau of Mont St Jean. When he raised his cocked hat and waved it in the air he was giving the signal for the final general onslaught on the French

Chassé opened up with enemy reserve batteries and launched 3,000 men of his Ditmer brigade into a bayonet charge against the assailants, rupturing their formations, crushing the Guard and throwing the survivors down the slopes.

The second echelon (4th Grenadiers) attacked the Halkett brigade and broke through the remnants of the 33rd and the 69th (English). But Halkett, though seriously wounded, rallied his men around the flag and held out against the Guard's assault.

The third echelon (3rd Chasseurs) reached the crest of the plateau almost without infantry opposition and marched on the Ohain ridge. Maitland's 2,000 Guards were waiting for them, lying on the ground. At the command 'Up Guards! At them!', they rose like a red wall, four lines deep, and fired, killing 300 of their assailants. The Guard took some time to reform, hampered by their dead comrades' bodies lying among them, and for ten minutes they were immobilized under English cannon and rifle fire. General Michel was shot dead. Wellington, seeing that the French were wavering, ordered Maitland's men to charge. They fell furiously upon this handful of survivors, threw them over and went down the slopes with them right up to Hougoumont in such close combat that the English artillery had to stop firing to spare its own infantry.

Suddenly, the English stopped short. The fourth Guard's echelon (4th Chasseurs) was coming to the rescue. Maitland's men retreated in disorder to climb back up the slopes as quickly as they had come down, with the Guard in close pursuit under renewed cannon fire. As the attackers reached the Ohain ridge, the Adam brigade came out firing on their flank, joined by the Colin Halkett brigade and Hanoverians coming up from behind Hougoumont. Fired upon from all sides, one French battalion deployed to face Maitland and the remnants of the other two turned to the Adam brigade. But they were mauled, depleted and overwhelmed by numbers (less than 3,000 against 8,000 to 10,000) and they retired in disorder.

Someone shouted: 'La Garde recule.' The cry was heard and the fact was being witnessed by the rest of the French army. Reille's infantry, the cuirassiers and the Guard's squadrons, who were on their way to support Ney's attack, stopped short. Everyone felt that it was the end. Donzelot's and Allix's men, who were fighting Kruse on the crests, began to lose ground and came down the slopes, taking Marcognet's division with them in their withdrawal. This movement amplified and spread gradually along the whole front. And,

simultaneously, Durutte was being fiercely attacked in Papelotte and La Haye Sainte by the Prussians coming out from Ohain.

Panic set in among the army's ranks, fearful of treason, having seen one general, one colonel and several officers going over to the enemy right at the beginning of the campaign and, indeed, that very afternoon (see pages 35 and 151). Soldiers were finding some of their cartridges filled with bran instead of powder. And whereas they were waiting for Grouchy's arrival, they were being attacked by Zieten's fresh Prussian corps. The rout began to spread as the Prussians rushed in to attack in force the French army's right flank. Amidst the debris of battle d'Erlon's four divisions were disrupting each other's movements in the crush, and in the valley all was utter confusion as English and Prussian shells and grape-shot were raining on them from all sides.

Wellington now decided to destroy this French army, which was already mortally wounded. He rode towards the edge of the plateau of Mont St Jean, raised his hat and waved it in the air. It was the signal for the first and the final general onslaught of the Anglo-Dutch army upon Napoleon's forces on that day. From right to left, 40,000 men, English, Hanoverians, Dutch, Belgians and Brunswickers, cavalry and infantry, came down the slopes like a torrent upon the French army, sabring, shooting and lancing the retreating French amongst the corpses, the wounded and the frightful debris littering the whole battlefield and shouting 'No quarter, no quarter!' The French abandoned Hougoumont and La Haye.

Napoleon saw the sudden crumbling of his battle line as he was organizing, in attack columns against La Haye Sainte, the 2nd Battalions of the 1st and 2nd Chasseurs and the battalions of the 2nd Grenadiers under Generals Cambronne, Roguet and Christiani respectively. Friant, wounded, had just arrived saying that 'all is well'. But Napoleon knew that he was beaten; from then on he hoped only to be able to organize his army's retreat (see page 32, plans of campaign). He formed the three battalions into three squares 100 yards away from La Haye Sainte. They were immediately surrounded by Vivian's hussars and other enemy cavalry who swarmed around them, but without being able to break through. Napoleon launched his four available squadrons against this flood.

On the road, brandishing his broken sword, Ney was on foot, his face blackened by powder, his uniform in shreds, one shoulder strap slashed off by a sabre. He shouted to d'Erlon, who was caught

153

in the rout: 'D'Erlon, if we come out of this, you and I will be hanged.' The 'Brave of Braves' looked like a wild beast, having done more during that day, in a superhuman effort, than any other commander in any battle. Twice he had led d'Erlon's infantry into attack. He had charged four times on the plateau at the head of the cuirassiers. And he had just led the Guards' desperate assault. Yet he still rushed to the Brue brigade (Durutte's division) of only two battalions, the only ones which seemed to be retreating in good order. He stopped the troops from retreating and led them once again against the enemy, shouting, 'Come and see how a Marshal of France dies!' The brigade was soon dispersed by the enemy. But, as death did not seem to be going to claim him on the battlefield, Ney resolved at least to be the last to leave it. He entered a Guard's square while Durutte, his forehead split open by a sabre slash, his right hand cut off, was caught in an English cavalry charge and brought back covered in blood to La Belle Alliance by his galloping horse.

The three Guards' battalions were standing up to the enemy cavalry, but the English infantry and artillery fire at sixty yards was making their position untenable. Napoleon ordered them to withdraw and galloped to La Belle Alliance with an escort of a few chasseurs. The three battalions, together with the 3rd Grenadiers, withdrew step by step in square formation, then in triangle formation, pushing their way with crossed bayonets through the mixed mass of English troops and cavalry and retreating French soldiers. Above the din, English officers were calling on the Guards to surrender. Cambronne, on horseback inside the 2nd Battalion, 1st Chasseurs, shouted back one single rude word, which is rendered in history books as: '*La Garde meurt et ne se rend pas!*' A few moments later, as he was reaching La Belle Alliance with his battalion, he fell seriously wounded with a bullet in his face.

On the French army's right and rear, Blücher was also making an all out attack, simultaneously with that of Wellington from Mont St Jean. Lobau's infantry and Domon's cavalry were thrown back towards La Belle Alliance by 15,000 Prussians of the Pirch corps (who had also come to reinforce Bülow) and were caught as in the jaws of a vice by the English coming from the opposite direction. At 9 p.m., as night fell, all was chaos and confusion. English dragoons were charged by German hussars, the Adam brigade was fired upon by a Prussian battery, Highlanders were turning French cannon against the retreating columns. And on the plateau the four Guard's battalions were being encircled and destroyed by English and Prussian cavalry and infantry.

Five hundred yards behind, the two battlions of the élite 1st Grenadiers were waiting under the command of General Petit, with Napoleon on horseback inside the first square. Napoleon ordered the 12-inch gun Guard battery to cover the formation's flanks and drums called all the Guards' detachments to rally. Crowds of routed French troops were straggling on the road closely pursued by the enemy. Each of the Guards' cannon had only one charge left. The last one struck and destroyed an enemy cavalry column at close range before another column fell upon the crews and sabred them. But the attacking cavalry squadrons broke on the solid square formations of the Guard, whose sides were further protected by the corpses of the enemy's men and horses.

In Plancenoit, the Young Guard and the 1st Battalions of the 2nd Chasseurs and 2nd Grenadiers were still resisting the combined attack of three Prussian divisions (von Hiller, Ryssel and Tippel-skirch). The French were fighting desperately (one against five) with all they had left: rifle butts, bayonets, knives, sticks and fists. One Young Guard battalion was wiped out in the cemetery redoubt. Hand-to-hand combat was raging in every house, every attic and every room in the village was set ablaze by the Prussian artillery. The French survivors who reached the plateau were slaughtered by English cavalry. General Pelet rallied a few chasseurs around an Imperial Eagle, all determined to save the Emperor's symbol or die. From Plancenoit, French and Prussians poured out on to the Charleroi road near the two grenadier squares which were protecting Napoleon. These two battalions repulsed all the combined attacks of the two enemy armies.

Napoleon finally gave the order to withdraw on Soult's insistence that the Emperor's life, at least, must be saved. Napoleon and Soult rode away at the head of the 1st Battalion with Drouot, Bertrand, Gourgaud and five or six mounted chasseurs while the 2nd Battalion continued to fight constant rearguard actions against the Prussians, who were in hot pursuit. At the farm of Caillou (Napoleon's headquarters that very morning), the 1st Battalion of the Guard's chasseurs joined up with Napoleon's escort, leaving behind the battlefield of Mont St Jean, where some 50,000 combatants (French and Anglo-Dutch–Prussian in about equal numbers) lay dead, together with the wounded and 10,000 dead horses, all intermingled with the frightful debris of this ten-hour savage and heroic Battle of Waterloo of 18 June 1815.[1]

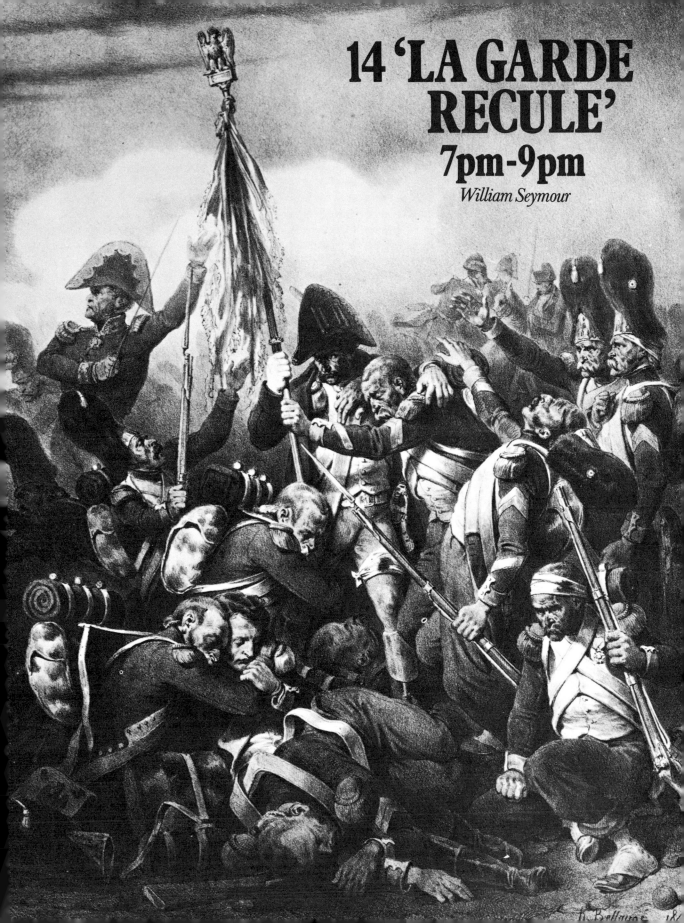

14 'LA GARDE RECULE'

7pm-9pm

William Seymour

Following the repulse of the extremely dangerous attack, after the fall of La Haye Sainte, there was a brief lull in the fighting, similar to that experienced by the allied army just before the great cavalry onslaught. Moreover, the tempo of the cannonading was less furious; gun teams had been diminished, some of the guns had become overheated and were no longer capable of firing, and ammunition stocks were dwindling.

Wellington seized the opportunity to make certain adjustments to lend what strength he could to his battered line. The five Brunswick battalions, which the commander-in-chief had personally brought up during the previous attack, were already in the line, and General Detmer's brigade from Chassé's division was now posted between Halkett's men and Kruse's Nassauers. D'Aubremé's brigade (also from Chassé's division) took the position recently occupied by the Brunswickers, and Vincke's Hanoverians were brought across to the area of the crossroads and placed in reserve on either side. Bolton's field brigade (since his death commanded by Captain Napier) came into position on the ridge half-way between La Haye Sainte and Hougoumont, from where it was to do great execution, and other artillery units were reorganized, guns were repaired where possible, and supplies of ammunition were replenished. Both Vivian's and Vandeleur's cavalry brigades were kept close up in line; Vivian's men had performed a useful service in the last fight by keeping the Brunswickers and Nassauers up to the mark, and they might have to do it again with troops freshly brought into the line whose reliability was suspect.

To meet Napoleon's last great throw Wellington probably had little more than 35,000 men capable of bearing arms; the casualties had been severe, many Dutch–Belgians were off the field, and there was a tendency among men escorting wounded to the rear not to be in too much of a hurry to return. But the flanks were secure – Hougoumont was untaken and Zieten's Prussian I Corps was just entering the field on the left – and although many of the best brigades in the centre, such as Pack's, Kempt's and Lambert's, were woefully reduced in numbers they were still valiant for battle. The front line, in what was to prove the most vital sector – that from the *chaussée* to Hougoumont – was held from east to west by Ompteda's much thinned battalions, Kielmansegge's and Kruse's brigades, the Brunswick battalions, Detmer's Dutch–Belgians, Colin Halkett's British battalions, Maitland's Guards, who were still strong, and Adam's brigade, which was almost completely fresh. There were now twice as many brigades in this sector as there had been in the morning and, in spite of heavy casualties, a greater weight of fire power. The artillery, though sadly thinned, was well placed to bring direct and flanking fire on any attacking column advancing to the east of Hougoumont.

It was a little after 7.30 p.m.; the sun, which had scarcely made an appearance during the afternoon, now peeped furtively through the heavy clouds that overhung Hougoumont, its dying rays glinting on the 5,000 bayonets of the Imperial Guard as they formed up for their last parade. Wellington had ridden to the junction of Maitland's and Adam's brigades, for his instinct told him that this was where the main attack would come – not that there were any indications yet that he would be right. The French artillery had stepped up its firing rate; Reille was preparing one more effort to get the Guards out of Hougoumont; d'Erlon's remnants were reforming once again in the centre; Durutte was keeping an anxious eye on Prince Bernhard's Nassauers and the Prussians, and the Guard was preparing to advance up the line of the *chaussée*. Yet again the seemingly endless supply of tirailleurs stretched a protective screen across the entire front.

It is scarcely surprising, after eight hours of so hard and fearful a battle, that wits should have become dulled and impressions blurred. Subsequently memories were allowed free licence, with the result that we have no really reliable contemporary account of this last phase, nor any two which agree in every detail. Indeed, when it comes to the numbers and composition of the Guard, its formation, line of approach and points of impact, almost every account has something different to say. One instinctively looks to the French for guidance, but in the long grey aftermath of disappointment everything became distorted, and each individual, having studied the possibilities, has now to determine for himself the probabilities.

The Young Guard had been engaged against the Prussians at Plancenoit and some of the Old Guard had been sent to help them, but Napoleon may still have had eleven fresh battalions with him and Wellington, searching the smoke-clouded valley with his telescope, probably saw the Emperor riding at the head of seven of those battalions. High and proud was the bearing of these magnificent troops, marching into battle in their long blue coats and tall red-plumed bearskin caps, rifles at the shoulder with bayonets gleaming. They marched in column on a two-company front, so that each battalion had a frontage of between sixty and seventy men and was at least nine ranks deep. Between each battalion came two field guns. When they reached the cutting in the road south of La Haye Sainte the Emperor handed them over to Marshal Ney, and they continued their march as though to strike the allied line somewhere close to the crossroads. But the head of the column had not long passed Napoleon when Wellington saw them swing to their left away from the *chaussée*.

Why Ney did this is not completely clear. One theory is that d'Erlon's troops were immediately to his front on his former axis, another that the road was too cluttered with debris, yet another that when the column broke formation the thick smoke and undulating ground would offer some protection. In fact the very reverse was the case, for marching through the churned up ground over heaped-up corpses he was to give the allied artillery a perfect target. The exact extent of that target has been argued over the years; if seven battalions went forward there would have been about 4,500 men on the march,[1] but if two were left in reserve on the intermediate ridge then the five attacking battalions – the number favoured by most authorities – could scarcely have contained more than 3,000 bayonets. Whatever the number of battalions there is no doubt that the column split shortly after leaving the *chaussée*, and advanced by battalions in echelon from the right; but instead of delivering their attack at five different points along the allied front they lost direction in the smoke and general confusion, and when they started to ascend the ridge they had come together in two columns and so offered Wellington's gunners exactly what they wanted.

Although many of the batteries were by now useless – muzzles bent, gunners dead, or ammunition exhausted – Lloyd's and Napier's teams still had plenty of life in them, and Chassé had wisely ordered van der Smissen's Dutch–Belgian battery to gallop forward and take up post on the right of Lloyd. This meant that as the leading column marched in the direction of Maitland's brigade there were quite a few guns capable of pouring shot into their exposed flank, and when these could no longer shoot first the tirailleurs and then the Guard presented an easy target for the frontal fire of Napier's battery. The effects of this canister, grape and shot hurtling into their densely packed ranks were very similar to those suffered by the cavalry earlier in the day; men went down like swathes of corn before the reaper. Ney had his fifth horse shot under him; the commander of the chasseurs, General Michel, was killed, and General Friant of the grenadiers fell wounded. But nothing daunted, and led by the gallant Ney, now on foot, the veterans of many battles came steadily on; for once more – so they thought – victory was at hand. Beyond the guns there was nothing, clearly their enemy had not waited to be assailed by the finest troops in the world; but the setting sun was casting a shadow of death across the ranks of these splendid warriors.

The storm of shot that ravaged the column did not deter those that survived, but it caused the battalions to lose distance and station, and one from the larger column seems to have dropped back a little and perhaps veered slightly to its left. The honour of being first to receive the attention of the Imperial Guard fell to Maitland's 1st Guards Brigade, whose soldiers, as a reward for their performance, were shortly to be given the title of Grenadier Guards – although it is more likely that their first assailants were not grenadiers but men from the 3rd Chasseurs of the Guard. Wellington had ordered the allied infantry to lie down behind the crest in four ranks, so the waiting men could see nothing; but the *rummadum, dummadum, dum* of the drummers beating the *pas de charge*, and the vibration of the earth from thousands of tramping feet, indicated plainly that the clash was imminent and that it would be savage. But for the French there was no such warning of impending doom; as they neared the top of the ridge all they could see was the occasional horseman, one of whom was the Duke of Wellington.

When the leading files were less than fifty yards from the country road – just a little to the west of where the Lion Hill now stands – the silence behind the ridge was broken by the commander-in-chief's 'Now, Maitland, now's your time!', and then, carried away by the excitement of the moment, he gave direct orders to the men, 'Stand up Guards!' Upon which Maitland's men rose from the ground in time for the next order, 'Make ready! Fire!', and some 600 muskets were discharged at the astounded and thoroughly unprepared French.

In the words of a 1st Guards survivor, 'We formed a line four deep, the first rank kneeling, the second also firing, the third and fourth loading and handling on to the front, and kept up such a continuous fire into the mass of heaped up Grenadiers . . . and this was the bouquet to all slaughter!' It certainly was, for some 300 Frenchmen, Grenadiers of the Middle Guard fell in the course of a minute.

Two battalions of Halkett's brigade, from the 69th and 33rd Regiments, which were on Maitland's immediate left, moved round to give him support with flanking fire, but at the same time the second column of the Guard attacked the left-hand battalions of this brigade, and for a while the situation here was confused and critical. It seems that the French at first gave way, probably owing to a blast of cannon fire from van der Smissen's guns, but that, quickly rallying and bringing their own light pieces into action, they then drove back the 2nd Battalions of the 30th and 73rd Regiments. The Brunswickers and Nassauers also gave ground, but were stopped by Vivian's cavalry, and Vandeleur performed a similar action when d'Aubremé's men in reserve panicked even before they were attacked. However, Detmer's Dutch–Belgians fought with much gallantry, and Chassé personally led up the guns of his horse artillery troops to fire into the flank of the attackers. Meanwhile, General Colin Halkett, displaying a high degree of courage and leadership, had steadied his two faltering battalions before having to retire because of a wound in the mouth; the Duke, seeing the dangerous situation, rode over to this point and once more brought the German troops back to their duty. A second attack in this sector of the line by the Guard, supported by some of d'Erlon's troops, was repulsed; and the French, leaving half their number dead among the blood-stained corn stalks, retired down the slope towards La Haye Sainte.

While Halkett's men were fighting so desperately, Maitland's Guards and Detmer's brigade cleared the enemy to their front from the crest, and Maitland's men pursued them down the slope. There now came another moment of crisis – Harry Smith, General Lambert's brigade-major, said of Waterloo that 'every moment was a crisis'[2] – when a fresh battalion of the Guard, coming up slightly to the left and deterred neither by the fire of the allied guns from near the Nivelles road nor by the disarray of their comrades, swung round into Maitland's flank. In the noise and confusion that followed, the call to retire was imperfectly understood, and the nearby presence of a squadron of cuirassiers (who had been ordered to charge the guns) caused at least one battalion to form square; but while the 23rd Dragoons took care of the cuirassiers the British Guards regained the crest, and being quickly formed into line again made ready to withstand this new attack by a fresh – probably grenadier – battalion of the Guard, and the battalions of chasseurs that had been rallied.

But now the splendid spirit and élan that had carried these superb French troops forward in pursuit of victory was to be eroded in adversity. It will be remembered that Adam's brigade was stationed immediately on the right of Maitland's, and Colonel Colborne's 52nd Regiment of Foot was the right battalion of the brigade, with two skirmishing companies of the 3rd Battalion of the 95th protecting its flank against the cuirassiers. Showing splendid initiative, and anticipating his commander-in-chief's orders, Colborne advanced his regiment in line four deep, and pivoting his men on the left files wheeled them into line opposite the flank of the advancing Guard – 'to make that column feel our fire', as he explained to his brigade commander. The movement was carried out with unhurried drill-book precision, and as soon as Adam appreciated its purpose he ordered the 71st and 95th to comply; but by then the 52nd had halted and the two front ranks had poured a withering volley into the flank of the Imperial Guard, with the two rear ranks passing through to fire in their turn.

The sudden appearance of fresh troops emerging through the smoke on its flank took the Guard by surprise, but, quickly recovering, the left-hand files faced outwards and returned the fire with devastating results, for 150 of Colborne's men fell. But it was to be the Guard's final throw; by now the 71st and 95th had come up, Maitland's reorganized battalions were slamming in frontal fire, and Hew Halkett's 3rd Hanoverian Brigade was emerging from the direction of Hougoumont's Hollow Way to take the chasseurs and grenadiers in rear.

Colborne saw his opportunity; as the Guard staggered under these repeated blows he checked his men's firing, and calling out to them 'Charge! Charge!' led them forward, closely supported by the other two regiments. The steadiest of troops could not prevail against this whirlwind attack; men whom no previous perils had daunted now turned and fled. The terrible and unheard-of cry went up, 'La Garde recule!', Adam's brigade swept diagonally across the field. In the smoky darkness there was an unfortunate incident involving Dornberg's 23rd Light Dragoons when friend fired upon friend, but there was no time for explanation; Wellington was close at hand with his 'Go on, Colborne, go on', and as the Duke rode back towards the centre of his line Adam's men were heading for La Haye Sainte.

It was a little after 8 p.m. when Wellington, sensing that the repulse of the Guard had had a fearful effect throughout the whole of the French army, judged it the moment to give the signal for the general advance. Nor was he to be deflected by those of his few remaining staff who advised caution, and only a limited advance; 'Oh, damn it! In for a penny, in for a pound,' he exclaimed. Then, in one of the great gestures of history, he raised his hat and waved it three times towards the French. Those who could see him let out a mighty cheer, for the long hours of patient endurance were over; others further to the west saw him riding towards them and urging them for-

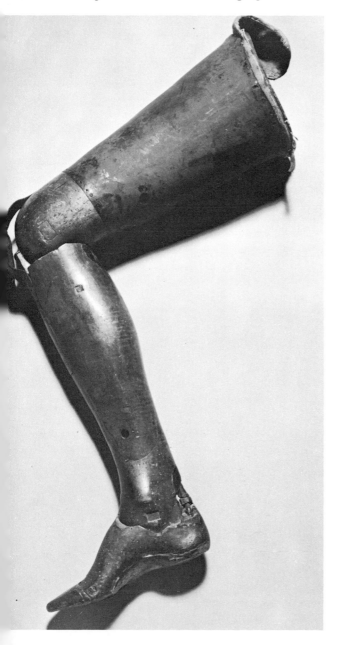

ward. Soon, in a moment of immortal glory, every man in the allied line capable of moving was advancing down the slope in pursuit of a broken enemy.

But before this triumphant advance had got properly under way, the forward-pressing troops on the right were already in conflict with the last pockets of resistance. Vivian's cavalry, riding through the smoke, suddenly found themselves confronted by two battalions of the Old Guard drawn up in square on the intermediate ridge. These troops had been left in reserve for just such a contingency as this,[3] and although somewhat demoralized by the failure of their comrades they knew that their duty was to stand firm and cover their Emperor's retreat. The Duke sent word that Vivian was not to attack unless he could break the squares, but turning to the messenger, Sir Colin Campbell, Vivian pointed out the need to drive the supporting cavalry off to enable the infantry to deal with the squares. Sir Colin agreed, so Vivian placed himself at the head of the 18th Hussars and shouted, 'Eighteenth, you will follow me,' to which Sergeant-Major Jeffs replied, 'Ay, General, anywhere you choose to lead us.' Straight into Kellermann's cuirassiers they then rode, scattering the cavalry and allowing Adam's and Hew Halkett's brigades to press the French Guardsmen back, step by step, in a fiercely contested rearguard fight. Then, as Vivian and Vandeleur swept the field with their hussars and dragoons, Adam's men pushed on towards La Belle Alliance, where Colborne's 52nd overran a battery, and Halkett's Hanoverians broke up the square formed by General Cambronne's 1st Regiment of Chasseurs, in which Napoleon had previously been sheltering, and made the General prisoner.

While these stubborn mopping-up operations were in progress the whole allied line came tumbling down the slope, sweeping through and past La Haye Sainte, driving the French before them. Now the proud Eagles of France, which had been carried forward with such devotion, hastened from the field amid a shattered and scattered army. Wellington and Uxbridge rode between the pockets of British and French troops, urging their victorious soldiers not to let the enemy stand, when a shot skimmed over Copenhagen's neck and struck Lord Uxbridge in the knee. 'By God! I've lost my leg,' he exclaimed. 'Have you, by God!' replied the Duke, as he hastily dismounted to assist his courageous cavalry commander. But the cavalry, now under the command of Vandeleur, rode on without their chief.

It seems possible that when the British troops had been withdrawn from the left of the line after Ney's last attack, the Duke put General von Müffling in command there. This able and tactful commander was instrumental in bringing the Prussians into line, although in the heat and excitement of victory there were to be unfortunate mistakes as the two armies came together. Prince Bernhard's Nassauers had fought with more determination and courage than any of the Dutch–Belgian troops, with the possible exception of Detmer's brigade, and it is sad that now, at the moment of total victory, they should have had to withstand a Prussian attack from the north-east. Before the mistake was corrected they had been driven back up the hill with casualties, and they were not able to play much part thereafter. Even more serious, although on a lesser scale, was the spirited exchange of fire in the murk between Mercer's troop and a Prussian battery. It must have been bad enough for Mercer, whose men had been fired on first, to suffer severe casualties, but unbearable when 'a tall man in the black Brunswick uniform came galloping up exclaiming ... "De Inglish kills dere friends de Proosiens! Vere is de Dook von Wellington? Oh, mine Gott! – mine Gott! vill you not stop sare?" '

But Zieten's corps was soon to make amends for these mishaps, and if his artillery did more harm to friend than foe that part of his infantry (probably no more than 5,000 men) now upon the field fought valiantly against Durutte's division, while Blücher and Bülow drove the French for the last time from Plancenoit. Soon their troops were mingling with British regiments on the *chaussée* near to La Belle Alliance; bands struck up 'God Save the King' and '*Nun danket Alle Gott*'. All around them was the smoke and carnage of the battlefield; the thudding of the guns had almost ceased; before them was a disorganized and demoralized army, now bent on *sauve qui peut*. Victory was complete, but it had been one of the toughest, cruellest and most destructive battles that had yet been fought.

It was about 9 p.m. when the two great commanders, Wellington and Blücher, met between La Belle Alliance and Rossomme. Both were on horseback, but leaning forward in the saddle the old Prussian warrior embraced his distinguished ally. Overcome with emotion he stammered out, '*Mein lieber Kamerad*', followed by '*Quelle affaire!*' – which Wellington always said was just about the only French Blücher knew.

The Prussians undertook the pursuit. What remained of the allied army mostly bivouacked on

79 Copenhagen, the Duke of Wellington's chestnut charger, which carried him at Victoria, the battles of the Pyrenees and Toulouse, and at the battle of Waterloo

the position occupied that morning by the French – though some regiments were too tired or too depleted to have come forward, and the Guards lay that night in a field behind the smoking ruins of the château they had so stubbornly defended.

The moon had risen by the time the Duke rode back to Waterloo and threw long, gruesome shadows across his path, lighting up the faces of the wounded, already pale with shock. Tears coursed down his cheeks. It had been a fearful battle; more than 40,000 men lay dead or wounded upon the field, of which nearly 15,000 were from his own army. Dismounting from Copenhagen, who had carried him unflinchingly throughout the long day, Wellington gave him a friendly pat on the quarters; the compliment was so unexpected that the great-hearted horse lashed out and broke loose. Entering the inn, the Duke went straight to see his dying friend and aide-de-camp, Colonel Alexander Gordon. Later that night Doctor Hume presented him with the tragically long casualty list. Deeply moved, he exclaimed, 'Well, thank God I don't know what it is to lose a battle. But nothing can be so painful than to gain one with the loss of so many friends.' Then he lay down and slept. Three miles away on the battlefield the ghouls were about their grisly business of ravishing the dead and killing the wounded.

15 THE PRUSSIAN VICTORY
7pm to early morning 19 June

Colonel E. Kaulbach

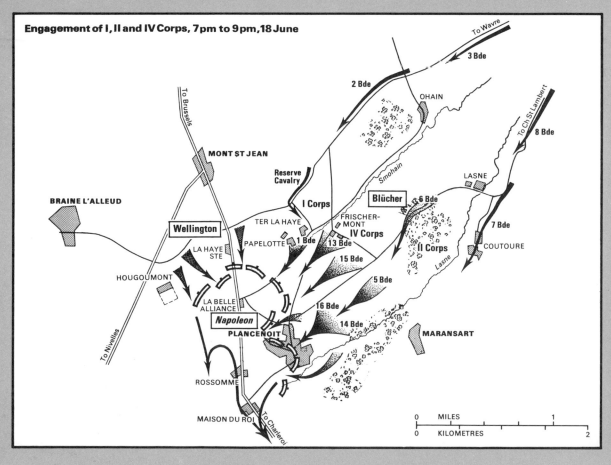

Engagement of I, II and IV Corps, 7pm to 9pm, 18 June

To Wavre

3 Bde

2 Bde

OHAIN

To Brussels

To Ch St Lambert

8 Bde

MONT ST JEAN

Reserve Cavalry

Smohain

LASNE

BRAINE L'ALLEUD

I Corps

Blücher

6 Bde

FRISCHER-MONT

Wellington

TER LA HAYE

IV Corps

7 Bde

PAPELOTTE

1 Bde

13 Bde

II Corps

COUTOURE

LA HAYE STE

15 Bde

Lasne

HOUGOUMONT

5 Bde

LA BELLE ALLIANCE

16 Bde

Napoleon

14 Bde

MARANSART

PLANCENOIT

To Nivelles

ROSSOMME

MAISON DU ROI

To Charleroi

0	MILES	1
0	KILOMETRES	2

The situation in which the armies found themselves at seven that evening was singular; all three armies had suffered reverses and all three had at some point enjoyed the hope that victory was still possible. Napoleon's attacks on Wellington's position during the past six hours had been unsuccessful but had resulted in heavy casualties for both attacker and defender; Wellington's line had withstood the attacks but had become very thin; Blücher's Prussians had been thrown out of Plancenoit for the second time; the breakthrough into the French rear had not yet succeeded. Hooper describes the situation as follows:

Blücher was not shaken by his reverses, the corps of Pirch I was now visible near the wood of Paris, and he prepared to renew the combat, to fight his way into the rear of the French. Napoleon, seeing the Prussians recoil before the onset of the Old Guard, thought that Bülow had exhausted his strength and that he still had the time and the means at his disposal wherewith to crush Wellington. Napoleon relied on his last reserve, 5,000 men of the Imperial Guard; Blücher relied more surely upon the corps of Pirch and the corps of Zieten – the latter now near Ohain; Wellington relied upon the promise of Blücher; but more upon the remains of the undaunted British and German infantry and horse, which had resisted so many charges, which had borne, without flinching, so murderous a fire.[1]

The height of the battle had been passed, and for Napoleon the prolonged struggle had been virtually ineffective; that which followed was the great, the final, dénouement, in which the chances – unknown to the participants – were already weighted against the attacker. Napoleon himself now had to do what in previous battles he had often forced upon his opponents – he had to commit his last reserves and then to make a stand without them while the enemy still had his own reserves at his back.[2] 'Napoleon,' comments von Ollech, 'was already beaten; the only question that remained was whether the victory over the French army could be turned into a total defeat.'[3]

While Napoleon, under the impression that his right flank was secure against the Prussians, brought up his last reserves, nine to ten battalions of the Guard, for a final attack, what the Prussian attackers had been aiming for at length came to pass; the reuniting on the battlefield of the army corps which had been approaching from different directions. The leading brigade of I Corps was to operate with the right wing of the Prussian IV Corps at Frischermont, as it arrived at the left wing of the English front; the leading 5th Brigade of II Corps joined up with the 16th and 14th Brigades on the left wing of IV Corps for a new

attack on Plancenoit. Blücher's army could finally move from the bloody and thankless task of holding down large numbers of the enemy – which is what IV Corps had been doing – to that active and decisive participation in the battle which he had prepared. In his impatience, the Field-Marshal had earlier sent his adjutant, Count Nostitz, to General von Zieten urging him to hasten his advance and attack;[4] later General von Grolmann also was sent up to spur on the Prussian right wing in their advance towards Belle Alliance.[5]

As the advance units of the 1st Brigade of I Corps reached the left wing of the English line, the attacking columns of the French Guard were moving up between La Haye Sainte and Hougoumont against the English centre; moving with them were also the divisions of the French right wing. The leading units of Durutte's division had taken Papelotte and La Haye. The unexpected arrival of new enemy forces on their right wing had a devastating effect upon the French. The Prussian advance battalion and the allocated infantry companies moved on Papelotte, which they captured. 24th Regiment under Colonel von Hofmann, which was following, was directed by General von Zieten on to La Haye; after capturing this village, the regiment continued to advance through the valley of the Smohain brook and along the ridge leading to Plancenoit. The batteries of the 1st Brigade had been placed in such a position on the heights to the north of Smohain and La Haye that they could fire on both the right wing of d'Erlon's corps and the left wing of the Lobau's corps.

This attack by the Prussians right wing took place at about the same time as the attack, the faltering and the retreat of the French Guards.[6] It caused a considerable shock to the French front *on the west* of the Brussels road, and in addition there now came the push against the salient right wing by the Prussian 1st Brigade, to which the battalions of the 15th and 13th Brigades of IV Corps had been attached.[7] While the British brigade under Adam followed up and pushed the French Guards back on to the Brussels road, the Prussian right wing attacked Durutte's and Lobau's troops in the direction of Belle Alliance and Plancenoit; the initial resistance of the French began to slacken, and gradually crumbled into a rout.

There have been conflicting interpretations of this attack by the Prussian I Corps and of the part it played in the defeat and collapse of Napoleon's

army. Charras gives an impressive account of the dismay caused among the French troops by the unexpected appearance of a new enemy – especially as they were, at first, believed to be Grouchy's men.

It is nearly eight o'clock. An enormous danger has just appeared at the right angle of the French front formed at Papelotte by their Goumont and Plancenoit lines. Marcognet, who was occupying the top of the plateau, and Durutte, who was contending with Prince Bernhard for La Haye, have just been suddenly attacked by two strong infantry columns advancing on the farm. Like the troops under them, they first took these to be Grouchy's columns, as they had been firing at Prince Bernhard's battalions, breaking them up and scattering them; but their error was short-lived. They now retreat from the new enemy; Durutte abandons Papelotte, and Marcognet goes back down the slope. Lobau is in danger of being cut off in the rear, a yawning gap is about to open up in the French lines. Cries of alarm ring out; confusion reigns in the divisions of Durutte and Marcognet; hundreds of soldiers break their lines and make their way, distracted, to Belle Alliance; thirty-two pieces of ordnance, ranged on the summit of the plateau, pound the battalions as they retreat across the valley; . . .[8]

Houssaye takes a very definite line on the question of the defeat, that is to say on the individual withdrawal and flight of specific parts of the French army:

Müffling and the German historians claim that it was Zieten's intervention which precipitated the rout. Captain Pringle and the English historians, on the other hand, maintain that it was Wellington's general attack. Since these two manoeuvres took place more or less at the same time, the argument could be endless. There were, however, three quite distinct movements in the retreat of the French army, of which the first and the third were due solely to the English. To begin with, the repulse of the central Guards entailed the sagging of more than two-thirds of the French line. Secondly, the Prussian break-through caused panic and disorder on the right (d'Erlon's corps). Finally, Wellington's advance precipitated the rout of the left (Reille's corps and what remained of the cavalry) . . .[9]

It is certainly essential to recognize the dramatic effect produced by the unexpected entry of the Prussian I Corps – that is to say Blücher's right wing – not only locally, but on the whole sequence of events, as Houssaye points out. Only then can we understand the importance of the co-operation of the two allied armies. In the larger, 'operational', framework, the mere approach of the Prussian army and the commitment of the leading IV Corps had a prompt influence on the enemy leadership, and by tying down the reserves, enabled a successful defensive battle on the English front to be maintained to the end and then made possible the change-over to a counter-attack. To this must be added the 'tactical' co-operation of the troops on the battlefield itself; this succeeded so well in the final phases of the battle that the enemy was not simply defeated, by being driven back, but was forced into flight and total collapse. This was no matter of casual coincidence, but of excellent co-operation. Again, one can agree with Houssaye's comment on the advance of the English line and the Prussian attackers: 'If Wellington, *at eight o'clock*, had stayed in his positions, Zieten's Prussians would in all likelihood have been contained. Likewise, if Zieten had not attacked, the Emperor would have been able to withstand the English at La Haye Sainte and on the road to Brussels as well as on the slopes of Belle Alliance.'[10]

Having overcome the French resistance, the pursuing Prussian infantry and cavalry, constantly held up by the flood of troops in flight, brought about a breakdown in enemy discipline and a rout of the French on the east side of the road.[11] English and Prussian units met on the Brussels road close to Belle Alliance.[12]

The final phase of the battle also reached a climax on the left wing of the Prussian army, at Plancenoit. The 16th and 14th Brigades of IV Corps had already suffered heavy casualties in the struggle for this village.[13] However, the situation allowed of no pause; the attack by the French Guards and the simultaneous advance, yet again, of the rest of the French army made plain what was at stake. Accordingly the Prussians did not wait for the arrival of all the brigades of II Corps. Tippelskirch's 5th Brigade on arrival took up the leading role in the new attack, while the weakened units of the 16th and 14th Brigades were used as support. The two leading batteries with the 5th Brigade co-operated with the artillery of IV Corps in the fight for Plancenoit.

The village of Plancenoit was jammed with French troops. Eleven battalions of the Guards, that is half the Corps of Guards, the large battle reserve of Napoleon, as well as parts of Lobau's corps were concentrated in this one village. These were the best troops of the Emperor's army, proud and determined to hold this key place. Plancenoit had become a corner stone, and had been well organized by its defenders. It was therefore obvious that this last attack was not going to be a rapid coup but rather a breaking down of stubborn resistance – and this could take a long time. Once again the village was attacked from several sides and encircled. The main attack on the church, which was a veritable fortress, was carried out by the battalions of the 1st Pomeranian Line Regiment; on the right was the 5th West-phalian Militia Regiment, while the 25th Line Regiment, formed from the former Lützow Free Corps, attacked the village from the south and encircled it.[14] House by house, farm by farm, the village had to be captured; the defenders had to be killed where they stood. Charras writes:

In the whole of Plancenoit and by the stream, eighteen Prussian battalions are now fighting the eleven battalions under Duhesme and Morand, and are throwing them back. They have just taken the church and the church-yard despite ferocious resistance, and they are continually moving forward. The fight rages on in gardens, orchards, streets and houses; they shoot and slaughter one another with a fury reminiscent of Ligny.[15]

The fighting lasted nearly one and a half hours, until the village was completely in the hands of the Prussians. The heroic resistance of the French, who fell where they stood like true Guards, meant that the mass of the French army, under pressure from Wellington's front and from the Prussian right wing, was able to escape by the road; it also meant that Napoleon, who had spent some time in one of the iron squares of the grenadiers near Rossomme, was able to escape capture.

It was getting dark by the time the fight for Plancenoit was over; the French and Prussians pressed on towards the road, to Maison du Roi.

The village once captured, [writes Charras], Lobau, Duhesme and Morand saw their battalions, frontally attacked, by-passed and encircled as they were, collapse

and seek safety in flight. . . . In the entire French army there was now not a single battalion or squadron left intact. The rout was complete and total. Napoleon had lost the most decisive battle of our time. The victory had been achieved by Wellington's unshakeable tenacity, Blücher's daring energy, and the military skill and collaboration of both men.[16]

Field-Marshal Blücher had reached the Brussels road with the leading troops of IV Corps. Here, between Belle Alliance and Rossomme, Wellington and Blücher met, greeted and congratulated each other.[17] In view of the exhaustion of the allied army, Blücher declared himself ready to take over the pursuit of the enemy with his troops during the night. He decided to 'allow no breathing time to the flying enemy and to deprive him of all power of rallying, at least on this side of the French frontier'.[18]

This decision by the old Field-Marshal, who by this time must have been close to the end of his strength, requires some explanation. Wellington's army, after nearly ten hours of incredible fighting, was certainly as Wellington said, *'fatigué à en mourir'*.[19] But this was no less true of the Prussian troops; contrary to what is often said, they were no fresher than Wellington's army. 'The Prussians had covered an average of five leagues by the worst paths and their fighting between Frischer-mont and Plancenoit was as ferocious as that of Wellington's soldiers at Mont St Jean' – that is

how Houssaye sees it.[20] In addition, the Prussian soldiers had been marching and fighting since 15 June without sufficient rest, unable to attend to their many wounded, and lacking adequate food. Baggage and supply trains had been sent away from the battlefield on the morning of the 18th in the direction of Louvain, and they were therefore without supplies. It certainly required the iron will of Blücher to commit these exhausted soldiers to a night pursuit. And there must have been some over-riding reasons for his decision. Firstly, there was the lesson gained from the previous year's fighting that one must never give Napoleon time to collect his scattered forces and organize them for a fresh attack. Furthermore, Blücher knew that, after Napoleon's collapse, the allied forces would have to advance on Paris at once, if renewed battles and endless political complications, of which they had experience enough in 1813 and 1814, were not to follow.

The Field-Marshal summoned the officers of the nearest troops and ordered them to take up the chase to the last gasp of man and horse in order 'to complete the victory they had wrung from the enemy by an annihilating pursuit'.[21] The wide dispersal of the Prussian army made it impossible to start off with all the troops; the bulk of I Corps remained on the battlefield; II Corps collected, to begin with, in the area around Maransart. But IV Corps, together with the 5th Brigade of II Corps and the cavalry of I Corps, immediately began to move off along the Brussels road in the direction of Genappe. Gneisenau had now taken command, and it was his energy that turned Blücher's wishes into action. The lead was taken by the two fusilier battalions of the 16th and 5th Brigades, who were the first to reach the road from Plancenoit and who, with a few squadrons, began the pursuit. They moved forward in bright moonlight.[22] Wherever the trumpets and drums of the Prussians sounded the enemy fled, frightened out of every new bivouac. Even in Genappe a few rounds from a Prussian battery were enough to quell any resistance. In the early hours of the morning the area of Frasnes was reached, and Gneisenau called a halt. The infantry could go no further. 'The troops were utterly exhausted and needed a few hours' rest,' writes Charras. 'Their exhaustion was the saving of the lives of many of our men.'[23] In the 'Zum Kaiser' inn, where Gneisenau stopped, he probably formulated his first thoughts about the continuing pursuit to Paris; in Gosselies, where he waited for Blücher, the first plans for this were made.[24] Blücher had remained in Genappe, and it was from here that the first reports of the victory were sent. To General von Knesebeck, military adviser to the King of Prussia, he wrote:

My friend! The finest of battles has been fought, and the most glorious victory has been won. Details will follow. I believe the Buonaparte affair is as good as over.

The 19th, early morning. I cannot write further; I am trembling in every limb. The strain has been too great. Blücher.[25]

16 THE AFTERMATH

Jacques Champagne

At 11 p.m. (18 June), Napoleon, with his depleted staff and Guard's battalions, reached Genappe, where he was hoping to rally some of his retreating troops. But the disorder was appalling and all his efforts were in vain. The Prussians were relentless in their pursuit. Bent on destroying the French army in full retreat, they gave no quarter, took no prisoners. The men belonging to the corps of Lobau and d'Erlon, to the divisions of Domon, Subervie and Jacquinot, and to the Young Guard were sabred, bayoneted or shot mercilessly. French cavalrymen shot their horses and then committed suicide rather than fall into Prussian hands. Five to six thousand men of Reille's corps marching on Genappe were killed or dispersed by constant Prussian attacks.

Finding it impossible to organize a defence, Napoleon rested his hopes on the Girard division (the 3rd of II Corps) which he had left on the battlefield at Ligny and to which he had sent orders to march on Quatre-Bras so as to back up the retreat. Napoleon left for Quatre-Bras on horseback, entrusting to Duhesme and a handful of soldiers the defence of Genappe, which was soon captured by the Prussians. They seized the Emperor's personal carriage containing a change of clothes, a toilet case, a sword and a folding iron camp bed, as well as diamonds worth 1 million francs.[1] Duhesme was wounded as he was about to be taken prisoner. Blücher visited him and recommended him to his personal surgeon, but this brave French general died of his wounds the next day.

Napoleon arrived at Quatre-Bras at 1 a.m. on 19 June. He expedited an officer to tell Grouchy that the battle had been lost at Mont St Jean and to order him to retreat on Namur. Until that moment, Napoleon had kept his composure, standing up in a frozen attitude, his arms crossed on his chest, looking intently in the direction of Mont St Jean during his rare moments of solitude. But that night, as he was having a light meal in the woods in front of a brazier, silent tears ran down his face. Of Girard's division there was no sign. General Nègre was at Quatre-Bras in charge of an artillery reserve depot with a small escort. A few hundred horses were rallied and, with them, Lobau organized a rearguard. The remnants of I and II Corps were retreating on the Marchiennes bridge, the Guard and VI Corps towards Charleroi. Napoleon sent Prince Jérôme to Marchiennes to rally the army between Avesnes and Maubeuge.

Napoleon went to Charleroi, arriving at 6 a.m. He stopped for an hour on the left bank of the Sambre to send out more orders, then rode to Philippeville (where he arrived at 9 a.m.) so as to be able to communicate more easily with Grouchy. He stayed there for four hours then went by carriage to Laon, arriving at 7 p.m. on 20 June. Ney, who had been dragged away from the battlefield at Mont St Jean by a corporal, joined him there.[2] Napoleon placed one of his own aides-de-camp, Count de Bussy, in charge of defending the town, sent Count Dejean to Guise and Flahaut (his main English interpreter), to Avesnes.

Dispatches from Prince Jérôme reported that he had rallied more than 25,000 men and about fifty cannon behind Avesnes; that Morand was now commanding the Foot Guard and Colbert the Guard cavalry; and that most of the generals had now arrived with more than half their artillery: 170 guns had been lost, but men and horses had arrived at Avesnes. Soult was ordered by Napoleon to set up General Headquarters in Laon, point of reunion of the army. Grouchy was ordered to rally there from Namur and Prince Jérôme from Avesnes.

The Prussians, exhausted by their pursuit, had stopped at Frasnes. The army's rout had been stemmed, and the French forces were getting organized again.

Paris was only twelve hours away from Laon and Napoleon decided to return to the capital, where he arrived on 21 June. He planned to use the next few days to organize the defence of Paris and to alert Lyon and the provinces, and then to return to the army in Laon on the 23rd or 24th. He was hoping that by this time Grouchy would have rallied there with his army corps, while the provincial forts and strongholds, which he had left well equipped and well manned, particularly in Flanders, would put up a good resistance to the advancing enemy.

Grouchy did arrive in Laon on 26 June with some 32,000 men, of whom 6,500 were cavalry, and 108 cannon, after a most remarkable retreat. He had finally reached Wavre on 18 June, attacked the rearguard of Zieten's corps as it was on its way to join Bülow and Pirch at St Lambert, attacked and beaten Thielemann's corps at Wavre and taken the town on the 19th. It was there that he received from Napoleon news of the loss of the battle at Mont St Jean, and his orders to rally first to Namur, then to Laon. When he read Napoleon's dispatch, Grouchy cried. He summoned his general staff and, in front of Vandamme and Gérard, made a point of explaining once again, but this time in a most apologetic way, the fateful decisions he had taken while the Battle of Mont St Jean was actually in progress.

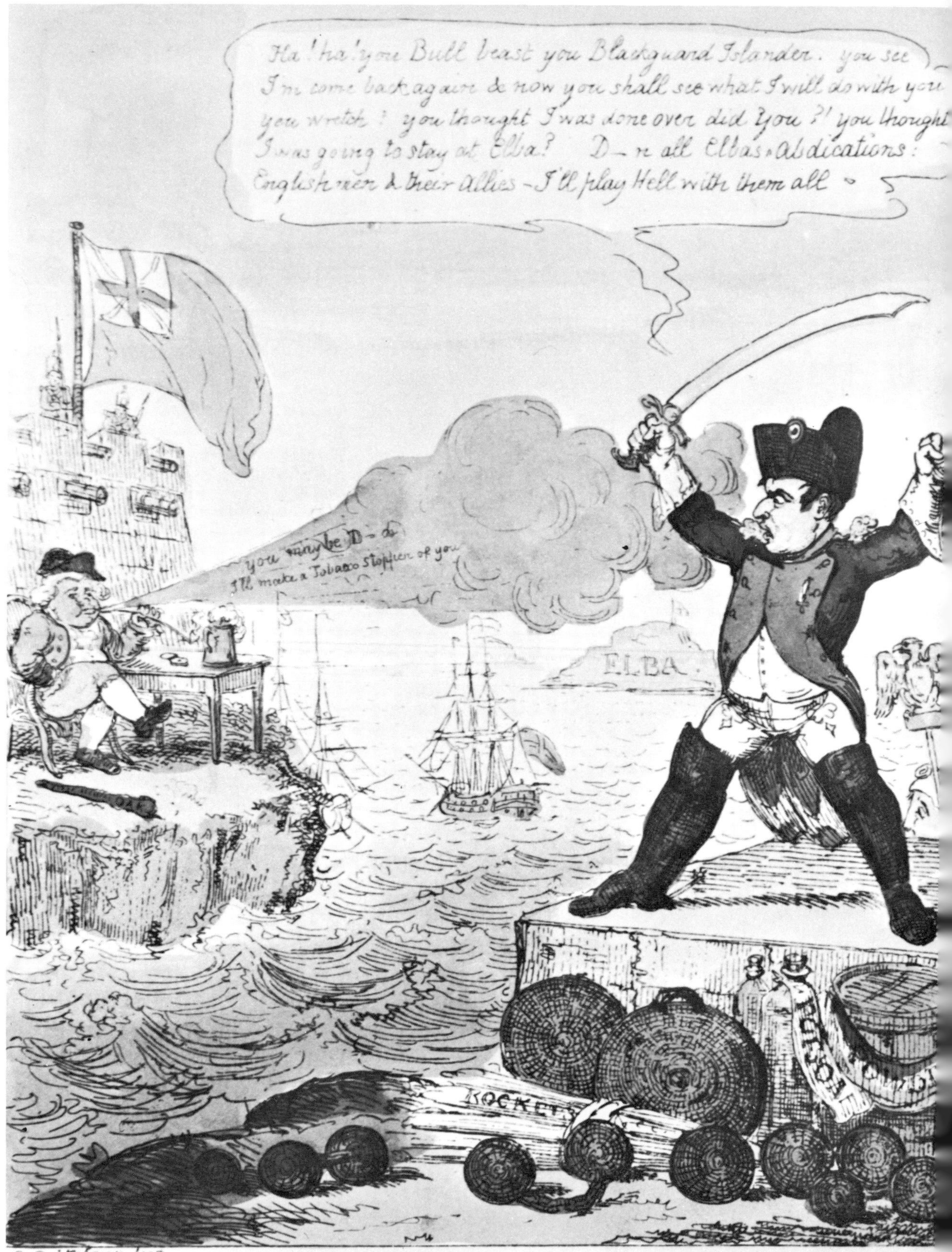

Buonaparte on the 17th of JUNE

84 Two views of Napoleon; defiant and, a month later, defeated. From a cartoon by George Cruikshank

85 Napoleon's coach, in which the Prussians found, among other things, a million dollars in diamonds and a cake of Windsor soap. It was later destroyed by a fire at Madame Tussauds in London in 1925

He then set out to rejoin the army, repulsing successfully all along the way every single enemy attack and displaying extraordinary strategic and tactical talents which, had he applied them on 17 and 18 June, would undoubtedly have turned the tables on the enemy at Mont St Jean and given victory to Napoleon. It must be said that, from the moment Grouchy more or less admitted his mistakes, he got the fullest co-operation from Vandamme and Gérard in executing his retreat to Laon, where he arrived with his forces almost intact.

But on 22 June Napoleon had abdicated at the Elysées Palace in Paris 'in favour of Napoleon II'. He left Paris on the 24th and King Louis XVIII returned to France on the 25th.

France was being invaded by the allied armies. On 21 June Blücher and Wellington crossed the frontiers. On the 22nd Avesnes surrendered, its main powder depot being blown up. On the 24th the Prussians were in Guise and the English in Cambrai, then both at Péronne on the 26th. All the Flanders forts were taken or surrendered.

Then, learning of the revolt of the Chambers (Representatives and Peers) in Paris, and of Napoleon's abdication, Blücher and Wellington marched on Paris, where they arrived in the last days of June 1815, with less than 90,000 men.

It was the end of the French army, of the French Empire and of the Emperor. Napoleon left France for Britain on 16 July. He was not allowed to land, and on 7 August 1815 he sailed for St Helena under strong English guard, protesting that 'England feigned to extend a hospitable hand to her enemy and, when she delivered himself to her in good faith, she immolated him'.[3]

H.M.S. *Northumberland* landed at St Helena on 15 October. As the faithful La Bédoyère had predicted, Napoleon was 'chained to a rock where, like Prometheus, his greatness would gnaw at him'.

On 5 May 1821 Napoleon died at Longwood. It was twenty years before his ashes were brought back to France and laid to rest in Paris at the Invalides, on 15 December 1840.

17

CONCLUSION

Colonel E. Kaulbach

So much has been written on the battle which has become world-famous as the 'Battle of Waterloo', so many detailed accounts of it have been published, that there seems no point in trying to extract anything new from the facts. It is the length of time that has elapsed between the student of today and the object of his study which justifies a further look, without national or personal bias, at the events of 1815 in their mutual relation to one another and their historic consequences.

Moreover, such a study contributes to a higher estimate of the great battle than was at one time thought to be justified. Looked at from the distance of a century and a half, the effects of the military conflict can clearly be seen to extend far beyond the battlefield, into the realms of politics. The collapse of Napoleon's supremacy and his immediate abdication following upon this battle, or partly caused by it, had instantaneous effects upon the political situation in Europe; England had thus successfuly brought to an end twenty years of bitter fighting against Napoleon's rule, and thereby established her dominion of the sea, as well as her pre-eminence in Europe, for a hundred years to come. But parallel with this, there was on the continent the beginning of a long period of restoration, and reaction to the Revolution, by national states and by means of imperialistic designs leading to the chaos of the twentieth century. It is a far cry indeed from the general applause of an earlier period; today the thoughtful observer of this battle and its consequences must ask himself '*Cui bono?*'[1]

The battle itself no longer looks like an isolated clash of arms, but rather like the magnificent and decisive conclusion of a series of operations. Chandler's conclusion compels our agreement:

> The so called Battle of Waterloo was in fact a composite action made up of no less than four contributory actions: two on 16 June, Quatre-Bras and Ligny; and two on the 18th, Waterloo and Wavre. A whole is the sum of its parts, and each of the three smaller actions had a most decided influence on what took place between La Belle Alliance and the ridge of Mont St Jean.[2]

Looking back one is first astonished at the great feats accomplished; there was an incredible readiness for action, a great fighting spirit, and an even greater fighting anger, among the units of all three armies, though springing from highly diverse motives. One is impressed by the power and élan of the French attacks,[3] by the steadfastness of the British soldiers, and by the endurance and willingness of the Prussian units, who had had little experience of battle. As one considers the 'leadership' of the manoeuvres and engagements of those days, one is struck by the unpredictable nature of the series of successes and failures, influenced by such factors as 'chance' and 'friction', to use the language of Clausewitz. In the whole sequence of events, two stages are discernable: the period up to 16 June; and the two following days, the 17th and 18th, which show completely different leadership.

To begin with the dominant factor is Napoleon's command – the rapid assembly of forces, the camouflaging of the concentration of his *Armée du Nord*, the surprise break-out – all these were as masterly as the plan of attack; it was exactly how a weaker force confronted by a stronger enemy should behave, trying to prevent Wellington and Blücher joining up forces and aiming at the defeat of their two armies singly. The following is Chandler's judgement: 'The original strategical conception was as brilliant as anything Napoleon ever devised, and until midday on the 16th – or even perhaps well into the 17th – everything appeared to be going well for his cause.'[4]

Compared with this, everything done by both British and Prussian commands appears inhibited and hesitant. 'It would seem,' says a nineteenth century Prussian account, 'as if both commanders wanted to miss the ordinary in order, later, to do the extraordinary.'[5]

In the two days following, the French and the Allied Commanders effected a complete exchange of characters. On the French side, Napoleon, as well as his subordinates, showed an increasing degree of mistaken assessment, uncertainty and negligence which, under such testing conditions, could not fail to have serious consequences. The allied command, on the other hand, seemed to gain in determination and purpose.

Napoleon believed the Prussian army to have suffered such severe defeat at Ligny as to be rendered incapable of coming to the aid of the English. He therefore decided against following up Blücher and neutralizing once and for all this dangerous enemy in a second battle. Confident in victory, he let the night of the 16th and the morning of the 17th pass without further action. 'Never waste time! *Activité, Vitesse, Vitesse*' – these had hitherto been the basic constituents of Napoleon's leadership.[6]

By comparison, the command of the allied armies seemed as if they had suddenly been shaken out of a deep sleep. For all their losses and exhaustion, there was no loss of morale in the Prussian army; rather there was a will to continue the fight alongside their ally, as shown in Gneisenau's difficult decision to withdraw to the north. To quote Sheppard: 'The Prussians showed great clear-sightedness and resolution in abandoning their communications after Ligny and staking all on retaining touch with their allies, and an equal determination and spirit animated the effort which brought them up at the right time and place to decide the fate of the day at Waterloo.'[7]

The decision of the Prussian command to withdraw to Wavre was the fruit of Gneisenau's far-sightedness and willingness to take responsibility.[8] The successes of the attack of the 18th on the French flank, and the achievement of bringing up the exhausted, hungry Prussian troops over the treacherous paths, were largely due to Blücher's energy. The success of Waterloo as a whole depended upon Wellington's cold-blooded, calculated, defensive leadership, and the steadfastness of his units. But it was probably the allies' greatest piece of luck that here, at Waterloo, the ideal conditions for the engagement of both armies were fulfilled: Wellington, the 'greatest defensive general that has ever lived',[9] had the task of holding off the enemy attack, while Blücher, the inveterate attacker, set off for the enemy flank, following the plan worked out by Gneisenau, who understood Napoleon's strategy of destruction more intimately than any man alive.

There has been much argument as to the lack of the usually overpowering quality of Napoleon's generalship at Waterloo. Illness and physical and mental exhaustion may have played their part.[10] But his 'leadership' during the battle demonstrates a departure from his own operational principles. The greatest successes of Napoleon's leadership were achieved during the twenty years of his rise to power, mainly through the development of the operation of 'internal lines', as Jomini has explained. This meant that the weaker aimed at dividing the stronger, and keeping him divided in order to defeat him piecemeal. It required decisiveness, mobility, the concentration of his own forces, the quest for superiority at the right time and in the right place, the relentless commitment of his own strength to the decisive stroke. Napoleon was able to ask this of the revolutionary armies and later of the imperial army. By putting these principles into practice, he achieved his total successes against the schematic leadership of the eighteenth century.[11]

If Napoleon's leadership from 15 to 18 June 1815 is looked at from this standpoint, a break becomes apparent. His use of the *Armée du Nord* was, at the beginning, completely in accordance with his principles, *but with Ligny a change begins to be seen*. The final phase of the battle shows Napoleon doing the complete opposite to what was required if success was to be achieved. The opponent who should have been broken up was able, despite defeat, to unify his forces and bring them into action to his own operational advantage. The attacker, on the other hand, had divided his forces and was unable to reunite them. Consequently, at a moment of great importance, in the decisive attack, Napoleon found himself at a disadvantage and in no position to recover himself. Such a situation had never arisen in his earlier battles. No matter what the reason, Napoleon had deviated from his own principles – and his enemy, realizing that the one thing that mattered here was to keep their forces together, had made every effort to achieve this end.[12]

If any conclusions are to be drawn from these considerations, it must first be realized that the Battle of Ligny, as it was fought, was an essential part of the development of the three days; *the result dazzled the victor and united the allies*. Without Ligny there might have been a victorious battle but it would hardly have been a 'Waterloo'.[13]

Moreover, without the co-operation of the Prussian army, the great battle itself would in all probability, not have been accepted by Wellington, and could not have been won. The weight of the French units was capable of shaking the resistance of the defenders right up to the culmination of the battle, even though the French were barely superior in numbers and tactical mistakes had weakened the attacks decisively.[14] If the French Guards, VI Corps and additional cavalry had remained fully available, the pendulum, by all human calculations, must have swung the other way; the English front would have been broken, exactly as the Prussians had been on the evening of the 16th at Ligny. Chandler comments: 'Wellington's army had hardly any chance of ultimate victory on its own, and the opportune arrival of a growing flood of Prussian troops on the French right flank undoubtedly swung the fortunes of the day'.[15] Lastly, there is no doubt that the pursuit immediately embarked upon by the Prussian troops, and going beyond Frasnes before morning light, was of great significance. It forestalled any pause in the headlong flight of the French *en masse*, it actively hindered the formation of collecting points both in front of the Sambre and on the river bank itself, and it stimulated the pursuit as far as Paris. The result was that the crushing defeat of the *Armée du Nord* became a rout and a dissolution. *It was from this and this alone that the political consequences stemmed; they could hardly have been so rapidly achieved by a normal 'victory'.*

Chandler thinks differently at this point. He believes that 'the effectiveness of this operation has been overestimated'.[16] I cannot agree with this. To arrive at a verdict, one has but to pose the question: what would have happened if after Ligny Napoleon had immediately pursued the Prussians on the night of the 16th–17th, or even in the early morning of the 17th? There would certainly have been no 'Waterloo'. It was precisely this that Gneisenau had learned from Napoleon's earlier campaigns – namely the importance of rapid pursuit immediately after a battle. The Prussian order to pursue after Waterloo was not prompted simply by the desire for revenge; it was the conviction that it was an operational necessity which was the driving force behind this final effort.

Once again let us quote Sheppard's verdict: 'Waterloo stands out in history with Jena as the classical instance in history of the complete exploitation of a victory by furious and relentless pursuit.'[17] And Clausewitz writes: 'Particular and very great merit attaches, however, to the unremitting pursuit throughout the night. There is no measuring the degree in which this contributed to the greater dissolution of the enemy forces and the magnitude and prestige of the trophies by which the Battle is distinguished.'[18]

Sometime after the battle, Blücher made the suggestion, from Genappe through General von Müffling, that the battle should be given the name of Belle Alliance. The Duke of Wellington did not agree – and, if one tries to put oneself in his place, this is understandable. After the tension of those days the performance of his own men must have been uppermost in his mind, not to mention the heavy casualties suffered by his troops, and by his own staff, and the stubbornness that made them hold out to the very last. There may also have been some sense of bitterness that the Prussians had not arrived earlier – a bitterness similar to that felt by the Prussian staff on the evening of Ligny when the English support, which they had counted on, for some unknown reason did not materialize. Wellington can have had no more idea of the losses, the trials and the performance of the Prussian army on 18 June than the Prussian command, on the evening of Ligny, had of the significance of Wellington's battle at Quatre-Bras. Nor could he have known that Napoleon had committed the bulk of his battle reserves against the Prussians: two cavalry divisions, Lobau's corps, and more than half of the Guards. All these – 17,000 to 18,000 men and considerable artillery – were missing from the French attacks on Wellington's line, and notably from the final great attack in the evening.

But even if Wellington had known of the efforts made by the Prussians and the casualties they had suffered, as well as of the effects of their arrival and engagement, what could all this have meant to him compared with the terrible battle his troops had fought? For him, quite apart from all personal and political considerations, this battle was an English achievement and should be honoured as such. Wellington therefore followed his usual custom and in his report called the battle after the site of his headquarters; and it became known as the 'Battle of Waterloo'.

At a distance of 150 years it is easier to view and honour achievements. Chesney has already written: 'To those who look fairly at its history, it stands proved that it was the fairly-won prize of a combination of valour, skill and mutual support, such as the world had never witnessed before in allied armies led by independent generals.'[19]

This was a battle where extraordinary success was achieved as a result of co-operation, of a classical mutual endeavour and effort. If there is anywhere, in history, an instance of a battle led and won on the foundations of a 'Belle Alliance', this is that battle.

18

CONCLUSION

Jacques Champagne

As witness the enormous bibliography available, there are one thousand and more different views about the Battle of Waterloo and the reasons for Napoleon's defeat at Mont St Jean.

Reaching a balanced conclusion requires a search for common, incontrovertible historical facts amidst a maze of views, comments and analyses, all of which might be held to be subjective or to be self-justifications according to the personal position, status and political, military or national standpoint of their authors.

Some controversies and arguments in the form of hypothetical possibilities must be discarded. Had they actually materialized, they would have created different circumstances and provoked new reactions and consequences on the battlefield and elsewhere. To deal adequately with them would require one to write several imaginary accounts of the Battle of Waterloo in conditions which did not actually prevail and with characters and personalities very different from those of the actual participants.

One must also avoid getting lost in exaggerated controversies about figures concerning the exact numbers of troops involved and the casualties on each side; the timing of the various operations; the distances, even between localities; and the hours of transmission and receipt of battle orders. Far more important than such slight discrepancies, which could not have affected crucially the disposition of the armies, their movements or the outcome of the battle, are the figures, times and distances on which the respective commanders based their assessments at the time and on the spot, and therefore their strategic and tactical decisions, for better or for worse.

From the moment that Napoleon decided to leave Elba and return to France, it was inevitable that the battles of Ligny, Quatre-Bras and Waterloo should take place. Napoleon's monumental political and diplomatic gamble, followed by his last, outstandingly brilliant military campaign, was thwarted – and victory turned into disaster – at the last minute, by the combination of three main factors:

1 Ney's incredible laxity and Grouchy's grossly timid incompetence. Together they prevented Wellington's and Blücher's armies from being decisively crushed at Quatre-Bras and at Ligny respectively, and allowed both enemies time and opportunity to recover from the most serious blows, and finally to join up again with overwhelming numerical superiority.

2 Wellington's self-imposed tenacity and defensive tactics against all odds and at whatever cost.

3 Blücher's army's brilliant recovery, followed by its outstanding contribution and massive succour to Wellington at the last, desperate hour.

It is, of course, the last hour of the last battle that counts, and the commanders-in-chief are held responsible in the last resort for the outcome of any battle. In this respect, the list of incidents, delays and mistakes' which plagued Napoleon's army during the three-day campaign which ended at Mont St Jean would appear so staggering as to have precluded any outcome other than certain defeat. The list runs briefly as follows:

Three desertions at times crucial both for the operations in hand and for the morale of the army; delays in crossing the Sambre; Ney's inactivity on the evening of 15 June and on the mornings of 16 and 17 June, which saved Wellington from what could easily have been a crushing blow and which denied Quatre-Bras to the French army before Napoleon's arrival there; d'Erlon's error of itinerary and confusion about contradictory orders in his march on St Amand, which prevented the destruction of the Prussian army; Napoleon's consequent ten-hour lull in Fleurus after the Ligny victory; the appalling weather at Mont St Jean on 17 June, which stopped the pursuit of Wellington's army, and the resulting condition of the terrain the next morning, which delayed Napoleon's attack by some four hours.

The diversionary attack on Hougoumont ordered by Napoleon, which was turned into a major, prolonged battle by Prince Jérôme; Ney's frontal attacks on Wellington with infantry in compact formations, which rendered them extremely vulnerable to enemy cannon and rifle fire; Ney's impetuous and massive cavalry charges without infantry support to the exhaustion of any cavalry reserve; improper use of French artillery fire, which spared the buildings of La Haye Sainte; failure to spike enemy cannon on the crests of Mont St Jean; Ney's belated use of infantry with exhausted cavalry; the non-availability of infantry reinforcements to Ney when Wellington's line faltered for the second time; the belated Guard's intervention by Napoleon coinciding with massive Prussian attacks; Grouchy's total and repeated failures, for two whole days, both to detect and foil the retreating Prussian army, and to join Napoleon at Mont St Jean himself.

And yet, by 7 p.m. on 18 June, to the honour of the French army and through the outstanding valour and courage of its troops and its commanders, all the aforesaid incidents, delays and mistakes – except that of Grouchy – had been repaired and made good. Napoleon's plans had been successful: concentration, surprise, separation, pursuit, frontal attack – all had come to fruition in the end. Wellington's line was breached, his situation was desperate, Bülow's 30,000 men had been repulsed and kept in check for three hours. The French army, fighting now against combined enemy forces twice its superior in numbers, was holding the Hougoumont position, occupying the Ohain ridge, Papelotte and La Haye Sainte, and had victory in sight for the second time that day (on Wellington's own admission). Blücher's 40,000 supplementary troops thrown into the scales at this juncture totally reversed the situation and clinched the final outcome of the battle. Grouchy's responsibility in this is incontrovertible.

The question arises as to the share of responsibility borne by the other French commanders and, in the first place, by Napoleon himself. At the outset, as we have seen, his choice of commanders was severely limited by the circumstances in which he had to make this choice. It is true, but idle, to say that Berthier would have made a better chief of staff than Soult, and Murat a better second-in-command to Napoleon than Ney. Berthier, the meticulous co-ordinator, who used if necessary to send ten dispatch riders with the same message from Napoleon to his army commanders, had followed King Louis XVIII in his flight from France. In a fit of depression he had thrown himself out of a window at the castle of his father-in-law, the Prince of Bavaria, just one month before Waterloo. As for Murat, Napoleon had never forgiven him for his pro-Austrian attitude in 1814, and he would not even hear of appointing him. Beaten and cast from the throne of Naples by the Austrians in April 1815, fugitive in Toulon, where he learned of the Waterloo disaster, then in Corsica and in Italy, Murat was soon to be summarily executed by a firing squad in Calabria within half an hour of his arrest by Italian gendarmerie.

In one respect only did Napoleon have a free choice which, in his memoirs, he rightly regretted not having made: i.e., that of Marshal Suchet, left behind in command of VI Observation Corps in Chambéry, in place of Grouchy. Even Ney and Grouchy finally redeemed their reputation; the first, by his heroic conduct at Waterloo; the second, by his most remarkable retreat on Laon against every Prussian attack and with all his forces practically intact. And, excepting Bourmont and the seven other traitors, all the other commanders did their duty, even to the supreme

179

sacrifice of their lives. Their names decorate the streets of Paris, of most French provincial towns and of many cities in foreign lands to this day, an honour which they richly deserved.

Napoleon himself can hardly be found at fault during the whole campaign, during the battle, or even during the retreat, which he stemmed before going on from Laon to Paris. On every occasion he was personally present in the forefront of his troops, and at every critical moment he personally corrected his commanders' mistakes. He never ceased to adapt his tactics to the constant and rapidly changing situation. That some of his crucial orders were not followed (as in the case of Ney), or rightly interpreted (as in the case of Grouchy), can hardly be laid at his door. Indeed, probably very conscious of Soult's limitations as a chief of staff, Napoleon was never more clear, precise or minutely detailed than when dictating to Soult his orders and dispatches. In this respect, he may be said to have taken too much upon himself. Many of his staff officers were also privately worried by the fact that on several occasions Napoleon showed equal and simultaneous interest in the military matters in hand and in the political news from Paris.

This happened particularly in Fleurus and at Ligny on the day after the victory over Blücher. But it does not appear to be more valid than the other speculative reason advanced by many critics and historians to explain Napoleon's ten-hour delay in sending Grouchy after the retreating Prussians, i.e., his lack of decision due to his supposed mental tiredness and bad state of health. It is true that Napoleon had a very bad spasmodic cough and that he was suffering from stomach pains and, more painfully, from haemorrhoids at this stage of the campaign. But, as Houssaye points out, a man of Napoleon's age who, out of ninety-six hours, can afford to stay thirty-seven hours in the saddle and only sleep twenty hours, can hardly be said to be in a bad state of health. Nor can Napoleon's activities during the three days 16, 17 and 18 June be said to reflect a state of mental tiredness or indecision.

On the morning of the first day, his information was that Ney was holding Quatre-Bras and that he himself was in the presence of a Prussian army corps. His plan was therefore to march on Brussels by the road which was supposed to be open. He gave orders to all his commanders to prepare to that effect, and told Ney to go on pushing forward. Attacked simultaneously in front and on its flank, the Anglo-Dutch army would be doomed, while the Prussians were simply to be kept in check.

By mid-morning, however, Napoleon learned that Ney was not at Quatre-Bras and that this position was being strongly reinforced by the enemy, while the whole of the Prussian army was appearing at Ligny and St Amand. Napoleon therefore modified his orders, telling Ney to contain Wellington, at least, while he himself gave battle to the whole Prussian army. And, to make it a crushing victory, Napoleon ordered Ney to detach d'Erlon on Blücher's rear before himself directing the attack on Ligny. By nightfall the Prussians were beaten and retreating, but there was still no news from Ney at 11 p.m.

At dawn on 17 June, Napoleon sent Pajol and Teste to shadow the Prussians who were (mistakenly) reported, two hours later, to be retreating on Liège and Namur. At 9 a.m. Napoleon visited his troops at Ligny, and at 11 a.m. he ordered Ney to renew his attack on Wellington pending his own arrival. He sent Grouchy with an army corps to follow the Prussians and to prevent them from joining up with Wellington. He then mounted up, arrived at Quatre-Bras before Ney, expelled Wellington, pursued him actively and drove him into a corner. Only the weather prevented Napoleon from acting further. He hardly slept that night for fear of the enemy's possible attempt to escape, and when he realized that Wellington was determined to give battle he prepared ceaselessly for it.

On 18 June Napoleon made good the delays in the general attack against Wellington by ordering a diversion on Hougoumont, and when this movement degenerated he set the position aflame with incendiary shells. He was the first to perceive Bülow's arrival at St Lambert, he took precautions to protect his right flank with Lobau's corps and, for the second time that day, he warned Grouchy to act. When Ney deprived him too early of his cavalry reserve, Napoleon felt duty-bound to support him, though reluctantly. It was on his renewed orders that Ney took La Haye Sainte and Durutte, Papelotte. When Wellington's line faltered, Napoleon engaged decisively the Guard, this now being his only reserve. The effect was dramatic. But the Prussian masses intervened simultaneously. Defeat and rout were the result. But Napoleon still did not give up.

At Genappe and at Quatre-Bras he stopped the rout. All along the way to Laon, he sent orders to all commanders to rally, and by 26 June some 70,000 officers and men of all arms, with 200 cannon were regrouped there. Together with the covering armies and the observation corps, Napoleon still disposed of some 120,000 officers and men of the line and 400 cannon to counter the approaching enemy invasion of about 90,000 men (Anglo-Dutch and Prussians). Paris itself was still defended by 36,000 National Guard, 30,000 fusiliers and 6,000 artillery men manning 600 guns. The lightning Belgian campaign had failed, but the French army, defeated but by no means crushed, was now in a better position than the Prussians after Ligny or Wellington's army after Quatre-Bras. This might have been enough to stop and repulse the approaching enemy in accordance with Napoleon's original alternative plan.

But, as he himself said in his memoirs:

The situation required firmness on the part of the officers, of the Government, of the Chambers and of the whole nation. It required the French people to be animated by the feeling of honour, of glory, of national independence; to have their eyes fixed on Rome after

Cannes, and not on Carthage after Zama. Had France risen to this occasion, she would have been invincible.

What in fact happened, however, was that 'the officers, the Government, the Chambers, indeed the whole French nation' required Napoleon to abdicate, which he did. And this may well be the most important conclusion to be drawn from the Battle of Waterloo. Perhaps Napoleon's only, though monumental, error was to misjudge the temper and the mood of the French, English and Continental European peoples at that particular time. By 1815, after a quarter of a century of internal revolution, foreign invasions, external war and imperial glory, the French people were physically, morally and ideologically exhausted. At the same time, most Europeans had come to hate the physical miseries and international upheavals brought to them in the wake, and in the name, of the French Revolution and its ideals of 'Liberté, Egalité, Fraternité' – even though these ideals still rang true and were still longed for. As for the European monarchs of that day, they were more than ever determined finally to subdue and to crush 'that little Corsican upstart who had the gall to proclaim himself their equal'.

Perhaps the Battle of Waterloo should rather be seen as 'la journée des dupes par excellence', for there is such a thing as 'le sort des armes' (the fate of battles) in which Napoleon firmly believed, as seen even in some of his dispatches. Marivaux himself could hardly have conceived a theatrical 'comedy of errors' such as the sinister one Mars, the God of War, playfully meddling, confusing and destroying all their arrogantly clever human plans, seems to have devised for the benefit of these two mortals, Napoleon and Wellington. Most of those present at Mont St Jean should not have been there at all, and those who should have been never arrived.

For Napoleon 'of all the battles he ever fought, perhaps the most famous turned out to be the one he lost'. To Wellington, Waterloo gave one of those rare and terrifying chances to make incarnate what the British are most proud of: resistance to the last man when finally cornered and with backs to the wall. Only on Blücher, who was seventy-three years old at Waterloo, did the gods really smile, perhaps to crown his long, famous and impetuous career.

Ney was tried by a court-martial of his peers and old comrades-in-arms; he was sentenced to death and shot on 6 December 1815. One will always wonder whether his flagrant contravention of Napoleon's orders in the field did not play a more important part in this awful verdict than the

88 Right: King Louis XVIII. When he returned to Paris he banished most of Napoleon's surviving commanding officers. He died in 1824
89 Below: General Rapp, later appointed personal lord-in-waiting to Louis XVIII

royal charge of treason on which he was tried. But for most of his illustrious comrades, Waterloo meant banishment by Louis XVIII's ordnance of 24 July 1815. This was followed by a partial amnesty four years later, and a full one some years after that granted by King Charles X.

D'Erlon took refuge in Bayreuth, where he managed an inn, and only returned to France under Charles X. Exelmans, Lobau and Soult returned to France in 1819, the first to be killed in a riding accident; the second, to succeed La Fayette as commander-in-chief of the Paris National Guard with the rank of marshal; the third, to become Prime Minister (President of the Council) under King Louis Philippe.

Cambronne, wounded at Waterloo and taken prisoner to England, was arrested on his return to France, court-martialled and sentenced to death for 'having betrayed the King and attacked France by force of arms' (the same indictment as that of Ney). He was acquitted on appeal after Louis XVIII's personal intervention in his favour. Davout was interned at Louviers and freed by the King on 7 August 1817. Rapp, who was in Strasbourg when he heard of Waterloo, made his submission to Louis XVIII, who appointed him his personal lord-in-waiting. Bertrand, returning from St Helena to France in 1821, was sentenced to death, but he was pardoned by the King to become commander of the Ecole Polytechnique in Paris. Drouot gave himself up, was acquitted by a court-martial, refused every offer of position made to him by the King and ended his days as president of the Agricultural Society in Nancy. Durutte retired to Belgium, and Gérard, pensioned out, was appointed marshal in 1830, and became a senator under Napoleon III. From St Helena, Gourgaud went to England, was expelled from there, and returned to France in 1821. Grouchy returned to France in 1819 after four years of comfortable exile in America.

And, exiled for life in St Helena, Napoleon was left to comment as follows on his last campaign:

Of his commanders: 'The character of several French generals had been distempered by the events of 1814.'

Of Ney: 'The bravery of a Commander-in-Chief must be different from that of a divisional general, which in turn must not be that of a Grenadier captain.'

Of Grouchy: 'With 34,000 men and 108 cannon, Grouchy found the matchless secret, on 18th June, of finding himself neither on the battlefield of Mont St Jean, nor in Wavre.'

90 Left: Napoleon's court sword
91 Below: The badge of an officer of Lancers, Garde Royale

Of the French army: 'Never has the French soldier shown more courage, good will and enthusiasm . . . He had full confidence in the Emperor, but he was suspicious and distrustful towards his other chiefs . . . Not a single soldier committed the crime of desertion.'

Of Wellington: 'The English general's decision to give battle at Waterloo was contrary to the interests of his nation, to the general war plan of the Allies and to all the rules of war . . . Strange whim of human events! The bad choice of his battlefield, which rendered any retreat impossible, was the cause of his success.'

Of the campaign: 'Singular campaign, where I saw the assured triumph of France escape three times from my hands. Without the desertion of a traitor, I would have crushed my enemies at the opening of the campaign. I would have crushed them at Ligny if my left had done its duty. I would have crushed them at Waterloo if my right had not failed me. Singular defeat where, despite the most horrible catastrophe, the vanquished's glory did not suffer, nor was that of the victor increased.'

19

CONCLUSION

William Seymour

'By God! I don't think it would have done if I had not been there!' These words were spoken to Thomas Creevey by the Duke in the course of a conversation in his hotel room on the day after the battle. There was nothing bombastic about them, for Wellington never arrogated to himself the principal honours of the day; but, albeit unintentionally, they very neatly summed up the battle. Without Wellington it most certainly would not have done. He was the rock amid the shifting quicksands of doubt and danger. Napoleon was out-fought and out-generalled by a man whose military prowess he despised. Wellington's capabilities as a commander have already been assessed (see Chapter 2); it is here only necessary to emphasize that at Waterloo it was his tactical genius and his personal example that did so much to win the day. A great exponent of the defensive battle, he was nevertheless always ready to go over to the offensive, and on this occasion, as on others, at the opportune moment he showed himself capable of striking hard.

The Duke's personal contribution to the victory cannot be too strongly stressed. First and foremost was the example he set. Here was one of the most powerful and privileged men in England calmly exposing himself to a greater degree of danger than any of his soldiers, and not through any meretricious display of bravado, but simply to animate those of his troops most in need of encouragement and leadership. Apart from the ability to mould and lead his fellow men – a gift that he shared with

Napoleon, who failed to exercise it at Waterloo – what key decisions did Wellington take that had a direct bearing on the victory? There was the decision to stand and fight in the best defensive position available; and there was also the decision to reinforce Hougoumont so that it could be held throughout. But Wellington's contribution to the victory was not so much through any single decision, as through the overall grip that he had on the battle, a grip that he never relaxed. He attended to every tactical detail; he was on hand to exploit every opportunity; his handling of the reserves, particularly his achievement in having fresh batteries available at critical moments, was superb; his courage never faltered, he remained calm throughout repeated crises, and above all he inspired his subordinate commanders with his confidence.

Wellington paid tribute to the worth of the British infantryman in Brussels before the battle, and it is certain that without the British and the King's German Legion infantry he could not have won. To say this is in no way to belittle the contribution of the other two arms, whose regiments and batteries fought with the greatest gallantry; but it is the infantry who gain, hold or abandon ground and are therefore the decisive factor in victory or defeat. The British and King's German Legion infantry were few in number, but they had been carefully positioned throughout the line, and with their superior training, their excellent fire discipline and their dogged determination they stood firm where lesser troops would have broken. There were many agonizing moments when the line was terrifyingly thin – one more push and it seemed that the French columns must be through – but somehow they stuck it and everywhere their commander-in-chief was at hand, sometimes with reinforcements, always with resolution and encouragement.

We have seen that in the mind of one combatant, Harry Smith (see p. 160), every moment of Waterloo was a crisis, but can we point a finger to any particular crisis or event upon the successful outcome of which the fate of the day hinged? In such a fiercely and bravely contested battle it may be invidious to do so. The gallant defence of La Haye Sainte, Colborne's magnificent sweep into the flank of the Imperial Guard, the glorious charge of the heavy brigades, the long hours of savage fighting by sternly embattled infantrymen – all are great epics in themselves. But Wellington evidently thought that Hougoumont was the key to victory. Some years after the battle the Rector of Framlingham left a bequest of £500 to the

92 Highlanders and French Lancers at Waterloo.
Wellington always acknowledged the courage of the
British infantrymen

bravest man in England, and Wellington was asked
to adjudicate. In making his award he said,

It is generally thought that the Battle of Waterloo was
one of the greatest battles ever fought; such is not my
opinion, but I say nothing upon that point. The success
of the Battle of Waterloo turned upon the closing of the
gates of Hougoumont. These gates were closed in the
most courageous manner in the very nick of time by the
efforts of Sir J. Macdonell. I cannot help thinking Sir
James is the man to whom you should give the five
hundred pounds.

Colonel Macdonell decided to share the money
with Sergeant Graham who so gallantly closed the
gates at Hougoumont.

There can be no proper appraisal of the allied
victory without a look at the Prussian intervention.
It is sometimes asserted that the Prussians won
the battle; this is not true, although the policy
formulated by Wellington and Blücher before
Ligny, and so loyally adhered to – in spite of many
grave difficulties – by Blücher, was indeed the
foundation of victory. The remark attributed to
Wellington, 'Would to God that night or Blücher
were come', was surely never made by him, but it
did accurately reflect the critical situation prevailing at the time. Their physical appearance on
the field may not have been felt until the evening,
but the Prussians had long since drawn off Lobau's
11,000 men, who never fired a shot at the Anglo-
Dutch army. Moreover, when the time came for
Wellington to go over to the offensive – never easy

after a long defensive battle – Bülow's and Zieten's
corps on his left flank, poised for a fatal thrust at
the French right, gave the necessary impetus to
victory that Wellington lacked through having no
fresh reserves. The Prussian losses of 7,000 men,
at Waterloo alone, pay ample tribute to the
importance of their presence and the courage of
their troops.

Focussing the spotlight principally on the Anglo-
Dutch army precludes any detailed examination
of the French troops that Napoleon commanded,
but the picture would be incomplete if no com-
parisons were drawn.

On his return to France Napoleon was quickly
faced with the Treaty of Alliance concluded between Great Britain, Austria, Russia and Prussia;
these allies could put into the field a total of over
700,000 troops, against which Napoleon was able
to muster little more than 200,000, and of those
only the Grand Army of 122,000 was in a proper
condition to take the field by the beginning of
June. But that army was very good indeed; two-
thirds of it consisted of veterans, and of the
remaining one-third most of the men had seen
service in 1813 and 1814. However, in the all-
important matter of regimental morale there was
something lacking, for there had been a number of
drastic reorganizations. Units had been recently
amalgamated, with the consequence that the component parts of divisions and brigades had not
had time to settle down and work together, and

there had been considerable inter-posting of senior and junior officers.

Over the years Napoleon's tactics had undergone a change; in his later battles he had come to rely on heavy concentrations of force. Artillery was used for massive bombardments; columns of infantry were sent against the enemy, and when the enemy were sufficiently demoralized they were subjected to shock cavalry charges. Such tactics were used at Waterloo, but Wellington over-simplified them when he said after the battle, 'Napoleon did not manoeuvre at all. He just moved forward in the old style, in columns, and was driven off in the old style.'

The essential ingredients of the tactical mixture were tirailleurs (skirmishers), columns, lines and squares. Much has been written in condemnation of the French column formation; it has often been said that the loss of fire power and the vulnerability to cannon suffered by battalions advancing to the attack in column formation contributed materially to Napoleon's defeat. In the light of what happened such criticism is justified; column of battalions proved disastrous for the French. But one hears less about another important reason for this disaster, which was the failure (except in d'Erlon's first attack, where in any event most of the infantry was not in close column) of the tirailleurs to allow the columns to get within striking distance comparatively unharmed.

Napoleon's infantry had usually attacked in column, but behind a mass of tirailleurs; these would adopt no formation and make as much use of the ground as possible, so as to occupy the enemy and cover the approach of the columns, thus allowing the latter to deliver a body punch at selected points almost before they had come under fire. Such tactics had been frequently successful in earlier battles, but the combination of good infantry and the fact that Wellington was able to neutralize, to a great extent, the efforts of the tirailleurs, caused them to fail at Waterloo. Usually a commander relied upon cavalry to sweep these skirmishers off the board, but Wellington was very short of cavalry after the débacle with the heavy brigades, and much of this work had to be done by his own skirmishers, whose performance against superior numbers was admirable. Occasionally, as we have seen, when the situation became too critical, Wellington would personally order a battalion forward to 'drive those fellows away'. The result was that the tirailleurs were seldom able to prevent the allied gunners from blasting the columns; the tactics of the reverse slope and the excellent fire discipline of the British infantry did the rest.

In the matter of command Wellington, for all his grumbles in the weeks preceding the campaign, had much the better team, especially in the higher echelons than Napoleon. The French fought superbly, and the men were well led by their regimental officers, who were devoted to the Emperor and were largely responsible for the smoothness of his return to power. But many of the senior officers had recently affirmed their loyalty to the Bourbons, and there was a certain amount of suspicion and mistrust between them. Some, like Ney, had everything to lose, which might have rendered them desperate, but not necessarily dependable. Ney himself could scarcely have shown more courage, but he was never a man to master-

186

mind a battle, which was what Napoleon left him
to do. With one or two exceptions, Wellington had
officers of the highest calibre; many of the senior
ones had fought under him before and had his
confidence, and if some of the foreign troops were
unreliable very few of their officers were. Wellington may have missed Murray, but he was much
better served by de Lancey than Napoleon was
by Soult.

Few battles are won where the opposition makes
no mistakes. After his brilliantly conceived and
speedily executed approach march to the frontier,
the genius that had raised Napoleon to the military
pinnacle of Europe seemed suddenly to desert him.
He made many mistakes; not all were fatal but a

few undoubtedly contributed to his defeat.

Waterloo was a campaign, not a single battle,
and as such it was lost to the French on 16 and 17
June. After the misunderstandings and indecisions
of those two days a victory on the 18th was certainly still possible, but it could never have been
decisive and the campaign would have continued
until Napoleon had been defeated. But any hope
of victory against the Anglo-Dutch army on the
18th was thrown away by a further series of
errors – all no doubt in part attributable to the
curious lethargy that seems to have overcome
Napoleon on that day. His first and greatest mistake was failing to gauge the determination and
loyalty of Blücher; he then hopelessly underestimated the courage and stubborn endurance of
the British and German troops. This led him to
disregard the advice of those of his generals who
had fought the British before and to insist on
attempting to bulldoze his way through the finest
infantry in the world, instead of manoeuvring – at
which his army was superior to the allies. For if
Wellington and Blücher could have been kept
apart, neither could have defeated Napoleon on
his own; the role of Grouchy's army is very
relevant in this context. Then there was the continued hammering at Hougoumont, which, originally intended as a diversion, became a harassment
that pinned down a corps for the whole day to little
purpose; while the failure to reinforce Ney after
the capture of La Haye Sainte, and the unsuitable
tactical formations of the infantry, were further
causes of defeat.

The continuing interest in the Battle of Waterloo
derives from the fact that it is one of the few great
battles up to modern times of which many of the
combatants have left an account of their experiences. Obviously most of these accounts are
slanted to favour the army to which the writer
belonged, and it is not always easy to obtain an
accurate picture from them. Wellington himself
was very averse to anyone trying to analyse the
battle and draw conclusions; writing from Paris
two months afterwards (see Chapter 11, p. 139)
he said, 'The history of a battle is not unlike the
history of a ball. Some individuals may recollect
all the little events, of which the great result is the
battle won or lost; but no individual can recollect
the order in which, or the exact moment at which,
they occurred, which makes all the difference as
to their value or importance.' To this we must
assent, even if in our obstinate way we persist in
the attempt to throw fresh chinks of light on a
battle unrivalled in interest, and perhaps in
importance, in the whole annals of war.

EPILOGUE

Lord Chalfont

History is the breeding ground of national pride. Generation after generation of children leave their schools firmly indoctrinated with the belief that they belong to the finest, bravest, most civilized nation on earth. Dr Johnson's reflection on this phenomenon was characteristically mordant, 'patriotism is the last refuge of the scoundrel'. It is not necessary to subscribe to this somewhat bilious doctrine to recognize that love of one's country – often an unexceptionable and even admirable emotion – tends sometimes to breed attitudes altogether less attractive – the nationalism, intolerance and xenophobia which are transformed in war into a violent hatred for those who have become, temporarily, 'the enemy'. Indeed, without this injection of artificial hostility, it is doubtful whether the concept of war between states would long survive.

Military history is perhaps the most potent creator of national stereotypes and of the chauvinism which they engender. The stories of great battles establish a pantheon of national heroes and weave a glowing tapestry of martial glory; and it is arguable that no battle exemplified this proposition more vividly than Waterloo. It is often said, not without justification, that to read the story of Waterloo in the history books of England, France and Germany is to read of three entirely different battles. The purpose of this book has been to try to reconcile these conflicting versions of what, it must be supposed, was objectively a single, observable, historical event. Yet even to state this is to raise all manner of philosophical doubts. There were three armies engaged at Waterloo, each with its own national traditions, its own *esprit de corps*, its own *Weltanschauung*; and, of course, each with its own leader, three men whose names are closely identified with the history and the psychology of the nations which bred them. It is not at all fanciful to suggest that for these three armies and the nations which raised them, Waterloo was a different experience, and in a very real sense a different event.

This great battle, with its compact battlefield, its confrontation of two of the great captains and its classical *dénouement* has given rise to questions which have preoccupied military historians for a century and a half. Most of the controversy has been concerned with questions of leadership, and most directly with the performances of the two leading actors in the drama – Napoleon and Wellington. Field Marshal Montgomery, with characteristic economy of style, has summed the matter up magisterially: 'It is a nice point as to who made the worse errors – Wellington or Napoleon.'

How much importance is to be invested in the fact that Wellington was dancing at a ball in Brussels on the evening of 15 June, when Napoleon's forces had already crossed into Belgium that morning? Did Napoleon throw away the opportunity which he had created by his masterly concentration at Charleroi by failing to pursue the retreating Prussians? Having launched the battle of Waterloo with what was ostensibly a diversionary attack on Hougoumont, why did Napoleon allow his brother Jérôme to persist with it long after it had clearly failed? Should Marshal Ney have attacked unbroken infantry at La Haye Sainte with unprotected cavalry? Should the Prince of Orange, a boy of twenty-three, have been in command of a corps? Was Napoleon, as Wellington concluded at a critical stage in the battle, a 'mere pounder'? This account of the battle has tried to answer some of these questions. They will, of course, never be definitively answered. Some of the flavour of the controversy which surrounds them emerges in the three contributions to this book, exemplified by three quotations, one from each of the three authors. William Seymour, the British historian, writes: '*Napoleon was outfought and out-generalled by Wellington . . . it is sometimes asserted that the Prussians won the battle; this is not true.*'

Eberhard Kaulbach, however, believes that: '*Without the co-operation of the Prussian army the great battle of Waterloo would probably not have been accepted by Wellington – nor could it have been won.*'

And, although no Frenchman would claim that Napoleon actually *won* the battle, Jacques Champagne notes that by 7 p.m. on the day of the battle, just an hour before it ended: '*The French army, fighting against combined enemy forces more than twice superior in numbers had victory in hand for the second time. . . .*'

Finally, it may be as well to note that personal experience is no guarantee of objective analysis. The young Prince of Orange, writing to his parents at The Hague on the morning after the battle, had his own version of the battle: '*We have had a magnificent affair against Napoleon today . . . it was my corps which principally gave battle and to which we owe the victory. . . .*'

Wellington's own assessment of Waterloo, often quoted, was that it was 'a damned nice thing – the nearest run thing you ever saw in your life'. Is it possible to arrive at any objective judgement from this array of subjective perceptions?

The literature of Waterloo is vast and comprehensive. The battle has been described and analysed in minute detail by hundreds of historians and biographers in dozens of languages. It would, therefore, be idle to expect three writers, working from the existing sources in the literature of their respective countries, to illuminate any facet of the battle which had not been scrutinized by some earlier observer. They could not be expected to cast any startling new light on events. That is, however, not the purpose of this present study. It is, rather, to bring together what has previously been dispersed – namely the images of the battle of Waterloo as they are normally presented to the citizens of those countries which took part in it; to demonstrate where they appear most to diverge; and to see at what points they are in agreement.

It might be well to begin a synthesis of this kind with a brief examination of the name of the battle as it has gone down in history. It is not surprising that the victors should have been responsible for naming the battle. Napoleon might have preferred some other style, but his views were not likely, at that moment in history, to carry much weight. Blücher, it is recorded, proposed that it should be called the battle of La Belle Alliance, commemorating at once the farmhouse at which the defeated Emperor had made his tactical headquarters, and the fact that in the eyes of the Prussians, the victory had been a triumph of allied cooperation. Wellington had other ideas. His view was that the victory had been brought about predominantly by English arms (indeed he said of Hougoumont that the

position could have been held by soldiers of no other nation). He, therefore, following a respectable tradition, headed his first despatch after the battle with the name of his own headquarters, and the battle of Waterloo was written into the history books. Suggestions by some historians that he was also influenced by the notorious inability of his countrymen to pronounce foreign words can probably be discounted; anyone who can anglicize Waterloo successfully should have had no difficulty with La Belle Alliance (although La Haye Sainte, another Prussian suggestion, might have posed more baffling problems).

The serious point which lies behind this apparently peripheral matter of naming the battle is one which has been at the heart of much of the national historical prejudice about Waterloo. To the British, for more than a century and a half, Waterloo has always been a great victory for Wellington and the British army, with Blücher and the Prussians appearing on the scene at the last moment to share the glory and participate in the political spoils. This is, for two reasons, somewhat at odds with the reality. The first reason, already fully recognized by most serious British historians, is that Wellington's army was British, or English, only in the most flexible interpretation of the word. It consisted, to quote Elizabeth Longford, of 'remarkably heterogeneous material' – a

judgement fully borne out by a study of Table 5 in this book. No more than a third of Wellington's troops were British, although it is probably true to say that, with the exception of the German Legion, they were the only troops who could be relied upon to perform creditably in battle. That the British soldiers *did* perform, not only creditably but for the most part magnificently, does not seem to be a matter of dispute. Wellington distributed his limited numbers of British infantry throughout the defensive line, and these stolid, unimaginative but incredibly brave soldiers did not let him down. Indeed, they were often engaged in two battles at once – one to repel the courageous onslaughts of the French and another to prevent some of their less militant comrades from taking precipitate leave of the battlefield. Although the Marquess of Anglesey is somewhat critical of the organization of the cavalry at Waterloo in his *History of the British Cavalry*, their élan and bravery were never in doubt, especially in the final, decisive assault. In this context Wellington was probably justified in his view of Waterloo as an English victory.

It is in the matter of the Prussian role in the battle that a little reassessment of historical viewpoints might legitimately be called for. Blücher's army almost certainly lived up to his own assessment of it. On 2 June 1815 – his men, he wrote, were 'in the best of shape and their morale is all

that can be wished for'. A year earlier a British officer, Colonel Hudson Lowe had written, 'Words fail me to describe my amazement at the fearlessness and discipline of these troops.' Furthermore, the Prussian army was efficiently organized and well led. Blücher himself was a sound strategist and tactician, loved by his soldiers, and he had a superb Chief of Staff in Gneisenau. This formidable army of 140,000 men played a part in the Waterloo campaign, not least in the final battle, which has been consistently underestimated by British historians. The English historian David Chandler has written that, 'Wellington's army had hardly any chance of ultimate victory on its own, and the opportune arrival of a growing flood of Prussian troops on the French right flank undoubtedly swung the fortunes of the day.' There was, however, much more to it than that.

It was not only that the Prussian attacks on the right flank of the French forces on the afternoon of the battle forced Napoleon to detach precious reserves to safeguard his flanks and to recapture Plancenoit; the advancing Prussian forces were a constant factor in the battle throughout the day – a persistent threat in the mind of Napoleon, who could not give his entire attention to Wellington, and a reassurance to Wellington, who could concentrate on repelling the initial French attacks in the knowledge that, sooner or later, the arrival of Blücher would decisively change the balance of forces. Indeed, it is arguable that some of Napoleon's apparent errors of judgement were brought about by the knowledge that if he could not crush Wellington before Blücher arrived, the day was lost. Furthermore, there was another less obvious Prussian influence on the course of the battle. The Prussian liaison officer on Wellington's staff was Baron von Müffling, an officer of great charm and ability who did much to ensure the timely arrival of Blücher at Waterloo. It is, indeed, clear that Waterloo was not an isolated battle, but the final decisive action in a coherent engagement which had begun at Ligny and Quatre-Bras and throughout which Blücher's Prussian army played a vital role.

It is arguable that the one subject upon which it is possible to arrive at a reasonably clear conclusion, undistorted by national pride or preconception, is that which concerns the overall political importance and impact of Waterloo. The historian's natural desire to impose some kind of order on the chaotic saga of the human condition tends to produce all manner of 'turning points', 'watersheds' and 'decisive confrontations' in the chronicle of events. From Alexander the Great's victory over Darius III at Arbela in 331 BC and Caesar's defeat of Vercingetorix at Alesia, to Montgomery's triumph at El Alamein and the French disaster at Dieu Bien Phu, it has been customary to claim that this or that battle had a dramatic effect on the course of history. After Blenheim or Rorke's Drift, Passchendaele or Arnhem, the historian is likely to claim 'nothing could ever be the same again'. In fact, with a few obvious exceptions, it can be persuasively argued that the clashes of arms celebrated in the annals of military history had no more than a marginal effect on the subsequent development of events; and Waterloo is no exception.

The battle was, of course, the final defeat of Napoleon and peace came to Europe after twenty-three years of war; and to that extent Waterloo was a history battle. After its defeat the Grande Armée was disbanded, and to erase the memory of the recent past, even the names of the regiments were done away with. David Howarth has gone as far as to describe the battle as 'the defeat of an Empire on a single Sunday afternoon', and it has been suggested that if Napoleon had been victorious at Waterloo, the course of nineteenth-century history would have been radically altered. On the other hand, it can be argued with equal conviction that even if Wellington and Blücher had abandoned Belgium, and the Waterloo campaign had never been fought, the defeat of Napoleon by the allies would not have been long postponed – possibly by a general offensive in 1816.

This is, however, no more than speculation. What is a matter of record is that the Waterloo campaign was the occasion of some of the bloodiest and fiercest fighting in the history of warfare. Some of the eye-witness accounts are horrifying in their stark revelations of the sheer destructive ferocity of war. An officer of Count Gérard's IV French Corps wrote:

The Prussian bullets swept us away by the dozen. Shot fell like hail, and the drums kept up their *pan-pan-pan*. It was a thousand times worse inside the houses, where the screams of rage mingled in the uproar. We rushed into a large room already packed with soldiers, on the first floor of a house. It was dark because they had covered the windows with sacks of earth, but we could see a steep wooden staircase at one end, down which the blood was running. We heard musket shots from above, and each moment the flashes showed us five or six of our men sunk in a heap

. . . and the others scrambling over their bodies with bayonets fixed trying to force their way up into the loft. The room was full of dead and wounded, the walls splashed with blood. Not one Prussian was left on his feet.

Another French officer – a member of Napoleon's suite at Ligny – described the battlefield on the morning after the battle:

The dead in many places were piled two or three deep. The blood flowed from under them in streams. Through the principal street [of Ligny] the mud was red with blood, and the mud itself was composed of crushed bones and flesh.

Roger Parkinson has described what Clausewitz saw at the village of St Amand:

Yet when the French tried to press on from St Amand, they were met with devastating grape and cannister shot from Prussian batteries on the hills beyond, and Napoleon's men swayed back again. A Prussian counter-attack, with four battalions of men shouting and screaming as they charged forwards, succeeded in holding the lower part of the village. By this time, the thunderous artillery duel between the two armies had reached a terrible crescendo. Shells were exploding upon the grassy slopes around Clausewitz, and the Prussian guns answered from behind him, shells whistling over his head to smash into the flanks of the enemy assault below. Clausewitz could see the effect of the cannister shot, which scythed into the French ranks and sprawled the cut and bloodied bodies in the dusty field and sent many running in fear. But most continued to advance.

But perhaps the most vivid and at the same time the most honest account of this terrible encounter was that of a very small British soldier, asked on the morning after Waterloo for his impressions of the battle. He replied: 'I'll be hanged if I know anything about the matter, for I was all day trodden in the mud, and ridden over by every scoundrel who had a horse'. The story, one might fairly say, of the infantryman's life through the ages.

Among all this slaughter, there were moments of incredible physical bravery – William Leeke of the 52nd Foot marching through the carnage of the evening unarmed, 'for an ensign needed both hands to carry the colour, and did not draw his sword'; Marshal Ney after the rout of Napoleon's Imperial Guard, dismounted, bareheaded and dirty, a broken sword in his hand, abandoned by his soldiers, rallying his men with the cry, 'Come and see a Marshal of France die'; Colonel Ponsonby of

97 Napoleon's embarkation from Rochefort on the British ship *H.M.S. Bellerophon*. The ship sailed to Plymouth and from there, on 8 August, Napoleon left for St Helena

the Scots Greys, who had been seen on the slopes below La Belle Alliance leading a cavalry charge against the French artillery with both his arms hanging useless and the reins in his teeth; and Blücher himself, wounded while leading a cavalry charge at Ligny and rescued unconscious by his troops from the counter-attacking French.

It is not easy to see clearly through the fog of this particular battle and of the remarkable courage of those who took part in it; to make judgements about tactical blunders or the contributions of individual commanders, regiments or armies. Certainly, as Wellington himself said, 'there was glory enough for all'. Yet Waterloo was a microcosm of the whole mysterious paradox of men at war – the glory and the squalor, the excitement and the boredom, the exaltation and the fear, the courage and the cowardice. It is a battle that contains the answers to some of the questions which the student of war is eternally asking himself. What is it that makes ordinary men (and women), normally gentle, unaggressive and kind, behave like ferocious animals when they put on a uniform and glare across a battlefield at other men and women who, they have been led to believe, are their enemies? Today, of course, the battlefield is vast and limitless; the weapons of destruction are complicated machines, released at the touch of a button to inflict their dreadful devastation thousands of miles away. Much of war is impersonal, remote, and the basic inhibitions against the maiming and killing of other human beings are correspondingly eroded.

At Waterloo, however, the battlefield was small, the weapons were the lance, the sword, the musket and the cannonball (which, according to the firm belief of the soldier of those days, you only saw coming if it was going to hit you). For hours of that day men charged at each other on foot or on horses, they hacked, slashed and stabbed each other to death; they fought with bare hands, often continuing to fight with shattered limbs and broken bodies. They suffered the agony of amputations without anaesthetics and, for the most part, they never contemplated any possible alternative to this incredible behaviour. The Duke of Wellington rode up to Major General Sir Colin Halkett during the French cavalry attacks on the afternoon of the battle, and asked him how the battle went. 'My Lord, we are dreadfully cut up', replied Halkett, 'can you not relieve us for a while?' 'Impossible', said the Duke. 'Very well', said the General, 'we'll stand till the last man falls.'

Yet 10,000 men under Wellington's command ran away; and the flower of the French army, after fighting with unbelievable courage all day, was, at the end of the battle, transformed in minutes into an undisciplined rabble. Explanations for these strange manifestations of resolute bravery and panic-stricken flight are often filtered through perceptions of nationalism, regimental pride or the image of some revered historical figure. Yet there can be no presumption that any army, any general or any regiment is intrinsically better or braver than any other.

Waterloo: Battle of Three Armies is an attempt to describe one of the great battles of history while at the same time liberating the mind of the reader from the shackles of national prejudice.

Appendix I

GUIDE TO THE BATTLEFIELD

William Seymour

General

The Battle of Waterloo was fought twelve miles to the south of Brussels on the Charleroi road and two miles south of the village of Waterloo. Waterloo is now virtually a suburb of Brussels, and the road from there to Mont St Jean is heavily built over on either side; but although new motorways are in the process of construction to the immediate north, the battlefield itself is protected by Belgian law and is very little changed from how it would have appeared on 18 June 1815. The principal exception is the Lion Hill. This artificial erection, built in the 1820s as a Netherlands memorial, a landmark for miles around, has greatly altered the appearance of Wellington's left centre, for in the removal of the vast quantity of soil required to build the hill the steep slope down to La Haye Sainte was graded and the high banks of the country road disappeared. Much of the excavation was done around the crossroads, where for part of the day Wellington had his headquarters, so the field from this position no longer looks as he saw it. The two memorials on either side of the Brussels–Charleroi road (Gordon's on the west and the Hanoverian on the east) stand approximately at the original level of the ground. Wellington's elm disappeared a long time ago, nor has the tree planted to replace it survived.

The battlefield can be reached by bus from the centre of Brussels, and various agencies organize coach tours, but a car is essential for those wishing to cover the whole field in a comparatively short time – and it is better if the student of the battle has someone else with him to act as chauffeur. The journey from Brussels is not a long one, but those unacquainted with Belgian roads and road users might find it pleasanter to stay locally. There are numerous hotels in the neighbouring towns, some excellent, such as the Château de Groenendaal at Hoeilaart, others not so good. There are restaurants catering for all tastes close to the Lion Hill.

At Waterloo, opposite the church (which contains many interesting memorials), in what was the inn where Wellington had his headquarters before and after the battle, are some Wellingtonian relics and a very fine display of illuminated maps showing the positions of the rival armies during each phase of the battle. This museum (the Wellington Museum) should be visited before a tour of the battlefield. Near the Lion Hill is the Panorama, in which is a large circular mural showing the battle during the French cavalry charges. David Howarth's brief but extremely comprehensive guide to the battlefield is on sale here; it contains a lot of interesting information.

Close to the Panorama is the Musée de l'Empereur, which has a collection of wax effigies of some of Napoleon's marshals and other figures. The Wellington Museum is closed between 30 September and 1 April (although it can be visited during these months on special application to the curator), but the other two are open all the year round. There is a small admission charge for these museums. The museum at Caillou, two miles south of the battlefield, which contains most interesting Napoleonic relics, is at present closed for restoration.

The visitor who has read this book will probably wish to look at the battlefield in much the same order as the chapters, and therefore the phases of the battle, unfold, starting with Hougoumont, then going on to the centre of Wellington's line, the French position, and Wellington's left flank. The more active, who also have time to spare, might like to climb the Lion Hill after visiting the Panorama. From this vantage point one gets an excellent impression of the whole battlefield – but it has to be remembered that no commander who fought in the battle had such a privileged view.

Hougoumont

Hougoumont is now a farm, the present occupiers of which are proud of its great historical connection and very willing to allow visitors to enter the courtyard and walk through what was the garden and orchard. But one must appreciate that these fields and enclosures, like all the rest of the battlefield, are private property. The farm is situated just to the east of the Nivelles road about two miles from where that road leaves the Charleroi one at Mont St Jean, and there is a sign marked Goumont. Basically the place has changed very little in the last 160 years; the chateau, cow house and stable block were never replaced after the fire, but the chapel, the large barn on the west side, the gardener's house (now the farmhouse) and the south gate are very much as they were. The north entrance (still the main one) no longer has any archway or building above it, and of course the great wooden doors have disappeared. The smaller gate in the west wall, through which Colonel Woodford led his Coldstream Guardsmen, is now blocked up, but clearly visible, as are the loopholes in the south wall of the garden.

To the south of the buildings, where there was a wood, there are now fields, but if one looks over the garden wall it is very easy to see the line of what was the wood – a few isolated trees remain – and the narrow strip of open ground which was the scene of so much slaughter when the French debouched from the wood and were faced by the Coldstreamers lining the wall. The Hollow Way can still be walked along (although the orchard hedges have gone), but this necessitates walking across what is usually a very muddy field. Indeed, the visitor wishing to make a thorough examination of Hougoumont is well advised to have a pair of wellingtons in the car at all but the driest times of the year.

Hougoumont is, perhaps, the most evocative part of the whole battlefield. It is very easy here to open a window on the past and to see through it the epic struggle that lasted on and off throughout the day, and to realize just how vital it was to Wellington that the Guards and Germans should have kept it safe.

Right centre of the line

From Hougoumont this is easily reached on foot. About 300 yards up the Nivelles road, just past a private house, one comes to a lane running towards the Lion Hill. At this point, where it meets the Nivelles road, the old country road, with its fairly deep cutting, is almost exactly as it was in 1815. It leads, after about a quarter of a mile, to the Lion Hill, but at the point where it comes out on to open ground – a little way beyond another track which runs south-east across the battlefield to La Belle Alliance – one is standing on that part of the line which was manned by Maitland's Guards brigade, with Adam's light infantry regiments a little way to the right. This ground is exactly as it was at the time of the battle, except for the house and woody enclosure immediately south of the lane, and from it one gets the same view of the undulating ground towards La Belle Alliance as those who defended the ridge in 1815 – at least those who were not forming square just behind the lane prior to the cavalry attack, or lying down prior to the advance of the Imperial Guard. Hougoumont can be seen through the trees to the right, but from this point La Haye Sainte is not visible.

A little further up the lane towards the Lion Hill one can see what is probably the very bank behind which Captain Mercer had his troop, and from most points along the lane it is easy to realize how close the French must have been before they became aware of the allied troops drawn up just behind the ridge.

Looking back towards the Nivelles road one sees the undulating ground in which the cavalry and reserves were placed, and it is obvious what a tactically sound position this was for them.

La Belle Alliance

Having examined part of the battlefield from the Anglo-Dutch army's viewpoint, it is interesting to cross the field and see how the ridge must have appeared to the attacking French troops. If the weather is fine and a car can be driven to meet the walker, it is suggested that having visited Hougoumont by car, the car could then be driven round to La Belle Alliance (situated on the east side of the Brussels–Charleroi road, two miles south of Mont St Jean), while the walker could take the track that crosses the battlefield diagonally from the area of the last vantage point to La Belle Alliance. This allows a good view of the Anglo-Dutch position first from the intermediate ridge and later from what was the French position along the ridge that runs east and west of La Belle Alliance. If this is not practicable it is easy to motor back to the crossroads and down the main road to La Belle Alliance, which at the time of the writer's last visit (October 1974) was still unspoilt – and with plenty of parking space.

The only fighting near La Belle Alliance took place at the very end of the day, when battalions of the Imperial Guard carried out an important delaying action with skill and courage. But a little further to the north is La Haye Sainte, the scene of some of the heaviest fighting of the whole day.

La Haye Sainte

The first part of the short drive to La Haye Sainte is over the route taken by the Guard as they marched, with Napoleon at their head, for what proved to be their last magnificent parade and bloody battle. La Haye Sainte, like Hougoumont, has changed very little since 1815. It is on a slightly smaller scale than Hougoumont, with the yard leading directly off the main road, and the occupiers – quite naturally – prefer to keep the premises private. But it is not necessary to invade their privacy in order to get a view of the buildings, for these can be seen quite well from the two monuments just below the crossroads. There is a lay-by close to the Hanoverian monument that can be used as a temporary car park, and by crossing the road (for which great care is necessary) the visitor can walk down to the open gateway and look inside. This gap was not there in 1815, but the site of the main gate (now permanently closed) just above it has not been altered. The Hanoverian monument is worth a visit before leaving the area, for it commands a good view of the battlefield to the south and east. This spot marks one of the largest graves on the battlefield, where some 4,000 men were buried.

99 Below left: The exterior of the Wellington Museum at Waterloo, in the building where Wellington had his headquarters. 100 Below right: Wellington's armchair and dispatch box

101 Following pages: The Waterloo mound commemorating the battle: in the foreground, the building which houses the panorama of the battlefield and various museums; in the background, the plain of Mont St Jean where Napoleon was finally and decisively defeated on 18 June 1815

Papelotte and Ter La Haye

Two hundred yards north of La Haye Sainte the visitor is back at the crossroads, where the Ohain road (at the time of the battle unpaved) runs west to the Lion Hill and the Nivelles road, and east towards the hamlet of Smohain, which is now called La Marache. In 1815 the lane just east of the crossroads had a hedge on each side of it, and the line of the road marks the approximate position of Sir Thomas Picton's 5th British Division, with Bylandt's Dutch–Belgian brigade on the forward slope. The 1st Battalion 95th Rifles were close to the crossroads, and on their left were the rest of Kempt's brigade and then Pack's Scotsmen. Standing just east of the crossroads, the visitor is more or less at the centre of d'Erlon's first massive infantry attack.

The road to La Marache is narrow and rather twisting, and there are few places where it is safe to stop; but driving slowly down the shoulder of the ridge one gets a good idea of the natural strength of this position. There is little of value to be learned from a visit to the Papelotte and Ter La Haye farmsteads, both of which are, of course, private property, and both of which have been somewhat altered. But the track running south-west to La Belle Alliance from the sunken road just south of Papelotte is exactly as it was at the time of the battle, and those with the time and energy to walk it will find themselves crossing that part of the field marched and fought over by Durutte's division. From La Marache there is a road running east and south to Plancenoit; the old part of the town and the church were the scene of very heavy fighting between the Prussians and the Young Guard.

Near Plancenoit there is a choice of roads; one hits the main Brussels road near Le Caillou, and the other at La Belle Alliance. This latter passes by – on the left side, and a very short way before La Belle Alliance – some steps leading up the bank to the place said to be Napoleon's viewpoint at midday. No doubt there were times when he stood on or near this spot, but for much of the afternoon he was further back, at Rossomme.

The chief viewpoints described above can be visited by car in two hours, or a little longer, but the student who wishes to absorb the detail and get the real feel of the battle should allow himself a full day – especially if he visits the museums. There are many excellent contemporary accounts of the fighting (Mercer's, Kennedy's, Leeke's, Harry Smith's and Gronow's, to name but a few), which although they may deal with only a narrow sector – being concerned with the individual's experiences – are well worth reading before a visit. The battlefield has changed so little that it is almost possible to relive the excitements and anxieties that these men experienced more than 160 years ago.

Appendix II

ORDERS & DISPATCHES

Jacques Champagne

15 June

Napoleon to Ney (verbal). Charleroi 3 p.m. Giving Ney command of French army's left flank, with orders to occupy Quatre-Bras and take up position there (p. 36).

Ney to Napoleon (verbal message). Gosselies 8 p.m. 'I occupy Quatre-Bras with a vanguard and my masses are camping behind.'

16 June

Napoleon (Soult) to Ney (p. 37). Charleroi 7 to 8 a.m. 'Monsieur le Maréchal, a lancers' officer has just told the Emperor that the enemy was showing masses towards Quatre-Bras. Group the corps of Counts Reille and d'Erlon with that of the Count of Valmy [Kellermann], who is starting out right now to join you. With these forces, you must beat and destroy all the enemy corps which may present themselves. Blücher was in Namur yesterday and it is not likely that he will have moved troops towards Quatre-Bras. So you have to deal only with what comes from Brussels. Maréchal de Grouchy is going to make the move on Sombreffe which I have announced to you. The Emperor is going to Fleurus. This is where you will address your reports to His Majesty.' (Received 11 a.m. in Frasnes, p. 38).)

Napoleon (Soult) to Ney (p. 37). Fleurus 11 a.m. Confirming previous dispatch. (Received Frasnes 1.30 p.m., p. 37.)

Napoleon (Soult) to Ney (p. 37). Fleurus 2 p.m. 'Monsieur le Maréchal, The Emperor entrusts me with warning you that the enemy has gathered a corps of troops between Sombreffe and Brye and that at 2.30 p.m., Marshal de Grouchy will attack them with III and IV Corps. His Majesty's intention is that you should also attack what is before you and that, after you have vigorously pushed the enemy, you should fall back on us to concur in the envelopment of the corps which I have just mentioned. If this corps is burst through before that, then His Majesty will have a manoeuvre made in your direction to hasten your operations also. Instruct the Emperor immediately of your dispositions and of what goes on on your front.' (Received Quatre-Bras 5 p.m., p. 40.)

Napoleon (Soult) to Ney (p. 37). Ligny 4.30 p.m. 'Monsieur le Maréchal, I wrote to you an hour ago that the Emperor would have the enemy attacked at 2 p.m. in the position he had taken between St Amand and Brye. At this moment, the engagement is very pronounced. His Majesty entrusts me with telling you that you must manoeuvre instantly in order to envelop the enemy's right and fall with might and main on his rear. This army is lost if you act vigorously. The fate of France is in your hands. So do not hesitate for an instant and do operate the movement which the Emperor orders you to make on the heights of Brye and St Amand in order to concur in what will perhaps be a decisive victory. The enemy is caught red-handed at the moment when he seeks to re-unite with the English.' (Received Quatre-Bras 6 a.m., when battle with Wellington was in full swing, p. 40.)

17 June

Napoleon (Bertrand) to Ney (p. 41). Ligny 11 a.m. Order to resume action on Quatre-Bras pending Napoleon's arrival with army. (Received Frasnes 1.30 p.m., note 24, p. 226)

Napoleon (Bertrand) to Grouchy (p. 41). Ligny 11 a.m. 'Proceed to Gembloux with the cavalry corps of Generals Pajol and Exelmans, the light cavalry of IV Corps (Gérard), the Teste infantry division and the III (Vandamme) and IV Infantry Corps. You will reconnoitre in the direction of Namur and Maestricht and you will pursue the enemy. Scout out his march and inform me of his movements to enable me to penetrate his intentions. I am transferring my headquarters at Quatre-Bras, where the English still were this morning. Our communications will therefore be by the paved road of Namur. If the enemy has evacuated Namur, write to the General commanding the 2nd Military Division at Charlemont in order to have this town occupied by a few battalions of the National Guard. It is important to penetrate Blücher's and Wellington's intentions and to know whether they propose to re-unite their armies to cover Brussels and Liège by tempting fate in a battle. In any case, keep your two infantry corps constantly together in two and a half miles of ground with several retreat exits; post intermediary cavalry detachments to communicate with General Headquarters.' (When Soult learned of this order on his way back from Fleurus to Ligny, he thought it a mistake so to detach almost one-third of the army to the sole pursuit of the Prussians.)

Napoleon modified his order to Grouchy in one respect only, less than half an hour later. He informed Grouchy that the Teste infantry division and Milhaud's cuirassiers would be subtracted from his command to take part instead in the action against Wellington. Only Milhaud was able to join Napoleon at Quatre-Bras and Mont St Jean. The Teste division was already too far away with Pajol's cavalry shadowing the retreating Prussians.

It was to distinguish itself in the capture of Wavre on 19 June.

Grouchy to Napoleon (p. 44). Gembloux 10 p.m. 'Sire, The enemy 30,000 strong continue to retreat. It seems from all reports that, from Sauvenières, the Prussians have divided into two columns. One must have taken the road to Wavre through Sart-a-Walhain, the other one seems to have taken the direction of Perwès [Liège]. A third one, with artillery, is retreating on Namur. One can infer that a portion is going to join Wellington and that the centre, which is Blücher's army, retreats on Liège. If the Prussians' mass retires on Wavre, I shall follow it in this direction to prevent it from reaching Brussels and to separate it from Wellington. If, on the contrary, their principal forces have marched on Perwès I shall follow them in pursuit through this town.' (Received at Caillou 4 a.m. 18 June, p. 45.)

18 June

Napoleon (Soult) to Grouchy (p. 79). Caillou 10 a.m. 'The Emperor has received your last report dated from Gembloux. You talk to His Majesty of two Prussian columns which have passed at Sauvenières and at Sart-a-Walhain. However, some reports say that a third column, quite a strong one, passed through Géry and Gentinnes marching towards Wavre. The Emperor enjoins me to warn you that at this moment he is about to have the English army attacked at Waterloo near the Forest of Soignes where it has taken up position. His Majesty therefore desires that you should direct your movements on Wavre so as to come nearer to us, to establish operational and liaison contact with us, pushing in front of you the Prussian army corps who have taken this direction and who might have stopped at Wavre, where you must arrive as soon as possible. You will have the Prussian army corps who have taken to your right followed by some light corps so as to observe their movements and to gather their stragglers. Instruct me immediately of your dispositions and of your march as well as of the information you possess on the enemy, and do not neglect to bind your communications with us. The Emperor desires to have news of you very often.' (Received 4 p.m. before Wavre, p. 103.)

Grouchy to Napoleon (p. 102). Gembloux 6 a.m. 'Sire, All my reports and information confirm that the enemy is retiring on Brussels to concentrate there or to give battle after joining Wellington. I and II Corps of Blücher's army seem to be marching, the first on Corbais, the second on Chaumont. They must have started yesterday evening (17 June) at 8 p.m. from Tourinnes and marched all night; fortunately the weather was so bad that they cannot have gone very far. I am leaving this instant for Sart-a-Walhain and from there to Corbais and Wavre.' (Received Rossomme 11 a.m., p. 82.)

Napoleon's Order of Battle (p. 81). Rossomme 11 a.m. 'Once the whole army is ranged in battle order, at about 1 p.m., and when the Emperor gives Marshal Ney the relevant order, the attack will begin in order to capture the village of Mont St Jean, which is the road junction. To this end, the 12-inch batteries of II and VI Corps will regroup with those of I Corps. These 94 cannon will fire on the troops of Mont St Jean and Count d'Erlon will begin the attack by bringing forward his left wing division, supporting it, according to the circumstances, by the other I Corps divisions. II Corps will advance so as to keep at the level of Count d'Erlon. The sapper companies of I Corps will be ready to entrench themselves immediately at Mont St Jean.'

Napoleon (Soult) to Grouchy (p. 83). Rossomme 1.15 p.m. 'Monsieur le Maréchal, You wrote to the Emperor this morning at 6 a.m. that you would march on Sart-a-Walhain. You were planning therefore to go to Corbais and Wavre. This movement is in accordance with His Majesty's dispositions which have been communicated to you. However, the Emperor orders me to tell you that you must always manoeuvre in our direction and seek to come closer to us in order to join us before any corps can come between us. I do not indicate any direction to you. It is for you to see the point where we are, to regulate yourself in consequence and to bind our communications, as well as always to be in a position to fall upon any enemy troops which would seek to worry our right flank, and to crush them. At this time, the battle is engaged on the line at Waterloo.' The following words were added by Soult: 'in front of the Forest of Soignes. The enemy centre is at Mont St Jean, so do manoeuvre to join our right.' Then followed a postscript added by Soult on Napoleon's order: 'P.S. A letter just intercepted says that General Bülow is going to attack our right flank. We think that we can perceive this corps on the heights of St Lambert. Do not lose one moment, therefore, in coming closer to us, in joining us and in crushing Bülow whom you will catch red-handed.' (Received before Wavre 7 p.m., Chapter 8, note 4, p. 229.)

(In his memoirs, Grouchy says that he read 'la bataille est *gagnée*' (the battle is *won*) instead of 'la bataille est *engagée*' (the battle is *engaged*). The

original manuscripted dispatch, perfectly preserved, leaves no doubt whatever that the word is in fact '*engagée*' (*engaged*).)

Grouchy to Napoleon (see pp. 102–3). Sart-a-Walhain 11 a.m. There is no trace of it having been received at La Belle Alliance, where it might have arrived between 5 and 6 p.m., at a time when the battle was raging at Mont St Jean.

19 June

Napoleon (Soult) to Grouchy (see p. 171). Quatre-Bras 1 a.m. (Received in Wavre later that morning, p. 171).

Note There is no doubt that certain written dispatches and verbal messages to and from Napoleon's various headquarters were not transcribed in Major-General Soult's register and that others did not arrive at their destinations, the dispatch riders being captured or killed by Prussian patrols in the 'operational triangle' during the three days 16–18 June.

But all the important dispatches did arrive or at least were transmitted, although sometimes rather late owing to distances, weather conditions, avoidance of enemy patrols and errors of itinerary. One crucial exception, however, constitutes a mystery which has never been solved

At about 9 p.m. on 17 June General Count Milhaud (IV Cavalry Reserve Corps), who was detached from Grouchy's mission to take part in the action against Wellington (see Orders and Dispatches, 17 June, Napoleon (Bertrand) to Grouchy), reported verbally to Napoleon at Caillou (see page 44) that during his march from Marbais to Quatre-Bras his right flank scouts had recognized a Prussian cavalry column retreating from Tilly to Wavre.

In his memoirs (confirmed in slightly different terms by General Gourgaud in his *Cahiers*), Napoleon specifically states that he sent a liaison officer to Grouchy at 10 p.m. on 17 June from Caillou to let him know:

that a great battle would probably take place on the next day [18 June]; that the Anglo-Dutch army was in position in front of the Forest of Soignes, its left flank leaning on to the hamlet of La Haye; that he [Napoleon] was ordering him [Grouchy] to detach before dawn from his camp in Wavre [where he was supposed to be by now] a division of 7,000 men of all arms with 16 cannon on St Lambert in order to join up with the army's right flank and to operate with it; that as soon as he [Grouchy] was certain that Blücher had evacuated Wavre, either to continue his march on Brussels or to march in any other direction, he [Grouchy] should march himself with the majority of his troops in support of the detachment he had sent to St Lambert.

In his memoirs, Grouchy declares that he never received this order, nor did he see any of Napoleon's liaison officers to that effect. Yet, in the same memoirs, Grouchy's son and grand-son (both Marquis de Grouchy) state that in the course of their long enquiry to establish the true role played by the Marshal during the campaign, they received from a M. le Tourneux the following letter dated 27 August 1840:

In 1815, during the Prussians' stay in Caen, Marshal Blücher's son, attached to his father's headquarters, often came to visit a cousin of his, hussar non-commissioned officer Lanken, who was billeted in my house, in the company of another young officer: Vousseaux. One day, the Marshal's son related as follows what had happened in his presence at Marshal Blücher's headquarters:

'An officer of the Imperial Headquarters was brought to Marshal Blücher. Had he been captured? Was he a traitor? This I do not know. But the fact is that he was carrying an order written in pencil addressed to Marshal de Grouchy saying that the latter must march on the point where the Emperor was and leave 6,000 men in front of the Prussian Army so as to mask his movement and to keep the enemy in check whilst making his move. In possession of this document, Marshal Blücher himself had made exactly this manoeuvre. And that is why the Emperor kept repeating, when perceiving an army corps coming from the side where he was expecting Monsieur le Maréchal de Grouchy: "It is Grouchy! It is Grouchy!"'

No one seems ever to have traced either the said message or any of the three young Prussian officers to obtain confirmation or denial of this story.

Appendix III/Tables

Table 1: Strength of the allied army of all nationalities at the commencement of the Battle of Waterloo

	Infantry	Cavalry	Artillery	Total men	Guns
British	15,181	5,843	2,967	23,991	78
King's German Legion	3,301	1,997	526	5,824	18
Hanoverians	10,258	495	465	11,220	12
Brunswickers	4,586	866	510	5,962	16
Nassauers	2,880	—	—	2,880	—
Dutch–Belgians	13,402	3,205	1,177	17,784	32
Total	49,608	12,408	5,645	67,661	156

Taken from Dorsey Gardener's *Quatre Bras, Ligny and Waterloo*.

THE FRENCH, ANGLO-DUTCH AND PRUSSIAN ARMIES OF THE LINE ON 1 JUNE
1815 (Archives de la Guerre, Paris)
AND AT MONT ST JEAN, 18 JUNE 1815 (Archives de la Guerre, Paris)

Table 2: French Army of the Line (Emperor Napoleon) (see pp. 28 and 31)

1 *Flanders Army* (for corps detail, see Table 4)

I Corps. Gen. Count d'Erlon	H.Q. Lille	18,640 inf. cav. art.	— 46 can.
II Corps. Gen. Count Reille	H.Q. Valenciennes	23,530 ,, ,, ,,	— 46 ,,
III Corps. Gen. Count Vandamme	H.Q. Mézières	15,290 ,, ,, ,,	— 38 ,,
IV Corps. Gen. Count Gérard	H.Q. Metz	14,260 ,, ,, ,,	— 38 ,,
Reserve Inf. Corps. (later known as VI Corps.) Gen. Count Lobau	H.Q. Laon	11,770 inf.	— 38 ,,
VII Corps. Marshal Grouchy (cavalry reserve)	H.Q. Aisne-Sambre	11,290 (4 cav. corps and art.)	— 48 can.
Imperial Guard Emperor Napoleon	H.Q. Paris	18,520 inf. cav. art.	— 96 ,,
Engineers, transport, supply etc.		2,200	
Total		115,500 officers and men—350 can.	

This army, numbering originally 122,400 officers and men, had to detach 6,900 men to the Army of the Vendée (see opposite).

2 Covering Armies

V Corps. Gen. Count Rapp	H.Q. Alsace	20,456	inf. cav. art.	— 46 can.	
VI Corps. Marshal Suchet	H.Q. Chambéry	15,764	,, ,, ,,	— 46 ,,	
	Total	36,220	,, ,, ,,	— 92 can.	
(less detached to the Army of the Vendée)		3,100			
	Total	33,120	,, ,, ,,	— 92 can.	

3 Observation Corps

I Corps. (Jura)	Gen. Lecourbe	H.Q. Belfort	5,392	inf. cav. art.	— 38 can.
II Corps. (Provence)	Marshal Brune	H.Q. Var	6,116	,, ,, ,,	— 22 ,,
III Corps. (Pyrenees)	Gen. Decean	H.Q. Toulouse	3,516	,, ,, ,,	— 24 ,,
IV Corps. (Gironde)	Gen. Clausel	H.Q. Bordeaux	3,516	,, ,, ,,	— 24 ,,
(IV Corps. in support of the Vendée Army)					
		Total	18,540	,, ,, ,,	—108 can.

4 Army of the Vendée (under Gen. Lamarque)

In Vendée	17,000	inf. cav. art.	—24 can.	
(including gendarmes and National Guard)				
From Flanders Army	6,900	inf. cav. art.		
From Covering Armies	3,100	,, ,, ,,		
Total	27,000	,, ,, ,,	—24 can. (and Gironde corps. support)	

Recapitulation				
	Flanders Army	115,500	officers and men	—350 can.
	Covering Armies	33,120	,, ,, ,,	— 92 ,,
	Observation Corps	18,540	,, ,, ,,	—108 ,,
	Army of the Vendée	27,000	,, ,, ,,	— 24 ,,
	Total Army of the Line	194,160	,, ,, ,,	—574 ,,

Table 3: French Special Auxiliary Army (see p. 31)

217,400 officers and men, infantry, cavalry and artillery, including 85,000 élite National Guard, manning 90 main French frontier strongholds, provincial forts, Paris and Lyon, and ports. Garrisoned all over France, mainly in the proximity of Flanders, Paris and Lyon.

Table 4: Flanders Army, later known as Armée du Nord (detail)

I Corps.	Count d'Erlon 4 inf. divs.	1st	Gen. Allix	4,120
	(32 battalions)	2nd	Gen. Donzelot	4,100
		3rd	Gen. Marcognet	4,000
	Total 16,220	4th	Gen. Durutte	4,000
1st Cav. Div. (11 squadrons)	Gen. Jacquinot 1,500			
Artillery: 46 can., crews	920		**Total I Corps**	**18,640**
II Corps.	**Count Reille** 4 inf. divs.	5th	Gen. Bachelu	5,000
		6th	Pce Jérôme	6,100
(with Chief of Staff div. Gen. Guilleminot)		7th	Gen. Girard	5,000
	Total 21,100	9th	Gen. Foy	5,000
2nd Light Cav. Div.	Gen. Piré 1,500			
Artillery: 46 can., crews	930		Total II Corps	23,530
III Corps.	**Count Vandamme** 3 inf. divs.	8th	Gen. Lefol	4,300
		10th	Gen. Hubert	4,430
	Total 13,030	11th	Gen. Berthézène	4,300
3rd Light Cav. Div.	Gen. Domon 1,500			
Artillery: 38 can., crews	760		Total III Corps	15,290
IV Corps.	**Count Gérard** 3 inf. divs.	12th	Gen. Pécheux	4,000
		13th	Gen. Vichery	4,000
		14th	Gen. Bourmont	4,000
	Total 12,000		then: Gen. Hulot	
6th Light Cav. Div.	Gen. Maurin 1,500			
Artillery: 38 can., crews	760		Total IV Corps.	14,260
VI Corps. (infantry reserve)	**Count Lobau** 3 inf. divs.	19th	Gen. Simmer	3,500
		20th	Gen. Jeanin	3,500
	Total 11,000	21st	Gen. Teste	4,000
Artillery: 38 can., crews	770		Total VI Corps.	11,770

Imperial Guard.	Infantry: Young Guard		Gen. Duhesme	3,800
	(chasseurs): Middle Guard		Gen. Morand	4,250
	(Old): Grenadiers		Gen. Friant	4,420
			Total infantry	12,470
	Light Cav. Div.		Gen. Lefèvre-Desnouettes	2,120
	Heavy Cav. Div.		Gen. Guyot	2,010
			Total cavalry	4,130
	Artillery (Gen. Devaux) 96 can., crews			1,920
			Total Guard	18,520

Cavalry reserve.	**Marshal Grouchy**			
I Corps.	**Count Pajol**	4th Div.	Gen. Soult, brother of Marshal Soult	1,280
(hussars and chasseurs)		5th Div.	Gen. Subervie	1,240
			Total I Corps.	2,520
II Corps.	**Count Exelmans**	9th Div.	Gen. Strolz	1,300
(dragoons)		10th Div.	Gen. Chastel	1,300
			Total II Corps.	2,600
III Corps.	**Count Kellermann**	11th Div.	Gen. Lhéritier	1,310
(cuirassiers)		12th Div.	Gen. Roussel	1,300
			Total III Corps.	2,610
IV Corps.	**Count Milhaud**	13th Div.	Gen. Wathier	1,300
(cuirassiers)		14th Div.	Gen. Delort	1,300
			Total IV Corps.	2,600

Total cavalry reserve	10,330	
Artillery: 48 can., crews	960	
Total under Marshal Grouchy	**11,290**	

Recapitulation Flanders Army		**Inf.**	**Cav.**	**Art.**	**Can.**	
I Corps.		16,220	1,500	920	46	
II Corps.		21,100	1,500	930	46	
III Corps.		13,030	1,500	760	38	
IV Corps.		12,000	1,500	760	38	
VI Corps. (infantry reserve)		11,000	—	770	38	
Imperial Guard		12,470	4,130	1,920	96	
Cavalry reserve		—	10,330	960	48	
	Total	85,820	20,460	7,020	350	= 113,300
		Engineers, sappers, supply				= 2,200
		Total Flanders Army			350 can.	—115,500

Table 5: Allied Armies of the line (Duke of Wellington)

1 ANGLO-DUTCH

24 infantry brigades	9 English, 10 German, 5 Belgian–Dutch	79,400
11 cavalry brigades	16 English regiments, 9 German, 6 Dutch	15,600
30 artillery brigades	mixed 30 English, 13 Belgian–Dutch	7,500
13 engineers, sappers	258 can.	

	Total Anglo-Dutch	102,500

I Corps. Prince of Orange
11 infantry brigades forming 5 divisions

	2 English	Maj. Gen. Cooke	5,000
		Lt. Gen. Alten	9,800
	3 Dutch	Lt. Gen. Chassé	7,400
		Lt. Gen. Perponcher	8,000
		Lt. Gen. Collaert	7,200

	Total I Corps.	37,400

II Corps. Lord Hill
13 infantry brigades forming 5 divisions

	4 English	Lt. Gen. Clinton	9,700
		Lt. Gen. Colville	9,300
		Lt. Gen. Picton	9,700
		Lt. Gen. Cole	8,000
	1 German	Duke of Brunswick	5,300

	Total II Corps.	42,000

Cavalry Corps. Lord Uxbridge

11 brigades	7 English	Maj. Gens. Somerset, Ponsonby, Dornberg, Vandeleur, Grant, Vivian and Colonel Arentschildt together	10,400	
	1 Hanoverian	1,200		
	2 Dutch	3,100		
	1 Brunswick	900		5,200

	Total Cavalry	15,600

Artillery and Service Corps.

	30 English brigades	180 can.	4,500 crews
	13 Belgian–Dutch brigades	78 can.	2,000 crews
	Sappers, miners etc.		1,000

	Total Artillery	258 can.	7,500

Recapitulation Anglo-Dutch Army

	Infantry	79,400	
	Cavalry	15,600	
	Artillery	7,500	258 can.
Total Anglo-Dutch Army		102,500	258 can.

2 PRUSSIAN–SAXON ARMY (Field-Marshal Blücher)

I Corps. Gen. Zieten	4 inf. divs.	34 battalions	27,200
	1 cav. div.	32 squadrons	4,800
		Total	32,000
II Corps. Gen. Pirch	4 inf. divs.	36 battalions	28,800
	1 cav. div.	36 squadrons	5,400
		Total	34,200
III Corps. Gen. Thielemann	4 inf. divs.	33 battalions	26,400
	1 cav. div.	32 squadrons	4,800
		Total	31,200
IV Corps. Gen. Bülow	4 inf. divs.	36 battalions	28,800
	1 cav. div.	48 squadrons	7,200
Artillery: 300 can., 8,500 crews		Total	36,000

Recapitulation Prussian–Saxon Army

	Infantry	111,200	
	Cavalry	22,200	
	Artillery	8,500	300 can.
Total Prussian–Saxon Army		141,900	300 can.

Recapitulation Allied Armies

	Anglo-Dutch	102,500	258 can.
	Prussian–Saxon	141,900	300 can.
Total Allied Armies of the Line		**244,400**	558 can.

Table 6: The Armies at Mont St Jean, 18 June 1815

1 Napolcon		Flanders Army	115,500	350 can. (see Table 4)
		Less	46,900	100 can.
			68,600	250 can.
Losses Ligny	8,500			
Losses Quatre-Bras	4,300			
Grouchy in Wavre with	34,100 and 100 can.			
2 Wellington		Army of the Line	102,500	258 can. (see Table 5
		Less	30,500	38 can. (1))
			72,000	220 can.
Losses Quatre-Bras	4,700	8 can.		
In Hal	16,500	30 can.		
In Brussels	2,200			
In Audenade and Ypres	1,500			
Disembarked in Ostend (see pp. 40 and 81)	5,600			
3 Blücher		Army of the Line	141,900	300 can. (see Table 5
		Less	24,500	? can. (2))
			117,400	250 can. (no less than)
Losses Ligny, Gosselies, runaways, Gilly (see pp. 35, 36 and 38)	24,500			

(of which: 30,000 at 4.30 p.m. plus 40,000 at 7 p.m. were engaged on Mont St Jean's battlefield with at least 175 cannon)

Appendix IV
THE CRISIS

There are few more vivid accounts of the last great crisis of the battle than those provided by Georgette Heyer and Victor Hugo: two novelists of very different styles and talents, one English, the other French. The late Sir John Wheeler Bennet regarded Georgette Heyer's account of the battle as one of the best he had ever read. Victor Hugo's is in its way equally dramatic, but perhaps the most moving passage is the last paragraph with its evocation of the 'visionary mist' and 'hallucination of the disaster.' A fitting conclusion to these two fictional accounts (taken respectively from *An Infamous Army* and *Les Misérables*) are Thackeray's four pungent paragraphs in *Vanity Fair*.

An Infamous Army

Georgette Heyer

104 The view from Mont St Jean, just before Wellington gave his order for the general advance

At seven o'clock things looked very serious along the Allied front. To the west, only some Prussian cavalry had arrived to guard the left flank; Papelotte and the farm of Ter La Haye were held by Durutte, whose skirmishers stretched to the crest of the Allied position; the gunners and the *tirailleurs* at La Haye Sainte were raking the centre with their fire; and although twelve thousand men of Reille's Corps d'Armée had failed all day to dislodge twelve hundred British Guards from the ruins of Hougoumont, all along the Allied line the front was broken, and in some places utterly disorganized.

The Duke remained calm, but kept looking at his watch. Once he said: 'It's night, or Blücher,' but for the most part he was silent. An Aide-de-Camp rode up to him with a message from his General that his men were being mowed down by the artillery fire, and must be reinforced. 'It is impossible,' he replied. 'Will they stand?'

'Yes, my lord, till they perish!'

'Then tell them that I will stand with them, till the last man.'

Turmoil and confusion, made worse by the smoke that hung heavily over the centre, and the débris that littered the ground from end to end of the line, seemed to reign everywhere. Staff Officers, carrying messages to brigades, asked mechanically: 'Who commands here?' The Prince of Orange had been taken away by March; three Generals had been killed; five others carried off the field, too badly wounded to remain; the Adjutant-General and the Quartermaster-General had both had to retire. Of the Duke's personal Staff, Canning was dead, Gordon dying in the inn at Waterloo; and Lord Fitzroy, struck in the right arm while standing with his horse almost touching the Duke's, had left the field in Alava's care. Those that were left had passed beyond feeling. It was no longer a matter for surprise or grief to hear of a friend's death: the only surprise was to find anyone still alive on that reeking plain. Horse after horse had been shot under them; sooner or later they would probably join the ranks of the slain: meanwhile, there were still orders to carry, and they forced their exhausted mounts through the carnage, indifferent to the heaps of fallen redcoats sprawling under their feet, themselves numb with fatigue, their minds focused upon one object only: to get the messages they carried through to their destinations.

Just before seven o'clock, a deserting Colonel of Cuirassiers came galloping up to the 52nd Regiment shouting: '*Vive le Roi*!' He reached Sir John Colborne, and gasped out: '*Napoléon est la avec les Gardes! Voila l'attaque qui se fait!'*

The warning was unnecessary, for it had been apparent for some minutes that the French were mustering for a grand attack all along the front. D'Erlon's corps was already assailing with a swarm of skirmishers the decimated line of Picton's 5th Division; and to the west of La Haye Sainte, on the undulating plain facing the Allied right, the Imperial Middle Guard was forming in five massive columns.

Colonel Audley was sent on his last errand just after seven. He was mounted on a trooper, and the strained and twisted strapping round his thigh was soaked with blood. He was almost unrecognizable for the smoke that had blackened his face, and was feeling oddly light-headed from the loss of blood he had suffered. He was also very tired, for he had been in the saddle almost continually since the night of the 15th June. His mind, ordinarily sensitive to impression, accepted without revulsion the message of his eyes. Death and mutilation had become so common that he who loved horses could look with indifference upon a poor brute with the lower half of its head blown away, or a trooper, with its fore-legs shot off at the knees, raising itself on its stumps, and neighing its sad appeal for help. He had seen a friend die in agony, and had wept over him, but all that was long past. He no longer ducked when he heard the shots singing past his head; when his trooper shied away, snorting in terror, from a bursting shell, he cursed it. But there was no sense in courting death unnecessarily; he struck northwards, and rode by all that was left of the two Heavy Brigades, drawn back since the arrival of Vivian and Vandeleur some three hundred paces behind the front line. An officer in the rags of a Life Guardsman's uniform, his helmet gone, and a blood-stained bandage tied round his head, rode forward and hailed him.

'Audley! Audley!'

He recognized Lord George Alastair under a mask of mud, and sweat, and blood-stains, and drew rein. 'Hallo!' he said. 'So you're alive still?'

'Oh, I'm well enough! Do you know how it has done with Harry?'

'Dead,' replied the Colonel.

George's eyelids flickered; under the dirt and the blood his face whitened. 'Thanks. That's all I wanted to know. You saw him?'

'Hours ago. He was dying then, in one of the Maitland's squares. He sent you his love.'

George saluted, wheeled his horse, and rode back to his squadron.

The Colonel pushed on to the chaussée. His horse slithered clumsily down the bank on to it; he held it together, and rode across the pavé to the opposite bank and scrambled up, emerging upon the desolation of the slope behind Picton's division. He urged the trooper to a ponderous gallop towards the rear of Best's brigade. A handful of Dutch–Belgians were formed in second line; he supposed them to be some of Count Bylandt's men, but paid little heed to them, wheeling round their right flank, and plunging once more into the region of shot and shell bursts.

He neither saw nor heard the shell that struck him. His horse came crashing down; he was conscious of having been hit; blood was streaming down his left arm, which lay useless on the ground beside him, but there was as yet no feeling in the shattered elbow-joint. His left side hurt him a little; he moved his right hand to it, and found his coat torn, and his shirt sticky with blood. He supposed vaguely that since he seemed to be alive this must be only a flesh wound. He desired nothing better than to lie where he had fallen, but he mastered himself, for he had a message to deliver, and struggled to his knees.

The sound of horse's hooves galloping towards him made him lift his head. An Adjutant in the blue uniform and orange facings of the 5th National Militia dismounted beside him, and said in English: 'Adjutant to Count Bylandt, sir! I'm directed by General Perponcher to – *Parbleu!* it is you, then!'

Colonel Audley looked up into a handsome, dark face bent over him, and said weakly: 'Hallo, Lavisse! Get me a horse, there's a good fellow!'

'A horse!' exclaimed Lavisse, going down on one knee, and supporting the Colonel in his arms. 'You need a surgeon, my friend! Be tranquil: my General sends to bear you off the field.' He gave a bitter laugh, and added: 'That is what my brigade exists for – to succour you English wounded!'

'Did you succeed in rallying your fellows?' asked the Colonel.

'Some, not all. Do not disturb yourself, my rival! You have all the honours of this day's encounter. *My* honour is in the dust!'

'Oh, don't talk such damned theatrical rubbish!' said the Colonel irritably. He fumbled with his right hand in his sash, and drew forth a folded and crumpled message. 'This has to go to General Best. See that it gets to him, will you? – or if he's been killed, to his next in command.'

A couple of orderlies and a doctor had come up from the rear. Lavisse gave the Colonel into their charge, and said with a twisted smile: 'You trust your precious message to me, my Colonel?'

'Be a good fellow, and don't waste time talking about it!' begged the Colonel.

He was carried off the field as the attack upon the whole Allied line began. On the left, Ziethen's advance guard had reached Smohain, and the Prussian batteries were in action, firing into Durutte's skirmishers; while somewhere to the south-east Bülow's guns could be heard assailing the French right flank. Allix and all that was left of Marcognet's division once more attacked the Allied left; Donzelot led his men against Ompteda's and Kielmansegg's depleted ranks; while the Imperial Guard of Grenadiers and Chasseurs moved up in five columns at rather narrow deploying intervals, in echelon, crossing the undulating plain diagonally from the chaussée to the Nivelles road. Each column showed a front of about seventy men, and in each of the intervals between the battalions two guns were placed. In all, some four thousand five hundred men were advancing upon the Allied right, led by Ney, *le Brave des Braves*, at the head of the leading battalion.

The sun, which all day had been trying to penetrate the clouds, broke through as the attack commenced. Its setting rays bathed the columns of the Imperial Guard in fiery radiance. Rank upon rank of veterans who had borne the Eagles victorious through a dozen fights advanced to the beat of drums, with bayonets turned to blood-red by the sun's last glow, across the plain into the smoke and heat of the battle.

Owing to their diagonal approach the columns did not come into action simultaneously. Before the battalions marching upon the British Guards had reached the slope leading to the crest of the Allied position, Ney's leading column had struck at Halkett's brigade and the Brunswickers on his left flank.

Over this part of the line the smoke caused by the guns firing from La Haye Sainte lay so thick that the Allied troops heard but could not see the formidable advance upon them. Colin Halkett had fallen, wounded in the mouth, rallying his men round one of the Colours; two of his regiments were operating as one battalion, so heavy had been their losses; and these were thrown into some confusion by their own Light troops retreating upon them. Men were carried off their feet in the surge to the rear; the Colonel, on whom the command of the brigade had devolved, seemed distracted, saying repeatedly: 'What am I to do? What would you do?' to the Staff Officer sent by the Duke to 'See what is wrong there!' The men of the 33rd, fighting against the tide that was sweeping them back, re-formed, and came on, shouting:

'Give them the cold steel, lads! Let 'em have the Brummagum!' A volley was poured in before which the deploying columns recoiled; to the left, the Brunswickers, rallied once more by the Duke himself, followed suit, and the Imperial Guard fell back, carrying with it a part of Donzelot's division.

Those of the batteries on the Allied front which were still in action met the advance with a fire which threw the leading ranks into considerable disorder. Many of the British batteries, however, were useless. Some had been abandoned owing to lack of ammunition; several guns stood with muzzles bent down, or touch-holes melted from the excessive heat; and more than one Troop, its gunner either killed or too exhausted to run the guns up after each recoil, had its guns in a confused heap, the trails crossing each other almost on top of the limbers and the ammunition wagons. Ross's, Sinclair's, and Snadham's were all silent. Lloyd's battery was still firing from in front of Halkett's brigade; so was Napier, commanding Bolton's, in front of Maitland; and a Dutch battery of eight guns, belonging to Detmer's brigade, brought up by Chassé in second line, had been sent forward to a position immediately to the east of the Brunswick squares, and was pouring in a rapid and well-directed fire upon the Grenadiers and the men on Donzelot's left flank.

As the Brunswickers and Halkett's men momentarily repulsed the two leading columns, which, on their march over the uneven ground, had become merged into one unwieldy mass, the Grenadiers and the Chasseurs on the French left advanced up the slope to where Maitland's Guards lay silently awaiting them. The drummers were beating the *pas de charge*, shouts of '*Vive l'Empereur!*' and '*En avant à la baïonnette!*' filled the air. The Duke, who had galloped down the line from his position by the Brunswick troops, was standing with Maitland on the left flank of the brigade, not far from General Adam, whose brigade lay to the right of the Guards. Adam had ridden up to watch the advance, and the Duke, observing through his glass the French falling back before Halkett's men, exclaimed: 'By God, Adam, I believe we shall beat them yet!'

At ninety paces, the brass 8-pounders between the advancing battalions opened fire upon Maitland's brigade. They were answered by Krahmer de Bichin's Dutch battery, but though the grapeshot tore through the ranks of the Guards the Duke withheld the order to open musketry-fire. Not a man in the British line was visible to the advancing columns until they halted twenty paces from the crest to deploy.

'Now, Maitland! Now's your time!' the Duke

said at last, and called out in his deep, ringing voice: 'Stand up, Guards!'

The Guards leapt to their feet. The crest, which had seemed deserted, was suddenly alive with men, scarlet coats standing in line four-deep, with muskets at the present. Almost at the point of crossing bayonets they fired volley after volley into the Grenadiers. The Grenadiers, in column, had only two hundred muskets able to fire against the fifteen hundred of Halkett's and Maitland's brigades, deployed in line before them. They tried to deploy, but were thrown into confusion by a fire no infantry could withstand.

On Maitland's left, General Chassé had brought up Detmer's brigade of Dutch–Belgians in perfect order. When the word to charge was given, and the sound of the three British cheers was heard as the Guards surged forward, the Dutch came up at the double, and, with a roar of 'Oranje boven!' drove the French from the crest in their front.

The Guards, scattering the Grenadiers before them, advanced until their flank was threatened by the second attacking column of Chasseurs. The recall was sounded, and the order given to face-about and retire. In the din of clashing arms, crackling musketry, groans, cheers, and trumpet-calls, the order was misunderstood. As the Guards regained the crest, an alarm of cavalry was raised. Someone shrieked: 'Square, square, form square!' and the two battalions trying to obey the order became intermingled. A dangerous confusion seemed about to spread panic through the ranks, but it was checked in a very few moments. The order to 'Halt! – Front! – Form up!' rang out; the Guards obeyed as one man, formed again four-deep, and told off in companies of forty.

In the immediate rear of Maitland's and Halkett's brigades, D'Aubremé's Dutch–Belgians, formed in three squares, appalled by the slaughter in their front, began to retreat precipitately upon Vandeleur's squadrons. The Dragoons closed their ranks until their horses stood shoulder to shoulder; Vandeleur galloped forward to try to stem the rout; and an Aide-de-Camp went flying to the Duke on a foaming horse, gasping out that the Dutch would not stand and could not be held.

'That's all right,' answered his lordship coolly. 'Tell them the French are retiring!'

Meanwhile, to the right, where Adam's brigade held the ground above Hougoumont, Sir John Colborne, without waiting for orders, had acted on his own brilliant judgement. As the columns advanced upon Maitland, he moved the 52nd Regiment down to the north-east angle of Hougoumont, and right-shouldered it forward, until it

stood in line four-deep parallel to the left flank of the second column of Chasseurs.

Adam, seeing this deliberate movement, galloped up, calling out: 'Colborne! Colborne! What are you meaning to do?'

'To make that column feel our fire,' replied Sir John laconically.

Adam took one look at the Chasseurs, another at the purposeful face beside him, and said: 'Move on, then! the 71st shall follow you,' and rode off to bring up the Highlanders.

The Chasseur column, advancing steadily, was met by a frontal fire of over eighteen hundred muskets from the 95th Rifles and the 71st High-landers, and, as it staggered, the Fighting 52nd, the men in third and fourth line loading and passing muskets forward to the first two lines, riddled its flank. It broke, and fell into hideous disorder, almost decimated by a fire it could not, from its clumsy formation, return. A cry of horror arose, taken up by battalion after battalion down the French lines: 'La Garde recule!'

Before the columns could deploy, Sir John Colborne swept forward in a charge that carried all before it. The officer carrying the Colour was killed, and a hundred and fifty men on the right wing, but the advance was maintained, right across the ground in front of the Allied line, the Imperial Guard being driven towards the chaussée in inextricable confusion. The 2nd and 3rd battalions of the Rifles, with the 71st Highlanders, followed the 52nd in support; the Imperial Guard, helpless under the musketry-fire, cast into terrible disorder through their inability to deploy, lost all semblance of formation, and retreated pele-mele to the chaussée, till the ground in front of the Allied position was one seething mass of struggling, fighting, fleeing infantry.

Hew Halkett brought up his Hanoverians into the interval between Hougoumont and the hollow road; the 52nd advanced across the uneven plain until checked by encountering some squadrons of Dornberg's 23rd Light Dragoons, whom, in the dusk, they mistook for French cavalry and fired upon.

The Duke, who had watched the advance from the high ground beside Maitland, galloped up to the rear of the 52nd, where Sir John, having ordered his Adjutant to stop the firing, was exchanging his wounded horse for a fresh one.

'It is our own cavalry which has caused this firing!' Colborne told him.

'Never mind! Go on, Colborne, go on!' replied the Duke, and galloped back to the crest of the position, and stood there, silhouetted against the glowing sky on his hollow-backed charger. He raised his cocked-hat high in the air, and swept it forward, towards the enemy's position, in the long-looked-for signal for a General Advance. A cheer broke out on the right, as the Guards charged down the slope. The crippled forces east of the chaussée, away to their left, heard it growing louder as it swelled all along the line towards them, took it up by instinct, and charged forward out of the intolerable smoke surrounding them, on to a plain strewn with dead and dying, lit by the last rays of a red sun, and covered with men flying in confusion towards the ridge of La Belle Alliance.

Cries of: '*Nous sommes trahis*!' mingled with the dismayed shouts of '*La Garde recule*!' Donzelot's division was carried away in the rush of Grenadiers and Chasseurs; the retreat had become a rout. Ney, on foot, one epaulette torn off, his hat gone, a broken sword in his hand, was fighting like a madman crying: 'Come and see how a Marshal of France dies!' and, to d'Erlon, borne towards him in the press: 'If we get out of this alive, d'Erlon, we shall both be hanged!'

Far in advance of the charging Allied line, Colborne, having crossed the ground between Hougoumont and La Haye Sainte, had reached the chaussée, and passed it, left-shouldering his regiment forward to ascend the slope towards La Belle Alliance.

To the right, Vivian had advanced his brigade, placing himself at the head of the 18th Hussars. 'Eighteenth! You will, I know, follow me!' he said, and was answered by one of his Sergeant-Majors: 'Ay, General! to hell, if you'll lead us!'

Taking up his position on the flank of the leading half-squadron, holding his reins in his injured right hand, which, though it still reposed in a sling, was just capable of grasping them, he led the whole brigade forward at the trot. As the Hussars cleared the front on Maitland's right, the Guards and Vandeleur's Light Dragoons cheered them on, and they charged down on to the plain, sweeping the French up in their advance past the eastern hedge of Hougoumont towards the chaussée at La Belle Alliance.

Through the dense smoke lying over the ground the Duke galloped down the line. When the Riflemen saw him, they sent up a cheer, but he called out: 'No cheering, my lads, but forward and complete your victory!' and rode on, through the smother, out into the sea of dead, to where Adam's brigade was halted on the ridge of La Belle Alliance, a little way from where some French battalions had managed to reform.

The Duke, learning from Adam that the brigade had been halted for the purpose of closing the files in, scrutinized the French battalions closely for a

moment, and then said decidedly: 'They won't stand: better attack them!'

Baron Müffling, looking along the line from his position on the left flank, saw the General Advance through the lifting smoke. Kielmansegg's, Ompteda's and Pack's shattered brigades remained where they had stood all day, but everywhere else the regiments charged forward, leaving behind them an unbroken red line of their own dead, marking the position where, for over eight hours of cannonading, of cavalry charges, and of massed infantry attacks the British and German troops had held their ground.

From Papelotte to Hougoumont the hillocky plain in front was covered with dead and wounded. Near the riddled walls of La Haye Sainte the Cuirassiers lay in mounds of men and horses. The corn which had waved shoulder-high in the morning was everywhere trodden down into clay. On the rising ground of La Belle Alliance the Old Guard was making its last stand, fighting off the fugitives, who, trying to find shelter in its squares, threatened to overwhelm them. These three squares, with one formed by Reille, south of Hougoumont, were the only French troops still standing firm in the middle of the rout. With the cessation of artillery-fire by the hollow road the smoke was clearing away, but over the ruins of Hougoumont it still rose in a slow, black column. Those of the batteries which had been able to follow the advance were firing into the mass of French on the southern ridge; musketry crackled as the Old Guard, with Napoleon and his Staff in the middle of their squares, retreated step by step, fighting a heroic rearguard action against Adam's brigade and Hew Halkett's Hanoverians. Where Vivian, with Vandeleur in support, was sweeping the ground east and south of Hougoumont, fierce cavalry skirmishing was in progress, and the Middle Guard was trying to reform its squares to hold the Hussars at bay.

Müffling, detaching a battery from Ziethen's Corps, led it at a gallop to the centre of the Allied position. He met the Duke by La Haye Sainte. His lordship called triumphantly to him from a distance; 'Well! You see Macdonnell has held Hougoumont!'

Müffling, detaching a battery from Ziethen's what the Guards at Hougoumont must have endured without a lump coming to his throat, knew the Duke well enough to realize that this brief sentence was his lordship's way of expressing his admiration, and nodded.

The sun was sinking fast; in the gathering dusk musket-balls were hissing in every direction.

Uxbridge, who had come scatheless through the day, was hit in the knee by a shot passing over Copenhagen's withers, and sang out: 'By God! I've got it at last!'

'Have you, by God?' said his lordship, too intent on the operations of his troops to pay much heed.

Colin Campbell, preparing to support Uxbridge off the field, seized the Duke's bridle, saying roughly: 'This is no place for you! I wish you will move!'

'I will when I have seen these fellows off,' replied his lordship.

To the south-east of La Belle Alliance, the Prussians, driving the Young Guard out of Plancenoit, were advancing on the chaussée, to converge there with the Allied troops. Bülow's infantry were singing the Lutheran hymn, *Now thank we all our God*, but as the columns came abreast of the British Guards, halted by the road, the hymn ceased abruptly. The band struck up *God Save the King*, and as the Prussians marched past they saluted.

It was past nine o'clock when, in the darkness, south of La Belle Alliance, the Duke met Prince Blücher. The Prince, beside himself with exultation, carried beyond coherent speech by his admiration for the gallantry of the British troops and for the generalship of his friend and ally, could only find one thing to say as he embraced the Duke ruthlessly on both cheeks: 'I stink of garlic!'

When his first transports of joy were a little abated, he offered to take on the pursuit of the French through the night. The Duke's battered forces, dog-tired, terribly diminished in numbers, were ordered to bivouac where they stood, on the ground occupied all day by the French; and the Duke, accompanied by a mere skeleton of the brilliant cortège which had gone with him into the field that morning, rode back in clouded moonlight to his Headquarters.

Baron Müffling, drawing abreast of him, said: 'The Field Marshal will call this battle Belle-Alliance, sir.'

His lordship returned no answer. The Baron, casting a shrewd glance at his bony profile, with its frosty eye and pursed mouth, realized that he had no intention of calling the battle by that name. It was his lordship's custom to name his victories after the village or town where he had slept the night before them. The Marshal Prince might call the battle what he liked, but his lordship would head his despatch to Earl Bathurst: 'Waterloo.'

* Published by William Heinemann Ltd, London and Toronto, 1937.

Les Misérables
Victor Hugo

106 'Night approaching, and death also . . .

Wellington felt that he was giving way. The crisis was upon him.

The cuirassiers had not succeeded, in this sense, that the centre was not broken. All holding the plateau, nobody held it, and in fact it remained for the most part with the English. Wellington held the village and the crowning plain; Ney held only the crest and the slope. On both sides they seemed rooted in this funebral soil.

But the enfeeblement of the English appeared irremediable. The haemorrhage of this army was horrible. Kempt, on the left wing, called for reinforcements. '*Impossible,*' answered Wellington; '*we must die on the spot we now occupy.*' Almost at the same moment – singular coincidence which depicts the exhaustion of both armies – Ney sent to Napoleon for infantry, and Napoleon exclaimed: '*Infantry! where does he expect me to take them! Does he expect me to make them?*'

However, the English army was farthest gone. The furious onslaughts of these great squadrons with iron cuirasses and steel breastplates had ground up the infantry. A few men about a flag marked the place of a regiment; battalions were now commanded by captains or lieutenants. Alten's division, already so cut up at La Haye Sainte, was almost destroyed; the intrepid Belgians of Van Kluze's brigade strewed the rye field along the Nivelles road; there were hardly any left of those Dutch grenadiers who, in 1811, joined to our ranks in Spain, fought against Wellington, and who, in 1815, rallied on the English side, fought against Napoleon. The loss in officers was heavy. Lord Uxbridge, who buried his leg next day, had a knee fractured. If, on the side of the French, in this struggle of the cuirassiers, Delord, l'Heritier, Colbert, Dnop, Travers, and Blancard were *hors de combat*, on the side of the English, Alten was wounded, Barne was wounded, Delancey was killed, Van Meeren was killed, Ompteda was killed, the entire staff of Wellington was decimated, and England had the worst share in this balance of blood. The second regiment of foot guards had lost five lieutenant-colonels, four captains, and three ensigns; the first battalion of the thirtieth infantry had lost twenty-four officers and one hundred and twelve soldiers; the seventy-ninth Highlanders had twenty-four officers wounded, eighteen officers killed, and four hundred and fifty soldiers slain. Cumberland's Hanoverian hussars, an entire regiment, having at its head Colonel Hacke, who was afterwards court-martialled and broken, had drawn rein before the fight, and were in flight in the Forest of Soignes, spreading the panic as far as Brussels. Carts, ammunition-wagons, baggage-wagons, ambulances full of wounded, seeing the French gain ground, and approach the forest, fled precipitately; the Dutch, sabred by the French cavalry, cried murder! From Vert-Coucou to Groenendael, for a distance of nearly six miles in the direction towards Brussels, the roads, according to the testimony of witnesses still alive, were choked with fugitives. This panic was such that it reached the Prince of Condé at Malines, and Louis XVIII, at Ghent. With the exception of the small reserve drawn up in echelon behind the hospital established at the farm of Mont Saint Jean, and the brigades of Vivian and Vandeleur on the flank of the left wing, Wellington's cavalry was exhausted. A number of batteries lay dismounted. These facts are confessed by Siborne; and Pringle, exaggerating the disaster, says even that the Anglo-Dutch army was reduced to thirty-four thousand men. The Iron Duke remained calm, but his lips were pale. The Austrian Commissary, Vincent, the Spanish Commissary, Olava, present at the battle in the English staff, thought the duke was beyond hope. At five o'clock Wellington drew out his watch and was heard to murmur these sombre words: *Blücher, or night!*

It was about this time that a distant line of bayonets glistened on the heights beyond Frischermont.

Here is the turning-point in this colossal drama.

SAD GUIDE FOR NAPOLEON; GOOD GUIDE FOR BÜLOW

We understand the bitter mistake of Napoleon; Grouchy hoped for, Blücher arriving; death instead of life.

Destiny has such turnings. Awaiting the world's throne, Saint Helena became visible.

If the little cowboy, who acted as guide to Bülow, Blücher's lieutenant, had advised him to debouch from the forest above Frischermont rather than below Planchenoit, the shaping of the nineteenth century would perhaps have been different. Napoleon would have won the battle of Waterloo. By any other road than below Planchenoit, the Prussian army would have brought up at a ravine impassable for artillery, and Bülow would not have arrived.

Now, an hour of delay, as the Prussian general Müffling declares, and Blücher would not have found Wellington in position; 'the battle was lost.'

It was time, we have seen, that Bülow should arrive. He had bivouacked at Dion le Mont, and started on at dawn. But the roads were impracticable, and his division stuck in the mire. The cannon

sank to the hubs in the ruts. Furthermore, he had to cross the Dyle on the narrow bridge of Wavre; the street leading to the bridge had been fired by the French; the caissons and artillery waggons, being unable to pass between two rows of burning houses, had to wait till the fire was extinguished. It was noon before Bülow could reach Chapelle Saint Lambert.

Had the action commenced two hours earlier, it would have been finished at four o'clock, and Blücher would have fallen upon a field already won by Napoleon. Such are these immense chances, proportioned to an infinity, which we cannot grasp.

As early as midday, the emperor, first of all, with his field glass, perceived in the extreme horizon something which fixed his attention. He said: 'I see yonder a cloud which appears to me to be troops.' Then he asked the Duke of Dalmatia: 'Soult, what do you see towards Chapelle Saint Lambert?' The marshal, turning his glass that way, answered: 'Four or five thousand men, sire. Grouchy, of course.' Meanwhile it remained motionless in the haze. The glasses of the whole staff studied 'the cloud' pointed out by the emperor. Some said: 'They are columns halting.' The most said: 'It is trees.' The fact is, that the cloud did not stir. The emperor detached Domon's division of light cavalry to reconnoitre this obscure point.

Bülow, in fact, had not moved. His vanguard was very weak, and could do nothing. He had to wait for the bulk of his *corps d'armée*, and he was ordered to concentrate his force before entering into line; but at five o'clock, seeing Wellington's peril, Blücher ordered Bülow to attack, and uttered these remarkable words: 'We must give the English army a breathing spell.'

Soon after the divisions of Losthin, Hiller, Hacke, and Ryssel deployed in front of Lobau's corps, the cavalry of Prince William of Prussia debouched from the wood of Paris, Planchenoit was in flames, and the Prussian balls began to rain down even in the ranks of the guard in reserve behind Napoleon.

THE GUARD

The rest is known; the irruption of a third army, the battle thrown out of joint, eighty-six pieces of artillery suddenly thundering forth, Pirch the First coming up with Bülow, Ziethen's cavalry led by Blücher in person, the French crowded back, Marcognet swept from the plateau of Ohain, Durutte dislodged from Papelotte, Donzelot and

Quiot recoiling, Lobau taken en echarpe, a new battle falling at night-fall upon our dismantled regiments, the whole English line assuming the offensive and pushed forward, the gigantic gap made in the French army, the English grape and the Prussian grape lending mutual aid, extermination, disaster in front, disaster in flank, the guard entering into line amid this terrible crumbling.

Feeling that they were going to their death, they cried out: *Vive l'Empereur!* There is nothing more touching in history than this death-agony bursting forth in acclamations.

The sky had been overcast all day. All at once, at this very moment – it was eight o'clock at night – the clouds in the horizon broke, and through the elms on the Nivelles road streamed the sinister red light of the setting sun. The rising sun shone upon Austerlitz.

Each battalion of the guard, for this final effort, was commanded by a general. Friant, Michel, Harlet, Mallet, Poret de Morvan, were there. When the tall caps of the grenadiers of the guard with their large eagle plates appeared, symmetrical, drawn up in line, calm, in the smoke of that conflict, the enemy felt respect for France; they thought they saw twenty victories entering upon the field of battle, with wings extended, and those who were conquerors, thinking themselves conquered, recoiled; but Wellington cried: '*Up, guards, and at them!*' The red regiment of English guards, lying behind the hedges, rose up, a shower of grape riddled the tricoloured flag fluttering about our eagles, all hurled themselves forward, and the final carnage began. The Imperial Guard felt the army slipping away around them in the gloom, and the vast overthrow of the rout; they heard the *sauve qui peut!* which had replaced the *vive l'Empereur!* and, with flight behind them, they held their course, battered more and more and dying faster and faster at every step. There were no weak souls or cowards there. The privates of that band were as heroic as their generals. Not a man flinched from the suicide.

Ney, desperate, great in all the grandeur of accepted death, bared himself to every blow in this tempest. He had his horse killed under him. Reeking with sweat, fire in his eyes, froth upon his lips, his uniform unbuttoned, one of his epaulettes half cut away by the sabre stroke of a horse-guard, his badge the grand eagle pierced by a ball, bloody, covered with mud, magnificent, a broken sword in his hand, he said: '*Come and see how a marshal of France dies upon the field of battle!*' But in vain, he did not die. He was haggard and exasperated. He flung this question at Drouet d'Erlon: '*What! are you not going to die!*' He cried out in the midst of all this artillery which was mowing down a handful of men '*Is there nothing, then, for me? Oh! I would that all these English balls were buried in my body!*' Unhappy man! thou wast reserved for French bullets!

THE CATASTROPHE

The route behind the guard was dismal.

The army fell back rapidly from all sides at once, from Hougoumont, from La Haye Sainte, from Papelotte, from Planchenoit. The cry *Treachery!* was followed by the cry: *Sauve qui peut!* A disbanding army is a thaw. The whole bends, cracks, snaps, floats, rolls, falls, crashes, hurries, plunges. Mysterious disintegration. Ney borrows a horse, leaps upon him, and without a hat, cravat, or sword, plants himself in the Brussels road, arresting at once the English and the French. He endeavours to hold the army, he calls them back, he reproaches them, he grapples with the rout. He is swept away. The soldiers flee from him, crying: *Vive Marshal Ney!* Durutte's two regiments come and go, frightened, and tossed between the sabres of the Uhlans and the fire of the brigades of Kempt, Best, Pack and Rylandt; rout is the worst of all conflicts; friends slay each other in their flight; squadrons and battalions are crushed and dispersed against each other, enormous foam of the battle. Lobau at one extremity, like Reille, at the other, is rolled away in the flood. In vain does Napoleon make walls with the remains of the guard; in vain does he expend his reserve squadron in a last effort. Quiot gives way before Vivian, Kellermann before Vandeleur, Lobau before Bülow, Moraud before Pirch, Domon and Lubervic before Prince William of Prussia. Guyot, who had led the emperor's squadrons to the charge, falls under the feet of the English horse. Napoleon gallops along the fugitives, harangues them, urges, threatens, entreats. The mouths, which in the morning were crying *Vive l'Empereur*, are now agape; he is hardly recognized. The Prussian cavalry, just come up, spring forward, fling themselves upon the enemy, sabre, cut, hack, kill, exterminate. Teams rush off, the guns are left to the care of themselves; the soldiers of the train unhitch the caissons and take the horses to escape; waggons upset, with their four wheels in the air, block up the road, and are accessories of massacre. They crush and they crowd; they trample upon the living and the dead. Arms are broken. A multitude fills roads, paths, bridges, plains, hills, valleys, woods, choked up by this flight of forty thousand men. Cries, despair, knapsacks and muskets cast into the rye, passage forced at the point of the sword; no more comrades, no more officers, no more generals; inexpressible dismay. Ziethen sabring France at his ease. Lions become kids. Such was this flight.

At Genappe there was an effort to turn back, to form a line, to make a stand. Lobau rallied three hundred men. The entrance to the village was barricaded, but at the first volley of Prussian grape, all took flight again, and Lobau was captured. The marks of that volley of grape are still to be seen upon the old gable of a brick ruin at the right of the road, a short distance before entering Genappe. The Prussians rushed into Genappe, furious, doubtless, at having conquered so little. The pursuit was monstrous. Blücher gave orders to kill all. Roguet had set this sad example by threatening with death every French grenadier who should bring him a Prussian prisoner. Blücher surpassed Roguet. The general of the Young Guard Duhesme, caught at the door of a tavern in Genappe, gave up his sword to a Hussar of Death, who took the sword and killed the prisoner. The victory was completed by the assassination of the vanquished. Let us punish, since we are history: old Blücher disgraced himself. This ferocity filled the disaster to the brim. The desperate rout passed through Genappe, passed through Quatre-Bras, passed through Sombreffe, passed through Frasnes, passed through Thuin, passed through Charleroi, and stopped only at the frontier. Alas! who now was flying in such wise? The Grand Army.

This madness, this terror, this falling to ruins of the highest bravery which ever astonished history, can that be without cause? No. The shadow of an enormous right hand rests on Waterloo. It is the day of Destiny. A power above man controlled that day. Hence, the loss of mind in dismay; hence all these great souls yielding up their swords. Those who had conquered Europe fell to the ground, having nothing more to say or do, feeling a terrible presence in the darkness. *Hoc erat in fatis*. That day, the perspective of the human race changed. Waterloo is the hinge of the nineteenth century. This disappearance of the great man was necessary for the advent of the great century. One, to whom there is no reply, took it in charge. The panic of heroes is explained. In the battle of Waterloo, there is more than a cloud, there is a meteor. God passed over it.

In the gathering night, on a field near Genappe, Bernard and Bertrand seized by a flap of his coat and stopped by a haggard, thoughtful, gloomy man, who, dragged thus far by the current of the rout, had dismounted, passed the bridle of his horse under his arm, and, with bewildered eye, was returning alone towards Waterloo. It was Napoleon endeavouring to advance again, mighty somnambulist of a vanished dream.

THE LAST SQUARE

A few squares of the guard, immovable in the flow of the rout as rocks in running water, held out until night. Night approaching, and death also, they waited this double shadow, and yielded unfaltering, to its embrace. Each regiment, isolated from the others, and having no further communication with the army, which was broken in all directions, was dying alone. They had taken position, for this last struggle, some upon the heights of Rossomme, others in the plain of Mont Saint Jean. There, abandoned, conquered, terrible, these sombre squares suffered formidable martyrdom. Ulm, Wagram, Jena, Friedland, were dying in them.

At dusk, towards nine o'clock in the evening, at the foot of the plateau of Mont Saint Jean, there remained but one. In this fatal valley, at the bottom of that slope which had been climbed by the cuirassiers, inundated now by the English masses, under the converging fire of the victorious artillery of the enemy, under a frightful storm of projectiles, this square fought on. It was commanded by an obscure officer whose name was Cambronne. At every discharge, the square grew less, but returned the fire. It replied to grape by bullets, narrowing in its four walls continually. Afar off the fugitives, stopping for a moment out of breath, heard in the darkness this dismal thunder decreasing.

When this legion was reduced to a handful, when their flag was reduced to a shred, when their muskets, exhausted of ammunition, were reduced to nothing but clubs, when the pile of corpses was greater than the group of living, there spread among the conquerors a sort of sacred terror about these sublime martyrs, and the English artillery, stopping to take their breath, was silent. It was a kind of respite. These combatants had about them, as it were, a swarm of spectres, the outlines of men on horseback, the black profile of the cannons, the white sky seen through the wheels and the gun-carriages; the colossal death's head which heroes always see in the smoke of the battle was advancing upon them, and glaring at them. They could hear in the gloom of the twilight the loading of the pieces, the lighted matches like tiger's eyes in the night made a circle about their heads; all the linstocks of the English batteries approached the guns, when, touched by their heroism, holding the death-moment suspended over these men, an English general, Colville, according to some, Maitland, according to others, cried to them: 'Brave Frenchmen, surrender!' Cambronne answered: '*Merde!*'

CAMBRONNE

Out of respect to the French reader, the finest word, perhaps, that a Frenchman ever uttered cannot be repeated to him. We are prohibited from embalming a sublimity in history.

At our own risk and peril, we violate that prohibition.

Among these giants, then, there was one Titan – Cambronne.

To speak that word, and then to die, what could be more grand! For to accept death is to die, and it is not the fault of this man, if, in the storm of grape, he survived.

The man who won the battle of Waterloo is not Napoleon put to rout; nor Wellington giving way at four o'clock, desperate at five; not Blücher, who did not fight; the man who won the battle of Waterloo was Cambronne.

To fulminate such a word at the thunderbolt which kills you is victory.

To make this answer to disaster, to say this to destiny, to give this base for the future lion, to fling down this reply at the rain of the previous night, at the treacherous wall of Hougoumont, at the sunken road of Ohain, at the delay of Grouchy, at the arrival of Blücher, to be ironical in the sepulchre, to act so as to remain upright after one shall have fallen, to drown in two syllables the European coalition, to offer to kings these privities already known to the Caesars, to make the last of words the first, by associating it with the glory of France, to close Waterloo insolently by a Mardi Gras, to complete Leinidas by Rabelais, to sum up this victory in a supreme word which cannot be pronounced, to lose the field, and to preserve history, after this carnage to have the laugh on his side, is immense.

It is an insult to the thunderbolt. That attains the grandeur of Aeschylus.

This word of Cambronne's gives the effect of a fracture. It is the breaking of a heart by scorn; it is an overplus of agony in explosion. Who conquered? Wellington? No. Without Blücher he would have been lost. Blücher? No. If Wellington had not commenced, Blücher could not have finished. This Cambronne, this passer at the last hour, this unknown soldier, this infinitesimal of war, feels that there is a lie in a catastrophe, doubly bitter; and at the moment when he is bursting with rage, he is offered this mockery – life? How can he restrain himself? They are there, all the kings of Europe, the fortunate generals, the thundering Joves, they have a hundred thousand victorious soldiers, and behind the hundred thousand, a million; their guns, with matches lighted, are agape; they have the Imperial Guard and the Grand Army under their feet; they have crushed Napoleon, and Cambronne only remains; there is none but this worm of the earth to protest. He will protest. Then he seeks for a word as one seeks for a sword. He froths at the mouth, and this froth is the word. Before this mean and monstrous victory, before this victory without victors, this desperate man straightens himself up, he suffers its enormity, but he establishes its nothingness and he does more than spit upon it; and overwhelmed in numbers and material strength he finds in the soul an expression – ordure. We repeat it, to say that, to do that, to find that, is to be the conqueror.

The soul of great days entered into this unknown man at that moment of death. Cambronne finds the word of Waterloo, as Rouget de l'Isle finds the Marseillaise, through a superior inspiration. An effluence from the divine afflatus detaches itself, and passes over these men, and they tremble, and the one sings the supreme song, and the other utters the terrible cry. This word of titanic scorn Cambronne throws down not merely to Europe, in the name of the Empire, that would be but little; he throws it down to the past, in the name of the Revolution. It is heard, and men recognize in Cambronne the old soul of the giants. It seems as if it were a speech of Danton, or a roar of Kleber.

To this word of Cambronne, the English voice replied: 'Fire!' the batteries flamed, the hill trembled, from all those brazen throats went forth a final vomiting of grape, terrific; a vast smoke, dusky white in the light of the rising moon, rolled out, and when the smoke was dissipated, there was nothing left. That formidable remnant was annihilated; the guard was dead. The four walls of the living redoubt had fallen, hardly could a quivering be distinguished here and there among the corpses; and thus the French legions, grander than the Roman legions, expired at Mont Saint Jean on ground soaked in rain and blood, in the sombre wheat-fields, at the spot where now, at four o'clock in the morning, whistling, and gaily whipping up his horse, Joseph passes, who drives the mail from Nivelles.

QUOT LIBRAS IN DUCE?

The battle of Waterloo is an enigma. It is as obscure to those who won it as to him who lost it. To Napoleon it is a panic;* Blücher sees in it only fire; Wellington comprehends nothing of it. Look at the reports. The bulletins are confused, the commentaries are foggy. The former stammer, the latter falter. Jomini separates the battle of Waterloo into four periods; Müffling divides it into three ties of fortune; Charras alone, though upon some points our appreciation differs from his, has seized with his keen glance the characteristic lineaments of that catastrophe of human genius struggling with divine destiny. All the other historians are blinded by the glare, and are groping about in that blindness. A day of lightnings, indeed, the downfall of the military monarchy, which, to the great amazement of kings, has dragged with it all kingdoms, the fall of force, the overthrow of war.

In this event, bearing the impress of superhuman necessity, man's part is nothing.

Does taking away Waterloo from Wellington and from Blücher, detract anything from England and Germany? No. Neither illustrious England nor august Germany is in question in the problem of Waterloo. Thank heaven, nations are great aside from the dismal chances of the sword. Neither Germany, nor England, nor France, is held in a scabbard. At this day when Waterloo is only a clicking of sabres above Blücher, Germany has Goethe, and above Wellington, England has Byron. A vast uprising of ideas is peculiar to our century, and in this aurora England and Germany have a magnificent share. They are majestic because they think. The higher plane which they bring to civilisation is intrinsic to them; it comes from themselves, and not from an accident. The advancement which they have made in the nineteenth century does not spring from Waterloo. It is only barbarous nations who have a sudden growth after a victory. It is the fleeting vanity of the streamlet swelled by the storm. Civilised nations, especially in our times, are not exalted nor abased by the good or bad fortune of a captain. Their specific gravity in the human race results from something more than a combat. Their honour, thank God, their dignity, their light, their genius, are not numbers that heroes and conquerors, those gamblers, can cast into the lottery of battles. Oftentimes a battle lost is progress attained. Less glory, more liberty. The drum is silent, reason speaks. It is the game at which he who loses, gains. Let us speak then, coolly of Waterloo on both sides. Let us render unto Fortune the things that are Fortune's, and unto God the things that are God's. What is Waterloo? A victory? No. A prize.

A prize won by Europe, paid by France.

It was not much to put a lion there.

Waterloo moreover is the strangest encounter in history. Napoleon and Wellington: they are not enemies. they are opposites. Never has God, who takes pleasure in antitheses, made a more striking contrast and a more extraordinary meeting. On one side, precision, foresight, geometry, prudence, retreat assured, reserves economised, obstinate composure, imperturbable method, strategy to profit by the ground, tactics to balance battalions, carnage drawn to the line, war directed watch in hand, nothing left voluntarily to intuition, inspiration, a military marvel, a superhuman instinct; a flashing glance, a mysterious something which gazes like the eagle and strikes like the thunderbolt, prodigious art in disdainful impetuosity, all the mysteries of a deep soul, intimacy with Destiny; river, plain, forest, hill, commanded, and in some sort forced to obey, the despot going even so far as to tyrannize over the battlefield; faith in a star joined to strategic science, increasing it, but disturbing it. Wellington was the Barrême of war, Napoleon was its Michael Angelo, and this time genius was vanquished by calculation.

On both sides they were expecting somebody. It was the exact calculator who succeeded. Napoleon expected Grouchy; he did not come. Wellington expected Blücher; he came.

Wellington is classic war taking her revenge. Bonaparte, in his dawn, had met her in Italy, and defeated her superbly. The old owl fled before the young vulture. Ancient tactics had been not only thunderstruck, but had received mortal offence? What was this Corsican of twenty-six? What meant this brilliant novice who, having everything against him, nothing for him, with no provisions, no munitions, no cannons, no shoes, almost without an army, with a handful of men against multitudes, rushed upon allied Europe, and absurdly gained victories that were impossible? Whence came this thundering madman who, almost without taking breath, and with the same set of combatants in hand, pulverised one after the other of the five armies of the Emperor of Germany, overthrowing Beaulieu upon Alvinzi, Wurmser upon Beaulieu, Melas upon Wurmser, Mack upon Melas? Who was this new-comer in war with the confidence of destiny? The academic military school excommunicated him as it ran away. Thence an implacable hatred of the old system of war against the new, of correct sabre against the flashing sword, and of the chequer-board against genius.

On the 18th of June, 1815, this hatred had the last word, and under Lodi, Montebello, Montenotte, Mantua, Marengo, Arcola, it wrote: Waterloo. Triumph of the commonplace, grateful to majorities. Destiny consented to this irony. In his decline, Napoleon again found Wurmser before him, but young. Indeed, to produce Wurmser, it would have been enough to whiten Wellington's hair.

Waterloo is a battle of the first rank won by a captain of the second.

What is truly admirable in the battle of Waterloo is England, English firmness, English resolution, English blood; the superb thing which England had there – may it not displease her – is herself. It is not her captain, it is her army.

Wellington, strangely ungrateful, declared in a letter to Lord Bathurst that his army, the army that fought on the 18th of June, 1815, was a 'detestable army.' What does this dark assemblage of bones, buried beneath the furrows of Waterloo, think of that?

England has been too modest in regard to Wellington. To make Wellington so great is to belittle England. Wellington is but a hero like the rest. These Scotch Grays, these Horse Guards, these regiments of Maitland and of Mitchell, this infantry of Pack and Kempt, this cavalry of Ponsonby and of Somerset, these Highlanders playing the bagpipe under the storm of grape, these battalions of Rylandt, these raw recruits who hardly knew how to handle a musket, holding out against the veteran bands of Essling and Rivoli – all that is grand. Wellington was tenacious, that was his merit, and we do not undervalue it, but the least of his foot-soldiers or his horsemen was quite as firm as he. The iron soldier is as good as the Iron Duke. For our part, all our glorification goes to the English soldier, the English army, the English people. If trophy there be, to England the trophy is due. The Waterloo column would be more just if, instead of the figure of a man, it lifted to the clouds the statue of a nation.

But this great England will be offended at what we say here. She has still, after her 1688 and our 1789, the feudal illusion. She believes in hereditary right, and in the hierarchy. This people, surpassed by none in might and glory, esteems itself as a nation, not as a people. So much so that as a people they subordinate themselves willingly, and take a Lord for a Head. Workmen, they submit to be despised; soldiers, they submit to be whipped. We remember that at the battle of Inkerman a sergeant who, as it appeared, had saved the army, could not be mentioned by Lord Raglan, the English military hierarchy not permitting any

hero below rank of officer to be spoken of in a report.

What we admire above all, in an encounter like that of Waterloo, is the prodigious skill of fortune. The night's rain, the wall of Hougoumont, the sunken road of Ohain, Grouchy deaf to cannon, Napoleon's guide who deceives him, Bülow's guide who leads him right, all this cataclysm is wonderfully carried out.

Taken as a whole, let us say, Waterloo was more of a massacre than a battle.

Of all great battles, Waterloo is that which has the shortest line in proportion to the number engaged. Napoleon, two miles, Wellington, a mile and a half; seventy-two thousand men on each side. From this density came the carnage.

The calculation has been made and this proportion been established: Loss of men: at Austerlitz, French, fourteen per cent; Russians, thirty per cent; Austrians, forty-four per cent. At Wagram, French, thirteen per cent; Austrians, fourteen. At La Moscowa, French, thirty-seven per cent; Russians, forty-four. At Bautzen, French, thirteen per cent; Russians and Prussians, fourteen. At Waterloo, French, fifty-six per cent; Allies, thirty-one. Average for Waterloo, forty-one per cent. A hundred and forty-four thousand men; sixty thousand dead.

The field of Waterloo to-day has that calm which belongs to the earth, impassive support of man; it resembles any other plain.

At night, however, a sort of visionary mist arises from it, and if some traveller be walking there, if he looks, if he listens, if he dreams like Virgil in the fatal plain of Philippi, he becomes possessed by the hallucination of the disaster. The terrible 18th of June is again before him; the artificial hill of the monument fades away, this lion, whatever it be, is dispelled; the field of battle resumes its reality; the lines of infantry undulate in the plain, furious gallops traverse the horizon; the bewildered dreamer sees the flash of sabres, the glistening of bayonets, the bursting of shells, the awful intermingling of the thunders; he hears, like a death-rattle from the depths of a tomb, the vague clamour of the phantom battle; these shadows are grenadiers; these gleams are cuirassiers; this skeleton is Napoleon; that skeleton is Wellington; all this is unreal, and yet it clashes and combats; and the ravines run red, and the trees shiver, and there is fury even in the clouds, and, in the darkness, all those savage heights. Mont Saint Jean, Hougoumont, Frischermont, Papelotte, Planchenoit, appear confusedly crowned with whirlwinds of spectres exterminating each other.

* Published, in an English Translation by Charles Wilbur, by The Modern Library, New York, in 1934

Vanity Fair
W.M.Thackeray

All that day from morning until last sunset, the cannon never ceased to roar. It was dark when the cannonading stopped all of a sudden.

All of us have read of what occurred during that interval. The tale is in every Englishman's mouth: and you and I who were children when the great battle was won and lost, are never tired of hearing and recounting the history of that famous action. Its remembrance rankles still in the bosoms of millions of the countrymen of those brave men who lost the day. They pant for an opportunity of revenging that humiliation; and if a contest, ending in a victory on their part, should ensue, elating them in their turn, and leaving its cursed legacy of hatred and rage behind to us, there is no end to the so-called glory and shame, and to the alternations of successful and unsuccessful murder, in which two high-spirited nations might engage. Centuries hence, we Frenchmen and Englishmen might be boasting and killing each other still, carrying out bravely the Devil's code of honour.

All our friends took their share and fought like men in the great field. All day long, whilst the women were praying ten miles away, the lines of dauntless English infantry were receiving and repelling the furious charge of the French horsemen. Guns which were heard at Brussels were ploughing up their ranks, and comrades falling and the resolute survivors closing in. Towards evening, the attack of the French, repeated and resisted so bravely, slackened in its fury. They had other foes besides the British to engage, or were preparing for a final onset. It came at last: the columns of the Imperial Guard marched up the hill of Saint Jean, at length and at once to sweep the English from the height which they had maintained all day, and spite of all: unscared by the thunder of the artillery which hurled death from the English line – the dark rolling column pressed on and up the hill. It seemed almost to crest the eminence, when it began to wave and falter. Then it stopped, still facing the shot. Then at last the English troops rushed from the post from which no enemy had been able to dislodge them, and the Guard turned and fled.

No more firing was heard at Brussels – the pursuit rolled miles away, Darkness came down on the field and city; and Amelia was praying for George, who was lying on his face, dead, with a bullet through his heart.

* Published by Smith, Elder & Co., London, 1875.

Notes

Chapter 1

1 Napoleon suffered from haemorrhoids and bouts of stomach pains. Bourienne, *Mémoires de Napoléon*.

2 Napoleon, however, never mastered his Italian accent when speaking French, and vice versa.

3 Berthier, Moncey, Masséna, Augereau, Jourdan, Bernadotte, Brune, Murat, Mortier, Bessières, Soult, Lannes, Ney and Davout. Created marshals in age order on 19 May 1804, the day after the proclamation of Napoleon as Emperor by the Senate (unanimously, less three votes). Only Soult and Ney were to accompany Napoleon in the 1815 campaign. Grouchy was appointed marshal just before the start of the campaign.

4 General Bruslart, ex-leader of the 'Chouan' (Vendéan) anti-Republican uprising, was to be in charge of a murderous landing party on Elba. Vaulabelle, *Histoire* . . .

5 Napoleon was never to see them again. Marie Louise never answered his many letters. Their son and heir, the Duke of Reichstadt, 'King of Rome', nicknamed 'L'Aiglon' (the Little Eagle), died of consumption in his late teens.

6 Vaulabelle, *Histoire* . . .

7 These troops, formed into three army corps in Franche-Comté, before Lyon and in the South of France, were actually on the move when Napoleon returned to France. Louis XVIII had ordered them to march against Murat (husband of Napoleon's sister Caroline), whose throne of Naples the King was claiming for the Bourbons. In Vienna, the Prussian Foreign Minister, Metternich, disdainfully doubted that 'Louis XVIII could muster 10,000 men without risking their mutiny against himself'. Talleyrand, from Napoleon, *Mémoires* . . .

8 Gourgaud, *Cahiers de Sainte-Hélène*.

9 On 16 February 1815, before leaving Elba, Napoleon had sent word to Murat asking him not to take any precipitate military action against Louis XVIII's threat to the throne of Naples. Murat was asked instead to inform the court in Vienna that Napoleon was specifically renouncing all his pretensions on Italy. But on 22 March, having learned that Napoleon was already in Lyon, Murat invaded the Vatican and Tuscany. The allied powers, hesitant until then, were convinced that Napoleon wanted the crowns of Belgium, of Italy and of the Rhine-land, despite the fact that on 25 March Napoleon had stated before the Conseil d'Etat in Paris: 'I have renounced the idea of the Great Empire of which, for fifteen years, I had only laid the foundations' (*Archives Nationales*). Austrian troops crossed the river Po, defeated Murat's Neapolitan troops and entered Naples on 12 May 1815.

10 There is ample evidence that Napoleon did not realize the importance of this step by which, for the first time in twenty-five years, the position of an allied commander matched his own position as commander-in-chief of all the forces at his disposal. In London, on 30 April, the House of Commons approved the 1815 defence budget: £3,169,622 'until peace be restored', and a further £2 million as a subsidy for the Prussian, Austrian and Russian armies.

11 There were only six foreign regiments in Napoleon's army: one Polish cavalry (800 officers and men of the Vistule Legion): one Irish infantry (401 officers and men): one Swiss infantry (500 men, whose officers, however, refused to wear the tricolor cockade); one Dutch–Belgian infantry (378 bayonets); one Italian and one German (the latter made up of deserters from the Prince of Orange's, Frimont's and Blücher's armies).

12 Even before Napoleon's intention to return from Elba was known to them, Davout was heading a Bonapartist conspiracy. Generals d'Erlon (military commander of the Lille region), Lallemand (commanding the department of Aisne) and Lefèvre-Desnouettes, together with Interior Minister Fouché, were planning to depose Louis XVIII and to force an unwilling Duke of Orleans to reign as a constitutional monarch in his place. When Napoleon landed in France, Soult, then War Minister, was signing the King's decrees branding Napoleon as a criminal and a traitor, and he himself was advocating the most violent action against the Emperor. At the court, Ney was saying loud and clear that Napoleon 'is mad and should be put in an iron cage', shortly before making his uneasy peace with him at the Auxerre Prefecture. Only General Grouchy, a noble marquis in his own right, and a distinguished cavalry officer in Napoleon's army, had been refused even an audience by Louis XVIII, who had deprived him of his command in 1814. Vaulabelle, *Histoire* . . .

13 Vaulabelle, *Histoire* . . .

14 Gourgaud, op. cit.

15 Napoleon, *Mémoires*.

16 With a France strongly under arms, Napoleon was also leaving behind him a comparatively liberal parliamentary government. On 3 June, before the two assembled Houses (Representatives and Peers), he had renounced dictatorship in a speech qualified as 'pretty good' even by his old political opponent La Fayette. Napoleon, *Mémoires*. And on 11 June Napoleon had appointed a Government Council composed of his brothers, Joseph (President) and Lucien, and eight ministers: Cambacérès, Carnot, Caulaincourt, Decrès, Fouché, Gaudin and Mollien, with four Ministers of State. Vaulabelle, *Histoire* . . .; *Archives Nationales*.

17 At 3 p.m., when Bourmont approached Blücher, who was talking with several of his staff officers, the old marshal refused to speak to him and exclaimed loudly in German: 'Never mind his white cockade. A blackguard will always be a blackguard!' Houssaye, *1815, Waterloo*, from German sources.

18 This symptomatic clash of personalities between the two commanders was to have far more dramatic consequences three days later when the Battle of Waterloo was in full swing (see p. 103).

19 'For the first time in his life, Ney had chosen to be cautious. Had he marched from Gosselies to Quatre-Bras at 4 p.m. with only a third of the forces which Napoleon had put under his command (two cavalry divisions, two infantry divisions and four batteries), he could have wiped out with these 14,000 men Prince

Bernhard of Saxe-Weimar's 4,000 Nassauer infantrymen, most of whom had no more than ten cartridges left.' Houssaye, op. cit.

20 *Archives de la Guerre.*
21 Ibid.
22 By the time d'Erlon received Ney's recalling order (later reiterated), it was too late for him to help Napoleon significantly against the Prussians and he was too far from Quatre-Bras to support Ney (see p. 37). During d'Erlon's corps' earlier march from Gosselies to Frasnes, there were two desertions. Colonel Gordon, chief of staff of the Durutte division, and Cavalry Major Gaugler went over to the Anglo-Dutch enemy, whom they joined at Nivelles.
23 Baudus' account from Houssaye, *1815, Waterloo.*
24 As on the evening of 15 June and the morning of the 16th, Ney had remained entirely inactive during the morning of the 17th, this time because Soult had failed to inform him of the victory at Ligny during the night. Ney had started preparing his corps to move only when receiving Napoleon's new strategic orders, sent from Ligny at 11 a.m. 17 June. Napoleon was later to say that at Quatre-Bras 'Ney was no longer the same man. He had become circumspect and temporizing to the point of inertia, whereas at Jena and Craonne he had attacked the enemy even before the appointed time'. Gourgaud, op. cit.
25 Captain Mercer, from Houssaye, *1815, Waterloo.*
26 'What would I not give today to have Joshua's power and retard the sun's march by two hours!' Napoleon, *Mémoires.*
27 Grouchy, *Mémoires.*
28 'As he passed by a bivouac fire in his grey over-coat and black bicorned hat, he asked for a potato which a Guard offered him out of a boiling pot. The Emperor tasted it with the philosophical relish of a simple soldier resting in the field between two battles. "After all", he said, "it is good . . . It is tolerable . . . With that, one can live anywhere and everywhere . . . That moment may not be all that far away . . . Themistocles! . . ." ' Bertrand, *Cahiers de Sainte-Hélène*; Gourgaud, op. cit.; Las Cases, *Mémorial de Sainte-Hélène.*
29 Gourgaud, op. cit.

Chapter 2

1 This figure excludes the detachment at Hal. For the detailed strength of the Anglo-Dutch army and the order of battle see Appendix III, Tables 1 and 2.
2 General Sir John Shaw Kennedy, who fought at Waterloo as a young officer, estimated the worth of the 38,000 foreign troops (which excluded the 5,824 men of the King's German Legion) to be equal to that of 11,000 British soldiers.
3 The King's German Legion was an integral part of the British army, having been formed originally from elements of the Electoral army of Hanover when the Electorate was overrun by French troops under Mortier in 1803.
4 A shell was a hollow iron ball filled with gunpowder with a fuse ignited by the firing of the charge; it exploded on coming to rest and scattered pieces of shell casing. Grape consisted of fifty to sixty one-inch diameter balls held in a cotton bag netted with twine; the firing of the gun burst the bag and the shot scattered. Case shot or canister was much the same as grape, only the canister was filled with smaller shot that carried further. Shrapnel was a shell containing balls and a small charge of powder that split the case apart in flight and propelled the balls forward and downward; very effective against troops concealed behind cover.
5 General Picton's tall black hat, which he wore at Quatre-Bras and Waterloo, can be seen at the National Army Museum, Chelsea.

Chapter 3

1 *Blüchers Briefe,* p. 277.
2 *Preussisches Heer,* p. 75 ff.
3 Jany, pp. 104–5: '*Am 3. Juni 1814 wurde auf Anregung Hardenbergs der Generalmajor v. Boyen zum Kriegsminister ernannt, . . . und aus seiner Feder ging das . . . Gesetz über die Verpflichtung zum Kriegsdienst vom 3. September 1814 hervor, das die allgemeine Wehrpflicht endgültig zur Grundlage der vaterländischen Kriegsverfassung erklärte.*' ('Major-General von Boyen was appointed Minister of War at Hardenberg's suggestion on 3 June 1814 . . . and it was his pen that drafted the . . . law of 3 September 1814 imposing obligatory war service, which finally decreed that general compulsory military service was to be the basis of the nation's military establishment.') *Preussisches Heer,* p. 221, app. 2.
4 Ollech, p. 14.
5 Ibid.
6 *Preussisches Heer,* p. 125 ff.
7 Ibid., p. 143 ff.
8 Ollech, p. 15; cf. Treuenfeld, p. 12; Lettow-Vorbeck, p. 162.
9 Lettow-Vorbeck, p. 163, app. 1; Treuenfeld, p. 13.
10 General von Pirch later commanded II Corps in place of General von Borstell.
11 Cf. Pertz, p. 409: '*Die Heere wuchsen ebenso sehr äusserlich der Zahl nach in das Vielfache, wie innerlich der Qualität des Soldatenstandes nach, seit sie die Vertheidiger und Repräsentanten der nationalen Unabhängigkeit geworden waren.*' ('Once they had become the defenders and symbols of national independence, the armies grew, both outwardly in the multiplication of their numbers and inwardly in the enhanced status of the soldier.')
12 *Preussisches Heer,* p. 522 ff.
13 Ibid., p. 166.
14 Pflug-Harttung, *Wochenblatt,* p. 376 ff.; Grolmann, pp. 90–4, esp. p. 92: '*Die grossen Anstrengungen der Feldzüge von 1813–1814 hatten die Kräfte des Staates so erschöpft, dass bei der Rückkehr Napoleons, wo noch grössere Anstrengungen effordert wurden, mit aller Aufopferung nur die eigentlichen Hilfsmittel zum Schlagen: Mannschaft, Pferde, Waffen und Schiessbedarf herbeigescgafft werden konnten; an Magazine und Verpflegungs-Anstalten im grossen Sinne war nicht zu denken. Den Sold musste man den Truppen schuldig bleiben, . . . Unter solchen Umständen bezog die Preussische Armee weitläufige Kantonnirungen in Belgien, was ihr oft zum Vorwurf gemacht, aber durch die Nothwendigkeit geboten wurde. In diesen Kantonnirungen gelang es ihr erst durch strenge Ordnung und Sparsamkeit, die Soldaten mit einem dreitägigen Bedarf an Brod und*

Lebensmitteln und die Pack-Colonnen mit einem ähnlichen Vorrathe zu versehen . . .'. ('The strenuous efforts of the campaigns of 1813–1814 had so exhausted the strength of the State that, on the return of Napoleon, which called for even greater exertions, only materials actually needed for battle, such as men, horses, arms and ammunition, could be acquired, despite every sacrifice. Ordnance and supply depots in the wider sense were out of the question. Pay had to be owed to the troops . . . It was under these circumstances that the Prussian army occupied widely scattered cantonments in Belgium, an action that has been often criticized but which was dictated by necessity. In these cantonments it was possible only by dint of rigid organization and frugality to provide the soldiers with a three-day supply of bread and food and to make similar provision for the supply columns . . .'.)

15 The details of this vary; mention is made of £50,000 sterling. The facts, however, are plain, and typical of the financial position.

16 *Preussisches Heer*, pp. 167–8.

17 Cf. the exchange of letters, in German, between Wellington and Gneisenau, in Ollech, p. 19 ff.; Wellington's letter of 5 April will be found on p. 20, Gneisenau's answer on p. 23, in which the following unambiguous statement is especially interesting: '. . . *vielmehr, Herr Herzog, können Sie im Fall eines Angriffs auf den Beistand aller unserer verfügbaren Streitkräfte rechnen. Wir sind fest entschlossen, das Loos der Armee zu theilen, welche unter den Befehlen Ew. Excellenz steht.'* ('. . . rather may you count, Your Grace, on the support of all our available forces in the event of your being attacked. We are firmly determined to share the lot of the army which is under Your Excellency's command.')

18 Müffling, *Leben*, p. 219 f.

19 *Befreiungskriege*, p. 164.

20 Lettow-Vorbeck, p. 179.

21 Cf. Grolmann, p. 91.

22 Lettow-Vorbeck, p. 204; cf., among others, Siborne, i, 26–7.

23 Chesney, p. 56: 'The will of the soldier is a more potent element in the combinations of war than military writers generally admit. If love for his general be needful for controlling it, Blücher had called this faculty out with no less success than Napoleon'; p. 64: 'They were, as before said, not behind the French in love for their general . . .'

24 Müffling, *Geschichte*, iv.

25 Pflugk-Harttung, *Vorgeschichte*, p. 7.

26 Hibbert, p. 40: 'Men will do anything and go anywhere for a fighting general, provided that he cares for their interests and touches their imagination.' This certainly applies to Blücher.

27 Cf. Pflugk-Harttung, *Vorgeschichte*, p. 273; Chesney, pp. 55–6.

28 Kaulbach, pp. 652–3.

29 Cf. Siborne, i, pp. 24–5 fn.

30 Cf. Pertz, p. 545 f.: letter to Hardenberg, 30 June 1815.

31 Unger, ii, p. 245.

32 Ibid., pp. 188–9.

33 Kaulbach, p. 650.

34 Kennedy; cf. Siborne, i, p. 55, n. 3; Lettow-Vorbeck, p. 199; Pflugk-Harttung, *Vorgeschichte*, p. 72 f.

35 Ollech, pp. 68 and 87 f.; Chesney, p. 50.

36 Hibbert, p. 141, quoting from Wellington's letter to Graham: 'I think we are now too strong for him . . .' Chesney, pp. 50–1; Lettow-Vorbeck, p. 176 ff., esp. pp. 178 and 192; and many others.

37 Clausewitz, pp. 39–40.

38 Ollech, p. 90; Lettow-Vorbeck, p. 199.

39 Concerning the 'friction' with IV Corps: in the Prussian army of that time seniority of service within the Officer Corps was of considerable importance. An officer of longer service would not readily tolerate being under the command of an officer lower in the list; already in 1813–14 Gneisenau had had to suffer considerable difficulties with commanding officers of greater seniority, e.g. Yorck von Wartenburg. Now, in 1815, the Prussian I, II and III Corps were commanded by less senior lieutenant-generals; only IV Corps had been entrusted, by the King, to General Count Bülow von Dennewitz. Consequently, Gneisenau's order of 14 June midnight to IV Corps was not couched in peremptory terms but rather in the form of a polite item of information. This may be one reason why General von Bülow, used to independence, chose to comply with it in his own way. The disadvantage which resulted, in the first major engagement at Ligny, was to have a permanent effect. See further, on this subject, Chesney, pp. 59–60; and details in Pflugk-Harttung, *Vorgeschichte*, p. 361 ff.; Müffling, *Leben*, pp. 226–7; Siborne, i, p. 55 ff., esp. p. 56, n. 2.

40 Lettow-Vorbeck, p. 199.

41 Ollech, p. 92.

42 Ibid.; Lettow-Vorbeck, p. 196.

43 Bernhardi, p. 278.

44 Siborne, i, p. 173.

45 On the question of co-operation, cf. Pertz, pp. 373–5; Pflugk-Harttung, *Vorgeschichte*, p. 241 ff.; Lettow-Vorbeck, p. 309 f.

46 Siborne, i, p. 170; but cf. Lehmann's completely different interpretation.

47 Siborne, i, p. 177.

48 Müffling, *Geschichte*, iv–v; cf. Freytag-Loringhoven, p. 134: '*Die preussische Armee von 1815 war eine Improvisation und ihre einzelnen Truppenteile von sehr verschiedenem Wert. Sie verbluteten sich in Ortskämpfen, in denen die Franzosen sich als gewandter erwiesen . . .'*. ('The Prussian army of 1815 was an improvisation, and its units were of widely varying worth. They spent themselves in local engagements, for which the French showed greater aptitude . . .').

49 Houssaye, pp. 170 and 180; Charras, p. 141 ff.; Chandler, p. 1044; Becke, p. 118; Siborne, i, p. 243; Bernhardi, p. 295 ff.; cf. the exact time sequence of the battle in Houssaye, p. 188 f.

50 Ollech, pp. 155–6; Treuenfeld, pp. 226–7.

51 Houssaye, p. 187.

52 Ollech, p. 160; Becke, p. 118; Houssaye, p. 189.

53 Becke, p. 121: '. . . but Blücher had also experienced a double disappointment, since neither Wellington nor Bülow had co-operated at Ligny.'

54 Wagner, p. 24; Siborne, i, p. 244; Pertz, p. 412.

55 Ollech, p. 152; Charras, pp. 152–3.

56 Clausewitz, p. 80; Houssaye, p. 180.

57 Chesney, p. 137.

58 On this important decision by Gneisenau,

opinions differ. Chandler, p. 1058, speaks, for example, of 'Gneisenau's fortuitous selection of Wavre'. It does, however, seem unlikely that such an experienced army staff as exemplified by Gneisenau and Grolmann would not have considered what could or ought to be done in the event of a mishap. Cf. Pertz, p. 394.

59 Siborne, i, p. 240 and 299 ff.
60 Unger, ii, p. 291.
61 Lettow-Vorbeck, p. 342: '*Eine Benachrichtigung Wellingtons über den angetretenen Rückzug ist preussischerseits im Drange der Ereignisse unterblieben, und Oberst Hardinge war daran durch eine noch vorher erhaltene schwere Verwundung verhindert.*' ('Owing to the pressure of events the Prussians omitted to inform Wellington of their withdrawal, and Colonel Hardinge was prevented from doing so by a serious wound he had received earlier.')
Treuenfeld, p. 275; Becke, p. 120, reports that shortly before Blücher's last attack Major von Winterfeldt had been sent by him to Wellington with the information that the Prussian army would have to withdraw. Winterfeldt is said to have been wounded on the way, and consequently the message did not reach the Duke. The fact of the dispatch of Winterfeldt is definite, but nothing is known for certain either of the time he was sent or of the contents of the verbal message; it does, however, seem unlikely that Blücher would have sent such a message *before* the French breakthrough or, moreover, without the knowledge of Gneisenau. Cf. Pertz, p. 661, Excursus IV: '*Die Benachrichtigung Wellingtons von dem Verlust der Schlacht bei Ligny*' ('The notification of Wellington of the loss of the Battle of Ligny').
62 Lettow-Vorbeck, pp. 343–4; the facts come from (the later) Colonel von Wussow, who related them in 1845.
63 Chandler, p. 1058 (cf. n. 59, above).
64 Ollech, p. 166.
65 Ibid., pp. 159–60; Lettow-Vorbeck, pp. 369–70; Siborne, i, pp. 282–5.
66 Lettow-Vorbeck, pp. 369–70, 386; Siborne, i, p. 283.
67 Ollech, p. 167; cf. Chesney, p. 144.
68 Siborne, i, p. 243–4; Lettow-Vorbeck, p. 360; the footnote on this page points out that Gordon's statement that he had spoken to General von Zieten at Tilly cannot be correct. The Prussian I Corps was on the way back to Wavre; the only troops left in the area of Tilly were von Sohr's brigade of II Corps. This is typical of the unreliability of many reports about these days.
69 Ollech, p. 180; cf. a similar statement in Lettow-Vorbeck, p. 360. Hofmann, p. 137 (communication of von Müffling). Siborne, i, p. 251: there is mention here of support by two Prussian army corps.
70 Lettow-Vorbeck, p. 360.
71 Ibid., p. 361.
72 Chesney, p. 159.
73 Lettow-Vorbeck, p. 370.
74 Ibid., p. 372.
75 Ollech, p. 186–7.
76 Lettow-Vorbeck, p. 527 (Appendix 11).
77 E.g. Ollech, pp. 168–70.

78 Ibid., p. 170; Lettow-Vorbeck, p. 374; Treuenfeld, p. 345.
79 Treuenfeld, p. 231; Damitz, i, pp. 181–2; Siborne, i, p. 301.
80 Hooper, p. 152: '. . . Blücher, worsted but not routed at Ligny, had rallied at Wavre nearly 90,000 men and 260 guns . . .'; Siborne, i, p. 302; Ollech, p. 202 fn., quotes De La Tour: '*Rien de semblable, il faut le dire, ne s'était vu dans les annales militaires d'aucun pays.*' ('It must be said that nothing like it had ever been seen in the military annals of any country.')
81 Lettow-Vorbeck, p. 365, quoted from *Suppl. Disp.*, p. 501; similarly Naylor, 106.
82 Lettow-Vorbeck, pp. 376–7.
83 Rose, ii, p. 478.
84 Unger, ii, p. 295.
85 Ollech, p. 189; Treuenfeld, p. 408.
86 Clausewitz, p. 96.
87 Nostitz, pp. 36–7.
88 Ollech, p. 23: exchange of letters, Wellington–Gneisenau.

Chapter 4

1 The light companies in each Guards brigade had been specially trained to work together as a battalion.

Chapter 5

1 Gourgaud, *Cahiers de Sainte-Hélène*.
2 Napoleon's younger brother, married to Catherine, daughter of the King of Wurtenburg.
3 Gourgaud, op. cit.; Napoleon, *Mémoires*; Grouchy, *Mémoires*; Soult, *Mémoires*.
4 *Archives de la Guerre*.

Chapter 7

1 Rose, ii, pp. 489 and 499; Pertz, pp. 401 and 402.
2 Treuenfeld, p. 411; and many other accounts.
3 Caemmerer, p. 135; Becke, pp. 163–4; and very many others.
4 Caemmerer, p. 135.
5 Lettow-Vorbeck, p. 450.
6 Hofmann, p. 83; Pertz, pp. 400–3.
7 Pertz, pp. 400–1.
8 Clausewitz, p. 108; cf. Pertz, pp. 400–2.
9 Chesney, p. 192.
10 Clausewitz, p. 107, writes of IV Corps moving off at seven o'clock, rather than at daybreak. This seems unlikely. One can hardly imagine Bülow, after the delayed departure from Liège, taking it upon himself to impose on his corps so serious a further delay. As chief of staff of III Corps, Clausewitz must have been with his corps or with the army high command (in command) in the early morning of 18 June, and therefore could not have been an 'eyewitness'. Houssaye, p. 289 fn., objects to Clausewitz's statement: '*Clausewitz qui dit à tort que le IV corps leva ses bivouacs seulement à sept heures.*' ('Clausewitz, who mistakenly states that IV Corps did not lift its bivouacs until seven o'clock.') Chesney, p. 173, and Becke, p. 184, have simply taken over Clausewitz's statement.
11 Ollech, p. 191.
12 The times stated vary.

Chapter 8

1 Colonel Frederick Ponsonby was wounded in both arms, but rode with the reins in his teeth until sabred to the ground. There he lay for the rest of the battle, and throughout the night. A lancer struck him through the back, a tirailleur robbed him, the Prussians galloped over him, but eventually – in a jolting cart – he was evacuated to Mont St Jean, and miraculously he lived.

2 Houssaye, *1815*, *Waterloo*, from regimental accounts.

3 Grouchy, *Mémoires*; Gourgaud, *Cahiers de Sainte-Hélène*; Baltus, from Houssaye, *1815*, *Waterloo*.

4 From Sart-a-Walhain, at midday, or even from Wavre at 4 p.m. 18 June, Grouchy could have 'marched to the guns' with his 34,000 men and 100 cannon, and arrived at about 3 p.m. or 7 p.m., respectively, at St Lambert, thus complying with Napoleon's orders to come closer to the army while pushing the Prussians in front of him. This is precisely the route Blücher was taking at this very moment with a fragment of Thielemann's and Pirch's corps to join Bülow at St Lambert, leaving Zieten in Wavre where Vandamme and Gérard (the latter to be wounded, although not too seriously, by a bullet in his chest) were already fighting the Prussians on the Dyle when Grouchy arrived. Napoleon's letter from Rossomme (1.15 p.m. 18 June) ordering Grouchy to join the army through St Lambert was carried by the same twenty-eight-miles roundabout way as the previous one (see Appendix II) and reached Grouchy, also six hours later, at 7 p.m.

Chapter 9

1 Gourgaud, *Cahiers de Sainte-Hélène*; Napoleon, *Mémoires*; Vaulabelle, *Histoire ...*; Soult, *Mémoires*.

2 Delort's citation, *Archives de la Guerre*.

3 Delort, Druot, Lhéritier, Guyot, Roussel, d'Hurbal, Dubois, Farine, Guiton, Picquet, Travers, Wathier and Colbert.

4 Napoleon, op. cit.

5 The 3rd Guards had the strongest battalion in the field with 1,131 all ranks; other Guards' battalions and the 52nd Foot were also above average in numbers.

6 According to Victor Hugo hundreds of horses and riders collapsed in a crumpled mass in the sunken road before they ever reached the squares, and the survivors rode over their bodies. There is no evidence from the many personal accounts (French or English) of the battle that this unlikely event ever occurred.

Chapter 10

1 Pertz, p. 402, says, among other things, significantly: '*Mittlerweile tobte die Schlacht. In der Umgebung Wellingtons sollen Stimmen laut geworden sein, die an dem guten Willen der Preussen zweifelten. Wellington wusste es besser. Er sah, dass sie durch ihren Flankenmarsch die Brücken hinter sich abgebrochen hatten und ihr eigenes Heil nur in der Verbindung mit ihm suchen konnten.*' ('Meanwhile the battle raged. Around Wellington, voices are said to have been heard expressing doubts of Prussian good will. Wellington knew better. He perceived that by making their flanking march they had burned their bridges behind them and could seek salvation only by joining up with him.')

Becke, p. 211: 'When troops were first seen issuing from the Paris wood their nationality was uncertain to the Anglo-Dutch army. The relief and delight can be imagined when the new-comers' guns opened fire on the French right. The long-expected Prussians had arrived. Such a reinforcement during an action was an occurrence so different from former days in the Peninsula, where everything centred on the British Army, that it appeared decisive of the fate of the day.' Chesney, p. 178.

2 Ollech, pp. 226 and 241; Pertz, p. 414; Hooper, p. 248; Siborne, i, pp. 399–400.

3 Clausewitz, pp. 134–5, states: '*Das Resultat dieser Betrachtungen für uns ist also: 1) dass am 17. Bonaparte die Mitwirkung Blüchers und Grouchys zur Schlacht vom 18. gar nicht im Auge gehabt, dass er gar nicht daran gedacht hat und dass er also am 18. durch Blüchers Erscheinen im Sinne der allgemeinen Anordhungen vollkommen überrascht worden ist; ...*' ('Thus, for us the result of these considerations is: (1) that on the 17th Bonaparte had never envisaged the participation of Blücher and Grouchy in the battle of the 18th, and was therefore, on the 18th, completely surprised, in his general dispositions, by Blücher's appearance.') Ollech, p. 241; Kennedy, pp. 161 and 165; Charras, pp. 348–9; Becke, pp. 205 and 211: 'Beyond giving a great increase of *moral* to Wellington's battered Army, Bülow's attack compelled Napoleon before 6 p.m. to divert against the Prussians 18,000 men from his general reserve.'

4 Hooper, pp. 160 and 242.

5 Ibid., p. 248.

6 Lettow-Vorbeck, p. 400; Siborne, i, p. 308 ff.

7 Nostitz, p. 40.

8 Ibid; Ollech, p. 227; Treuenfeld, p. 413.

9 Blücher had received, through IV Corps, messages from Müffling in which he made suggestions for the advance of the Prussian army corps. When Napoleon's attack against the English centre became apparent, Müffling had suggested that one of the Prussian army corps should be sent to the English left wing and another to make a third column of march to the south, on Couture. At this time I Corps was on the move in the direction of Mont St Jean. Of these suggestions, the move further to the south may have been taken up by the Prussian high command. Cf. Müffling, *Geschichte*, p. 22 f.; Unger, ii, p. 297 ff.; Ollech, pp. 215–16; Lettow-Vorbeck, pp. 401–2.

10 Lettow-Vorbeck, p. 429; and many others.

11 Ollech, p. 192.

12 Kennedy, p. 136; Chesney, p. 178; Houssaye, p. 378 ff.; Damitz, i, p. 289.

13 Nostitz, p. 40.

14 Damitz, i, p. 289: '*Bei den erst vorhandenen geringen Kräften wird daher der Entschluss, die Truppen dessen ungeachtet unmittelbar gegen Rücken und Flanke des Feindes zu dirigiren, zu den entscheidenden Massregeln bei Führung der Schlacht gerechnet werden müssen ...*'. ('Considering the original severe limitation of manpower, the resolve to commit the forces

notwithstanding directly against the enemy flanks and rear must be regarded as one of the crucial command decisions taken in the conduct of this battle . . .'.) Ollech, p. 242.

15 Houssaye, p. 379. According to other accounts, Napoleon did not allow his VI Corps to advance until after 4 p.m.

16 Ollech, p. 242. The order for the advance of IV Corps was, like almost all Prussian orders, given by word of mouth. Von Ollech gives the contents of the order approximately as follows: 'The 15th (Losthin) Brigade will take the lead and deploy to the west of the wood in battalion strength, the right wing, the Tirailleurs, leading. They will be followed by the Brigade Battery and the Reserve Artillery, who will advance as far as the next elevation, their front being covered by the 2nd Silesian Hussar Regiment 6 and the Brigade Cavalry (two militia squadrons) of the 15th Brigade. The 16th (Hiller) Brigade will follow, and pull out left and form the left wing. H.R.H. Prince Wilhelm's Reserve Cavalry will be drawn up behind the 16th Brigade. The 13th (von Hake) Brigade will then become the Reserve.' Cf. Treuenfeld, p. 476 ff.

17 Ollech, p. 242.
18 Houssaye, p. 380.
19 Ibid., p. 381; Lettow-Vorbeck, p. 430.
20 Unger, ii, p. 302.
21 Hofmann, p. 118; Lettow-Vorbeck, pp. 431–2. Houssaye, p. 381, states that the Prussian troops were able, in the first attack, to take Plancenoit and throw out the troops in occupation. Thus threatened, Napoleon sent in the Young Guard with orders to recapture Plancenoit, which they did. Rose, ii, p. 503, similarly describes the beginning of the fight for Plancenoit: 'Bülow pressed on with his 30,000 men, and, swinging forward his left wing, gained a footing in the village of Plancenoit, . . . This took place between 5.30 and 6 o'clock, and accounts for Napoleon's lack of attention to the great cavalry charges. To break the British squares was highly desirable; but to ward off the Prussians from his rear was an imperative necessity. He therefore ordered Duhesme with the 4,000 footmen of the Young Guard to regain Plancenoit. Gallantly they advanced at the charge, and drove their weary and half-famished opponents out into the open.'

22 Ollech, p. 196.
23 Treuenfeld, p. 416 (following Weltzien, ii, p. 208).
24 Weltzien, ii, pp. 209–10.
25 One infantry and one cavalry regiment were left behind under the command of Major von Stengel. The orders for Stengel's detachment vary. Mention is made of their being left in Bierges to guard the bridge there, as well as of their being dispatched to Limal. The probability is that they remained in the region of Bierges. Cf. Weltzien, ii, p. 219.
26 Ollech, p. 194.
27 Ibid., p. 194 f.
28 Treuenfeld, pp. 432–3.
29 Ibid., p. 433; Lettow-Vorbeck, p. 452.
30 Treuenfeld, pp. 434–5: details of the formation of III Corps.
31 Lettow-Vorbeck, p. 453.
32 Becke, p. 212.

Chapter 11

1 *The Dispatches of Field Marshal the Duke of Wellington*, Vol. XII, pp. 590, 609 and 610. Compiled by Lieutenant-Colonel Gurwood, London, 1838.

2 It is certain that Baron Ompteda was killed in this way and at approximately this time; but it is probable that earlier in the battle some other German troops were killed near La Haye Sainte in almost identical circumstances. Captain Kincaid's account of the incident obviously refers to the one related above, for it happened after the fall of the farmhouse, although Kincaid's timings are all wrong. Two eminent authorities on the battle (Dorsey Gardner, *Quatre Bras, Ligny and Waterloo*, p. 295, and J. W. Fortescue, *History of the British Army*, Vol. 10, pp. 381 and 383) state that the Prince of Orange ordered two separate attacks, both with equally disastrous results. This seems most unlikely. The present writer believes that apart from the charge led by Ompteda there was only one other occasion when French cavalry caught a German battalion unawares and that was at the time of d'Erlon's first attack (see Chapter 8, p. 100).

Chapter 12

1 Lettow-Vorbeck, p. 434, n. 1.
2 Houssaye, p. 389.
3 Lettow-Vorbeck, p. 431.
4 Becke, p. 211.
5 Cf. Lettow-Vorbeck, p. 448, and Ollech, p. 118. Later commentators have regarded the Prussian attack on Plancenoit as doubtful. Lettow-Vorbeck, for example, calls the low lying village a *Mausefalle* ('mousetrap'). He is inclined to think that it would have been better to hold back the Prussian left wing, and instead to combine with the English to attack with a strong right wing over the high ground to the north of Plancenoit in the direction of Belle Alliance. In his opinion this would have achieved quicker results and cost fewer lives. On the other hand, considering the magnetic effect produced upon Napoleon's behaviour by the fighting for Plancenoit – the commitment of the bulk of his reserves against the dogged Prussian attacks on the village, his final over-hasty attack with the remaining, inadequate reserves, and the collapse of the French army – one wonders whether perhaps Blücher's decision at that moment was not fully justified. Ollech, p. 249, quotes with approval the French statement: '*La destruction entière des Français dépendait de la prise de Plancenoit*.' ('Upon the capture of Plancenoit hung the total rout of the French.')

6 Treuenfeld, p. 481; Hofmann, p. 120; Unger, ii, p. 302; Damitz, i, p. 301; Lettow-Vorbeck, p. 433; Ollech, p. 243.

7 Lettow-Vorbeck, p. 434, n. 1, shares this view, and bases the statement on the report of the 2nd Brigade (formerly available in the Prussian Military Archives) that they received the order to turn off while under way and then, later, the order to resume the old direction. Treuenfeld, p. 488; Hofmann, p. 120; Weltzien, ii, pp. 211–13. In many accounts, the reason for the change of direction is said to have been the

(erroneous) report of an officer who had been sent ahead that the English army was retreating. It seems, however, quite unlikely that General von Zieten would have changed his orders to his corps on the basis of an unconfirmed report, without at least going forward to see for himself.

8 Hofmann, p. 119.
9 Müffling, *Geschichte*, p. 35.
10 Weltzien, ii, p. 212; Lettow-Vorbeck, p. 433; Treuenfeld, p. 487; Chesney, p. 134, commenting on the von Reiche memoirs (Weltzien, ii, pp. 211–13)
11 Ollech, p. 244; Treuenfeld, p. 488; Hofmann, p. 120; Müffling, *Leben*, p. 248.
12 Treuenfeld, p. 488; Ollech, p. 244; both quote the words of von Müffling, which Major Count Gröben asserts that he heard with his own ears. Houssaye, p. 400.
13 Lettow-Vorbeck, p. 434; Ollech, p. 244.
14 Ollech, p. 248 (report from Colonel von Hiller).
15 Wagner, p. 89.
16 Houssaye, p. 394; Chandler, p. 1086; compare the rather different version in Siborne, ii.
17 Wagner, loc. cit.; Damitz, i, p. 299; Houssaye, pp. 394–5.
18 Becke, p. 212.

Chapter 13

1 There were about 22,000 dead on each side. This is the best estimate, from all official sources, of those killed in action during the battle. The number of wounded, which was considerable, has never been accurately assessed because robbers about their grisly business killed many of them as they lay helpless and moaning on the battlefield during the night. Nor has the total number of deserters and runaways in each army ever been either assessed or revealed. No one has ever challenged, however, that apart from Bourmont and the officers mentioned in the text, there were no deserters or runaways in the ranks of the French army either during the battle or in the three previous days of fighting.

The French losses during the rout and the retreat up to Paris, including 8,500 taken prisoner, were considerable. Taking these into account, the French army lost some 41,000 officers and men as from 15 June 1815. During that same period, the allied armies lost 60,800 officers and men: 22,800 Anglo-Dutch (11,300 English, 3,500 Hanoverians, 8,000 Belgians, Nassauers and Brunswickers) and 38,000 Prussians. *Archives de la Guerre.*

Chapter 14

1 This figure is close to Henry Lachouque's 6,500, which included 1,500 horse. *The Anatomy of Glory, Napoleon and his Guard*, p. 487.
2 H. Smith, *Autobiography*, Vol. I, p. 271.
3 The presence of these two fresh battalions adds strength to the suggestion that only five of the seven battalions originally led forward by Napoleon actually attacked.

Chapter 15

1 Hooper, p. 225.
2 Damitz, i, pp. 295–6.
3 Ollech, p. 245.
4 Nostitz, p. 43.

5 Ollech, p. 252; Damitz, i, p. 309.
6 Lettow-Vorbeck, p. 436.
7 Wagner, p. 93; Damitz, i, pp. 307–9; Lettow-Vorbeck, p. 437.
8 Charras, pp. 299–300; see also Becke, p. 228.
9 Houssaye, p. 414, n. 1.
10 Ibid.
11 Damitz, i, pp. 309–10.
12 Lettow-Vorbeck, p. 438.
13 The exact figures of IV Corps's losses can be found in Siborne, ii, p. 519. (app. XV). According to these, the 16th Brigade suffered, between about 5.30 and 9 p.m., some 1,800 casualties in the three infantry regiments; the 14th Brigade, just under 1,400. The losses suffered during the same period by the 15th and 13th Brigades fighting against the Corps Lobau were, respectively, 1,800 and 800.
14 Unger, ii, p. 304; Wagner, pp. 94–5; Beitzke, ii, pp. 310–11; Damitz, i, pp. 311–12; Ollech, pp. 248–9.
15 Charras, pp. 303–4; Housaye, p. 422.
16 Charras, p. 305.
17 Wagner, p. 95; Siborne, ii, p. 246; Houssaye, p. 427 ff.
18 Siborne, ii, pp. 246–7.
19 Wellington to Lady Webster – Bruxelles 19.6.1815; 8.30 o'clock – in the *Suppl. Disp.*, X, p. 531; quoted by Houssaye, p. 428, n. 1.
20 Houssaye, p. 428.
21 Damitz, i, p. 316: '*um den erkämpften Sieg durch eine vernichtende Verfolgung zu vollenden.*'
22 Pertz, p. 708 (from the Army Report of the Prussian army): '*Der Mond schien hell und begünstigte ungemein die Verfolgung. Der ganze Marsch war ein stetes Aufstöbern des Feindes in den Dörfern und Getreidefeldern . . .*' ('The moon was bright and was uncommonly helpful to the pursuit. The entire march was just a continual routing out of the enemy in villages and cornfields.')
23 Charras, p. 312.
24 Ollech, p. 254.
25 Ibid., cf Treuenfeld, p. 495.

Chapter 16

1 These were the jewels belonging to Napoleon's second sister, Pauline. Abandoning her husband, Prince Borghese, and her luxurious life in Italy, Pauline had brought them to Napoleon in Elba on 31 May 1814, to help him financially. She gave him also the news of the Empress Josephine's death two days before.
2 According to Colonel de Ladrière, dragoons' officer, who was present at dinner that evening in an inn, 'Ney, holding his head in both his hands, seemed to be in a state of extreme agitation, mumbling incoherently and exclaiming from time to time: "Ah, Grouchy! Ah, Grouchy!" Suddenly, the Emperor turned to him and told him brusquely: "Keep quiet. Keep quiet. If, because of a fatality which I cannot understand, he has not arrived in time to save us, [nevertheless] I consider him as a man of heart and of honour, who has always done his duty, like you, and I shall allow no one to attack him in my presence." Ney kept silent.' Grouchy, *Mémoires.*
3 Napoleon, *Mémoires*; Gourgaud, *Cahiers de Sainte-Hélène.*

Chapter 17

1 Cf. Peball; Fuller, p. 56; Hibbert, p. 256.
2 Chandler, p. 1008.
3 Cf. Chesney, pp. 63–4: '. . . if we make every possible deduction for the high colouring of national historians, it may still be assumed that no such compactly formidable mass of troops ever moved into the field before.'
4 Chandler, pp. 1091–2; cf. among others, Chesney, p. 51; Hibbert, pp. 160 and 168; Clausewitz, pp. 52–3.
5 Hofmann, p. 36.
6 Fuller, p. 50: 'The loss of time is irreparable in war.'
7 Sheppard, p. 13.
8 Chesney, pp. 112–13 and 137.
9 Pertz, p. 413: '*Er ist der grösste Defensiv-General der je gelebt hat.*' Freytag-Loringhoven, p. 135, comments on Wellington's defensive leadership on 18 June: '*Sein Vertrauen in Wellington hat ihn nicht getäuscht, denn was dieser vorher durch mangelndes operatives Verständnis für die Gesamtlage gefehlt hatte, das ersetzte er durch die mustergültige Leitung der Verteidigungsschlacht am 18. Juni 1815.*' ('His confidence in Wellington did not let him down; for the latter, though previously in error owing to his insufficient operational grasp of the general situation, made up for this by his exemplary conduct of the defensive battle of 18 June 1815.')
10 But cf. Lettow-Vorbeck, p. 383: '*Napoleon hat bei seinem letzten Waffengang gegen das verbündete Europa mindestens dieselbe Spannkraft des Körpers und Geistes gezeigt wie auf der Höhe seiner Feldherrnlaufbahn. Was ihm aber in sehr merklicher Weise fehlte, das war die Unterstützung so ausgezeichneter Unterführer, wie Soult, Davout und mit Einschränkungen Murat und Bernadotte.*' ('During his last campaign against the European allies, Napoleon certainly showed as much physical and mental energy as he had when at the height of his career as a military commander. What, however, he did miss most notably was the support of such outstanding subordinate commanders as Soult, Davout, and, with reservations, Murat and Bernadotte.')
11 Cf. Fuller, p. 49.
12 Hofmann, p. 77; Damitz, i, p. 232; Lettow-Vorbeck, pp. 242–3.
13 Ollech, p. 179, gives his opinion: '*Wir erörterten schon früher, wie Wellington ohne die Schlacht bei Ligny unaufhaltsam nach Brüssel zurückgeworfen worden wäre; ja er hätte ohne dieselbe den Kampf bei Quatre Bras gar nicht aufnehmen können.*' ('Earlier we have discussed how Wellington, but for the battle of Ligny, would have been inexorably thrown back on Brussels; indeed, without that engagement he could not have given battle at Quatre-Bras.') Cf. Beitzke, ii, p. 248.
14 Clausewitz, pp. 107–10; Treuenfeld, p. 483; Kennedy, pp. 164–6.
15 Chandler, p. 1093.
16 Ibid., p. 1090.
17 Sheppard, p. 13; Clausewitz, p. 145; Pertz, p. 420, concerning Gneisenau's willingness to take up the pursuit.
18 Chesney, p. 209.
19 Chesney, p. 209.

Bibliographies

SELECT BIBLIOGRAPHY (William Seymour)

Becke, A. F., *Napoleon and Waterloo*, Vols. I and II, London, 1914.
Bryant, Arthur, *Jackets of Green*, London, 1972.
Bryant, Arthur, *The Great Duke*, London, 1971.
Chandler, D. G., *Campaigns of Napoleon*, London, 1967.
Cotton, Sergeant-Major Edward, *A Voice from Waterloo*, London, 1854.
Fortescue, J. W., *History of the British Army*, Vol. X, London, 1920.
Gardner, Dorsey, *Quatre Bras, Ligny and Waterloo*, London, 1882.
Gronow, Captain, *Reminiscences and Recollections*, (2 vols.), London, 1892.
Heyer, Georgette, *An Infamous Army*, London, 1961.
Howarth, David, *A Near Run Thing*, London, 1968.
Jomini, General Baron de, *The Campaign of Waterloo*, New York, 1853.
Lachouque, Henry, *The Anatomy of Glory: Napoleon and his Guard*, London, 1961.
Longford, Elizabeth, *Wellington: The Years of the Sword*, London, 1969.
Maurice, Major-General Sir F., *The History of the Scots Guards*, Vol. II, London, 1934.
Mercer, General Cavaliér, *Journal of the Waterloo Campaign*, William Blackwood, 1870.
Morris, William O'Connor, *The Campaign of 1815*, London, 1900.
Oman, C. W. C., *Wellington's Army*, London 1913.
Rogers, Col. H. C. B., *Artillery Through the Ages*, London, 1972.
Shaw-Kennedy, General Sir James, *Notes on the Battle of Waterloo*, London, 1865.
Sloane, Wm., *Life of Napoleon* (4 vols.), New York, 1901.
Smith, Lieutenant-General Sir Harry, *Autobiography*, Vol. I, edited by G. C. Moore Smith, London, 1902.
Stanhope, Fifth Earl of, *Notes of conversations with the Duke of Wellington 1831–1851*, London, 1888.
Weller, Jac, *Weapons and Tactics*, London, 1966.
Weller, Jac, *Wellington at Waterloo*, London, 1967.

BIBLIOGRAPHY (Jacques Champagne)

Ain, Girod de l', *Vie militaire du général Foy*, Paris, 1900.
Archives de la Guerre (Correspondance générale par armée et par général).
Archives des Affaires Etrangères (Correspondance diplomatique, mémoires et documents).
Archives Nationales (Rapports et procès-verbaux).
Bas, de, *Campagne de 1815*, Holland, 1908.
Bertrand, Général, *Cahiers de Sainte-Hélène, Campagne de 1815*, Paris, 1925.
Bourienne, de, *Mémoires de Napoléon*, Paris, 1829.
Bourienne, de, *Mémoires de Napoléon*, Paris, 1836.
Charras, Colonel, *Histoire de la campagne de 1815*, Paris, 1869.
Constant, Benjamin, *Mémoires sur les Cent Jours*, Paris, 1829.
Gérard, Général, *Dernières observations sur la bataille de Waterloo*, Paris, 1830.
Gérard, Général, *Quelques documents sur la bataille de Waterloo*, Paris, 1829.

Gourgaud, Général, *Cahiers de Sainte-Hélène, Campagne de 1815*, Paris, 1925.

Grouard, Colonel, *Critique de 1815*, Paris, 1907.

Grouard, Colonel, *Stratégie Napoléonique*, Paris, 1904.

Grouchy, Maréchal, *Mémoires: le Maréchal du 16 au 18 Juin*, Paris 1873–4.

Houssaye, *1815, Waterloo*, Paris, 1907.

Jomini, *Récit politique et militaire de la campagne de 1815*, Paris, 1839.

Jourdan, Maréchal, *Journal d'un soldat du 71ème régiment*, Paris, 1822.

Las Cases, *Mémorial de Sainte-Hélène*, London, 1823.

Lenient, *La solution des énigmes de Waterloo*, Paris, 1915.

Mauduit, de, *Les derniers jours de la Grande Armée*, Paris, 1847.

Napoleon, *Mémoires pour servir a l'Histoire de France en 1815*, Paris, 1820.

Navez, *Quatre-Bras, Ligny, Waterloo, Wavre*, Paris, 1910.

Pascal, Adrien, *Bulletins de la Grande Armée*, Paris, 1843.

Quinet, Edgar, *Histoire de la campagne de 1815*, Paris, 1861.

Rogniat, Général, *Considérations sur l'art de la guerre*, Paris, 1916.

Ségur, Comte de, *Histoire de Napoléon et de la Grande Armée*, Paris, 1824.

Soult, *Mémoires*, Paris, 1854.

Thiers, *Histoire du Consulat et de l'Empire*, Paris, 1862.

Tour d'Auvergne, Prince de la, *Waterloo*, Paris, 1870.

Vaulabelle, Tenaille de, *1815, Ligny, Waterloo*, Paris, 1883.

Vaulabelle, Tenaille de, *Histoire des deux Restaurations*, Paris, 1857.

Novels

Erckmann-Chatrian, *Waterloo*.

Hugo, Victor, *Les Misérables*.

Stendhal, *La Chartreuse de Parme*.

Thackeray, W. M., *Vanity Fair*.

BIBLIOGRAPHY (Col. E. Kaulbach)

List of works cited in notes

Becke, A. F., *Napoleon and Waterloo: The Emperor's Campaign with the Armée du Nord 1815*, London, 1946.

Befreiungskriege. Deutsche Gesellschaft für Wehrpolitik und Wehrwissenschaften (ed.), *Die Befreiungskriege* (The Wars of Liberation), Berlin, 1938.

Beitzke, Heinrich, *Geschichte des Jahres 1815* [History of the Year 1815], 2 vols., Berlin, 1865.

Bernhardi, Theodor von, *Geschichte Russlands und der europäischen Politik in den Jahren 1814 bis 1831* (History of Russia and European Politics 1814–1831), Part I: *Vom Wiener Congress bis zum zweiten Pariser Frieden* (From the Congress of Vienna to the Second Treaty of Paris), Leipzig, 1863.

Blüchers Briefe. Wolfgang von Unger (ed.), *Blüchers Briefe*: Vervollständigte Sammlung des Generals E. von Colomb (Blücher's Letters: Complete Edition by General E. von Colomb), Stuttgart and Berlin, 1913.

Caemmerer, Rudolf C. F. von, *Die Befreiungskriege 1813–1815: Ein strategischer Überblick* (The Wars of Liberation 1813–1815: A Strategical Survey), Berlin, 1907.

Chandler, D. G., *The Campaigns of Napoleon*, London, 1967.

Charras, Jean-Baptiste A., *Histoire de la campagne de 1815: Waterloo* (History of the Campaign of 1815: Waterloo), Brussels, 1857.

Chesney, Charles C., *Waterloo Lectures: A Study of the Campaign of 1815*, London, 1868.

Clausewitz, Carl von, *Hinterlassene Werke über Krieg und Kriegführung* (Posthumous Works on War and the Conduct of War), Vol. 8: *Der Feldzug von 1815 in Frankreich* (The French Campaign of 1815), Berlin, 1862.

Damitz, Karl von, *Geschichte des Feldzugs von 1815 in den Niederlanden und Frankreich als Beitrag zur Kriegsgeschichte der neuern Kriege* (History of the Campaign of 1815 in the Netherlands and France: A Contribution to the History of Modern Warfare), 2 vols., Berlin, Posen and Bromberg, 1837–8.

Freytag-Loringhoven, Hugo von, *Feldherrngrösse: Vom Denken und Handeln hervorragender Heerführer* (Great Generalship: Thoughts and Actions of Eminent Military Commanders), Berlin, 1922.

Fuller, J. F. C., *The Conduct of War 1789–1961: A Study of the Impact of the French, Industrial, and Russian Revolutions on War and Its Conduct*, London, 1961.

Grolmann, C. von, 'Bemerkungen über die im englischen Parlamente von dem Herzog von Wellington gethanen Äusserungen über die Disziplin in der preussischen und englischen Armee' (Remarks upon the Duke of Wellington's observations made in the English Parliament on Discipline in the Prussian and English Armies), in *Militair-Wochenblatt* (Weekly Journal of Military Affairs), 1836, pp. 90–4.

Hibbert, Christopher, *Waterloo: Napoleon's Last Campaign*, London, 1967.

Hofmann, Georg W., *Zur Geschichte des Feldzuges von 1815 bis nach der Schlacht von Belle-Alliance* (A Contribution to the History of the 1815 Campaign up to the Battle of Belle Alliance), second enlarged edition, Berlin, 1851.

Hooper, George, *Waterloo: The Downfall of the First Napoleon. A History of the Campaign of 1815*, London, 1862.

Houssaye, Henry, *1815, Waterloo*, 66th edition, Paris, 1910.

Jany, Curt, *Geschichte der Königlich Preussischen Armee* (History of the Royal Prussian Army), Vol. 4: *Die Königlich Preussische Armee und das Deutsche Reichsheer 1807 bis 1914* (The Royal Prussian Army and the German Imperial Army 1807–1914), Berlin, 1933.

Kaulbach, Eberhard, 'Gneisenau: Zur geistigen Entwicklung und Leistung des grossen Soldaten' (Gneisenau: Reflections upon the Spiritual Development and Achievements of a Great Soldier), in *Wehr-Wissenschaftliche Rundschau* (Review of Military Science), 11 (1965), pp. 641–56.

Kennedy, James Shaw, *Notes on the Battle of Waterloo*, London, 1865.

Lehmann, Max, 'Zur Geschichte des Jahres 1815' (On the History of the year 1815), in *Historische Zeitschrift* (Historical Journal), New Series, Vol. 2, pp. 274–94, Munich, 1877.

Lettow-Vorbeck, Oskar von, *Napoleons Untergang 1815* (Napoleon's Downfall 1815), Vol. 1: *Elba–Belle-Alliance* (From Elba to Belle Alliance), Berlin, 1904.

Müffling, *Geschichte. Geschichte des Feldzuges der englisch-hannövrisch-niederländisch-braunschweigschen Armee unter Herzog Wellington und der preussischen Armee unter dem Fürsten Blücher von Wahlstadt im Jahre 1815* (History of the Campaign of the English Hanoverian Netherlands and Brunswick Army under the Duke of Wellington and of the Prussian Army under Prince Blücher von Wahlstadt in the Year 1815), von C. V. W. ('by C. von W.'), Stuttgart and Tübingen, 1817.

Müffling, *Leben.* Friedrich Carl Ferdinand, Freiherr von Müffling, genannt von Weiss, *Aus meinem Leben* (For My Life), Berlin, 1851.

Naylor, John, *Waterloo*, London, 1960.

Nostitz, 'Das Tagebuch des Generals der Kavallerie Grafen von Nostitz, II. Theil' (Journal of General Count von Nostitz, Part 2), in *Kriegsgeschichtliche Einzelschriften des Grossen Generalstabes* (Monographs of the Supreme General Staff on the History of War), Vol. I, part 6, Berlin, 1885.

Ollech, Carl R. von, *Geschichte des Feldzuges von 1815 nach archivalischen Quellen* (History of the Campaign of 1815 Based on Documentary Sources), Berlin, 1876.

Peball, Kurt, 'Waterloo – 18. Juni 1815: Die historische Symptomatik einer Schlacht' (Waterloo – 18 June 1815: the Battle in its Historical Context), in *Österreichische Militarzeitschrift* (Austrian Army Journal), 1965, Part 6.

Pertz. Hans Delbrück, *Das Leben des Feldmarschalls Grafen Neithardt von Gneisenau* (The Life of Field-Marshal Count Neithardt von Gneisenau), continued by Georg Heinrich Pertz, Vol. 4: *1814, 1815*, Berlin, 1880.

Pflugk-Harttung, Julius von, *Vorgeschichte der Schlacht bei Belle-Alliance. Wellington* (Prelude to the Battle of Belle Alliance. Wellington), Berlin, 1903.

Pflugk-Harttung, Julius von, 'Über die Ausrüstung der norddeutschen Heere 1815' (On the Equipment of the North German Armies 1815), in *Beihefte zum Militär Wochenblatt* (Supplements to the Army Weekly Journal), 1910, pp. 376 ff.

Preussisches Heer. Grosser Generalstab (ed.), *Das Preussische Heer der Befreiungskriege* (The Prussian Army in the Wars of Liberation), Vol. 3: *Das Preussische Heer in den Jahren 1814 und 1815* (The Prussian Army in the Years 1814–15), Berlin, 1914.

Rose, John Holland, *The Life of Napoleon I including new materials from the British Official records*, 2 vols., London, 1902.

Sheppard, E. W., *The Study of Military History*, Aldershot, 1952.

Siborne, William, *History of the War in France and Belgium in 1815*, 2 vols., London, 1844.

Treuenfeld, Bruno von, *Die Tage von Ligny und Belle Alliance* (The Days of Ligny and Belle Alliance), Hanover, 1880.

Unger, Wolfgang von, *Blücher* Vol. 2: *Von 1812 bis 1819* (1812–1819), Berlin, 1908.

Wagner, August, *Plane der Schlachten und Treffen, welche von der preussischen Armee in den Feldzügen der Jahre 1813, 14 und 15 geliefert worden* (Plans of the Battles and Engagements Fought by the Prussian Army in the Campaigns of 1813, 1814 and 1815), Part 4, Berlin, 1825.

Weltzien. *Memoiren des königlich preussischen Generals der Infanterie Ludwig von Reiche.* Herausgegeben von seinem Neffen Louis von Weltzien, grossherzoglich oldenburgischem Hauptmann und Brigademajor (Memoirs of Ludwig von Reiche, General in the Royal Prussian Infantry. Edited by his nephew, Louis von Weltzien, Captain and Brigade Major in the army of the Grand Duchy of Oldenburg), two parts in one volume, Part 1: *Von 1775 bis 1814* (1775–1814), Part 2: *Von 1814 bis 1855* (1814–1855), Leipzig, 1857.

Other sources consulted but not cited

Aldington, Richard, *Wellington: being an account of the Life & Achievements of Arthur Wellesley, 1st Duke of Wellington*, London, 1946.

Bornstedt, von, *Das Gefecht bei Wavre an der Dyle am 18. und 19. Juni 1815* (The Action at Wavre on the Dyle on 18–19 June 1815), Berlin, 1858.

Cardinal von Widdern, Georg, *Belgien, Nordfrankreich, der Niederrhein und Holland als Kriegsfeld* (Belgium, Northern France, the Lower Rhine and Holland as Theatre of War), Breslau, 1870.

Fuller, J. F. C., *The Decisive Battles of the Western World and Their Influence upon History*, 3 vols, London, 1954–6.

Gourgaud, Gaspard, *Campagne de Dix-huit Cent Quinze; ou, Relation des Opérations Militaires qui ont eu lieu en France et en Belgique, pendant les Cent Jours: écrite à Sainte-Hélène* (The Campaign of 1815; or, A Narrative of the Military Operations in France and Belgium during the Hundred Days; written on Saint Helena), Paris, 1818.

Groote, Wolfgang von, and Müller, Klaus-Jürgen (eds), *Napoleon I und das Militärwesen seiner Zeit* (Napoleon I and the Military System of His Period), Freiburg im Breisgau, 1968.

Güth, Rolf, 'Betrachtungen über den unbekannten Gneisenau' (Reflections upon the Unknown Gneisenau), in *Zeitschrift für Religions- und Geistesgeschichte* (Journal of Religious and Intellectual History), vol. 27, part 3, pp. 222–39, Cologne, 1975.

Heyer, Georgette, *An Infamous Army*, London, 1966.

Horsetzky, Adolf von, *Kriegsgeschichtliche Übersicht der wichtigsten Feldzüge seit 1792* (Historical Review of the Most Important Military Campaigns since 1792), seventh edition, Vienna, 1913.

Jomini, Antoine H., *Vie politique et militaire de Napoléon, recontée par lui-meme, au tribunal de César, d'Alexandre et de Frédéric* (The Political and Military Life of Napoleon, as Related by Himself before the Judgement Seat of Caesar, Alexander, and Frederick the Great), Paris, 1827.

Klessmann, Eckart (ed.), *Deutschland unter Napoleon in Augenzeugenberichten* (Eyewitness Reports on Germany under Napoleon), Düsseldorf, 1965.

Königer, Julius, *Der Krieg von 1815 und die Vertrage von Wien und Paris* (The War of 1815 and the Treaties of Vienna and Paris), Leipzig, 1865.

Las Cases, Emmanuel A. D. M. J., *Mémorial de Sainte-Hélène; ou, Mon Séjour auprès de l'Empereur Napoléon* (Memoir of Saint Helena; or, My Stay with the Emperor Napoleon), 4 vols, London, 1823.

Mitchell, Joseph B., *Decisive Battles of the Civil War*, New York, 1962.

Ollech, Carl R. von, *Carl Friedrich Wilhelm von Reyher, General der Kavallerie und Chef des Generalstabes der*

Armee (Carl Friedrich Wilhelm von Reyher, General of Cavalry and Chief of the Army General Staff), Part Three, Berlin, 1874.

Pflugk-Harttung, Julius von, 'Elba und die Hundert Tage' (Elba and the Hundred Days), in *Napoleon I: Das Erwachen der Volker* (Napoleon I and the Awakening of the Nations), ed. von Pflugk-Harttung, Berlin, 1901.

Pflugk-Harttung, Julius von, 'Das I. Korps Zieten bei Belle-Alliance und Wavre' (The First (von Zieten's) Corps at Belle Alliance and Wavre), in *Jahrbücher für die Deutsche Armee und Marine* (Annals of the Germany Army and Navy), 1903: January–June, pp. 196–209, Berlin.

Pflugk-Harttung, Julius von, 'Das I. preussische Korps bei Belle-Alliance' (The First Prussian Corps at Belle Alliance), in *Jahrbücher für die Deutsche Armee und Marine* (Annals of the German Army and Navy), 1905: July–December, pp. 143–68, and 209–39, Berlin.

Pflugk-Harttung, Julius von, 'Archivalische Beiträge zur Geschichte des Feldzuges 1815 (16. bis 24. Juni 1815)' (Notes from Documentary Sources on the History of the 1815 Campaign (16–24 June)), in *Jahrbücher für die Deutsche Armee und Marine* (Annals of the German Army and Navy), 1906: July–December, pp. 509–22 and 608–24, Berlin.

Pflugk-Harttung, Julius von, 'Das Kampfgelände der Preussen bei Belle-Alliance' (The Prussians' Fighting Terrain at Belle Alliance), in *Jahrbücher für die Deutsche Armee und Marine* (Annals of the German Army and Navy), 1910: July–December, pp. 34–40, Berlin.

Pflugk-Harttung, Julius von, 'Wellington und Blücher am 17. Juni 1815' (Wellington and Blücher on 17 June 1815), in *Jahrbücher für die Deutsche Armee und Marine* (Annals of the Germany Army and Navy), 1911: January–June, pp. 371–88, Berlin.

Thornhill, Patrick, *The Waterloo Campaign*, London, 1965.

Yorck von Wartenburg, Maximilian, *Napoleon als Feldherr* (Napoleon as Military Commander), Part Two, Berlin, 1886.

108 The allegory of the fleur-de-lis and the violet. Napoleon adopted the violet as an emblem while in exile, as a herald of his return in the spring

Index

238

A Note About the Authors

Lord Chalfont (editor) is a distinguished author, broadcaster and journalist, and a former minister of the 1964–70 Labour Government in Great Britain. He now sits in the House of Lords as an independent peer. During World War II he served with the South Wales Borderers in Burma and India, and later in Malaya and Cyprus. Further military service included regimental, staff and intelligence posts in the Middle East, in Paris and with the Rhine Army. In 1961 he became defence correspondent of *The Times*—a post relinquished in 1964 on his appointment as Minister of State for Foreign Affairs. He is general editor of *The Great Commanders*, a series of military biographies. He is also author of a biography of Field Marshal Montgomery, published in 1976.

William Seymour, formerly a regular soldier in the Scots Guards, and Staff College trained, contributes regularly to *History Today* and has written articles for the *Army Quarterly* and other military papers. He is at work on a history of the British monarchy and its cultural heritage. His other published works include *Battles in Britain*, *Ordeal by Ambition*, and *Lands of Spice and Treasure*.

Eberhard Kaulbach joined the 9th Infantry at Potsdam in 1921, and three years later became an officer. From 1934 to 1936 he attended the War Academy in Berlin, and later held various General Staff positions. During World War II he rose to the post of Chief of Staff of division and army corps. From 1957 to 1968 he taught military history at the Fuhrungsakademie der Bundeswehr, Hamburg Blankenese. He has published works on the German military campaigns of 1866 and 1870, and essays on Gneisenau, Schlieffen and von Seeckt.

Jacques Champagne, a journalist and broadcaster, was a reporter in Paris before World War II. Invalided out of the French Air Force in 1939, he became a member of the French Resistance a year later. In 1943 he joined the Allied Special Forces in France and served as an officer until 1945. Since 1947 he has been permanent London correspondent of daily papers in Paris and Brussels, and of Radio-Lausanne. He is an active lecturer on international affairs and has appeared on the BBC as a military commentator.

GAYLORD RG